PAGE 50

ON THE ROAD

YOUR COMPLETE DESTINATION GUIDE
In-depth reviews, detailed listings
and insider tips

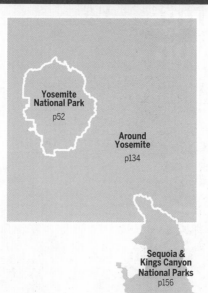

Yosemite
National Park
p52

Around
Yosemite
p134

Sequoia &
Kings Canyon
National Parks
p156

PAGE 221

SURVIVAL GUIDE

VITAL PRACTICAL INFORMATION TO
HELP YOU HAVE A SMOOTH TRIP

Health & Safety

Keeping safe while visiting
the parks depends on your
predeparture preparations,
daily routines and how you
handle any dangerous
situations that develop.
While the potential problems
can seem quite frightening,
in reality few park visitors
experience anything worse
that a skinned knee.

call center before seeking
help. Be sure to keep all
receipts and documentation.
For travel insurance,
see p225.

Websites
Yosemite National Park –
Your Safety (www.nps.gov
/yose/blanyourvisit/yoursafe
.htm)
Sequoia & Kings
Canyon National
Your Safe...

BEFORE YOU GO

THIS EDITION WRITTEN AND RESEARCHED BY

Beth Kohn
Sara Benson

welcome to Yosemite, Sequoia & Kings Canyon

Backcountry Bonanza

All the usual trappings of civilization can be found within the Sierra Nevada, a mountain range spanning 400 miles roughly north to south across Central California. But take a turn and you'll find yourself in one of its dazzling mountain canyons, face-to-face with some of the highest peaks in the country. Trails branch out and lure you to verdant valleys of wildflowers and desolate lightning-prone pinnacles. Bears tear open logs, marmots whistle in warning, and crickets and frogs harmonize to a nightly fever pitch. Something about spending time in the wilderness resets your brain. You step back, assess the situation with fresh eyes and put things into perspective. Maybe it has something to do with the timelessness of the landscape – the ancient glaciers or the glow of the lakes at dusk and dawn. Civilization can wait. The wilderness? Maybe not.

Time Warps

You might come for the beauty of the mountains, but this region has a past both wide and deep. Glaciers, although receding, gnaw at granite shoulders as they have for millennia. Prehistoric forests loom within the parks and at inhospitable heights beyond them. The volcanic forces that moved these mountains to life still rumble underfoot, and simmering hot springs serve as a reminder that the earth's core continues to

Yosemite and neighboring Sequoia & Kings Canyon occupy the most spectacular region of one of the most spectacular mountain ranges on the planet.

(left) Autumnal view of Half Dome (p64)
(below) Wildflowers in Kings Canyon National Park (p174)

stir. Humans have left their mark as well. Trails show the routes taken by indigenous Californians – the Sierra Miwok, the Paiute and the Shoshone – who traded between the western foothills and the Eastern Sierra; grinding stones and ancient petroglyphs have endured. Pioneers discarded mining camps to the elements, creating desolate ghost towns and the remains of forgotten railway lines. Of course, history is as much in the making as it is in the past, and visitors need to be mindful of their own impact on the parks' preservation.

Winter Wonderland

For solitude and serenity, winter rules. Summer may be high season in the parks, but after seeing snow in the Sierras you might well question why. The peaks are some of the highest in the US, regularly rising above 11,000ft, occasionally bursting to 14,000ft, and blanketed by snow for much of the year. Snow paints the trees and splatters the mountains, and your breath turns into moist puffy clouds. In the parks, there's full-moon snowshoeing and cross-country adventures, plus the chance to camp under a giant sequoia. Go swooshing across the hushed backcountry, barreling down some powdery slopes or just stay inside and warm your toes by a roaring wood fire. Whatever your energy level, there's something fun to fill your days.

› Yosemite, Sequoia & Kings Canyon

Top Experiences ›

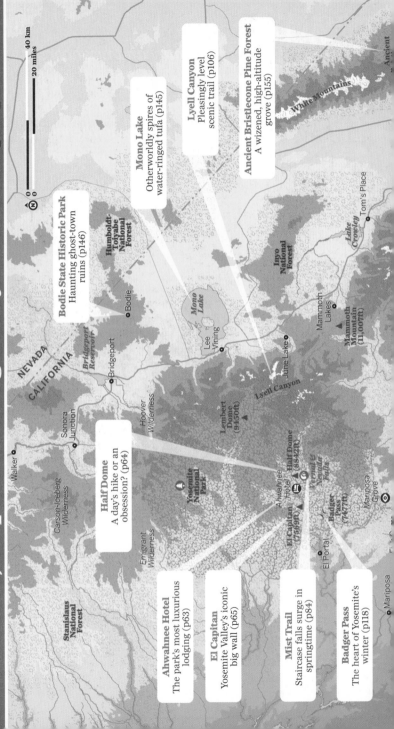

Bodie State Historic Park
Haunting ghost-town ruins (p146)

Mono Lake
Otherworldly spires of water-ringed tufa (p145)

Lyell Canyon
Pleasingly level scenic trail (p106)

Ancient Bristlecone Pine Forest
A wizened, high-altitude grove (p155)

Half Dome
A day's hike or an obsession? (p64)

Ahwahnee Hotel
The park's most luxurious lodging (p63)

El Capitan
Yosemite Valley's iconic big wall (p65)

Mist Trail
Staircase falls surge in springtime (p84)

Badger Pass
The heart of Yosemite's winter (p118)

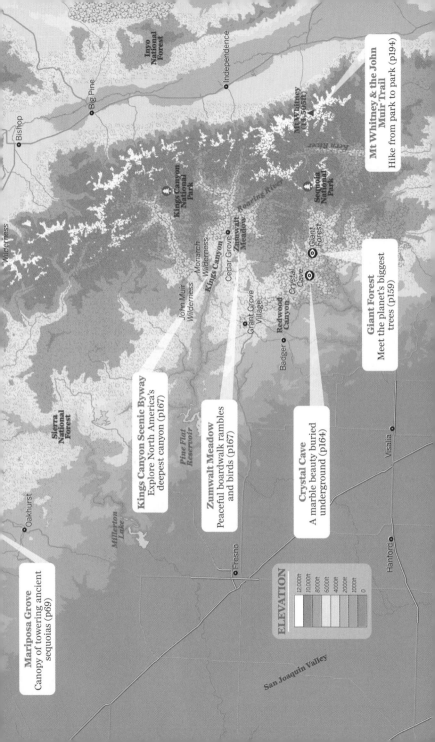

Mt Whitney & the John Muir Trail Hike from park to park (p194)

Mariposa Grove Canopy of towering ancient sequoias (p69)

Kings Canyon Scenic Byway Explore North America's deepest canyon (p167)

Zumwalt Meadow Peaceful boardwalk rambles and birds (p167)

Crystal Cave A marble beauty buried underground (p164)

Giant Forest Meet the planet's biggest trees (p159)

ELEVATION

12,000ft
10,000ft
8000ft
6000ft
4000ft
2000ft
1000ft
0

Inyo National Forest

Independence

Big Pine

Bishop

Mt Whitney (14,505ft)

Kings Canyon National Park

Roaring River

Kern River

Sequoia National Park

Monarch Wilderness

Kings Canyon

Cedar Grove

Zumwalt Meadow

John Muir Wilderness

Wilderness

Pine Flat Reservoir

Grant Grove Village

Redwood Canyon

Crystal Cave

Giant Forest

Badger

Sierra National Forest

Oakhurst

Millerton Lake

Fresno

Visalia

Hanford

San Joaquin Valley

20
TOP
EXPERIENCES

Spring Waterfalls

1 Nothing can strike you speechless like water plunging off a cliff. Standing at the base of a massive waterfall, hearing its roar and reveling in its drenching mist is simultaneously invigorating and humbling. Yosemite holds some of the world's greatest collections of waterfalls and, in springtime, Yosemite Valley is spray central. In addition to the seasonal creeks tumbling over the Valley's walls, the iconic cataracts of Yosemite Falls (p64) and Bridalveil Fall (p64) will satisfy any falls fanatic.

Climbing Half Dome

2 Just hold on, don't forget to breathe and – whatever you do – don't look down. A pinnacle so popular that hikers now need a permit to scale it, Half Dome (p64) lives on as Yosemite Valley's coveted cocked-top jewel and a must-reach-it obsession for millions. It's a day hike longer than an average work day, an elevation gain equivalent to almost 480 flights of stairs, and a final stretch of near-vertical steps that melts even the strongest legs and arms to masses of quivering jelly.

Giant Forest

3 When it's time to pay your respects to the most massive trees on the planet, there's nowhere better than in Sequoia National Park. Giant sequoias can live for 3000 years, and some of those ancient ones standing in the Giant Forest (p159) have been around since the fall of the Roman Empire. Go on, give 'em a hug – if you can even get your arms around their ginormous trunks.

El Capitan

4 A pale fortress rising abruptly from the Valley floor, the glow of dusk on El Capitan is a majestic spectacle. A formation most formidable, summiting the sheer granite and splintering cracks of this monolith (p65) is the vertigo-conquering achievement of a lifetime. Now the world standard for big-wall climbs, it was once deemed impossible to ascend. Strain your eyes to find the glowing moth-like bivvies dangling from its face at night, and bite your nails tracking the climbers' progress by day.

DOUGLAS STEAKLEY/LONELY PLANET IMAGES ©

PHOTOLIBRARY/GETTY ©

KENNAN WARD/CORBIS ©

Kings Canyon Scenic Byway

5 Marvel at soaring granite walls and river-carved clefts deeper than the Grand Canyon on this scenic drive (p169), which connects the Grant Grove and Cedar Grove areas of Kings Canyon National Park. Arrive at Junction View just before dusk or dawn to truly appreciate this glacier-smoothed canyon, which John Muir called 'a rival to the Yosemite.' Twisting hairpin turns, sheer drop-offs and mile-high cliffs are all part of the thrill as you wind down to the bottom of the canyon alongside the rushing Kings River.

Crystal Cave

6 Step through the creepy Spider Gate to explore the subterranean tunnels and cool passageways of this rare marble cave (p164). Among hundreds of caves that have been discovered in Sequoia and Kings Canyon National Parks, only this one is open to the public. A hotspot for biodiversity, this creek-polished cave is stuffed full of stalagmites and stalactites, appearing frozen in time, as well as even more impressive hanging curtains and flowstone formations. Ranger-guided tours are given daily during summer – don't forget to dodge those bats!

Merced River

7 Yosemite Valley's main artery, the Merced River, is also its undulating centerpiece. A wild and undeveloped river pitted with immense boulders, this is where families frolic in summer, splashing on the sandy banks at Cathedral Beach and Devil's Elbow, and rafting its gentle waters. Whether you're dipping your toes in or tracing its ribbony curves from atop Glacier Point, its beauty never fails to impress. Look for level marker signs from the 1997 New Year's flood, when it escaped its banks and washed away trees and campgrounds.

Badger Pass

8 Play like a puppy dog at California's oldest ski resort (p118) where fun is paramount and the hills are gentle. Its the center of winter activity in Yosemite, so bring the kids to get them started on skis, or send them tubing down an easy slope. With a convenient shuttle from the Valley, it's also an easy-to-reach terminus for ranger-led snowshoe walks to Dewey Point and overnight cross-country trips to Glacier Point Ski Hut. At the end of the day, don't forget to treat everyone to hot chocolate piled high with whipped cream.

LEE FOSTER/LONELY PLANET IMAGES ©

PHOTOLIBRARY/GETTY ©

Yosemite High Sierra Camps

9 Who said you had to bust your back to trek overnight in the mountains? In the tradition of European hut-to-hut hikes, each of Yosemite's five tent cabin camps (p128) sits in the spectacular high country, spaced one day's walk from another in a splendid alpine loop. Spend each day bouncing almost weightlessly down the trail, and then end it with a hot meal – prepared by someone else – and the possibility of a hot shower. Warning: this may be addictive.

Hiking the Mist Trail

10 This hike (p84) was made for springtime, when the thundering waters of the Merced River form the 'Giant Staircase,' ricocheting 594ft from Nevada Fall and then 317ft down from Vernal Fall on the way to meet Yosemite Valley. Pack your lunch, and maybe a rain jacket for the trail's namesake mist. With water gushing all around you, the panoramic views are certain to boggle your brain.

Mariposa Grove

11 Pace the needle-carpeted trails in a cathedral of ancient trees, where almost 500 hardy specimens rocket to the sk (p69). In the early evening, after the crowds have gone, you can explore in solitude and contemplate the thousands of years they've witnessed. Fire scars blaze the trunks, and yo can walk through the heart of the still-living California Tunnel Tree and wonder at the girth of the Grizzly Giant. Hike here after the road closes for winter to see its yearly hibernation and snow camp beneath a giant.

WADE EAKLE/LONELY PLANET IMAGES ©

PHOTOLIBRARY/GETTY ©

KANWARJIT SINGH BOPARAI/ALAMY ©

Ahwahnee Hotel

12 Hushed and elegant, the soaring ceilings and tapestried walls of the 1927 Ahwahnee (p63) epitomize luxury – in a dignified, National Historic Landmark kind of way. The iconic lodging in the nation's most iconic park, its muted grandeur is thankfully on sight for all to see, not only the lucky overnighters lounging on its stuffed sofas. Dress up for dinner in its grand, high-beamed dining room, or stop in for evening drinks at the piano bar.

Zumwalt Meadow

13 There's something magical about Zumwalt Meadow (p167). Secreted deep inside Kings Canyon and hedged against soaring granite walls, abundant bird life peacefully flits between trees, and hikers have a good chance of spotting mule deer or even a black bear and her cubs munching on grasses and berries. Zumwalt Meadow is a living geology lesson, wildlife primer and Zen meditation all wrapped into one.

Lyell Canyon

14 Not a fan of uphill slogs to reach the best scenery? This level and easy section of the John Muir Trail was perhaps made with you in mind. Daydream away as you walk through a subalpine meadow buffeted by tree-covered granite peaks and cut by the snaking Lyell Fork of the Tuolumne River. The trail traverses the flat and picture-perfect Lyell Canyon (p106), from where you can admire 13,114ft Mt Lyell, site of one of the park's two remaining glaciers.

Tuolumne Meadows & Tioga Road

15 Winter makes you wait to take in Tuolumne's beauty, but it's so worth it. In summer, after Tioga Rd has been plowed and the roadside walls of snow recede, make a beeline for Yosemite's high country (p73) for carpets of outrageous wildflowers and a cornucopia of alpine lakes. Climbers clip in to tackle the park's high peaks, backpackers lace their eager boots and mules plod the trails to stock the High Sierra Camps. Explore the granite eye candy at one of the Cathedral Lakes or just roam Tuolumne's creek-laced main meadow.

JOHN MOCK/LONELY PLANET IMAGES ©

WES WALKER/LONELY PLANET IMAGES ©

Rae Lakes Loop

16 Get a crush on the skyscraping back-country of Kings Canyon National Park on this jaunt between sparkling alpine lakes. This multiday backpacking expedition (p176) isn't for the faint of heart, especially not along high-country stretches of the John Muir Trail, with the narrow saddle of alpine Glen Pass (11,978ft) to haul yourself over. But the scenic rewards are unmatched. Bed down beside lush meadows or beneath the towering faces of granite domes to watch the stars shine brighter than you've ever seen them before.

Ancient Bristlecone Pine Forest

17 Respect your elders and pay homage to the oldest living things on earth (p155). With some estimated to be about 4000 years old, these gnarled and wind-battered stalwarts have certainly stood the test of time. From Independence, wind your way up the high-altitude road to the White Mountains, stopping midway to admire the distant spiked ridge of the Sierra Nevada and the valley below. At the solar-powered Schulman Grove visitor center, get your bearings and catch your breath before admiring these wizened survivors.

WOODS WHEATCROFT/LONELY PLANET IMAGES ©

Mono Lake

18 Brought back from the brink of extinction by local conservationists battling the might of Los Angeles, this enormous basin (p145) – the second-oldest lake in North America – is truly a sight to ponder. Salty tufa castles rise from subterranean springs, standing watch where mountains meet the desert. Migrating birds feast on clouds of lake flies once relished by local Native American tribes, and bubbly volcanic craters and deep rock fissures buffer this vast blue bowl.

Mt Whitney & the John Muir Trail

19 In for the long haul? Load up that pack and connect the dots from the heart of Yosemite to the pinnacle of Mt Whitney (p194), the highest peak in the contiguous USA. A true adventure, this 200-mile-plus trek (p34), goes step-by-step up and over six Sierra passes topping 11,000ft. Cross chilly rivers and streams between bumper-to-bumper Yosemite Valley, the roadless backcountry of Kings Canyon and Sequoia and the oxygen-scarce summit of Mt Whitney.

Bodie State Historic Park

20 Hopscotch back in time to the era of the lawless Wild West, and imagine the quick-draw bar-room brawls and frenzied gold strikes of this former boom town (p146). One of the West's most authentic and best-preserved ghost towns, it's accessed via a long road that bumps towards a desolate high valley. Now a serene landscape dotted with weather-battered wooden buildings, in its heyday it was renowned for its opium dens and more than five dozen saloons.

need to know

Entrance Fees

» Yosemite: $20 per car, $10 per person on foot, bicycle or motorcycle

» Sequoia & Kings Canyon: as above; admits to both parks

Number of Visitors

» Yosemite: 4.05 million (2010)

» Sequoia & Kings Canyon: 1.25 million (2010)

When to Go

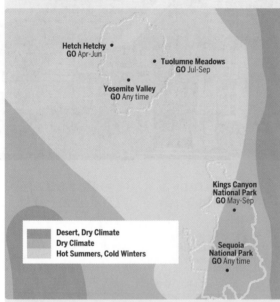

Hetch Hetchy
GO Apr-Jun

Tuolumne Meadows
GO Jul-Sep

Yosemite Valley
GO Any time

Kings Canyon National Park
GO May-Sep

Sequoia National Park
GO Any time

- Desert, Dry Climate
- Dry Climate
- Hot Summers, Cold Winters

Your Daily Budget

Budget less than

$100

» Campsite $15–20

» Daily shower in park $5

» Dine at inexpensive restaurant outside park or fast-food option inside park $10

» Buy food to cook from markets in or outside parks

Midrange

$100– 250

» In-park lodging, midrange hotel or B&B $80–200

» Non-fast-food meal in a park restaurant $20

Top end over

$250

» Room in a top park hotel $200–450

» Meal in a park hotel restaurant $40–60

High Season
(Jun–Aug)

» Temperatures in Yosemite Valley and lower areas of Sequoia and Kings Canyon soar above 90°F (32°C), but higher altitudes are sublime.

» Yosemite waterfalls can dry up entirely.

» All park trails and facilities are open.

» Shoulder (Apr–May & Sep–Oct)

» Autumn is splendid, with fall foliage. Temperatures drop in late October.

» Spring is Yosemite's waterfall season, with crowds usually at weekends only. High country and Sierra passes are inaccessible.

Low Season
(Nov–Mar)

» Winter snows close the high-elevation roads. Most facilities shut down in and around the parks and crowds disappear.

Money

» Yosemite: ATMs in Yosemite Valley and Wawona; credit/debit everywhere

» Sequoia & Kings Canyon: ATMs at Lodgepole, Grant Grove, Cedar Grove and Stony Creek; credit/debit everywhere

Cell phones

» Yosemite: Reception is sketchy; AT&T, Verizon and Sprint have the best coverage

» Sequoia & Kings Canyon: Coverage is nonexistent; some limited reception at Grant Grove

Driving/ Transport

» Major roads are paved in all parks

» Ample parking and year-round frequent free shuttle service in Yosemite Valley

Year Founded

» Yosemite: 1890

» Sequoia & Kings Canyon: 1890

Websites

» **Yosemite National Park** (www.nps.gov/yose) Official park website.

» **Sequoia & Kings Canyon National Parks** (www.nps.gov/seki) Official park website.

» **@YosemiteNPS** (www.twitter.com/yosemitenps) Yosemite's official Twitter feed.

» **High Sierra Topix** (www.highsierratopix.com) Excellent Sierra Nevada forums.

» **Yosemite Online** (www.yosemite.ca.us) By folks in the know.

» **Lonely Planet** (www.lonelyplanet.com/usa) Travel summaries and advice forum.

Exchange Rates

Australia	A$1	US$1.04
Canada	C$1	US$1.01
Europe	€1	US$1.42
Japan	¥100	US$1.27
New Zealand	NZ$1	US$0.84
UK	£1	US$1.63

For current exchange rates see www.xe.com

Important Numbers

Yosemite National Park	209-372-0200
Sequoia & Kings Canyon National Parks	559-565-3341
Delaware North Companies (DNC) at Yosemite (lodging)	801-559-4884
Recreation.gov (camping reservations, all parks)	877-444-6777
California road conditions	800-427-7623

Opening Dates

» **Yosemite**
Park open year-round, 24 hours a day. Tioga Rd closes mid-October until summer. Glacier Point Rd beyond Badger Pass closes November through May. Road to Mariposa Grove closes November through April.

» **Sequoia & Kings Canyon**
Parks open year-round, 24 hours a day. Scenic Byway closes mid-November through mid-April. Mineral King Rd closes late October through late May. Crystal Cave closes November through mid-May.

Public Transportation

In Yosemite, free and frequent shuttle buses ply Yosemite Valley year-round, making car travel unnecessary; free shuttles also travel in the Mariposa Grove and Tuolumne Meadows areas when those roads are open.

In Sequoia National Park, three free shuttle-bus routes run in summer: Giant Forest Museum to Moro Rock and Crescent Meadow; General Sherman Tree parking areas to Lodgepole Village; and a loop covering Lodgepole, Wuksachi Lodge and Dorst Campground.

Yosemite Area Regional Transportation System (YARTS) buses connect Yosemite with the Hwy 140 corridor to Merced year-round and to Mammoth Lakes via Hwy 120 E and Hwy 395 in summer. Amtrak trains run to Merced year-round.

The Sequoia Shuttle connects Visalia to the Giant Forest area of Sequoia National Park in summer. Amtrak service runs to the park gateway of Visalia (via Hanford) year-round.

what's new

For this new edition of Yosemite, Sequoia & Kings Canyon National Parks, our authors have hunted down the fresh, the transformed, the hot and the happening. These are some of our favorites. For up-to-the-minute recommendations, see lonelyplanet.com/usa/yosemite -national-park and lonelyplanet .com/usa/california/sequoia -national-park.

Half Dome Permits

1 Something had to be done about the traffic on Half Dome, where backups on the climbing cables led to lengthy climbing times and potentially hazardous conditions. To scale the cables, day hikers now need to obtain a permit in advance, and backpackers can pick one up at the same time as their wilderness permit. At the time of writing, the system was still being refined to account for no-shows and cancellations.

Mammoth Yosemite Airport

2 Fly directly to the Eastern Sierra all year round from Los Angeles, or in ski season from the San Francisco Bay area.

Mt Whitney Permits

3 Save your stamps: the Mt Whitney permit lottery has forsaken its leafblower-in-a-stairwell shuffling method and gone paperless. Go online to throw your hat into the ring for a permit during peak climbing season.

Yosemite Walk-in Wilderness Permits

4 No longer distributed right when the wilderness centers open their doors, unreserved wilderness permits are now handed out at 11am the day before a hike.

Yosemite Science

5 Check out this online publication to learn about the latest research being done in the park. You'll find it at www .nps.gov/yose/naturescience.

Mammoth Lakes Bike Paths

6 Feel the mountain air fill your lungs as you set off from town on this network of paved bicycle paths.

Solar Energy in Yosemite

7 In 2011 Yosemite completed a 2800-panel photovoltaic array project that's expected to meet 12% of its energy needs, making it the largest solar energy system in US national parks.

Sequoia National Park Shuttles

8 Forget about driving in jam-packed traffic along the Generals Hwy and in the Giant Forest. Take a ride on the park's expanding summer shuttle-bus system.

Boyden Cavern

9 Kings Canyon's only publicly accessible cave just got even more thrilling: sign up for rappelling and canyoneering adventures by day, or camp in the cave overnight.

Ancient Bristlecone Pine Forest

10 Rebuilt following an arson fire, the Schulman Grove Visitor Center is completely powered by solar energy and features a small theater, bookstore and research library.

if you like...

Waterfalls

Mesmerized by springtime flow? Grab a camera and a rain jacket and let the never-ending spray work its magic.

Yosemite Falls The thundering cascades draw stares from across Yosemite Valley. Conquer the tough switchback trail for impressive top-down views (p64)

Waterwheel Falls Turning like a turbine – traipse the high country to reach these unusual cascades (p111)

Mist Falls Who says Yosemite has all the water? Kings Canyon has a trick or two up its sleeve, and this is one of its largest (p175)

Bridalveil Fall After thundering in spring, its wispy summer trickle shows you how it got its name (p64)

Vernal & Nevada Falls The steps of the 'Great Staircase' leap and plunge. An absolute must-do hike in spring (p84)

Rainbow Falls Be wowed by the prism that jets off its waters. Don't miss it when you visit Devils Postpile (p152)

Hiking

Though the sights may look lovely from the car, you need to stop, smell and touch to really experience the landscape.

Shadow Lake Get a small taste of the big wilderness at one of the most accessible lakes in the Ansel Adams Wilderness (p149)

Mt Hoffman Share the sights with marmots at the midpoint of Yosemite, a stark high peak that's easy to summit. Pay your regards to May Lake along the way (p91)

Zumwalt Meadow Mosey around the wildflowers between river and canyon, listening for birds and looking for wildlife (p174)

Panorama Trail With falls aplenty, this picturesque trek descends from Glacier Point to Yosemite Valley (p87)

Mirror Lake Who could resist an easy hike to a sight like this? In spring, stop to contemplate its famed reflection of Half Dome (p82)

Winter Activities

Revel in the hushed pine forests or scream down a powdery mountain chute. The bears may be slumbering, but you don't have to!

Mammoth Mountain Steel yourself for a gondola ride to 11,053ft and some of the most accessible views in the Sierra. The mountain's high and the season practically lasts until summer begins (p149)

Badger Pass California's oldest ski resort is still a charmer. Learn to ski, prepare to fall and then start all over again. Beginners will love the gentle hill (p118)

Winter ski huts Strap on the skins and set out over snowy cross-country hills and valleys. At the end of the journey, snuggle down in a rustic stone cabin in Yosemite (p119)

Ice-Skating A favorite Yosemite tradition where you can practice those rusty pirouettes *al fresco* under the gaze of Glacier Point. Twirl around the ice and watch the ice resurfacer tidy it up (p119)

» A climber ascending the East Buttress of El Capitan (p65)

Swimming

Chock-full of deep lakes, careening rivers and veins of gentle streams, there are endless water adventures to choose from. You can swan dive into pools, simmer in boiling liquid or plunge into an icy pond.

Hume Lake Sandy coves and beaches lure families to this pleasant lake and campground (p168)

Merced River Suit up and wander down to Yosemite's best summer splashing. Rent a raft and paddle the wild and scenic waterway, or sit on boulders and soak up some sun (p116)

Eastern Sierra Hot Springs Toe-test that tub before jumping in, it could be a doozy! Prowl around for a solitary soaking spot with a mountain view and then strip down to your birthday suit (p150)

Muir Rock Cannonball off John Muir's lecture site and do laps from shore to shore in the lazy summer sunshine. The current is gentle and you can float the day away (p167)

Tenaya Lake Build sand castles on the beach and coax those toes into the chilly water. At these altitudes, it's never going to feel balmy, so jump in quickly (p116)

Giant Sequoias

The biggest trees you'll ever see, thankfully preserved, and the original reason why these parks were created. They're living lightning rods and habitats for incredible ecosystems.

Mariposa Grove Over 500 giants live on, including a walk-through tunnel tree (p69)

Giant Forest Don't miss a gander of the hefty General Sherman Tree, by volume the largest living tree on earth (p159)

General Grant Grove A virtual sequoia playground of hollow specimens and the site of the country's first ranger station, it also holds 'the nation's Christmas tree' memorial (p166)

Redwood Mountain Grove In a land full of superlatives, this out-of-the-way grove earns another: the largest sequoia grove in the world (p166)

Tuolumne Grove One of Yosemite's less visited forests, kids can tromp through a hollowed-out tunnel. Cross-country skiers make tracks here in winter (p89)

History

Take a few steps back in time to see who and what has come before.

Bodie State Historic Park Whoa, who stopped the clock? Journey down a back road to this beautifully preserved ghost town, among the best in California (p146)

Laws Railroad Museum If you've ever wondered what life was like in late-1880s Eastern Sierra, take a look around this assemblage of old buildings, myriad artifacts and a historical railway station (p154)

Ancient Bristlecone Pine Forest Who could pass up the chance to see the world's most mature trees? Some of these specimens have been standing for over 4000 years (p155)

Eastern California Museum The work of Paiute and Shoshone basket makers, pioneer alpinists and Manzanar artists provides a fuller look at the landscape and its people (p195)

If you like... spelunking
Crystal Cave's otherworldly stalactites, domes and curtains trace a fantastical underground river (p164)

Views

Lift your eyes and adjust your road-weary pupils to stark mountains, ethereal lakes and vertiginous canyon cliffs. You could gaze for a lifetime – it never gets old.

Glacier Point Spin around in circles at the dizzying sight to behold. Salute Half Dome, and spy on the falls pouring from all sides (p65)

Mono Lake A little salty for swimming, but get an eyeful of all that crazy tufa! Canoe through this beautiful blue bowl and discover why locals refused to let it die (p145)

Alabama Hills You've seen the movies, now take a ride into the sunset on this famous Wild West movie set. Blazing orange hills give way to soaring snow-tipped peaks of granite (p193)

Buck Rock Lookout Summit this remote fire lookout atop a rocky mountain perch. The Great Western Divide and the John Muir Wilderness stretch out before you (p166)

Backpacking

Break out that bag and put some distance between you and everyday life. With a wilderness permit, you're ready to roam.

Rae Lakes Loop Get acquainted with the Kings Canyon backcountry on a jaunt between a chain of sparkling lakes, and find out why this is the most popular loop hike in the park (p176)

High Sierra Camps Lighten the load and give in to soft beds and real showers. Feel a spring in your step as you trek in without the weight of a tent or food (p128)

Rancheria Falls Dodge bear scat during a spring hike past raging Wapama Falls, Hetch Hetchy Dome and Kolana Rock to this tumbling cascade that spills into the Hetch Hetchy Reservoir (p112)

Whitney Back Door Route Sneak up on Mt Whitney from Sequoia and forego the lottery system. The very hard-to-get Whitney permits don't apply to hikers summiting from the peak's west side (p192)

Extreme Adventures

Not one to seek out creature comforts or follow the pack? Up your adrenaline level with a few local favorites, but feel free to invent your own.

Ice Climbing Steady your ice axe and strike a pose in a frozen waterfall. Lee Vining Canyon and the arrested cascades along the June Lake Loop area are the spots to be (p144)

Rafting the Merced River Canyon Know what happens to all that spring runoff? It ends up here in Class III and IV rapids, and you'll be bouncing over its fury (p116)

Canyoneering Boyden Cavern Rappel and wade in the chilly darkness, looking out for things that go bump (p168)

Hang Gliding If you're certified to fly, there's no better thrill than leaping off a cliff at Glacier Point. Float down to the Valley as bystanders clutch their handkerchiefs (p117)

month by month

Top Events

1 **Horsetail Fall**, February

2 **Strawberry Music Festival**, May

3 **Autumn Foliage**, October

4 **Yosemite Facelift**, September

5 **Bracebridge Dinner**, December

January

Short days and freezing temperatures mostly empty out the parks, and ice-quiet solitude has never looked so stunning. Skiing and other snow sports reign supreme.

 Chefs' Holidays
At the Ahwahnee Hotel, meet top chefs from around the country as they lead cooking demonstrations and offer behind-the-scenes kitchen tours in January and February. It's all topped off by a sumptuous gala dinner (www.yosemitepark.com).

February

Daytime temperatures gradually begin to inch up the thermometer as the days get longer. The ski and snowboarding season hits its stride and the long Presidents' Day weekend brings out the snowhounds.

 Horsetail Fall
For two weeks at the end of the month, this thin, seasonal cascade becomes Yosemite's most-photographed attraction. When the sun sets on clear evenings, the flow lights up like a river of fire.

March

When it's sunny, Yosemite Valley can top out at almost 60°F (15°C), though ice forms in the evenings. Spring feels like it's creeping closer at lower elevations.

Yosemite Springfest
Badger Pass Ski Area hosts this winter carnival on the last weekend of each ski season, usually in late March or early April. Events include slalom racing, costume contests, obstacle courses, a barbecue and snow-sculpting (www.badgerpass.com).

April

Don't forsake the tire chains – there's still the possibility of snowstorms during winter's last gasp. But by the end of the month, the dogwoods start to bloom and the waterfalls begin awakening.

 Fishing Season Begins
Anglers froth at the mouth counting the days until the last Saturday of the month. Why? It's the kickoff date of the fishing season, and the trout are just waiting to bite (www.dfg.ca.gov).

May

Things really start stirring on Memorial Day weekend, when flocks of vacationers flood the area and the spring snowmelt courses through park waterfalls. Chilly nights punctuate the occasional 70°F (21°C) day.

Strawberry Music Festival
Each Labor Day and Memorial Day weekend, lovers of country and folk music beeline to this wildly popular music festival held in a meadow at Camp Mather near Hetch Hetchy. Children's programs constitute half the fun (www.strawberrymusic.com).

June

The high country has begun to thaw, and the

summer visitor influx begins. It's the best time to explore trails below 8000ft, though you'll want snow gear to hike much higher.

🏃 Tioga Road Opens

Though it varies year-to-year, by now this crucial trans-Sierra highway is usually plowed and open. The Eastern Sierra suddenly feels a little closer, and hikers feel that itch to strike the trail.

July

Snow has usually receded from the higher elevations, though mosquitoes often wait to greet you there. At exposed lower ground, summer heat may leave you wilting at midday.

✨ Badwater Ultramarathon

About 30 years ago someone came up with a preposterous idea: why not run a race between the highest and lowest points in the continental US? Over 60 hours, runners attempt a nonstop course from Death Valley (35 miles southeast of Lone Pine) to Whitney Portal (www .badwater.com).

August

Temperatures in Yosemite Valley and the lower areas of Sequoia & Kings Canyon keep rising, making an escape to the higher altitudes a refreshing relief.

✨ Tuolumne Meadows Poetry Festival

A poetry festival on the grass in Tuolumne Meadows. How can you beat that? Sponsored by the Yosemite Conservancy, wildflowers and words take center stage during a weekend of workshops and readings (www.yosemiteconservancy .org).

September

The summer heat begins to fizzle as the month progresses, giving way to brisk days and frigid evenings. The crowds recede and waterfalls are at a trickle.

✨ Yosemite Facelift

The biggest volunteer event of the year – in Yosemite or any other national park – sees climbers and other grateful souls descend for a major clean up at the end of the season. The result? Over 100,000 pounds of garbage removed (www.yosemite climbing.org).

October

The weather's hit-and-miss, with either Sierra Nevada sunshine or bucketfuls of chilling rain. Mountain businesses wind up their season and diehards take one last hike before the first snowflakes appear.

👁 Autumn Foliage

Fall colors light up the Sierra Nevada and leaf-peeping photographers joyride looking for the best shot. Black oaks

blaze dramatically in the undulating foothills, but it's the stands of aspen that steal the show as they flame gold under blue high-elevation sky.

November

Deep snow shuts Tioga Rd and – ta-da! – it's the unofficial start of winter. The Thanksgiving holiday reels in families, and backcountry campers tune up their cross-country skis.

✨ Vintners' Holidays

Toast the close of the year's harvest with prominent winemakers and fruits of their labor. Wine-lovers descend upon the Ahwahnee Hotel each November and December for this annual wine- and food-tasting extravaganza, with seminars and wine tastings galore (www.yosemitepark.com).

December

Vacationers inundate the resorts during the week between Christmas and New Year's Day, though otherwise the parks remain frosted and solitary. Think snowshoe hikes and hot chocolate.

✨ Bracebridge Dinner

Held at the Ahwahnee Hotel, this traditional Christmas pageant is part feast and part Renaissance fair. Guests indulge in a multicourse meal while being entertained by more than 100 actors in 17th-century costume (www .bracebridgedinners.com).

Whether you've got six days or 60, these itineraries provide a starting point for the trip of a lifetime. Want more inspiration? Head online to lonelyplanet.com /thorntree to chat with other travelers.

itineraries

At Least Two Weeks
Grand Tour – Sequoia to Alabama Hills

> Kick off the trip with three to four days in **Sequoia & Kings Canyon National Parks**, touring its ancient trees, ethereal caves and show-stopping river canyon. Heading north up Hwy 41, camp at **Wawona** and budget a day for the southern reaches of **Yosemite National Park**. Spend *at least* three days exploring the miraculous falls and granite monoliths of **Yosemite Valley**, then hike the trails of Yosemite's high country while camped out at **Tuolumne Meadows**. Just east of the park, take a full day to explore the surreal countryside around **Saddlebag Lake**, and then journey over to **Mono Lake**. Detour north to the ghost-town ruins of **Bodie State Historic Park**, and then continue back south to lap up the mountain vistas buffering the **June Lake Loop**. Using **Mammoth Lakes** as a base, spend a day hiking to the bizarre formation of the **Devils Postpile National Monument** and then to the delicious **hot springs**, located southeast of town, as the sun sets. Next, wind up the road to the **Ancient Bristlecone Pine Forest** to breathe the thin air and marvel at the gnarled time-capsule trees. On your final day tour the solemn remains of **Manzanar**, and catch a film-worthy sunset at the **Alabama Hills** in **Lone Pine**.

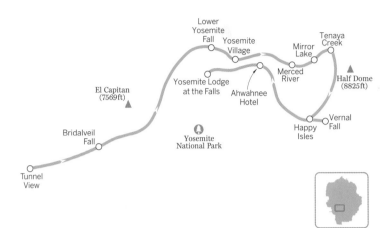

One Day
Yosemite Valley in a Day

If you really, really only have one day to see Yosemite, there are two stops you should make before heading into the Valley. At **Tunnel View** you can drink in views of the entire Valley, with the iconic Half Dome front and center and Bridalveil Fall plunging in the distance. The heavenly **Bridalveil Fall** up close is the other must-see; put on some flip-flops or galoshes and pack raingear if it's spring, because the spray turns the sidewalk into a flowing creek. Aim your camera at its misty rainbows and yell over the thundering water. Afterward, pull over just east along Southside Dr and try to spot the microscopic-sized climbers working their way up the sheer granite of El Capitan. Keep your eyes peeled for wildlife wandering about the meadows, and then park in one of the Valley's day-use parking lots. Rent a bicycle from Yosemite Lodge or Curry Village and ride to the viewing area at the base of **Lower Yosemite Fall**. Follow the bike path to **Yosemite Village**, and hitch up at Degnan's Deli for a lunch of fresh sandwiches and soup.

Saunter over to the Yosemite Valley Visitor Center and explore the center's exhibits of park geology and wildlife and peruse the Yosemite Conservancy Bookstore. Saddle up again and ride east on the dedicated bike path, crossing the **Merced River** and eluding four-wheeled traffic. Continue on to **Mirror Lake** and snap a photo of Half Dome's dignified reflection in its shallow waters, and stroll along **Tenaya Creek** to find quiet nooks to sit along its shore. Pedal south to **Nature Center at Happy Isles** to hear what sounds the park animals make, and consider a longer hike up the short but steep trail to **Vernal Fall**. If you don't have time for the 2.4-mile round-trip, you could stop at the footbridge below the fall. Zip over to the historic **Ahwahnee Hotel** for a well-deserved cocktail or coffee, and then return the bike before indulging in the excellent food and views at the Mountain Room Restaurant at **Yosemite Lodge at the Falls**.

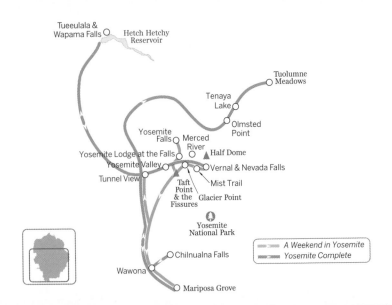

Tueeulala & Wapama Falls
Hetch Hetchy Reservoir
Tuolumne Meadows
Tenaya Lake
Olmsted Point
Yosemite Falls
Merced River
Half Dome
Yosemite Lodge at the Falls
Yosemite Valley
Vernal & Nevada Falls
Tunnel View
Mist Trail
Taft Point & the Fissures
Glacier Point
Yosemite National Park
Chilnualna Falls
Wawona
Mariposa Grove

A Weekend in Yosemite
Yosemite Complete

Seven to 10 Days ·
Yosemite Complete

Spend your first day strolling the re-markably crowd-free **Yosemite Valley looptrails**. Next day, experience mind-altering views hiking the drenched **Mist Trail** to **Vernal and Nevada Falls**. Be a lazy toad the following day, floating around the **Merced River** – the best views from a raft you'll ever have. Reserve day four to huff and puff the Four Mile Trail to **Glacier Point** for vistas from the park's most famous viewpoint. Or go climb a rock: take a climbing class with the Yosemite Mountaineering School. Remember where San Francisco's water comes from? Drive out to Hetch Hetchy for a day trip and hike along the city's infamous **reservoir** to **Tueeulala and Wapama Falls**. Next morning gobble down a giant buffet breakfast in style at the historic **Wawona Hotel**, and then humble yourself exploring the ancient **Mariposa Grove**. Pack a lunch and hike to thundering **Chilnualna Falls**, near Wawona. Don't forget the high country! The following day stop to marvel at **Olmsted Point** from the Tioga Rd viewpoint, and sun your buns while taking in the dazzling views from the sandy shores of **Tenaya Lake**. Wind up your trip with a wander around the Sierra Nevada's biggest alpine meadow while camped at **Tuolumne Meadows**.

Two Days
A Weekend in Yosemite

On Saturday, pack a lunch and head out pronto to conquer the long up-ward climb of either the **Mist Trail** or the **Yosemite Falls Trail**, giving yourself oodles of time and lots of scenic breather stops along the way. Take the shuttle bus to and from either trailhead. Back in the Valley, quench your thirst post-hike with a celebratory drink at the festive Mountain Room Bar in **Yosemite Lodge at the Falls**, and in the evening, hear the rangers spin park tales around the flames at a convivial Campfire Program. On your final day, pack up and motor to **Glacier Point**, stopping en route for a leisurely stroll to vertigo-inducing **Taft Point and the Fissures**. Save lunch for when you get to road's end, in full view of **Half Dome** and **Vernal and Nevada Falls**. Continue south into **Wawona**, ditching the car for the shuttle to take a gander at the giant sequoias of **Mariposa Grove**. Return to the historic Wawona Hotel for a dinner in its classy dining room. On your way home, catch the remains of the day at the magnificent **Tunnel View** lookout, taking in one last Valley eyeful before leaving.

Sequoia National Park
Kings Canyon National Park

One Day
Sequoia National Park

Start your day at the **Foothills Visitor Center**, stopping long enough to get oriented and scoop up late-afternoon tour tickets for Crystal Cave. Head north on the Generals Hwy, hitting the brakes at **Tunnel Rock** – visualize squeezing through with a Tin Lizzie – and to see Native American pictographs and grinding holes at **Hospital Rock**. Arriving in **Giant Forest**, let yourself be dwarfed by the majestic General Sherman Tree, the largest tree in the world. Learn about the life cycles of giant sequoias at the Giant Forest Museum, then let your kids go nuts at the Beetle Rock Education Center, take a photo of your car driving through the Tunnel Log archway, or leave your car behind and hop on the park shuttle for an easy wildflower walk around Crescent Meadow after scaling the puff-and-pant stairs up Moro Rock for bird's-eye canyon and peak views. Picnic at **Lodgepole Village**, then get back in your car and make your way to the chilly underground wonderland of **Crystal Cave**. Marvel at delicate marble formations while easing through eerie passageways, sucking it in and squeezing your shoulders on tight corners.

One Day
Kings Canyon National Park

Start in **Grant Grove Village** at the northern end of the Generals Hwy, which conveniently connects Sequoia and Kings Canyon National Parks. Take a walk in the mammoth sequoia grove encompassing the **General Grant Tree** and gigantic Fallen Monarch. Traverse the length of the park by driving the Kings Canyon Scenic Byway, which passes through the **Giant Sequoia National Monument**, where you can bump over a dirt road to **Converse Basin Grove** and take a wistful hike to the lonely Boole Tree. Wash off all that sweat with a dip at **Hume Lake**. Back on the scenic byway, which precipitously descends all the way into Kings Canyon, pull over to survey the canyon depths and distant peaks from the shoulder of lofty **Junction View**. Take a tour of **Boyden Cavern**, then cruise through **Cedar Grove Village**. Feel waves of spray from roadside **Roaring River Falls** or stroll alongside the Kings River and admire striking granite canyon views from verdant **Zumwalt Meadow**, a bird-watching hotspot with a boardwalk nature trail. Last but not least, cool off on the beach at **Muir Rock** before catching a canyon sunset from historic **Knapp's Cabin**.

Activities

Best Times to Go

Backpacking June–September
Cycling May–October
Hiking May–October
Horseback Riding June–August
Mountain Biking June–September
Rock Climbing April–October
Swimming July–August
White-water Rafting April–September
Winter Sports December–March

Top Outdoor Experiences

Backpacking John Muir Trail and summiting Mt Whitney
Cycling Around Yosemite Valley's paved loop trails
Hiking Half Dome, high above Yosemite Valley
Mountain biking Mammoth Mountain in the Eastern Sierra
Rock climbing El Capitan in Yosemite Valley
Swimming, tubing, kayaking Merced River in Yosemite Valley
Skiing Downhill at Badger Pass or cross-country along Glacier Point Rd
Snowshoeing Among giant sequoias in Sequoia's Giant Forest
Stargazing From Yosemite's Glacier Point
White-water rafting Merced River outside Yosemite

Every time you get home from a trip to the Sierra Nevada, all you can think about for weeks is your *next* trip. Maybe it's the granite. Or the big, big trees. Whatever it is, the Sierra Nevada is not just for climbers and mountaineers. Hikers, skiers, horseback riders and river runners all have that same eager look in their eye here. It's as if everyone knows you *could* do these same outdoor activities anywhere in the world, but the setting just wouldn't match up.

As far as summer activities go, the Sierra Nevada is a dream: few mountain ranges anywhere can boast the same perpetually beautiful, gloriously mild summer weather. As for winter, the snow gets thick and the Sierras offer everything from world-class downhill skiing and snowboarding (think Mammoth) to scenic cross-country skiing and snowshoeing inside the parks. If you don't mind some occasional wet weather, spring and fall can be sublime, with fewer crowds hitting the trails.

Hiking & Backpacking

Whether strolling leisurely along the floor of Yosemite Valley or schlepping a 60lb pack over a high pass, hiking is the way most visitors experience the Sierra Nevada. And it's no wonder: over 1600 miles of trails traverse a diverse and spectacular landscape, ranking the region's national parks among the world's most incredible hiking and backpacking destinations.

Some of the parks' most spectacular sights can be visited via short, easy trails; a few are even wheelchair-accessible. For

HOW HARD IS THAT TRAIL?

Sierra Nevada hikes in this book are rated by three levels of difficulty to help you choose the trail that's right for you.

» **Easy** Manageable for nearly all walkers, an easy hike is under 4 miles, with fairly even terrain and no significant elevation gain or loss.

» **Moderate** Fine for fit hikers and active, older children, moderate hikes have a modest elevation gain in the range of 500ft to 1000ft and are usually less than 7 miles long.

» **Difficult** Hikes have elevation gains of over 1000ft, are mostly steep, may have tricky footing and are often over 8 miles long. Being physically fit is paramount.

All hikes included in this book, from day hikes to backcountry treks, follow marked, established trails and unless otherwise noted, the distance listed in each hike description is for a *round-trip* journey. The actual time spent hiking will vary with your ability. When in doubt, assume trails will be harder and take longer than you think.

our top 10 hikes with kids, see p43. Many of the most famous hikes in Yosemite are day hikes, but they often involve steep ascents and descents. Avoid the crowds and blistering afternoon heat by starting early if you're tackling those trails in summer. Depending on last winter's snowpack, some trails may be closed until late spring or even midsummer, especially in the high country.

Permits are not required for day hikes into the backcountry, with the exception of Yosemite's Half Dome (see p63) and Mt Whitney (p192). All overnight backcountry trips in the parks require permits. If you're planning on hiking the most popular trails in summer, apply for permits many months in advance. For park-specific wilderness regulations and permit information, see the 'Overnight Hikes' sections of the park chapters.

Maps, Books & Online Resources

Bulletin boards posted with trail maps and safety information are found at major trailheads. For short, well-established hikes, free maps handed out at park entrance stations and visitor centers are usually sufficient, as are the hiking maps in this guide. Occasionally a more detailed topographical map may be necessary, depending on the length and difficulty of your hike. These are usually sold at park bookstores, visitor centers and wilderness permit desks.

US Geological Survey (USGS; www.store .usgs.gov) offers topographic maps as free downloadable PDFs, or you can order print copies online. Complete, in-depth hiking

and backpacking guides include Wilderness Press' excellent *A Complete Hiker's Guide* series, with titles for Yosemite and Sequoia & Kings Canyon. To stay current on trail-access issues, visit the website of the non-profit **High Sierra Hikers Association** (www.highsierrahikers.org).

Group Hikes & Courses

All national parks offer free ranger-guided walks and day hikes year-round. Ask at visitor centers or check the seasonal park newspapers for current programs and schedules. The following is a list of paid guided hikes and outdoors classes:

Yosemite Conservancy (www.yosemite conservancy.org) Guided natural history, wildflower, photography and twilight hikes, plus overnight backpacking trips, including to Half Dome.

Sequoia Natural History Association (www.sequoiahistory.org) 'Ed Venture' backpacking trips, natural history hikes and backpacking skills courses, including for women only.

Sierra Club (www.sierraclub.org, http://sierra clubcalifornia.org) Day hikes, backpacking trips and volunteer vacations in the Sierra Nevada.

Road Scholar (www.roadscholar.org) Educational hiking trips for travelers aged 50-plus.

DNC Parks & Resorts at Yosemite (www .yosemitepark.com) Private and group guided hikes and overnight backpacking trips, including for beginners.

Southern Yosemite Mountain Guides (www.symg.com) Long-established outfitter offering expensive guided hiking and backpacking trips, as well as backcountry skills courses.

HIKING IN YOSEMITE NATIONAL PARK

NAME	REGION	DESCRIPTION	DIFFICULTY
Lukens Lake	Big Oak Flat Rd & Tioga Rd	Quick hike to small but attractive lake; lots of wildflowers	easy
Tenaya Lake	Big Oak Flat Rd & Tioga Rd	A level stroll around one of biggest lakes in the high country	easy
Tuolumne Grove	Big Oak Flat Rd & Tioga Rd	Descend along a portion of Old Big Oak Flat Rd to a small sequoia grove	easy-moderate
Merced Grove	Big Oak Flat Rd & Tioga Rd	The park's least visited sequoia grove; downhill with a stiff ascent on the return	easy-moderate
Harden Lake	Big Oak Flat Rd & Tioga Rd	Follow the old Tioga Rd and the Tuolumne River for a rare warm lake swim	easy-moderate
North Dome	Big Oak Flat Rd & Tioga Rd	Astounding views of Yosemite Valley, Half Dome and Tenaya Canyon; includes 1000ft descent	moderate
May Lake & Mt Hoffmann	Big Oak Flat Rd & Tioga Rd	Short hike to May Lake High Sierra Camp, plus more challenging summit to nearby peak	moderate-difficult
Clouds Rest	Big Oak Flat Rd & Tioga Rd	Yosemite's largest expanse of granite; arguably its finest panoramic viewpoint	difficult
Tenaya Lake to Yosemite Valley	Big Oak Flat Rd & Tioga Rd	Includes 6321ft cumulative descent, with the option to summit Clouds Rest	difficult
Old Big Oak Flat Rd to Yosemite Falls	Big Oak Flat Rd & Tioga Rd	Inspiring hike from the heights of the Valley's north rim	difficult
McGurk Meadow	Glacier Point & Badger Pass	Short, flat walk to lush meadow; lots of wildflowers and old log cabin	easy
Taft Point & the Fissures	Glacier Point & Badger Pass	Major Valley viewpoint with interesting geological features	easy
Sentinel Dome	Glacier Point & Badger Pass	Easiest hike to top of a dome with amazing 360-degree views	easy-moderate
Panorama Trail	Glacier Point & Badger Pass	Descends from Glacier Point to Valley floor, with postcard views the whole way down	moderate-difficult
Pohono Trail	Glacier Point & Badger Pass	Passes numerous Valley viewpoints; requires car shuttle	moderate-difficult
Ostrander Lake	Glacier Point & Badger Pass	Out-and-back wildflower trail with distant views leads to a backcountry hut and amphitheater lake	moderate-difficult
Carlon Falls	Hetch Hetchy	Falls feed into two swimming spots on the western edge of the park	easy-moderate
Tueeulala & Wapama Falls	Hetch Hetchy	Undulating trail to base of Hetch Hetchy's roaring waterfalls; boasts views aplenty	easy-moderate
Rancheria Falls	Hetch Hetchy	A popular introduction to Hetch Hetchy's lower altitude backcountry and waterfalls; best in spring	moderate-difficult
Dog Lake	Tuolumne Meadows	Picnicking and brisk swimming await at the end of this pine-forest trail	easy-moderate
Lyell Canyon	Tuolumne Meadows	Flat trail; superb views of Mt Lyell and its eponymous glacier	easy-moderate
Lembert Dome	Tuolumne Meadows	One of the best places to watch the sun set in Yosemite is atop this granite dome	moderate
Gaylor Lakes	Tuolumne Meadows	Short, steep hike with epic scenery of high country and lakes above Tioga Pass	moderate
Elizabeth Lake	Tuolumne Meadows	Great jaunt for acclimatizing in Tuolumne; superb views; lots to explore	moderate
Cathedral Lakes	Tuolumne Meadows	Easily one of Yosemite's most spectacular hikes	moderate

  Wildlife Watching   *View*   *Great for Families*   *Waterfall*   *Restrooms*   *Drinking Water*

DURATION	ROUND-TRIP DISTANCE	ELEVATION CHANGE	FEATURES	FACILITIES	PAGE
1hr	1.6 miles	+200ft			90
1hr	2 miles	+50ft			90
1½hr	2 miles	+500ft			89
1½-2hr	3 miles	+600ft			90
2-3hr	5.8 miles	+400ft			91
4½-5hr	8.5 miles	-1000/+422ft			93
4-5hr	6 miles	+2004ft			91
6-7hr	14.4 miles	+2205ft			92
2 days (one way)	17.2 miles (one way)	+2205ft			104
2 days (one way)	18.8 miles (one way)	+3080/-2700ft			103
1hr	1.6 miles	+150ft			85
1hr	2.2 miles	+250ft			86
1hr	2.2 miles	+370ft			86
5hr (one way)	8.5 miles (one way)	-3200/+760ft			87
7-9hr (one way)	13.8 miles (one way)	-2800ft			87
2 days	12.4 miles	+1550ft			102
2hr	2.4 miles	+300ft			99
2½-3hr	5.4 miles	+400ft			98
7hr-2days	13 miles	+786ft			112
2hr	2.8 miles	+520ft			94
2 days	17.6 miles	+200ft			106
2-3hr	2.4 miles	+850ft			94
2-3hr	3 miles	+560ft			97
2½-4hr	5.2 miles	+800ft			94
4-7hr	8 miles	+1000ft			95

  Transportation to Trailhead   *Ranger Station*   *Backcountry Campsite*   *Picnic Sites*   *Swimming*

HIKING IN YOSEMITE NATIONAL PARK (CONTINUED)

NAME	REGION	DESCRIPTION	DIFFICULTY
Glen Aulin	Tuolumne Meadows	Follow Tuolumne River past waterfalls to one of the High Sierra Camps	moderate
Young Lakes	Tuolumne Meadows	Sweeping views of the Cathedral Range lead to a trio of lovely lakes	moderate
Mono Pass	Tuolumne Meadows	Outstanding day hike into high country above Tioga Pass	moderate-difficult
Vogelsang	Tuolumne Meadows	Multiday, high-country trip with astounding views of Cathedral Range	moderate-difficult
Mt Dana	Tuolumne Meadows	Lung-busting, thigh-burning hike to the park's second-highest peak	difficult
Waterwheel Falls	Tuolumne Meadows	Splendid series of waterfalls at head of Grand Canyon of the Tuolumne River	difficult
Wawona Meadow Loop	Wawona	Loop around meadow shaded and flat, but lots of horse manure	easy
Mariposa Grove to Wawona	Wawona	Woodsy, downhill alternative to shuttle bus	easy-moderate
Chilnualna Falls	Wawona	Uncrowded trail along cascading creek to top of waterfalls over Wawona Dome's shoulder	moderate-difficult
Mirror Lake	Yosemite Valley	Best in spring, a relaxed stroll to the lovely sight of reflective Mirror Lake and beyond	easy
Yosemite Valley Loops	Yosemite Valley	Surprisingly uncrowded trails that pass all the major Valley sights	easy
Inspiration Point	Yosemite Valley	Some of the finest views of Yosemite Valley; easily extended to include other viewpoints	moderate-difficult
Vernal & Nevada Falls	Yosemite Valley	Justifiably popular hike to two of Yosemite's finest falls; mind-blowing scenery	moderate-difficult
Four Mile Trail	Yosemite Valley	One of the grandest viewpoints in the entire country; also accessible by car or shuttle	difficult
Yosemite Falls	Yosemite Valley	Sweat yourself silly and enjoy the views hiking to the top of Yosemite's highest falls	difficult
Half Dome	Yosemite Valley	The park's most difficult day hike is a strenuous push to the top of Yosemite's iconic dome	difficult

Wildlife Watching　　View　　Great for Families　　Waterfall　　Restrooms　　Drinking Water

Long-Distance Trails

Several long-distance trails pass through Yosemite, Sequoia and Kings Canyon National Parks, most famously the 211-mile John Muir Trail, which starts in Yosemite Valley and follows the Sierra Crest all the way to Mt Whitney (14,505ft). The daunting 2650-mile Pacific Crest National Scenic Trail extends from Canada to Mexico, passing through the High Sierra en route. The province of experts, these trails can be a lifetime achievement for those who manage to thru-hike the entire distance, but many people choose to hike them in smaller, more manageable sections. For more information on both trails, consult the **Pacific Crest Trail Association** (www.pcta.org); for trail conditions, call ☏888-728-7245.

Biking

Bicycles are an excellent way to explore Yosemite Valley (rentals available; see p113). Twelve miles of mostly flat, paved trails pass nearly all of the Valley's most famous sights. Wear a helmet and ride defensively – the path isn't always clearly marked, and many visitors pay more attention to gawking than steering.

DURATION	ROUND-TRIP DISTANCE	ELEVATION CHANGE	FEATURES	FACILITIES	PAGE
6-8hr	11 miles	-600ft			96
2 days	13 miles	+1300ft			107
4hr	7.4 miles	+915ft			97
3 days	27 miles	+3852ft			109
6-7hr	5.8 miles	+3108ft			97
2 days	18 miles	+2260ft			111
1-1½hr	3.5 miles	+200ft			88
2-3hr (one way)	6.5 miles (one way)	-2000ft			88
4-5hr	8.6 miles	+2240ft			89
1hr	2 miles	+100ft			82
varies	varies	+330ft			81
1½-2½hr	2.6 miles	+1000ft			83
4-7hr	6.5 miles	+1900ft			84
4-8hr	9.2 miles	+3200ft			84
5-6hr	6.8 miles	+2400ft			83
10-12hr	17 miles	+4800ft			101

Transportation to Trailhead — *Ranger Station* — *Backcountry Campsite* — *Picnic Sites* — *Swimming*

For serious road cyclists, Yosemite's Glacier Point Rd ascends almost 2000ft over 16 miles. Tioga Rd/Hwy 120 is a more grueling route, climbing almost 6000ft from Yosemite Valley to lung-busting Tioga Pass, then dropping dramatically – make that *frighteningly* – down Lee Vining Canyon to finish at Hwy 395 near Mono Lake, a 45-mile total trip.

From Lee Vining, you can ride south on Hwy 395 and pick up Hwy 120 east again to knock out a spectacular Eastern Sierra loop by taking Benton Crossing Rd back west to Hwy 395. This is the route of the annual, open-registration **High Sierra Fall Century** (www.fallcentury.org). The 16-mile June Lake Loop offers outstanding cycling, too, as does the road to Twin Lakes.

Sequoia and Kings Canyon don't offer many places for cycling, although some paved roads in Sequoia's Giant Forest and from Cedar Grove to Roads End in Kings Canyon make for easy, mostly level rides – just watch for traffic. Hard-core cyclists could ride the Kings Canyon Scenic Byway/Hwy 180, which drops over 2000ft in 36 miles as it nerve-wrackingly winds its way down to the Kings River. Of course, you have to turn around and climb back up in order to get out – whew!

PLAN YOUR TRIP ACTIVITIES

NAME	REGION	DESCRIPTION	DIFFICULTY
Marble Falls	Foothills	Lower-elevation hike parallels a river canyon to a thundering cascade	moderate
Moro Rock	Giant Forest	Steep granite dome ascent for panoramic peak and canyon views	easy
Big Trees Trail	Giant Forest	Paved, kid-friendly interpretive trail circling a sequoia-bordered forest meadow	easy
Crescent Meadow Loop	Giant Forest	Beautiful subalpine meadow ringed by giant sequoias and summer wildflowers	easy
General Sherman Tree to Moro Rock	Giant Forest	Huge sequoias, peaceful meadows and the pinnacle of Moro Rock	moderate
High Sierra Trail to Bearpaw Meadow	Giant Forest	Gorgeous sequoia-grove and canyon-view hike crossing mountain streams	difficult
Tokopah Falls	Lodgepole	One of Sequoia's largest, most easily accessed scenic waterfalls	easy
Monarch Lakes	Mineral King	High-country hike to two alpine lakes at base of Sawtooth Peak	difficult
Zumwalt Meadow Loop	Cedar Grove	Flat, meadow boardwalk loop traces the Kings River beside canyon walls	easy
Mist Falls	Cedar Grove	Partly shaded forest and granite hike to a gushing waterfall	moderate
Rae Lakes Loop	Cedar Grove	Passes a chain of jewel-like lakes in the heart of the Sierra Nevada high country	difficult
General Grant Tree Trail	Grant Grove	Paved interpretive loop through a giant sequoia grove	easy

🦌 Wildlife Watching   🔭 View   👪 Great for Families   🌊 Waterfall   🧗 Rock Climbing   🚻 Restroom

Note that all trails within the national parks are off-limits to mountain bikes. You'll need to head to Mammoth Mountain for this, with over 80 miles of single track, from downhill runs to free rides, plus shuttles, gondolas and chairlifts (p149).

Rock Climbing & Bouldering

With 3000ft granite monoliths, sheer spires, near-vertical walls and a temperate climate, Yosemite is no less than the world's holy grail of rock. Camp 4, Yosemite Valley's cheap, no-reservations walk-in campground, has for decades been the hangout for some of climbing's legendary stars. Yosemite's granite, mostly deemed impossible to climb until the 1940s, necessitated entirely new techniques, equipment and climbing styles. In 1947, using hand-forged steel pitons, Swiss climber John Salathé and Anton 'Ax' Nelson became the first to climb the Lost Arrow Chimney, regarded as the most

difficult climb of its day. Next came a team of illustrious climbers who changed the sport forever, including Royal Robbins, a pioneer of clean climbing techniques, and Yvon Chouinard, founder of Patagonia.

Attacking the world's greatest single slab of granite in stages between July 1957 and November 1958, big-wall pioneer Warren Harding took 45 days to climb El Capitan's now world-famous Nose route. In 1994 Lynn Hill free-climbed the route in less than 24 hours. In 2010, Dean Potter and Sean Leary speed-climbed the Nose in just over 2½ hours. Needless to say, climbing has come a long way.

Today, the climbing spirit soars as high as ever. During spring and fall, climbers flock to Yosemite Valley, and boulder-strewn Camp 4 remains ground zero. Need a climbing partner? Check the Camp 4 bulletin board. Looking for used climbing equipment? Camp 4. Want route information from fellow climbers? You guessed it.

DURATION	ROUND-TRIP DISTANCE	ELEVATION CHANGE	FEATURES	FACILITIES	PAGE
3-4hr	7 miles	+2000ft			173
40min	0.5 miles	+300ft			170
45min	1.2 miles	+100ft			170
1hr	1.6 miles	+200ft			171
2½-4hr	6 miles	+1600ft			171
2 days	22 miles	+2200ft			176
2hr	3.5 miles	+500ft			171
4-6hr	8.5 miles	+2700ft			173
1hr	1.5 miles	+100ft			174
3-5hr	8 miles	+800ft			175
5 days	40 miles	+7000ft			176
30min	0.5 miles	+100ft			174

Drinking Water   Transportation to Trailhead   Ranger Station   Backcountry Campsite   Swimming

Come summer, many climbers relocate to gentler, high-elevation Tuolumne Meadows, where temperatures are cooler than in the Valley and where there's an abundance of glacially polished granite domes. Bulletin boards at the Tuolumne Meadows Store and the campground are information hubs.

With so much glacial debris scattered about, Yosemite is also outstanding for bouldering, the sport of climbing without a rope at short distances above the ground. The only equipment necessary are shoes, a chalk bag and a bouldering mat, so it's a great way to enter the sport of climbing. Yosemite Valley and Tuolumne Meadows are the park's most popular bouldering spots.

Yosemite doesn't have a monopoly on rock climbing. Sequoia & Kings Canyon have some outstanding climbing with a fraction of the crowds. In the Eastern Sierra, Mammoth Lakes, and the Owens River Gorge and the Buttermilks near Bishop are top climbing areas. There's also plenty of high-altitude climbing between Saddlebag Lake and Yosemite's east entrance near Tioga Pass.

Yosemite Mountaineering School & Guide Service (www.yosemitemountaineering .com) If you're new to climbing, or want to build on your techniques and knowledge, come here. Based at the Curry Village Mountain Shop and, during summer, the Tuolumne Meadows Sport Shop, ask about big-wall weekend climbing seminars and 'Girls on Granite' boot camps.

Sierra Rock Climbing School (www.sierra rockclimbingschool.com) Check here for climbing courses and guides in the Eastern Sierra; based in Mammoth Lakes.

Horseback Riding

There's ample opportunity to saddle up within the parks. But don't imagine yourself galloping across a meadow with the wind at your back, though – stock animals must stick to the trails. Keep in mind that unless you're bringing your own horses, any

LEAVE NO TRACE

Before you hit the trail, learn how to minimize your impact on the environment by talking with park rangers and visiting **Leave No Trace Center for Outdoor Ethics** (www.lnt.org) online.

Food

» Store food in a bear-resistant canister (see p242).

» Never feed wildlife and avoid leaving any food scraps behind. Wild animals can become dependent on hand-outs, causing disease, starvation and aggressive behavior toward people.

Hiking & Camping

» Stay on the trail – making and taking shortcuts contributes to erosion.

» Camp at least 100ft from water and, if possible, the trail.

» Always yield to stock animals.

» Camp in existing sites or on durable surfaces. Keep campsites small.

Fires

» Don't start any campfires over 9600ft or above the tree line.

» Below the tree line, collect only dead and downed wood. Use only sticks that can be broken by hand, not logs.

» If you make a campfire, utilize existing fire rings only – don't build new ones.

Waste

» Discard all grey-water at least 100ft from all water sources. Don't put any soap in the water (even biodegradable soap pollutes).

» Carry out all trash, including toilet paper. Toilet paper burns poorly, and animals will dig up anything scented.

» Relieve yourself at least 200ft from any water source. For solid waste, dig a hole 6in deep (in snow, dig down to the soil).

'horseback rides' offered within the parks are usually on tough, surefooted mules.

From late spring through early fall, the Yosemite Valley, Tuolumne Meadows and Wawona Stables offer two-hour to full-day trail rides in Yosemite (p115). In Kings Canyon, Grant Grove Stables offers one-and two-hour guided trail rides, while Cedar Grove Pack Station (also in Kings Canyon) and Horse Corral Pack Station (in the Sequoia National Forest) offer half- and full-day trips further afield (see p179).

If you want to get out into the wilderness, both the Cedar Grove Pack and Horse Corral Pack Stations can arrange multiday backcountry trips, including for fishing. In Yosemite, the most popular pack trips go to the park's High Sierra Camps, which require reservations far in advance.

The Eastern Sierra is ideal for horseback adventuring, with its mountain vistas, lakes and valleys. Several outfitters run trips out of Mammoth Lakes and Bishop, putting riders within easy reach of the gorgeous Ansel Adams and John Muir Wilderness Areas.

Swimming

Few sensations top the joy of jumping into a river or swimming in a mountain lake. However, you'd better be able to tolerate cold water here: rivers swollen with spring snowmelt don't become safe enough for swimming until midsummer, and alpine lakes stay chilly year-round.

In rivers, always swim near other swimmers unless you're absolutely certain about the nature of the current. People drown every year in Sierra Nevada rivers. Watch out for slippery boulders, and never swim around or below a waterfall, as you could drown if the current carries you over the top or if you're hit by rockfall.

Public swimming pools with lifeguards are open in summer at Curry Village and

Yosemite Lodge. The following are some good spots to swim:

Merced River Yosemite's warmest waters are found along sandy beaches in the Valley; more swimming holes are hidden around Wawona too (p116).

Tenaya Lake This high-elevation lake is partly bordered by a sandy beach (p116).

Eastern Sierra Take your pick between Lundy Lake or June Lake, or visit local hot springs.

Kings River Near Cedar Grove in Kings Canyon, Muir Rock and the Red Bridge are popular swimming holes (p179).

Hume Lake – Outside the Kings Canyon park boundaries; family-friendly swimming beaches and water-sports equipment rental (p179).

Rafting

During the summer months, floating the Merced River in Yosemite Valley (p116) is a fun way to beat the heat (inflatable raft rentals available at Curry Village). But all the white-water action happens outside the park boundaries, where runoff from spring snowmelt creates massive flows and lots of rapids along the Merced and Tuolumne Rivers.

The Yosemite region's white-water rafting season kicks off in April. Typically, the Tuolumne River runs into September, while the Merced wraps up by July, and both are well suited for beginner to intermediate rafters. For experts, there's renowned Cherry Creek, a nine-mile stretch of the upper Tuolumne, offering nearly nonstop Class IV to V+ rapids marked by narrow shoots, huge boulders, sheer drops, ledges and vertical holes.

In the Sierra National Forest, Kings River offers a scenic 10-mile stretch of exciting, mostly Class III rapids that are good for beginners. With its headwaters in Sequoia National Park, the Kaweah River kicks out challenging Class III to V rapids west of the park. Depending on snowmelt, these rivers' rafting season runs from mid-April until mid-July.

Guided River Trips

Several outfitters in the region offer one- to three-day white-water rafting trips, with prices that vary by season and day of the week. Generally, rafters must be at least 12 years old. All rafters should be strong swimmers.

All-Outdoors Whitewater Rafting (www .aorafting.com) One of two companies that runs to Cherry Creek; also does the Merced, Tuolumne and Kaweah Rivers.

ARTA River Trips (www.arta.org) Nonprofit running one-day and multiday Tuolumne trips, as well as day trips on the Merced.

Kaweah Whitewater Adventures (www .kaweah-whitewater.com) Small local operator offering half- and full-day Kaweah River trips.

Kings River Expeditions (www.kingsriver .com) Small local operator offering one- and two-day Kings River trips.

OARS (www.oars.com) Worldwide rafting operator with a solid reputation and admirable environmental ethics. Offers trips on the Tuolumne and Merced Rivers.

Sierra Mac (www.sierramac.com) One of two outfitters offering trips on Cherry Creek. Also does the upper Tuolumne.

Whitewater Voyages (www.whitewater voyages.com) Runs trips on the Tuolumne, Merced, Kaweah and Kings Rivers.

Zephyr Rafting (www.zrafting.com) Large, reputable outfitter offering trips on the Merced, Tuolumne and Kings Rivers.

Winter Activities
Downhill Skiing & Snowboarding

When it comes to downhill skiing and snowboarding, Mammoth Mountain in the Eastern Sierra reigns supreme. A top-rate mountain with excellent terrain for all levels of ability, Mammoth is known for its sunny skies, vertical chutes, airy snow and laid-back atmosphere. For a more local vibe, hit June Mountain nearby. Not for adrenaline junkies, Yosemite's Badger Pass is a historical spot: it was California's first ski resort. Gentle slopes, terrain parks, consistent snow, an excellent ski school and rental gear for the whole family make it an incredible spot for beginners.

Cross-Country Skiing

Outstanding cross-country skiing is found throughout the Sierras. Yosemite is an invigorating place for skiers of all skill levels, with options ranging from scenic half-mile loops to challenging backcountry trails. Cross-country skiers can take their pick of almost 350 miles of well-marked trails and roads, with over 25 miles of groomed trails accessed from Badger Pass. Other popular park ski trails are found at Crane Flat and Mariposa Grove. Experienced skiers can

LEAVES OF THREE, LET IT BE!

Watch out for western poison oak on the western slopes of the Sierra Nevada below 5000ft elevation. This poisonous shrub is most easily identified by its shiny, reddish-green tripartite leaves, which turn crimson in the fall, and its white berries. In winter, when the plant has no leaves, it looks brown and twiggy, and can still cause a serious allergic reaction if it touches your skin. If you accidentally brush against poison oak, scrub the area immediately with soap and water or an over-the-counter remedy such as Tecnu, a soap specially formulated to remove the plant's itchy urushiol oils.

overnight at the no-frills backcountry ski huts at Glacier Point, Ostrander Lake or Tuolumne Meadows (see p119).

In Sequoia & Kings Canyon, some 50 miles of marked but ungroomed trails crisscross the Giant Forest and Grant Grove areas, with rental skis available at Wuksachi Lodge and Grant Grove Village. Backcountry skiers can try the challenging trail from Lodgepole to Pear Lake Ski Hut. In Sequoia National Forest, ski rentals and groomed trails await at Montecito Sequoia Resort.

In the Eastern Sierra, Mammoth Lakes has some top-rated cross-country skiing, particularly off Sawmill Cutoff Rd and Lake Mary Rd and around Inyo Craters. The Ansel Adams and John Muir Wilderness Areas, Saddlebag Lake and Mt Dana offer endless exploring opportunities for experienced backcountry skiers.

Badger Pass Cross-Country Center & Ski School (www.yosemitepark.com) Highly regarded school offers a wide range of instruction (including snow camping, backcountry skiing and skate skiing), rentals, guided overnight trips to Glacier Point and trans-Sierra ski tours.

Montecito Sequoia Resort (www .montecitosequoia.com) Old-fashioned family-oriented resort offers lessons, rents cross-country and skate skis, and maintains over 30 miles of groomed trails for all skill levels in the Sequoia National Forest.

Tamarack Cross-Country Ski Center (www.tamaracklodge.com) Operates a busy cross-country ski center, with lessons, rentals and over 19 miles of groomed trails (with restrooms!) accessible from Tamarack Lodge at Mammoth Lakes in the Eastern Sierra.

Snowshoeing

One of the easiest ways to explore the winter wilderness is to don a pair of snow-shoes and head out on any of the hiking or cross-country skiing trails. Just be sure not to tramp directly in ski tracks, which destroys them for any cross-country skiers who come after you.

You can rent snowshoes at Yosemite's Badger Pass and explore on your own or join a fun guided trip, ranging from two-hour moonlight walks to an all-day trek out to Dewey Point and back. If you bring your own snowshoes, Yosemite Valley, Mariposa Grove and Crane Flat are all scenic spots. Near Hetch Hetchy Valley, Evergreen Lodge rents out snowshoes and offers guided snowshoe hikes inside and outside the park.

In Sequoia & Kings Canyon, ranger-led snowshoe walks (you can borrow snow-shoes for free!) depart from Giant Forest and Grant Grove and fill up fast, so reserve a spot by calling ahead or signing up in person in advance. Rental snowshoes are available at Sequoia's Wuksachi Lodge and Kings Canyon's Grant Grove Village. For a backcountry adventure, score overnight reservations for Pear Lake Ski Hut (p183), accessible on snowshoes and cross-country skis.

The cross-country ski centers listed in the previous section rent snowshoes, as does Mammoth Mountain in the Eastern Sierra.

Other Winter Activities

One of the most memorable winter activities for families in Yosemite is skating on Curry Village's open-air rink (rentals available; p119). Or rent a snow tube and send yourself spinning downhill at Yosemite's Badger Pass or Sequoia's Wolverton Meadow. At Montecito Sequoia Lodge in the Sequoia National Forest and at Mammoth Mountain in the Eastern Sierra, you can rent a snow tube, grab a rope tow and go rocketing downhill. Sledding and tubing are also popular at designated snow-play areas throughout all three parks and in nearby national forests, but you'll have to bring your own snow-play gear.

BUT WAIT, THERE'S MORE!

ACTIVITY	LOCATION	DESCRIPTION	PAGE
Canoeing & Kayaking	Yosemite Valley	Bring your own kayak to paddle the Merced River during early summer.	116
	Tenaya Lake	Bring your own watercraft and launch into this alpine lake in Yosemite's high country	116
	Tioga & Saddlebag Lakes	Easy DIY put-ins at an alpine lake off Tioga Rd, east of Yosemite	143
	Mono Lake	Paddle past bizarre-looking tufa formations; rentals and guided tours available	145
	June Lake	Marinas rent canoes and kayaks	147
	Mammoth Lakes	Eastern Sierra's best paddling is at Crowley Lake, Convict Lake and Lakes Basin; marinas rent canoes and kayaks	148
	Hume Lake	Rent a canoe and paddle across this family-friendly lake in Kings Canyon	168
Caving	Crystal Cave	Explore Sequoia's most famous marble cave, carved by an underground river.	164
	Boyden Cavern	Go for a wet-and-wild guided walk or a rappelling adventure in Kings Canyon	168
Fishing*	Yosemite Valley	Catch trout on the Merced River between Happy Isles and Foresta Bridge	117
	Tuolumne Meadows	Trout swim the Lyell and Dana Forks of the Tuolumne River	117
	Hetch Hetchy	Trout fishing along the Tuolumne River	117
	Eastern Sierra	Trout fishing in lakes, rivers and streams, especially June Lake and Mammoth Lakes	147 & 149
	Kings Canyon	Cast for trout at Hume Lake and along the Kings River	180
Golf	Wawona	Yosemite's historic nine-hole 'organic' golf course, open spring through fall	117
Hang Gliding	Yosemite	Advanced pilots with own equipment can soar from Glacier Point to Yosemite Valley	117
Stargazing	Glacier Point	Join amateur astronomers and park rangers high above Yosemite Valley	68
Tennis	Wawona	Tree-shaded outdoor court in southern Yosemite	125

* California fishing license required for anyone over age 16; state fishing laws apply (see www.dfg.ca.gov). Ask for local fishing regulations at visitor centers and ranger stations.

PLAN YOUR TRIP ACTIVITIES

Travel with Children

Best Regions for Kids

Yosemite National Park

Drop by the Happy Isles Nature Center, be awestruck by Yosemite Valley's waterfalls, drink in views of Half Dome from Glacier Point, wander among giant sequoia trees at Mariposa Grove and picnic at Tuolumne Meadows.

Around Yosemite

Ride a historic narrow-gauge railroad through pine forests, explore an Old West mining ghost town, ski the powder slopes of Mammoth Mountain and touch ancient bristlecone pine trees.

Sequoia & Kings Canyon National Parks

In Sequoia, traipse through the Giant Forest and learn all about giant sequoias at Beetle Rock Nature Center, scramble up Moro Rock and explore the creepy-crawly underground at Crystal Cave. In Kings Canyon, scramble inside the Fallen Monarch tree in Grant Grove, cool off at family-friendly Hume Lake, tour Boyden Cavern and spot wildlife in Zumwalt Meadow.

Kids love the parks, and bringing them along is a no-brainer. There's loads for them to do. You could spend your days swimming, rafting, biking or hiking. How about spying on the wildlife, marveling at waterfalls, peering over tall cliffs or exploring some crazy-cool caves? For many kids, just sleeping in a tent for the first time – and listening to all the strange noises of the night – is the biggest adventure of all.

The parks organize lots of children's activities and programs. To find kid-oriented events, check the free seasonal park newspapers and look at the daily calendars posted at visitor centers and some campgrounds.

In Yosemite Valley, keep free shuttle buses in mind. When your kids get tired, simply hop on the bus and head back to your car, campsite or lodge.

Children's Highlights

Biking

» **Yosemite Valley** – Rent bikes or bring your own for the Valley's mostly level bike paths.

» **Mammoth Mountain** – Older kids and teens will go bananas over this giant summer mountain-biking park.

Classes

» **Yosemite Conservancy** – Park partner offers all types of outdoor classes where kids can learn about ecology, wilderness skills and more.

KEEPING KIDS SAFE & HEALTHY OUTDOORS

Travel with kids always requires extra safety measures, but with a little preparation and common sense, your family can make the most of your park visit.

» Dress children (and yourself) in layers so they can peel clothing on or off as needed – mountain weather can change suddenly.

» Bring along lots of high-energy snacks and drinks, even for short outings and easy hikes. Remember kids can dehydrate more quickly than adults. See p237 for more advice on dehydration.

» When hiking, make sure your kids stay within earshot (if not sight). They may want to rush ahead, but it's easy to miss a trail junction or take a wrong turn.

» As an extra precaution while hiking, have each kid wear brightly colored clothes and carry a flashlight and safety whistle.

» Make sure kids know what to do if they get lost on the trail (eg stay put, periodically blow the whistle) or anywhere else in the parks (eg ask a ranger for help).

» Be extra cautious with kids around waterfalls, cliff edges and at viewpoints, not all of which have railings; the same goes for any peaks or domes.

» At higher elevations, kids may experience altitude sickness. Watch them for symptoms (see p235), especially during outdoor activities. Descend to lower elevations if any symptoms arise.

» Ensure your kids know what to do if they see a bear (see p236).

» Children are more vulnerable to spider and snake bites (see p236). Remind them not to pick up or provoke snakes (eg with sticks), and never put their hands anywhere they can't see.

» Teach children to identify poison oak (p40).

» **Yosemite Art and Education Center** – Low-cost art classes in Yosemite Valley (sign up the day before); children under 12 must be accompanied by an adult.

» **Ansel Adams Gallery** – Photography walks for budding shutterbugs in Yosemite Valley.

» **Yosemite Mountaineering School** – Kids aged 10 and up can take a beginners rock-climbing class in Yosemite Valley.

» **Sequoia Natural History Association** – Park partner leads field classes and natural history talks and walks, plus family-oriented living history programs.

Hiking
Yosemite

» **Vernal Falls** – It's less than a mile to the footbridge below the Valley's famous falls.

» **Mirror Lake** – Best in spring or early summer, when the lake's waters reflect iconic Half Dome.

» **Sentinel Dome** – Yosemite's easy granite-dome scramble, worth it for the panoramic views.

» **Mariposa Grove** – Walk just as far as the kids feel like among majestic giant sequoia trees.

» **Tuolumne Meadows** – Stroll by wildflowers to Soda Springs, or climb nearby granite domes.

Sequoia & Kings Canyon

» **Big Trees Trail** – Hug giant sequoia trees along a short paved trail.

» **Crescent Meadow Loop** – Spy on black bears and peer inside the Chimney Tree.

» **Tokopah Falls** – Scenic riverside hike to a 1200ft cascade tumbling over cliffs.

» **General Grant Tree Trail** – Stare up at giant sequoias and scramble inside the Fallen Monarch.

» **Zumwalt Meadow** – A peaceful riverside ramble, with a good chance of spotting wildlife.

History

» **Yosemite Valley Visitor Center** – Child-friendly, interactive natural and cultural history exhibits, plus evening living-history presentations in the outdoor theater during summer.

» **Yosemite Museum** – Explore Yosemite's indigenous heritage, including at the reconstructed Native American village. Don't miss the cross-section of a giant sequoia (count the rings!) out front.

» **Pioneer Yosemite History Center** – Wawona's great old buildings, stagecoaches and covered bridge are worth a look. In summer, take a short stagecoach ride.

» **Yosemite Mountain Sugar Pine Railroad** – South of Yosemite, ride historic narrow-gauge trains into the forest or take part in a reenacted train robbery.

» **Hospital Rock** – Inspect ancient pictographs and Native American grinding holes in the Foothills area of Sequoia National Park.

» **Bodie State Historic Park** – The ghostly ruins of a real 19th-century mining town that went from boom to bust in the Eastern Sierra.

» **Laws Railroad Museum** – A fun whistle-stop for train enthusiasts in the Eastern Sierra; check the website for family-friendly special events.

Horseback Riding

» **Yosemite** – Hitch up in summer for a scenic two-hour trip to Mirror Lake in Yosemite Valley, or a short ride around Tuolumne Meadows.

» **Kings Canyon** – In summer, one- or two-hour horseback trips into the giant sequoia forest depart from Grant Grove.

Nature Centers

» **Nature Center at Happy Isles** – In Yosemite Valley, has great hands-on exhibits and dioramas depicting natural environments. Kids can learn about pine cones, rub their hands across some granite, check out different animal tracks and even snicker at the display on animal scat.

» **Beetle Rock Education Center** – In Sequoia's Giant Forest, has lots of stuff to touch, play with and explore, from microscopes for examining bugs up close to binoculars for spotting wildlife on guided walks for kids in the Giant Forest outside.

» **Discovery Room** – In Kings Canyon, at the back of Grant Grove's visitor center, kids can practice pine-cone identification and play a spot-the-species game with bilingual (Spanish/English) murals.

Swimming & Water Sports

» **Merced River** – In summer, go rafting or kayaking in Yosemite Valley, or just splash around by the sandy shore.

» **Curry Village** – Yosemite Valley's outdoor public swimming pool lets families cool off.

» **Tenaya Lake** – Build sandcastles on the beach of Yosemite's roadside high-altitude lake (warning: the water is chilly, even in summer!).

» **Hume Lake** – Along the Kings Canyon Scenic Byway, take a dip in this pretty forest lake with sandy beaches always crowded with families.

» **Muir Rock** – Later in summer, this swimming spot along the Kings River near Roads End in Cedar Grove offers a small, sandy beach.

» **June Lake** – In the Eastern Sierra, hang out by the beach in summer, or launch a canoe, kayak or paddleboat.

Winter Sports

» **Badger Pass** – The gentle slopes and groomed cross-country tracks in Yosemite's Badger Pass are excellent for beginners. The 'Badger Pups' kids downhill program offers lessons for little skiers and boarders from four to six years old. Babysitting services available.

» **Curry Village** – Go ice-skating on an outdoor rink with superb scenery in Yosemite Valley.

» **Giant Forest** – In Sequoia National Park, rent snowshoes and take the whole family for a hike around giant sequoia groves, or join a ranger-guided snowshoe walk.

» **Mammoth Mountain** – In the Eastern Sierra near Mammoth Lakes, this superb skiing and snowboarding resort has kids lessons and child-care services; lift passes are also valid at tamer June Mountain ski resort nearby.

» **Montecito Sequoia Lodge** – In the Giant Sequoia National Monument, this family camp offers cross-country ski trails, snow tubing,

---

BE A JUNIOR RANGER!

The Junior Ranger booklet is a park-specific activity book that helps children of different ages learn about wildlife, history and conservation. All in all, it's one of the best bundles of things for kids to do, and includes scavenger hunts, crossword puzzles and assignments like picking up a bag of trash on the trail or interviewing a real ranger. Upon completion, kids get a badge. It's an educational and neat way to experience the parks, and it's open to all ages (even adults!). The booklets are available for a small fee from park visitor centers and bookstores.

snow biking, ice-skating and daily children's activities.

Planning

When planning what to do and see in and around the parks, try not to overdo things. Packing too much into your trip can cause frustration and spoil the adventure. Try to include the kids in the trip planning from the get-go. If they have a hand in choosing activities, they'll be much more interested and excited when you finally arrive.

For more advice and anecdotes, especially for families hitting the road together for the first time, read Lonely Planet's *Travel with Children*. The *Sierra Club Family Outdoors Guide,* by Marlyn Doan, includes helpful checklists and is especially handy for parents who are new to the outdoors.

To easily find family lodgings, restaurants, activities, attractions and more throughout this guide, just look for the family-friendly icon (👪).

Before You Go

Some great resources for getting kids psyched-up about your trip:

» Yosemite's official website (www.nps.gov/yose/forkids) lists upcoming family-friendly events and links to all kinds of Junior Web Ranger online activities.

» Sequoia & Kings Canyon's official website (www.nps.gov/seki/forkids) lists kid-friendly activities and educational programs, and also includes a link to the *Sequoia Seeds* kids' newspaper.

» A cute resource for taking kids to the park, www.visitsequoia.com/just-for-kids.aspx includes downloadable coloring pages and an *I Spy* checklist for those long car rides.

» Phil Frank's comic-strip books *Fur and Loafing in Yosemite* and *Eat, Drink & Be Hairy* are compilations of hilarious, bear-filled park adventures.

Sleeping & Eating

Parks and nearby gateway towns cater for families well. Most lodgings allow kids under 12 to sleep for free in the same room as their parents, but a rollaway cot may cost extra. Alternatively, a child-sized inflatable mattress or portable sleeping crib will fit into most motel or hotel rooms. Almost all restaurants in and around the parks have kids menus with smaller portions and significantly lower prices. Dress codes are casual almost everywhere (except at Yosemite's Ahwahnee Hotel dining room).

Travel with Pets

Best Regions for Pets

Yosemite National Park

Dogs are allowed on most paved hiking trails, including the scenic Yosemite Valley Loop. Many park campgrounds accept pets; a few have facilities for horses too. Popular stock trips leave from high-country Tioga Rd in summer.

Around Yosemite

Mammoth Lakes and the Eastern Sierra offer an abundance of dog-friendly trails and scenic backcountry stock trips, especially in the Inyo National Forest.

Sequoia & Kings Canyon National Parks

Dogs are prohibited on all park trails, but are allowed at park campgrounds. Backcountry stock trips are popular, with scenic trails starting from Mineral King, Cedar Grove and the Sequoia National Forest nearby. The national forest allows dogs on hiking trails and in campgrounds.

If you want to experience the outdoors with your pets, it's paramount to ensure they are comfortable and safe. Considerations include availability of accommodations that accept your pet, possible interactions with other animals and local restrictions on recreational use (eg hiking and camping). Be sure to check the different regulations governing each of the areas you plan to visit.

Policies & Regulations

Pets are allowed in the parks, though restrictions are limiting. Dogs aren't allowed on park shuttles, on most hiking trails or in wilderness areas. Dogs are generally permitted in campgrounds and picnic areas, but must be kept on a 6ft leash and accompanied at all times. Don't sneak dogs into backcountry or leave them tied up and unattended at campgrounds; it's illegal and you will be cited. Remember to clean up your pooch's poop.

In the Sequoia National Forest, leashed dogs are permitted on trails, but they must sleep inside a tent or vehicle at night. Dogs aren't allowed at developed swimming areas.

Up-to-date policies are at the following:

Yosemite (www.nps.gov/yose/planyourvisit /pets.htm)

Sequoia & Kings Canyon (www.nps.gov/seki /planyourvisit/pets.htm)

Sequoia National Forest (www.fs.fed.us/r5 /sequoia/faq/)

Service animals (eg guide dogs) *are* welcome in the parks. They may accompany visitors with disabilities on park shuttles, inside

---

KEEPING PETS SAFE & HEALTHY

» Pets are extremely susceptible to overheating. Never leave your pet alone in a hot car, where they may experience brain and organ damage after only 15 minutes.

» Follow park regulations and keep your dog leashed at all times. Off-leash there's more opportunity for your dog to roll in poison oak or get in a fight with another pet or wild animal.

» Keep your dog healthy by periodically checking for ticks and being prepared for weather extremes. Bring plenty of water on hot days and blankets for chilly evenings.

» Remember that pet food is potentially bear food. Store your pet's food properly at all times (eg use bear lockers at campgrounds, trailheads and parking lots).

---

museums and visitor centers, and on hiking trails and into the backcountry. Ask about current regulations to see if any special permits are required of if any areas are off-limits. To prevent misunderstandings, make sure your service animal always wears its official vest and is kept on a 6ft-long leash.

Trails & Campgrounds

In Yosemite, dogs are allowed on fully paved trails, unless otherwise signposted – they're prohibited on paved trails leaving the Valley floor, for instance. Dogs are not allowed on any unpaved trails (Wawona Meadow Loop and parts of Old Big Oak Flat Rd excepted).

You can bring pets into most campgrounds in Yosemite, except Tamarack Flat, Porcupine Flat and any walk-in campgrounds (eg Camp 4).

In Sequoia & Kings Canyon, dogs are allowed in all developed campgrounds, but never on any trails, paved or unpaved.

Most national forests allow dogs at campgrounds and on trails, with the possible exception of wilderness areas; inquire at the nearest USFS ranger station.

Bodie State Historic Park in the Eastern Sierra allows leashed dogs into the town site.

Dog-Friendly Lodgings & Kennels

Except for service animals, dogs are not allowed inside any park lodgings. Some hotels and motels outside the parks accept pets, although a nightly surcharge, weight limits and breed restrictions may apply. To find accommodations that welcome pets in this guide, look for the pet-friendly icon 🐾.

Yosemite Valley has a **dog kennel** (☑209-372-8348; ⊙Memorial Day–Labor Day), though it's bare-bones. Dogs are kept in outdoor cages and stay unattended. Board runs $9.50 for the day, or overnight. You must provide a written copy of vet immunization records. Reservations are recommended.

Horse Trails & Facilities

On backcountry trails, stock users must follow strict guidelines on group size, grazing and dispersal of manure, as well as feed restrictions to prevent the introduction of invasive plant species. Many trails are horse-friendly unless posted otherwise, but you'll need a special wilderness stock-use permit.

In Yosemite, a number of trails leave from Tioga Rd. Sequoia & Kings Canyon have several trails for stock trips, including those starting from the Mineral King and Cedar Grove areas. If you don't want to bring your own animals, talk to pack outfits in and around the parks about stock rentals and guided trips (see p37).

Up-to-date policies are at the following:

Yosemite (www.nps.gov/yose/planyourvisit/stock.htm)

Sequoia & Kings Canyon (www.nps.gov/seki/planyourvisit/stockreg.htm)

Sequoia National Forest (www.fs.fed.us/r5/sequoia/maps/brochures/horse_sense.html)

In Yosemite, a handful of developed campgrounds have stock facilities, and the **park concessionaire** (☑209-372-1000) has some overnight board facilities available by advance reservation.

There's a primitive **Horse Camp** (www.fs.fed.us/r5/sequoia/recreation/campgrounds.html) in the Sequoia National Forest, off the Generals Hwy. There are more horse camps in the Eastern Sierra, such as **Agnew Horse Camp** (reservations ☑877-444-6777; www.recreation.gov) in the Inyo National Forest.

regions at a glance

With fierce granite mountains standing watch over high-altitude lakes, the Sierra Nevada forms an exquisite topographical barrier embracing magnificent natural landscapes. In the majestic parks of Yosemite, Sequoia and Kings Canyon, visitors will be humbled by the enduring groves of solemn giant sequoias, the ancient rock formations and valleys, and the omnipresent opportunity to see wildlife.

In the Eastern Sierra, cloud-dappled hills and sun-streaked mountaintops dabbed with snow typify a landscape of slashing peaks, pine forests, lush meadows, ice-blue lakes and simmering hot springs.

The foothill towns still bear the trappings of the Gold Rush days, with old-time Western saloons and the vestiges of mining and railroads.

Yosemite National Park

Hiking ✓✓✓
Waterfalls ✓✓✓
Rock Climbing ✓✓✓

Pick a Trail

Saunter the high country and bag alpine lakes or stop for lunch beside a burbling stream. With 95% of its land designated as wilderness, you can still find solitude by leaving your car behind.

Lively Waterfalls

Winter depth equals spring-time volume, so pray for snow. A visit to the Valley during peak season is a volley of spray, but don't stop there. Wawona, Hetch Hetchy and late-season Tuolumne Meadows all have something to show.

Climb a Rock

Take your pick from leisurely hikes to polished domes, heart-racing ascents of granite cliffs and lots of viewpoint scrambles in between. Rock faces and pinnacles dot the landscape – the hardest choice is deciding where to start.

p52

Around Yosemite

History ✓✓✓
Geology ✓✓✓
Outdoor Activities ✓✓✓

The Old Days
Ramble off the beaten path to explore crumbling ghost towns, railroad remnants and wooden Gold Rush–era saloons. Native American petroglyphs can be discovered in craggy rock canyons, and mule packers head to the hills as they have for over a century.

Hot Stuff
Volcanic activity has shaped the Sierra Nevada landscape, and the evidence is everywhere. Need a crash course in geology? Hike to Devils Postpile, explore the Mono Lake formations and then dip in a steaming hot-springs pool.

Nature's Playground
If the Eastern Sierra double-dares you, it's easy to oblige. Tear downhill on a world-class powder mountain or trail run from peak to peak. Summit a chalky boulder or climb a frozen waterfall. With fishing, mountain biking and swimming galore, you'll feel like a kid over and over again.

p134

Sequoia & Kings Canyon National Parks

Wildlife ✓✓✓
Outdoor Activities ✓✓✓
Scenic Drives ✓✓✓

Not Just Giant Trees
Ancient groves of giant sequoias are the prime reason to visit, but they're not the only flora and fauna thriving here. Watch black bears munching berries and acorns, spot rare birds or surprise a curious marmot in the high country.

Take a Hike
Less crowded than Yosemite, both parks offer peaceful hiking trails for all ages and abilities. Ramble around wildflower-strewn meadows or take a waterfall day hike. Backpackers have hundreds of miles of trails to choose from, including to skyscraping peaks and alpine lakes.

Mountain Highs, Canyons Deep
Mile for mile, the Generals Hwy, which dramatically rises into the Giant Forest, and the Kings Canyon Scenic Byway, which dizzyingly descends into North America's deepest canyon, are the parks' most memorable scenic drives.

p156

Every listing is recommended by our authors, and their favourite places are listed first

Look out for these icons:

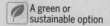 Our author's top recommendation

A green or sustainable option

FREE No payment required

On the Road

Yosemite National Park

Best Hikes

» Vernal & Nevada Falls (p84)

» Tueeulala & Wapama Falls (p98)

» May Lake & Mt Hoffmann (p91)

» Old Big Oak Flat Road to Yosemite Falls (p103)

» Lyell Canyon (p106)

Best Places to Stay

» High Sierra Camps (p128)

» Ahwahnee Hotel (p123)

» Evergreen Lodge (p127)

» Yosemite Creek (p126)

» Wawona Hotel (p125)

Why Go?

The jaw-dropping head-turner of USA national parks, Yosemite (yo-*sem*-it-tee) garners the devotion of all who enter. From the waterfall-striped granite walls buttressing emerald green Yosemite Valley to the skyscraping giant sequoias catapulting into the air at Mariposa Grove, you feel a sense of awe and reverence that so much natural beauty exists in one place. It is a Unesco World Heritage Site that makes even Switzerland look like God's practice run. As far as we can tell, America's third-oldest national park has only one downside: the impact of the four million visitors annually who wend their way here. But lift your eyes ever so slightly above the crowds, seek out the park's serene corners or explore its miles of roadless wilderness and you'll feel your heart instantly moved by unrivaled splendors.

When to Go
Yosemite Village

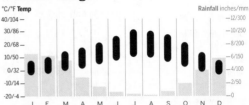

May & Jun Spring runoff pumps up the show at the spectacular Yosemite waterfalls.

Jul & Aug Head for the high country for wilderness adventures and glorious sunshine.

Dec–Mar Take a wintertime romp through snowy forests on skis, boards or snowshoes.

Entrances

The park has four main gates: Big Oak Flat Entrance (Hwy 120 West) and Arch Rock Entrance (Hwy 140) from the west, South Entrance (Hwy 41) near Wawona and Tioga Pass Entrance (Hwy 120 East) from the east.

Tioga Pass (9945ft) is the highest roadway across the Sierra, and Tioga Road/Hwy 120 East is usually open only between early June and mid-November, though the dates vary every year. In high snow years, the road may not open until July, so definitely don't expect to drive across the park in springtime without checking on the status of the road.

DON'T MISS

For two of the best views over Yosemite Valley, you don't even need to stroll far from your car. The best all-around photo op of the Valley can be had from Tunnel View (Map p58), a large, busy parking lot and viewpoint at the east end of Wawona Tunnel, on Hwy 41. It's just a short drive from the Valley floor. The vista encompasses most of the Valley's greatest hits: El Capitan on the left, Bridalveil Fall on the right, the green Valley floor below, and glorious Half Dome front and center. This viewpoint is often mistakenly called Inspiration Point. That point was on an old park road and is now reachable via a steep hike from the Tunnel View parking lot.

The second view, known as Valley View (Map p58), is a good one to hit on your way out. It offers a bottom-up (rather than top-down) view of the Valley and is a lovely spot to dip your toes in the Merced River and bid farewell to sights like Bridalveil Fall, Cathedral Rocks and El Capitan. Look carefully to spot the tip-top of Half Dome in the distance. As you head west out of the Valley on Northside Dr, look for the Valley View turnout (roadside marker V11), just over a mile past El Capitan Meadow.

When You Arrive

» The $20 vehicle entrance fee is valid for one week; keep your receipt if you plan to exit and enter the park during your stay.

» You'll receive a park map and the seasonal *Yosemite Guide* newspaper with information on activities, camp-grounds, lodging, shuttles, visitor services and more.

» The park is open 24 hours daily. If you arrive at night and the gate is unattended, pay the entrance fee when you leave.

PLANNING TIPS

For 24-hour recorded information, including winter road conditions and summer road-construction updates, call ☑209-372-0200.

The park website (www.nps.gov/yose) offers free downloads of the park newspaper and helpful trip-planning tips.

Fast Facts

» Total area: 1169 sq miles

» Designated wilderness area: 1101 sq miles

» Yosemite Valley elevation: 3955ft

Reservations

NPS & USFS Camp-grounds (☑518-885-3639, 877-444-6777; www.recreation .gov) For all campgrounds within Yosemite and those in the surrounding national forests.

Delaware North Companies (DNC; ☑801-559-4884; www.yosemitepark .com) For all Yosemite National Park lodgings.

Resources

Yosemite Conservancy (☑209-379-2317; www .yosemiteconservancy.org) A nonprofit educational organization with the specific purpose of supporting the park. It organizes educational and recreational programs and activities and operates the wilderness permit reservation system.

Yosemite National Park Highlights

1 Explore **Mariposa Grove** (p69) and its towering giant sequoias

2 Stand beneath the spray of Hetch Hetchy's roaring **Wapama Falls** (p98)

3 Hike to **Vernal & Nevada Falls** (p84) in spring via the Mist and John Muir Trails

4 Bask in the summer sun on the shore of Tuolumne's **Cathedral Lake** (p95)

5 Shed the crowds at scenic **Chilnualna Falls** (p89) in Wawona

6 Peer down from **Glacier Point** (p65) at the eye-level peaks, deep Valley and the high country beyond

---

Bridgeport

Lundy

Mono Village (historical)

Dunderberg Mill

Inyo National Forest

Saddlebag Lake

Mt Dana (13,057ft)

Mt Gibbs

Tioga Lake

Tioga Pass (9945ft)

Tioga Pass Entrance

120

Lembert Dome (9450ft)

Mt Conness (12,649ft)

Tuolumne Meadows

Pothole Dome

Tuolumne Falls

Conness Creek

Pacific Crest Trail

Camiaca Peak (11,739ft)

Twin Peaks (12,323ft)

Matterhorn Peak (12,264ft)

Virginia Peak (12,001ft)

Stanton Peak (11,699ft)

Finger Peaks (11,498ft)

Sawtooth Ridge

Crown Point (11,346ft)

Kettle Peak (11,010ft)

Ehrmbeck Peak (11,240ft)

Acker Peak (10,988ft)

Slide Mountain (11,118ft)

Wells Peak (11,118ft)

Bath Mountain (10,558ft)

Doghead Peak (11,102ft)

Cold Mountain (10,295ft)

Wildcat Point (9455ft)

Waterwheel Falls

Volunteer Peak (10,479ft)

Rodgers Lake

Benson Lake

Piute Mountain (10,541ft)

Pacific Crest Trail

Tower Peak (11,755ft)

Forsyth Peak (11,180ft)

Keyes Peak (10,670ft)

Tilden Lake

Lake Vernon

Grizzly Peak (10,365ft)

Bigelow Peak (10,539ft)

Cascade Falls

The Roughs

Humboldt-Toiyabe National Forest

Stanislaus National Forest

Emigrant Lake

Twin Lakes

Huckleberry Lake

Spotted Fawn Lake

Laurel Lake

Rancheria Falls

Hetch Hetchy Reservoir

Hetch Hetchy Dome (6197ft)

Wapama Falls

Tueeulala Falls

Kolana Rock (5772ft)

Smith Peak (7730ft)

White Wolf

Tuolumne Peak (10,858ft)

N

5 miles

10 km

(p69)

(p98)

(p84)

(p95)

(p89)

(p65)

7 Cycle past traffic on the flat trails throughout **Yosemite Valley** (p113)

8 Soak up epic views while swimming in **Tenaya Lake** (p116)

9 Launch into fresh powder on the slopes of **Badger Pass** (p118) or set off on a cross-country trail adventure

Orientation

Though the park encompasses nearly 1200 sq miles of land (about the size of Rhode Island), 95% of Yosemite is designated wilderness and, therefore, inaccessible by car. Elevations range from below 3000ft at Hetch Hetchy to 13,114ft atop Mt Lyell, the park's tallest peak.

The most popular region is Yosemite Valley, a relatively small sliver of the park at the heart of Yosemite. Along with spectacular scenery, you'll find the largest concentration of visitor services, including lodges, campgrounds, stores and restaurants.

About 55 miles northeast of the Valley, near the east end of Tioga Road, is Tuolumne Meadows (elevation 8600ft), the focal point of Yosemite's high country and summertime home to a small hub of visitor services.

Crane Flat sits at the junction of Tioga and Big Oak Flat Rds. You'll find limited visitor services here and to the north at the park's Big Oak Flat Entrance. Between Crane Flat and Tuolumne Meadows is a stretch we've labeled 'Along Tioga Road,' which covers camping, hiking and other activities along this section of Hwy 120. North of Tioga Rd lies the park's vast northern wilderness, accessible only by serious backpackers. To the west, a short drive from the Big Oak Flat Entrance, is Hetch Hetchy Reservoir.

Perched 3200ft above Yosemite Valley, Glacier Point is the park's prime viewpoint, reachable during summer via a trail from the Valley or by car along Glacier Point Rd. Also on Glacier Point Rd is the Badger Pass Ski Area, which is open in winter only.

Thirty-six miles south of Yosemite Valley is Wawona, home to a historic hotel and other services for those visiting the giant sequoias of nearby Mariposa Grove. The southeastern corner of the park harbors another large wilderness area.

Park Policies & Regulations

WILDLIFE

There's one main rule regarding Yosemite's wildlife: don't feed the bears...nor the deer, chipmunks, raccoons, skunks, squirrels, jays, marmots or mountain lions. Giving wild animals treats may be fun, but they learn to associate humans with food. That can lead to trouble, especially for the bears, who are often killed if they become serious nuisances. Remember, small critters can bite, while deer (no matter how cute and tame they seem) may charge people who get too close.

FOOD STORAGE

Store all food and scented items – cosmetics, toothpaste, soda cans and any other food-related trash – in the bear-proof storage lockers provided at each campsite and in major parking lots. Never leave anything in your car, including canned goods. Bears have a powerful sense of smell and are adept at breaking into locked vehicles. They also recognize coolers and grocery bags, so even if these are empty and clean, at least cover them with a blanket. Failure to follow these rules can lead to a citation (or the trashing of your car). When cooking at your campsite, avoid leaving the locker hanging open and the food spread out. That's an open dinner invitation. Treat the locker like a fridge – pull out only what you need, then shut and latch the door. For backpackers, bear-resistant food canisters are required throughout most of the park's backcountry. For more on bears, including what to do if you encounter one, see p236.

CAMPFIRES

Everyone loves a campfire, but take note of a few rules. Fires in Yosemite campgrounds are allowed only within established fire rings or barbecue pits. Wood and kindling gathering is illegal in the Valley, so you'll have to buy firewood. To improve air quality, campfires are allowed only between 5pm and 10pm from May 1 through September. Those staying in campgrounds outside the Valley are allowed to gather wood, but it must be downed (on the ground) and dead. It's often easier (and always more environmentally sound) to simply buy a bundle, preferably from within a 50-mile radius to thwart invasive pests.

After having a campfire, make sure it's completely out. Stir the fire and coals with water a half-hour before going to bed or leaving the site, then hold your hand close to check for any lingering hot spots.

WILDERNESS CAMPING & PERMITS

A whopping 95% of Yosemite National Park is designated wilderness. Anyone can hike into it, but those wishing to spend the night in it must obtain the proper wilderness permit. For complete information on how to do so, see p99. Wilderness permits are not required for day hikes.

SIGHTS

Yosemite Valley

Yosemite Valley is the park's crown jewel. It's home to what most people think of when they imagine Yosemite: Half Dome, Yosemite Falls, El Capitan, the Royal Arches – all those mind-boggling sights that draw over four million people to the park each year. But the numbers can be deceiving. Most visitors come in July and August, and many of them stay only for the day. Sure, the stores, the dining rooms and the food stands at Yosemite Village and Curry Village are a complete nightmare, and the traffic is maddening, but come sundown, when the day-trippers and tour buses disappear, you can stroll the loop trails along the Valley floor and feel the tranquil magic that has always been here. Of course, visiting the Valley outside of summer makes finding solitude a cinch. If you don't mind nippy nights, then springtime, when the waterfalls are raging, is one of the very best times to visit. Winter is quiet, and the snow lends a serenity to the Valley that few people experience.

Orientation

Meadow-carpeted Yosemite Valley is 7 miles long and 1 mile wide (at its widest point). The Merced River meanders down its middle, within sight of Half Dome on the east end, westward past El Capitan, and out of the park into the Merced River Canyon.

Northside Dr and Southside Dr parallel the valley on either side of the river, each one way for most of its route (the former heads west, the latter heads east). Four bridges span the river, including Sentinel Bridge, which leads to Yosemite Village, the Valley's commercial center.

The Ahwahnee Hotel sits about a half-mile east of the village, while Yosemite Lodge is near the base of Yosemite Falls, less than a mile west of the village. Curry Village and the three Pines campgrounds lie south of the river, about a mile east of Sentinel Bridge.

Three highways diverge at the west end of the Valley. Big Oak Flat Rd leads north to Crane Flat (where it meets Hwy 120), Hetch Hetchy and Tuolumne Meadows; Hwy 140 heads west out of the park to El Portal and Mariposa; and Hwy 41 runs south to Glacier Point Rd, Wawona and Mariposa Grove.

NATIVE AMERICAN BASKET WEAVERS

Handwoven baskets were an integral part of indigenous Californian life. The exquisitely wrought baskets were so tightly woven that they could be used for drawing and carrying water. They also served as cooking vessels and dinner plates.

Ironically, the survival of the craft owes something to its commercial exploitation by mid-20th-century art collectors. Artists like Lucy Parker Telles, a descendant of Southern Miwok and Mono Lake Paiute, wove larger and more ornate baskets than those of their ancestors, fetching a higher price from collectors. Intricate geometric designs were painstakingly created along the sides of bulb-shaped baskets using natural dyes and special weaves. Larger baskets could span as wide as 3ft and often had narrow openings at their tops. The craft was also given a boost by that era's Yosemite Indian Field Days, when survivors of ancient tribes gathered to demonstrate their crafts.

Though Indian Field Days are no longer held, organizations like the **California Indian Basketweavers Association** (www.ciba.org) seek to preserve the craft and reaffirm its spiritual significance. One sacred part of that practice is the gathering of traditional materials – sedge, bracken fern, redbud, willow and waterproofing elements such as pine pitch and soap root. Thus, recent efforts have focused on environmental restoration of traditional gathering sites.

Lucy Parker Telles' daughter-in-law, Julia Parker, is a renowned basket weaver and teacher who makes traditional Kashaya Pomo baskets. Through marriage, she also learned the cultural traditions of her mother-in-law's Yosemite Miwok and Mono Lake Paiute ancestors, passing this knowledge to her daughter, Lucy Parker. Both Julia and Lucy continue to teach their craft and display their baskets and jewelry at Yosemite. The Yosemite Museum has a collection of extraordinary baskets, some of which took several years to weave.

Yosemite Valley

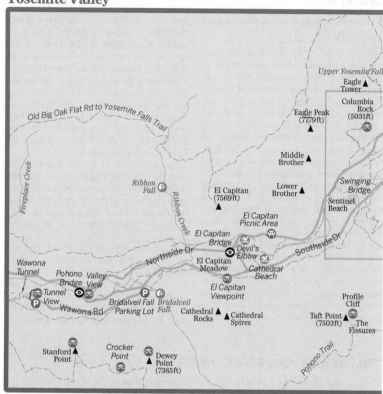

YOSEMITE VILLAGE & AROUND

Regardless of your feelings toward commercial development in one of the world's natural wonders, you'll probably wind up here at one point or another, as the village offers just about every amenity – from pizzas and ice cream to fire wood and wilderness permits.

Commercial development began in the Valley almost as soon as the public became aware of the park. Quite a few hotels opened around the turn of the 20th century, and by the 1920s a collection of businesses – including hotels, photo studios, a dance pavilion and even a cinema – had risen just south of the river near Sentinel Bridge. This was the original Yosemite Village. By the 1950s, however, it was downgraded to the 'Old Village,' as businesses moved north of the river. The site of the Old Village has since reverted to meadow (look for road marker V20), though the chapel remains, albeit in a slightly different spot. A few buildings were moved to the Pioneer History Center in Wawona, and Best's Studio was moved to the present-day village and eventually renamed the Ansel Adams Gallery.

The Village Store has a huge range of groceries – including produce, vegetarian items and deli foods. It's more expensive than your local store but has a surprisingly good selection. It also carries camp supplies, booze, maps and an overwhelming supply of Yosemite-emblazoned souvenirs. Head to **Sport Shop** (Map p60; ⊘9am-6pm, reduced hrs in winter) for last-minute camping supplies.

Yosemite Valley Visitor Center

(Map p60 ☐209-372-0299; ⊘9am-7:30pm summer, shorter hrs rest of year) Rarely do visitors spend much time in the Valley without a stop at the park's main visitor center. If you've never been to Yosemite, it's an excellent place to load up on information.

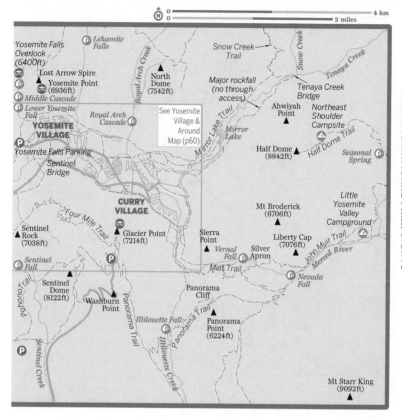

At the main desk, rangers answer tourists' questions (remaining amazingly friendly amid the barrage) and can pretty much settle any query you might have. A rudimentary hiking map is available, and weather reports, trail conditions and road conditions are posted behind the desk.

To the right of the help desk is the exhibit hall, which offers an interactive walk through Yosemite's history from the dinosaurs to the present.

To the left of the visitor center help desk, the **Yosemite Conservancy Bookstore** (www.yosemiteconservancystore.com) stocks an outstanding assortment of Yosemite-related books and maps and a smattering of Yosemite paraphernalia.

Yosemite Theater THEATER
(Map p60; performances adult/child $8/4; ⊙9am-7:30pm summer, shorter hrs rest of year) Behind the visitor center stands this theater, which screens the painfully dramatic, but beauti-

fully photographed, 22-minute film *Spirit of Yosemite*. The movie starts every half-hour or so between 9:30am and 5:30pm, and offers a free, air-conditioned respite from the summer heat. On Sundays, the first screening is at noon.

In the evening, take your pick from a rotating cast of performers, including Wawona Hotel pianist Tom Bopp, the fascinating life and philosophy of John Muir as portrayed by actor Lee Stetson, and Park Ranger Shelton Johnson re-creating the experiences of a Buffalo Soldier (see the boxed text, p206). There are also special children's shows.

FREE **Yosemite Museum** MUSEUM
(Map p60; ⊙9am-4:30pm or 5pm) Next to the visitor center, the Yosemite Museum features a series of cultural and historical exhibits on the Valley's native Miwok–Ahwahneechee and Paiute people, covering

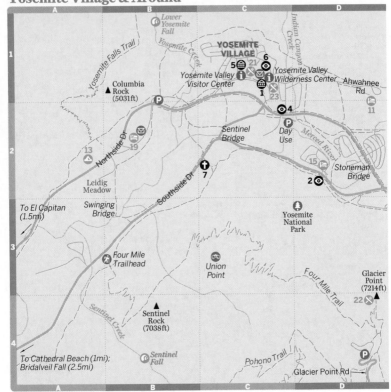

the period from 1850 to today. It's worth a visit just to see the giant, intricately woven **Miwok–Paiute baskets** dating from the 1920s and '30s. The baskets were woven (some over periods as long as three years) by famous weavers such as Lucy Parker Telles, Carrie Bethel and Alice Wilson. A basket by Telles, the largest in the collection, took four years to make. She later declined an offer by Robert Ripley (of *Ripley's Believe It or Not!*) to purchase the basket.

The museum also features paintings and photographs from its permanent collection, including some Ansel Adams prints, and has a small hands-on area where kids can play with Miwok games and ask Miwok interpreters questions.

Behind the museum, a free, self-guided interpretive trail winds through the **Indian Village of Ahwahnee**, where you can peek inside full-size, reconstructed Miwok buildings, including a traditional roundhouse.

The building and the sweat lodge behind it are used for ceremonial purposes by the Miwok.

A couple of items in front of the museum are worth a look: a cross section of a **giant sequoia** has been marked with rings to show its age. Its center is marked 'AD 923.' Nearby, a **time capsule** awaits the year 2090, when rangers will open it and use the materials inside to evaluate changes in the park since the capsule was created in 1990.

FREE **Ansel Adams Gallery** GALLERY
(Map p60; ☎209-372-4413; www.anseladams .com; ⊗9am-6pm summer, to 5pm rest of year) East of the visitor center, this privately run art gallery is housed in a building that was originally Best's Studio, founded in 1902. Owner Harry Best was the father of Virginia Best, who married Adams in 1928. The gallery has since moved from its original site south of the river and been extensively

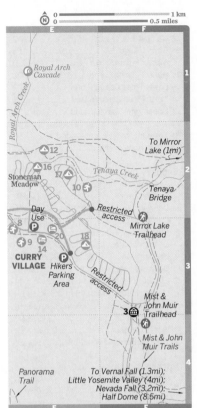

donation; ☺10am-2pm Tue-Sat Apr-Oct) nearly every day that feature a different artist and medium (watercolor, pastel, acrylic etc) each week. Classes usually take place outside, and students must bring their own supplies or purchase them at the center. No experience is necessary. Children under 12 must be accompanied by an adult. Sign up at least a day ahead to ensure a spot.

Yosemite Valley Chapel   CHURCH
(Map p60; www.yosemitevalleychapel.org) Built in 1879, this chapel is Yosemite's oldest structure that still remains in use. The church originally stood near the base of Four Mile Trail, and in 1901 was moved about a mile to its present site. Sunday morning services are nondenominational.

CURRY VILLAGE & AROUND
Lying directly below Glacier Point, Curry Village is home to the Valley's second-biggest collection of restaurants, stores and overnight accommodations. Originally called Camp Curry, it was founded in 1899 by David and Jennie Curry as a place where everyday visitors could find 'a good bed and a clean napkin at every meal.' Starting with just a handful of tents, the camp quickly grew, thanks in large part to David Curry's entrepreneurial drive and booming personality. One of his biggest promotional schemes was the Firefall (p69), a nightly event and significant tourist draw. Curry Village is now owned and run by Delaware North Companies (DNC).

More than 100 years later, the Camp Curry sign still hangs over the entrance, but this sprawling complex retains few traces of its turn-of-the-20th-century roots. From the parking lot, a sea of tent cabins fans out toward the base of Glacier Point, radiating from a central cluster of stores and snack bars – not exactly a vision of rustic glory. Still, it's pleasant to settle in for pizza and beer on the patio that faces the amphitheater out back. There's even a small cocktail bar. Or you can head to the charming deck of the old Camp Curry Lounge for a catnap in one of the rocking chairs.

Curry Village Mountain Shop (Map p60; ☎209-372-8396) offers the Valley's best selection of camping, mountaineering and backpacking supplies and is the home of the Yosemite Mountaineering School (p115). It's also world-renowned for its selection of big-wall climbing gear.

remodeled. Today, instead of Best's paintings, it specializes in Adams' photographs and the work of other contemporary artists; it also houses a great selection of art and ecology books and other gift items. Though the gallery sells original Adams pieces, it doesn't display many of them, exhibiting works by other nature photographers instead.

On Mondays (from the Ahwahnee), Tuesdays, Thursdays and Saturdays, the gallery hosts free **photography walks** at 8:30am, where you'll pick up tips on composition, technique and the best spots to shoot. Walks are for 15 people max, so sign up over the phone or in person.

Yosemite Art & Education Center   ART CENTER
(Map p60; ☎209-372-1442; ☺9am-noon & 1-4:30pm) In late spring, summer and fall, this center holds **art classes** ($5 suggested

Yosemite Village & Around

LeConte Memorial Lodge HISTORICAL BUILDING
(Map p60; ☎209-372-4542; www.sierraclub.org
/education/leconte; ⊙10am-4pm Wed-Sun May-
Sep) Built by the Sierra Club in 1903, this
small, rustic, granite-and-wood lodge offers
a glimpse into a relatively unknown chapter of California architecture. Designed by
Berkeley architect John White, the building sits firmly within a style known as the
First Bay Tradition, a movement that was
intimately linked with the 20th-century
Arts and Crafts Movement. The First Bay
Tradition placed great importance on
reflecting the natural world and insisted
each work of architecture be specific to its
surroundings.

The Sierra Club built the lodge in honor
of Joseph LeConte (1823–1901), a University
of California Berkeley geologist and a co-
founder of the Sierra Club. The building was
initially erected in Camp Curry, then moved
here in 1919. LeConte Lodge is one of three
National Historic Landmarks in Yosemite,
along with the Ahwahnee Hotel and the
Rangers' Club (a Valley building currently
used as employee housing).

Sierra Club members staff the lodge,
which houses exhibits and information on
LeConte, Muir and Ansel Adams, along with
an excellent library of park-related ecology,
geology and other nature books free for the
browsing. There's also a fun children's corner. Evening activities are posted out front
and in the *Yosemite Guide.*

FREE **Nature Center at
Happy Isles** NATURE CENTER
(Map p60; ⊙9:30am-4pm May-Sep; ⊛) Happy
Isles lies at the Valley's southeast end,
where the Merced River courses around
two small islands. The area is a popular spot for picnics, swimming and short
strolls in the woods. It also marks the
start of the John Muir Trail (JMT) and

9781741794069

Mist Trail, where hikers begin treks to Vernal Fall, Nevada Fall and Half Dome.

On the site of a former fish hatchery, the nature center features great hands-on exhibits that will enthrall kids and adults alike. Displays explain the differences between the park's various pinecones, rocks, animal tracks and (everyone's favorite subject) scat. Out back, don't miss an exhibit on the 1996 rock fall, when an 80,000-ton rock slab plunged 2000ft to the nearby Valley floor, killing a man, felling about 1000 trees and seriously damaging the nature center.

Happy Isles is about a mile from Curry Village. The road is closed to cars (except those with disabled placards); instead, reach it by either an easy walk, bike ride or the free shuttle bus. There's a small snack bar at the shuttle stop and the islands themselves are wheelchair accessible.

AHWAHNEE HOTEL

Almost as iconic as Half Dome itself, the elegant Ahwahnee Hotel (Map p60) has drawn well-heeled tourists through its towering doors since 1927. Of course, you needn't be wealthy in the least to partake of its many charms. In fact, a visit to Yosemite Valley is hardly complete without a stroll through the **Great Lounge** (aka the lobby), which is handsomely decorated with leaded glass, sculpted tile, Native American rugs and Turkish kilims. You can relax on the plush but aging couches and stare out the 10 floor-to-ceiling windows, wander into the **Solarium**, or send the kids into the walk-in fireplace (no longer in use) for a photo. You can even sneak up the back stairs for a peek into the private **Tudor Room**, which has excellent views over the Great Lounge.

Take a wander around the outside, too. The hotel was built entirely from local granite, pine and cedar – against the backdrop of the Royal Arches it's truly a sight to see. There's no mistaking the reasoning behind its National Historic Landmark designation. Dropping in for a meal at the restaurant or a drink and a snack at the bar are great ways to experience this historic hotel without coughing up three car payments' worth of cash in order to spend the night.

The Ahwahnee was built on the site of a former Ahwahnee–Miwok village. In order to promote the relatively young national park, National Park Service (NPS) director Stephen Mather dreamed up the idea of a majestic hotel to attract wealthy guests. The site was chosen for its exposure to the sun and its views of Half Dome, Yosemite Falls and Glacier Point. The hotel was designed by American architect Gilbert Stanley Underwood, who also designed Zion Lodge, Brice Canyon Lodge and Grand Canyon North Rim Lodge. If the Ahwahnee's lobby looks familiar, perhaps it's because it inspired the lobby of the Overlook Hotel, the ill-fated inn from Stanley Kubrick's *The Shining*.

YOSEMITE LODGE AT THE FALLS

Near the base of Yosemite Falls, the collection of buildings known as Yosemite Lodge (Map p60) includes modern, motel-like accommodations, restaurants, shops, a bar, a bicycle-rental stand, a public pool, a tour desk and other amenities. The amphitheater hosts regular evening programs, and the pool is open to the public.

Unlike the Ahwahnee, it's not a very striking development. Despite efforts to blend it into the natural surroundings, the place feels strangely like a suburban condo development. Though it doesn't appear very old, the lodge dates back to 1915. It underwent extensive redesign and remodeling in 1956 and 1998, retaining little to suggest its history.

The Yosemite Valley shuttle bus stops right out front, as do Yosemite Area Regional Transport System (YARTS) buses. All guided tram tours, ski shuttles and hiker buses also leave from here; tickets are available from the tour desk in the lobby.

MANDATORY HALF DOME PERMITS

To stem lengthy lines (and increasingly dangerous congestion) on the vertiginous cables of Half Dome, the park now requires that all day hikers obtain an advance **permit** (877-444-6777; www.recreation.gov; fee per person $1.50) to climb the cables or go beyond the base of the subdome. Permits go on sale four months in advance, and the 300 available per day sell out almost immediately. You can get up to four permits per reservation. Backpackers can obtain permits when they pick up wilderness permits, without the advance reservation process. Be warned that rangers are stationed to check permits. See www.nps.gov/yose/planyourvisit/hdpermits.htm for the latest information.

YOSEMITE NATIONAL PARK SIGHTS

THE LEGEND OF HALF DOME

According to Native American legend, one of Yosemite's early inhabitants came down from the mountains to Mono Lake, where he married a Paiute named Tesaiyac. The journey back to the Valley was difficult, and by the time they reached what was to become Mirror Lake, Tesaiyac decided she wanted to return to her people at Mono Lake. Her husband refused to live on such barren, arid land with no oak trees where he could get acorns. With a heart full of despair, Tesaiyac fled toward Mono Lake, her husband in pursuit. When the spirits heard the couple quarreling, they grew angry and turned the two into stone: he became North Dome and she became Half Dome. The tears she cried made marks as they ran down her face, forming Mirror Lake.

YOSEMITE FALLS

One of the world's most dramatic natural spectacles, Yosemite Falls (Map p58) is a marvel to behold. Naturalist John Muir devoted entire pages to its changing personality, its myriad sounds, its movement with the wind and its transformations between the seasons. No matter where you are when you see it (and it regularly pops into view from all over the Valley), the falls will stop you in your tracks.

In spring, when snowmelt gets Yosemite Creek really pumping, the sight is astounding. On those nights when the falls are full and the moon is bright, you might spot a 'moonbow.' In winter, as the spray freezes midair, an ice cone forms at the base of the falls.

Dropping 2425ft, Yosemite Falls is considered the tallest in North America. Some question that claim, however, as Yosemite Falls comprises three distinct tiers: towering 1430ft Upper Yosemite Fall, tumbling 675ft Middle Cascade and the final 320ft drop of Lower Yosemite Fall. If you want to make the grueling hike to the top, see p83. The easternmost route of the loop trail is wheelchair-accessible.

To get to the base of Lower Yosemite Fall, get off at shuttle stop 6 (or park in the lot just north of Yosemite Lodge) and join the legions of visitors for the easy quarter-mile stroll. Note that in midsummer, when the snowmelt has dissipated, both the upper and lower falls usually dry up – sometimes to a trickle, other times stopping altogether.

HALF DOME

Rising 8842ft above sea level, and nearly a mile above the Valley floor, Half Dome (Map p58) serves as the park's spiritual centerpiece and stands as one of the most glorious and monumental (not to mention best-known) domes on earth.

Its namesake shape is, in fact, an illusion. While from the Valley the dome appears to have been neatly sliced in half, from Glacier or Washburn Points you'll see that it's actually a thin ridge with a back slope nearly as steep as its fabled facade. As you travel through the park, witness Half Dome's many faces. For example, from Mirror Lake it presents a powerful form, while from the Panorama Trail it looks somewhat like a big toe poking out above the rocks and trees.

Half Dome towers above Tenaya Canyon, a classic, glacially carved gorge. Across this canyon rise North Dome and Basket Dome, examples of fully intact domes. In contrast, Half Dome's north face shattered along cracks as a small glacier undercut the dome's base. The resulting cliff boasts a 93% vertical grade (the sheerest in North America), attracting climbers from around the world. Hikers with a permit can reach its summit from the Valley via a long series of trails (see p101). The final 45-degree stretch to the top was first made accessible by George Anderson, a local blacksmith who drilled holes in the granite in 1875 and installed a rope system (later replaced by the steel cables in use today).

BRIDALVEIL FALL

In the southwest end of the Valley, Bridalveil Fall (Map p58) tumbles 620ft. The Ahwahneechee people call it Pohono (Spirit of the Puffing Wind), as gusts often blow the fall from side to side, even lifting water back up into the air. This waterfall usually runs year-round, though it's often reduced to a whisper by midsummer. Bring rain gear or expect to get soaked when the fall is heavy.

Park at the large lot where Wawona Rd (Hwy 41) meets Southside Dr. From the lot, it's a quarter-mile walk to the base of the fall. The path is paved, but probably too rough for wheelchairs, and there's a somewhat steep climb at the very end. Avoid climbing on the slippery rocks at its base – no one likes a broken bone.

If you'd rather walk from the Valley, a trail (part of the Loop Trails) follows Southside Dr, beginning near the LeConte Memorial Lodge and running about 3.8 miles west to the falls.

EL CAPITAN

At nearly 3600ft from base to summit, El Capitan (Map p58) ranks as one of the world's largest granite monoliths. Its sheer face makes it a world-class destination for experienced climbers, and one that wasn't 'conquered' until 1958. Since then, it's been inundated. Look closely and you'll probably spot climbers reckoning with El Cap's series of cracks and ledges, including the famous 'Nose.' At night, park along the road and dim your headlights; once your eyes adjust, you'll easily make out the pinpricks of headlamps dotting the rock face. Listen, too, for voices.

The road offers several good spots from which to ogle El Capitan. The Valley View turnout is one. For a wider view, try the pull-out along Southside Dr just east of Bridalveil Fall. You can also park on Northside Dr, just below El Capitan, perhaps the best vantage point from which to see climbers, though you'll need binoculars for a really good view. Look for the haul bags first – they're bigger, more colorful and move around more than the climbers, making them easier to spot. The **Yosemite Climbing Association** (www .yosemiteclimbing.org) began an 'Ask-a-Climber' program in 2011, where it sets up a telescope at El Capitan Bridge for a few hours a day (mid-May through mid-October) and answers visitors' questions.

Glacier Point & Badger Pass

Constructed to replace an 1882 wagon road, the modern 16-mile stretch of Glacier Point Rd leads to what many people consider the finest viewpoint in Yosemite. A year-round destination, winter attracts skiers galore who whoosh down the Badger Pass slopes and traverse the unplowed road as a cross-country route. In warmer months, gawkers flock to the end of the road for its satiating Half Dome views and hikers file out from its many trailheads.

Orientation

From Yosemite Valley, it's 30 miles (about an hour's drive) to Glacier Point. Glacier Point Rd runs east from the Chinquapin junction on Hwy 41, dead-ending at Glacier Point itself. The road rises from about 6000ft at Chinquapin to 7700ft at the Sentinel Dome parking lot, then down again to 7214ft at Glacier Point. From the Chinquapin turnoff, Badger Pass Ski Area lies about 5 miles to the east; in winter, Glacier Point Rd is closed east of the ski area.

Glacier Point lies at the far eastern end of winding Glacier Point Rd. Along the road, hiking trails lead to more spectacular viewpoints such as Dewey Point and Sentinel Dome. The road also passes Bridalveil Creek Campground, adjacent to Bridalveil Creek, which runs north and drops into Yosemite Valley as Bridalveil Fall.

The only services in the area are at Glacier Point, where there's a small **snack bar** (Map p66; ☺9am-5pm) and gift shop. Rangers are stationed at viewpoint areas but the closest visitor center is in Yosemite Valley. No wilderness permits are available in the vicinity (except at Badger Pass in the winter); you must backtrack to either Yosemite Valley or Wawona if you develop warm-weather backcountry urges.

A Valley–Glacier Point bus service operates in summer, and there's also a Valley–Badger Pass service in the winter; see Getting Around, p132.

GLACIER POINT

The views from 7214ft Glacier Point can make you feel like you cheated somehow –

DON'T MISS

HORSETAIL FALL

For two weeks in late February, if the sky's clear and the water flow is just right, visitors can behold a fiery spectacle at Horsetail Fall. A seasonal ribbon of water dropping off the eastern edge of El Capitan, when the fall catches the sunset during this time of year its thin flow blazes like a stream of molten lava. Many compare it to witnessing the Glacier Point Firefall (p69), and photographers flock to the El Capitan Picnic Area to get the best views.

Glacier Point & Badger Pass

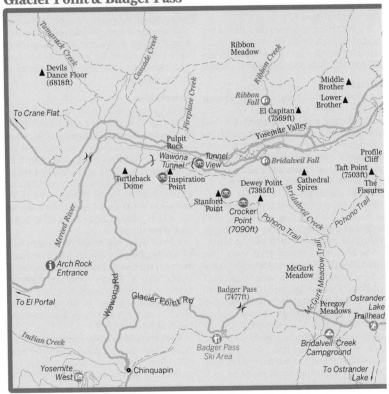

a huge array of superstar sights present themselves without any physical effort. A quick mosey up from the parking lot and you'll find the entire eastern Yosemite Valley spread out before you, from Yosemite Falls to Half Dome, as well as the distant peaks that ring Tuolumne Meadows. Half Dome looms practically at eye level, and if you look closely you can spot ant-sized hikers on its summit. The cable approach is not visible, however.

To the left of Half Dome lies the glacially carved Tenaya Canyon, and to its right are the wavy white ribbons of Nevada and Vernal Falls. On the Valley floor, the Merced River snakes through green meadows and groves of trees. Sidle up to the railing, hold on tight and peer 3200ft straight down at Curry Village. The aqua rectangle of its swimming pool is clearly visible, as is the Ahwahnee Hotel just to the north. Basket Dome and North Dome also rise to the north of the Valley, and Liberty

Cap and the Clark Range can be seen to the right of Half Dome.

Almost from the park's inception, Glacier Point has been a popular destination. It used to be that getting up here was a major undertaking. That changed once the Four Mile Trail (p84) opened in 1872. While not exactly an easy climb – neither then nor today – the trail did offer a more direct route to the point. James McCauley, an early Yosemite pioneer, financed formation of the trail, for which he charged a toll; he later took over the reins of the Mountain House hotel, built in 1873 atop Glacier Point. In the 1870s he also conceived the famous Firefall, though Curry Village later picked up and heavily promoted the event.

A wagon road to the point was completed in 1882, and the current Glacier Point Rd was built in 1936. As far back as 1929 (and again in the 1970s), there was talk of building an aerial tramway to ferry tourists from Yosemite Valley to Glacier Point. But since

you'll round a corner to a view of El Capitan and Yosemite Valley's western half. Serious switchbacks begin below this point.

Drivers should go in the morning to avoid the idling afternoon backup from the parking lot.

WASHBURN POINT

Named for the brothers who built the Wawona Hotel, this viewpoint along Glacier Point Rd is magnificent, though not quite as expansive as Glacier Point. The point faces east toward the Clark Range and lacks the sweeping view of Yosemite Valley. Still, a stop here serves as a great warm-up to Glacier Point, less than a mile down the road.

BADGER PASS

The California ski industry essentially got its start in Yosemite Valley, and Badger Pass was California's first alpine ski resort. After Yosemite's All-Year Highway (now Hwy 140) was completed in 1926 and the Ahwahnee Hotel opened its doors the following year, the Valley quickly became a popular winter destination.

As the 1929 Winter Olympics approached, the newly formed Curry Company and the Yosemite Winter Club submitted an impassioned bid to host the games. They lost, and instead the events were held at Lake Placid, New York – where, in a freakish irony, no snow fell that winter. Bales of hay were used in lieu of snow, while the Sierra saw record snowfalls.

When Wawona Tunnel opened in 1933, skiers began congregating at Badger Pass. In 1935 a new lodge opened on Glacier Point Rd, and a newfangled device called 'the upski' was installed at the pass. The crude lift consisted of nothing more than two counterbalanced sleds, but it worked, and Badger Pass became California's first alpine ski resort.

In winter a free shuttle bus runs between the Valley and Badger Pass (see p132). Also in winter, wilderness permits are available by self-registration at the **A-frame building** (209-372-0409), where the first-aid station and ski patrol are also situated. Rangers usually staff the office from 8am to 5pm, but coverage can be hit and miss. See p118 for details on the Badger Pass Ski Area.

the cables would be an eyesore and the system would disturb fragile ecosystems, plans thankfully were abandoned. The spectacularly situated Glacier Point Hotel stood on the point from 1917 until 1969, when it burned down along with the adjacent McCauley Mountain House.

At the tip of the point is **Overhanging Rock**, a huge granite slab protruding from the cliff edge like an outstretched tongue, defying gravity and once providing a scenic stage for daredevil extroverts. Through the years, many famous photos have been taken of folks performing handstands, high kicks and other wacky stunts on the rock. You'll have to stick to the pictures though, as the precipice is now off-limits.

To escape the crowds, consider a short hike down the first half-mile or so of the Four Mile Trail, which drops gently into a quiet forest and – at this point at least – isn't too steep. After about 10 or 15 minutes,

Wawona

Yosemite's historical center, Wawona was home to the park's first headquarters (supervised by Captain AE Wood on the site of the

DON'T MISS

GREETINGS, STARGAZERS

On many Friday and Saturday nights in summer, the Glacier Point amphitheater hosts various astronomy clubs, which set up telescopes and let the public take a closer-than-usual look at what's deep in the night sky – from the moon's mottled surface to fuzzy, faraway star clusters. These programs are accompanied by 'Stars Over Yosemite' discussions, during which rangers point out constellations in the sky above Glacier Point. Bring the kids.

On most summer nights, there are also four-hour **stargazing tours** (☏209-372-4386, 209-372-1240; www.yosemitepark.com; adult/senior/child over 4/child under 4 $41/35/23/free) from the Valley to Glacier Point that include an hour-long astronomy program.

Throughout the summer, astronomy walks are also regularly hosted by amateur astronomers in Tuolumne Meadows, Yosemite Valley and Wawona. In Tuolumne you get to walk out into the meadow, lay on granite still warm from the afternoon sun and gaze up at the star-blazoned sky.

Check the *Yosemite Guide* for schedules.

Wawona Campground) and its first tourist facilities. The latter was a simple wayside station run by Galen Clark, who homesteaded in Wawona in 1856. A decade later, Clark was appointed state guardian of the Yosemite Grant, which protected Yosemite Valley and the Mariposa Grove. In 1875 he sold his lodge to the Washburn brothers, who built what's known today as the Wawona Hotel. The Washburns also renamed the area Wawona – thought to be the local Native American word for 'big trees.'

Completed in 1875, the original Wawona Rd opened the floodgates for tourists curious to see the big trees – as well as wondrous Yosemite Valley to the north. The road was modernized in 1933, following construction of the Wawona Tunnel.

From 1891 to 1906, the current Wawona campground site was home base for the US cavalry, who were appointed as the first official protectors of the newly formed national park. The cavalry moved its headquarters to Yosemite Valley in 1906. Curiously, considering its significant role in the park's history, Wawona remained private property for decades and wasn't incorporated into the boundaries of Yosemite National Park until 1932. Some parts of the area are still in private hands, including the houses that line Chilnualna Falls Rd.

A blend of Victorian elegance and utilitarian New England charm, the Wawona Hotel is the commercial hub of the area. The unassuming white wooden building sits behind a large, manicured green lawn and a fountain inhabited by very vocal frogs.

The **Wawona Information Station** (☏209-375-9531; ◷8:30am-5pm late May-early Oct) doubles as the area's visitor center and wilderness center. It issues wilderness permits and bear canisters, answers general park questions and sells some maps and books. The station is located inside Hill's Studio, a historic 1886 building (it was the studio of landscape painter Thomas Hill) adjacent to the Wawona Hotel. Small exhibits in the studio include reproductions of his work. When the office is open for the season, it issues wilderness permits for all areas of the park. When it's closed (about October through May), backcountry-bound visitors can self-register for wilderness permits for trailheads in Wawona and Glacier Point Rd only. Bear canisters can be rented at the general store when the office is closed.

Orientation

Wawona lies on Hwy 41 (Wawona Rd), 4 miles north of the park's South Entrance, which is about 63 miles north of Fresno. Yosemite Valley is a 27-mile drive north. No public transportation serves Wawona; DNC's Grand Tour (see p227), which originates and ends in the Valley, is the only scheduled option for getting to Wawona without a car.

The South Fork of the Merced River passes through Wawona, running northwest out of the park. Most visitor services lie just to its south. Across Hwy 41, there's the Wawona Golf Course (p117) and the expansive Wawona Meadow, which doubled as the local airport in the early 20th century.

At the corner of Hwy 41 and Forest Dr, just north of the hotel, are a general store, post office, ATM and gas station (24-hour with credit card).

North of the river is Chilnualna Falls Rd, which runs east into a development of private homes and rental properties. The horse stables, the Pioneer Yosemite History Center and a small Campground Reservation Office are along Chilnualna Falls Rd, as are the Bassett Memorial Library (with free internet access) and the year-round Pine Tree Market, about a mile northeast of Hwy 41.

Some 6 miles southeast of Wawona stands the Mariposa Grove of giant sequoias, the park's largest and deservedly popular sequoia grove.

FREE **Pioneer Yosemite**
History Center   HISTORICAL CENTER
(⊙24hr) In the 1960s, a large number of Yosemite's historic wooden buildings – including some from the original site of Yosemite Village – were transferred to the Pioneer Yosemite History Center, forming a period village along the South Fork of the Merced River just north of the Wawona Hotel. Mostly furnished, the buildings include a Wells Fargo office, a jail and the Hodgdon homestead cabin. An evocative covered bridge (it dates from 1857 but was modified with walls and a ceiling by Vermont native Henry Washburn in 1875) crosses the river, and a barn south of the river holds a collection of vintage stagecoaches. In a reminder of daffy past land-management practices, there's also a 'mosquito wagon' that once sprayed oil on Tuolumne Meadows ponds to control bugs!

In the spring, elementary school teachers and their students can spend the night and learn about pioneer life as part of the Environmental Living Program (www.nps .gov/yose/forteachers/elp.htm).

A nice spot to trip back in time, the center gives you a sense of what local life was like a century ago. For fun, hop aboard a 10-minute stagecoach ride (adult/child $4/3; ⊙Wed-Sun Jun-Sep). For summer events like blacksmithing demonstrations or the occasional barn dance, check the *Yosemite Guide*.

MARIPOSA GROVE
With their massive stature and multimillennium maturity, the chunky high-rise sequoias of Mariposa Grove will make you feel rather insignificant. The largest grove of giant sequoias in the park, there are approximately 500 mature trees towering over 250 acres, with a number of mammoths right in the parking lot. A few walking trails wind through this very popular grove, and you can usually have a more solitary experience if you come during the early evening in summer or anytime outside of summer. The Mariposa Grove Rd closes to cars from about November to

THE FIREFALL

Imagine the ruckus that would ensue today if someone built a bonfire and sent it toppling over Glacier Point. Rangers and fire crews would swarm the scene, and rangers would no doubt press arson charges. So it's hard to believe that this was a Yosemite evening tradition for 88 years, inciting public rapture and no official park condemnation. It sounds horrific to those schooled in the 'leave no trace' wilderness ethic, but countless Valley campers still testify to the beauty and excitement of the Firefall, regarded as a sublime summer moment in the enchantment of a summer's evening. Even the echoing signal call to Glacier Point from the Camp Curry campfire, 'Let the fire fall!' became a spine-tingling element of the tradition.

The Firefall originated around 1872, when a hotel was being built at the top of James McCauley's new 4-mile toll trail to Glacier Point. Perhaps as an advertisement for his enterprise, McCauley pushed his campfire off the cliff, creating a glowing waterfall of sparks that was so appealing that tourists in Yosemite Valley called on McCauley to repeat it. His sons transformed the Firefall into a family business, collecting $1.50 from each person who wanted to see it happen. When they found enough takers, a fire builder went up the trail to build a large fire of fir bark and pushed it off the cliff just after nightfall.

The McCauleys left Yosemite in 1897, but two years later David Curry reintroduced the Firefall as a way to draw business to his newly created Camp Curry. Apart from two brief hiatuses, one in 1913 and the other during WWII, the Firefall continued to hold a place in Yosemite evening activities until the National Park Service ended it in 1968, finally declaring the tradition to be incompatible with natural land management.

To read a compilation of Firefall memories, visit http://firefall.info.

Wawona

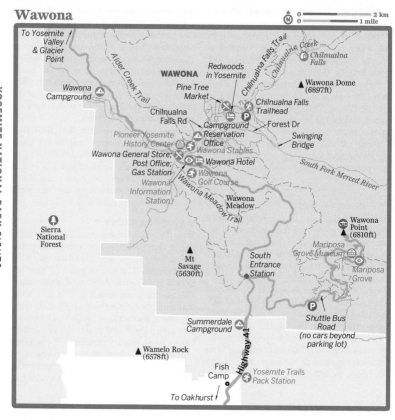

April, but you can always hike in (2 miles, 500ft of elevation gain) and experience it in its quiet hibernation.

Walk a half-mile up to the 2700-year-old **Grizzly Giant**, a bloated beast of a tree with branches that are bigger in circumference than most of the pine trees in this forest. The walk-through **California Tunnel Tree** is close by, and the favored spot for 'I visited the tall forest' photos. Incredibly, this tree continues to survive, even though its huge portal was hacked out back in 1895. The more famous **Fallen Wawona Tunnel Tree**, however, fell over in a heap in 1969 – its 10ft-high hole gouged from a fire scar in 1881. Other notable specimens include the **Telescope Tree** and the **Clothespin Tree**. Three miles from the parking lot, the wide-open overlook at **Wawona Point** (6810ft) takes in the entire area. It's about a mile round-trip from the Fallen Wawona Tunnel Tree.

Depending on your energy level, you could spend half an hour or a few hours exploring the forest. Between the parking lot and the Wawona Tunnel Tree in the upper grove, the elevation gain is about 1000ft, but the trail is gentle.

Parking can be very limited, so come early or late, or take the free shuttle bus from the Wawona General Store or the park entrance. You can also explore the grove on a one-hour guided tour aboard a noisy open-air **tram** (☎209-375-1621; adult/child $25/18; ☺usually May-Sep) that leaves from the parking lot.

Allow at least an hour to get to the grove from Yosemite Valley.

Mariposa Grove Museum   MUSEUM
(☺10am-4pm May-Sep) The upper grove is home to this small building, further dwarfed by the scale of the surrounding trees. The museum has exhibits on sequoia ecology.

Big Oak Flat Road & Tioga Road

Those arriving on Hwy 120 first encounter this section of the park. While not the most spectacular part of Yosemite, it has a steady flow of visitors. Many just pass through, but the campgrounds at Hodgdon Meadow and Crane Flat keep the area humming with people.

Big Oak Flat Rd was the second route into the park, completed in 1874, just a month after Coulterville Rd. Both were toll roads. Today, Big Oak Flat Rd follows a modified route into the Valley, though a portion of the old road remains open to cyclists and hikers headed for Tuolumne Grove. In winter the road is popular with cross-country skiers.

Going east on Big Oak Flat Rd (Hwy 120) past the Big Oak Flat Entrance, you'll find the **Big Oak Flat Information Station** (Map p71; ☎209-379-1899; ☺8am-5pm May-Sep). It serves as a mini visitor center with a good variety of books, maps and postcards for sale. The staff can answer questions and there is a courtesy phone inside to check available concessionaire-run lodging inside the park. In the same office is the **wilderness permit desk** (☺8am-5pm May-Sep), which issues permits and doles out bear boxes ($5).

At Crane Flat junction, the **Crane Flat Service Station & General Store** (Map p71; ☺8am-8pm summer, approx 9am-5pm winter) sells firewood, ice, beer and a smattering of groceries and last-minute camping supplies. Perhaps most importantly, it also has decent fresh coffee. Hurrah! The gas station operates 24 hours year-round with a credit card, and there's a pay phone outside.

Orientation

From the entrance, Big Oak Flat Rd descends southeast into the Valley, passing through several tunnels that offer great overlooks of the Merced River Canyon.

Going north, Tioga Rd (Hwy 120 East) rises from 6200ft at Crane Flat to 9945ft at Tioga Pass. Because of the high elevation, snow closes the road (and everything along it) in winter; the road's generally plowed and open from late May or mid-June to mid-November. Exact dates are impossible to predetermine, so always call ahead. From the Crane Flat junction until Tenaya Lake, there are few visitor services.

A half-mile from Crane Flat (going east on Tioga Rd toward Tuolumne Meadows) is the turnoff for Tuolumne Grove, a small grove containing two dozen mature giant sequoias.

Big Oak Flat Road / Crane Flat

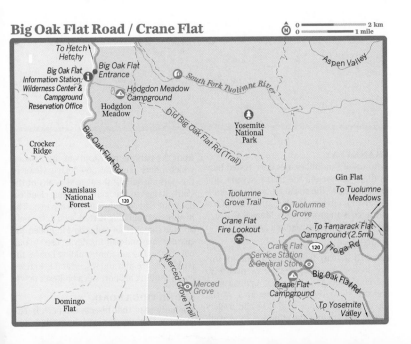

Along Tioga Road

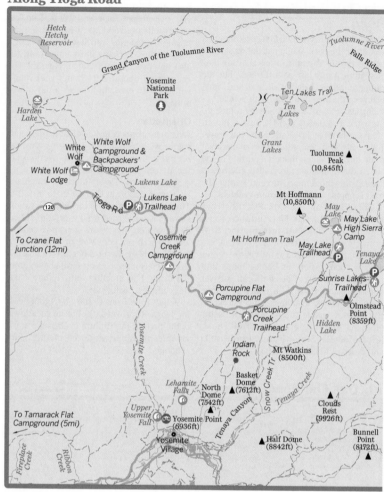

CRANE FLAT

Throngs of sandhill cranes once rested here as they crisscrossed the Sierra Nevada, and the birds gave the meadow (and surrounding area) its name. About 4 miles east of the entrance is the road to the Merced Grove, a seldom-visited giant sequoia grove.

Crane Flat Fire Lookout LOOKOUT

(Map p71) It's easy to miss the turnoff for this fire lookout, so keep your eyes peeled to the north between Crane Flat Campground and the Merced Grove parking area. At the top of a 1.5-mile spur road (RVs and trailers should not attempt the climb), a short walk

from the parking area leads to the lookout, which offers fantastic 360-degree views of the park, including the jagged peaks of the Clark Range to the south and (on cloudless days) the San Joaquin Valley to the west. The historic 1931 building here is open to the public and contains an Osborne Firefinder, the circular map and plotting device used to pinpoint fires. The adjacent building houses the park's crack search and rescue and fire crews, and a working heliport sits a bit lower down.

ALONG TIOGA ROAD

The only road that bisects the park is Tioga Rd, a 56-mile scenic highway that runs

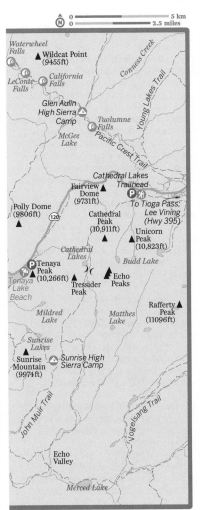

found, and the mine closed soon after the road was completed. Tioga Rd was realigned and modernized in 1961. Only a few sections of the original roadbed remain, including the rough, 4.5-mile stretch that leads to Yosemite Creek Campground. Head down this narrow, tortuous road for a glimpse of how much more treacherous park roads used to be – and not even that long ago. You'll return to Tioga Rd with newfound respect for this engineering marvel.

As Tioga Rd heads east toward Tuolumne Meadows, it passes four campgrounds. Some 15 miles northeast of Crane Flat is White Wolf (Map p72), with a small lodge tent cabins and a store that sells mostly snacks and drinks. White Wolf sits on a short spur road a mile north of Tioga Rd.

During summer the Tuolumne Meadows Tour & Hikers' Bus (p133) is an excellent transportation option for one-way hikes that depart from Tioga Rd.

For information on Tioga Pass and the eastern stretch of Tioga Rd, see p142.

Olmsted Point   LOOKOUT

This 'honey hit the brakes!' viewpoint is a lunar landscape of glaciated granite with a stunning view down Tenaya Canyon to the backside of Half Dome. Midway between the May Lake turnoff and Tenaya Lake, the point was named for Frederick Law Olmsted (1822–1903), who was appointed chairman of the first Board of Commissioners to manage the newly established Yosemite Grant in 1864. Olmsted also helped to design Central Park in New York City and did some landscaping for the University of California and Stanford University.

To experience an even better view, and without the company of your awestruck compatriots, stroll a quarter-mile down to the overlook, where you can get past the tree cover and see even deeper into the canyon. Because of extreme avalanche hazards, Olmsted Point is the last area of Hwy 120 to be plowed before the road opens.

Looming over the canyon's eastern side is 9926ft **Clouds Rest**, a massive mountain comprising the largest exposed chunk of granite in Yosemite. As its name implies, clouds often settle atop the peak. Rising 4500ft above Tenaya Creek, it makes a strenuous but rewarding day hike (see p92).

Tenaya Lake   LAKE

Just east of Olmsted Point, Tenaya Lake (8150ft) takes its name from Chief Tenaya, the

between Crane Flat in the west (starting from Crane Flat junction) and Hwy 395 at Lee Vining, about 12 miles east of Tioga Pass, the park's easternmost gate. Along the way it traverses a superb High Sierra landscape. Be prepared to pull over regularly to gawk at sights such as glorious Tenaya Lake, mighty Clouds Rest and Half Dome from Olmsted Point.

Initially called the Great Sierra Wagon Rd, the road was built by the Great Sierra Consolidated Silver Company in 1882–83 to supply a mine at Bennettville near Tioga Pass. Ironically, no significant silver was ever

YOSEMITE'S ARTISTS

From its very beginnings as a park, Yosemite has inspired a body of art nearly as impressive as the landscape itself. The artists who came to Yosemite with the first generation of tourists revealed a world of extraordinary beauty, even as miners, ranchers and lumbermen were tearing it apart in their lust for profit. From the illustrations of Thomas Ayres to the photographs of Carleton Watkins, art played a key role in the bid to establish Yosemite as a national park.

In the mid-19th century, the Hudson River School and related movements in American art strived to capture the face of God in the wild magnificence of nature. A parallel trend in literature expressed a distinctly American spiritualism tied to the wilderness; writers who explored such transcendental themes included Ralph Waldo Emerson, Walt Whitman, Emily Dickinson and Henry David Thoreau. Into this intellectual moment, which flourished on the East Coast, came the first paintings of Yosemite by a recognized artist, Albert Bierstadt, in 1863.

At that time, San Francisco was becoming the epicenter for a distinctly Californian school of art. Inspired by the vistas that Bierstadt and the photographers were capturing in Yosemite, many other artists embraced the Sierra as a subject matter. Mountain landscapes by Charles Nahl, Thomas Hill and William Keith soon adorned Victorian mansions in San Francisco and Sacramento, and painters became a regular fixture in the haunts of John Muir, who occasionally led groups of them on sketching expeditions into remote locations. Hill set up a studio at Wawona in 1884, beginning the tradition of resident artists and galleries in the park.

While the painters were often content to set up their easels in the meadows, photographers became known for seeking out more inaccessible regions. Sierra Club photographer-mountaineers such as Joseph LeConte and Norman Clyde captured extremely remote areas of the park. Yosemite's best-known photographer, of course, was Ansel Adams, who developed a level of craft not seen in the work of his predecessors. An early proponent of the idea that photography could adhere to the same aesthetic principles used by fine artists, he also became a strong advocate for the preservation of the wilderness, working on the frontlines of the growing conservation movement.

In 1929 Adams married Virginia Best, whose father's gallery in Yosemite Valley was the precursor to the Ansel Adams Gallery, found today in Yosemite Village. In 1940 Adams held a photography workshop at the gallery with fellow photographer Edward Weston, beginning a tradition of photography education that continues to this day.

Three of Adams' assistants – John Sexton, Alan Ross and Ted Orland – are lesser known but equally important to the greater body of Yosemite photography. Photographer-mountaineer Galen Rowell, who Adams himself highly regarded, took some of the most extreme photos of the park, continuing to expose those faraway places to the public eye.

Ahwahneechee chief who aided white soldiers, only to be driven from the land by white militias in the early 1850s. Tenaya allegedly protested use of his name, pointing out that the lake already had a name – Pywiack, or 'Lake of Shining Rocks,' for the polished granite that surrounds it. The lake's shiny blue surface looks absolutely stunning framed by thick stands of pine and a series of smooth granite cliffs and domes. Dominating its north side is **Polly Dome** (9806ft). The face nearest the lake is known as **Stately Pleasure Dome**, a popular spot with climbers – you may see them working their way up from the road. Sloping up from the lake's south shore are Tenaya Peak (10,266ft) and Tresidder Peak (10,600ft).

Tuolumne Meadows

Arriving at Tuolumne (too-*ahl*-uh-mee) Meadows after the drive up from the Valley is like stepping into another world, even though the two areas are only about 55 miles apart. Instead of being surrounded by waterfalls and sheer granite walls, you emerge in a subalpine wonderland marked by jagged peaks, smooth granite domes, brilliant blue lakes and the meadows' lush grasses and wildflowers. The flowers, which peak in July, are truly a highlight of any visit to Yosemite.

Flowing from the Sierra Crest, the Lyell and Dana Forks of the Tuolumne River – not to mention creeks such as Budd, Unicorn and Delaney – all converge at Tuolumne Meadows (8600ft elevation). At 2.5 miles long, the main flat cradles the Sierra's largest subalpine meadow. The surrounding peaks and domes make Tuolumne a paradise for climbers and hikers, with trails stretching in all directions.

Lying deep in the high country of the Sierra, the Tuolumne Meadows region enjoys a brief but glorious summer and, depending on weather conditions, is only accessible roughly between June and November. Despite the short season, Tuolumne is far quieter than the Valley, although the area around the store, campground and visitor center can get crowded, especially on midsummer weekends. Many hiking trails, such as Dog Lake, are also well traveled, but with a little effort you'll quickly find solitude.

At the **Tuolumne Meadows Visitor Center** (☑209-372-0263; ☺9am-6pm Jul-Aug, to 5pm spring & fall), about a mile west of the campground, rangers answer questions, sell books and hiking maps, and have helpful handouts describing local trails. There are a few good displays that explain common glacial features. Especially handy is the wildflower display, which will help you identify what you see on your hikes. For further information about wildflowers, see p216.

The **Tuolumne Meadows Wilderness Center** (Map p76; ☑209-372-0309; ☺approx 7:30am-5pm Jul & Aug, 8am-4:30pm spring & fall) is the place to go for wilderness permits and trail information. Since Tuolumne's mountains, lakes and trails are such a draw for backpackers, it's often a busy spot. It stocks a small selection of books and maps, and has information on current trail conditions. The center sits on the south side of Tioga Rd just east of Lembert Dome, on the spur road leading to Tuolumne Meadows Lodge.

The Tuolumne Meadows Store stocks groceries and supplies and has a post office. The **Tuolumne Meadows Sport Shop** (☺8:30am-6pm Jul-Sep), next door at the gas station, sells a variety of climbing gear, some backpacking supplies, maps, dehydrated food and bear-resistant food containers.

Orientation

Tuolumne Meadows sits along Tioga Rd (Hwy 120) west of the park's Tioga Pass Entrance. Limited parking is available for hikers and meadow meanderers in pullouts along Tioga Rd (or you can take the shuttle bus). You'll find larger parking lots near Lembert Dome, the visitor center and the wilderness center.

Temperatures in Tuolumne Meadows and the surrounding high country are 15°F to 20°F cooler than in Yosemite Valley, a benefit for hikers and anyone else who struggles in the heat. At the same time, nights are much chillier up here, so pack warm clothes. And remember, snow can fall here in any month of the year, though typically no later than June and no earlier than September.

MAIN MEADOW

Stretching nearly 3 miles from Pothole Dome in the west to Lembert Dome in the east, Tuolumne's main meadow is a beautiful sight to behold, especially during sunset, when golden light ripples across the green grass and lashes up the sides of distant peaks into the still blue sky. Grab a fishing pole and dip into the gently rolling **Tuolumne River** as the sunlight drifts away, or just find a quiet spot to sit and stare at the landscape as the mood shifts and the colors shimmer.

While the meadow is a perfect place for quiet contemplation, there's actually a lot of activity going on here. Blanketed in snow for most of the year, the meadow explodes to life in summer, when the wildflowers, taking full advantage of the short growing season, fill the grassy expanse with color. For an explanation of what's happening beneath the meadow's deceptively still surface, check out the interpretive signs that line the dirt road between the stables and Soda Springs.

Soda Springs NATURAL SPRINGS

Above the northern shore of the Tuolumne River, carbonated mineral water burbles silently out of Soda Springs, a small natural spring that turns its surroundings into a cluster of mineral-crusted, rust-red puddles. People (and animals) used to drink the stuff, though the park service now discourages the practice due to possible surface contamination – no big deal as it's not exactly an appealing method for quenching your thirst anyway.

The springs are a short, pleasant walk across the flat middle of the meadow. There

Tuolumne Meadows

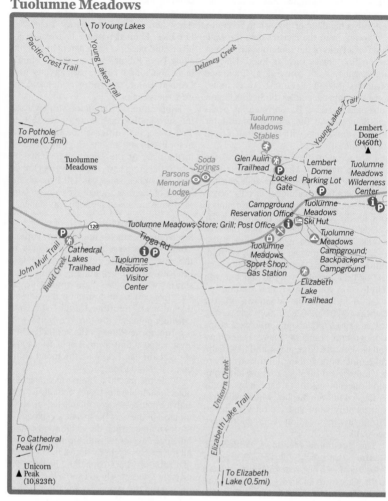

are two approaches, both about 0.5 miles long. The first starts opposite the visitor center on Tioga Rd. The other begins in the Lembert Dome parking area.

Parsons Memorial Lodge HISTORICAL BUILDING
Nearby Soda Springs stands this simple but beautifully rugged cabin built in 1915 from local granite. It initially served as a Sierra Club meeting room and was named for Edward Taylor Parsons (1861–1914), an adventurer and active Sierra Club member who helped found the club's outings program. Today, it opens as a shelter during thunderstorms (there's a huge fireplace inside), as well as for special events, ranger talks and other programs. See *Yosemite Guide* for the current schedule.

POTHOLE DOME

Pothole Dome marks the west end of Tuolumne Meadows. It's small by Yosemite standards, but the short, 200ft climb to the top offers great views of the meadows and surrounding peaks – especially, of course, at sunset. Park along Tioga Rd, then follow the trail around the dome's west side and up to its modest summit. It's a fairly quick trip and well worth the effort.

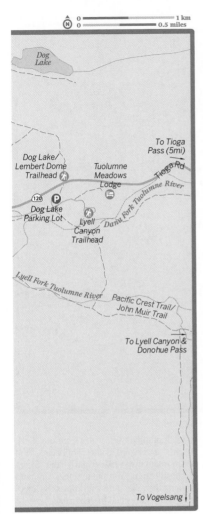

Jean-Baptiste Lembert, who homesteaded in Tuolumne Meadows.

CATHEDRAL RANGE

Dominating the views to the south of Tuolumne Meadows, the jagged Cathedral Range runs roughly northwest from the Sierra Crest, marking the divide between the Tuolumne and Merced Rivers. Its granite pinnacles are immediately striking, in particular **Cathedral Peak** (10,911ft), visible from numerous spots in the region, including along Tioga Rd. At certain angles, its summit appears to be a near-perfect pinpoint, though in reality it's a craggy, double-pronged affair. Other mountains in the range include Tresidder Peak, Echo Peaks, the Matthes Crest and Unicorn Peak (10,823ft), another standout with a horn-shaped protuberance, just east of Cathedral Peak. Soda Springs offers a particularly good vantage point for viewing the range, as does the trail up to Young Lakes (p107). The Cathedral Lakes hike (p95) is the classic must-do hike into the range itself.

TIOGA PASS

East of Tuolumne Meadows, Tioga Rd (Hwy 120) climbs steadily toward Tioga Pass, which at 9945ft is the highest auto route over the Sierra. The short ride by car or free shuttle bus from Tuolumne Meadows takes you across dramatic, wide open spaces – a stretch of stark, windswept countryside near the timberline. You'll notice a temperature drop and, most likely, widespread patches of snow.

Tioga Rd parallels the Dana Fork of the Tuolumne River, then turns north, where it borders the beautiful Dana Meadows all the way to Tioga Pass. To the east you'll see great views of Mt Gibbs (12,764ft) and 13,057ft Mt Dana, the park's second-highest peak after Mt Lyell (13,114ft).

For coverage of the spectacular area beyond Tioga Pass, see p142.

LEMBERT DOME

Prominently marking the eastern end of the main meadow, Lembert Dome towers about 800ft above the Tuolumne River. Its summit, which chalks in at 9450ft above sea level, is easily one of the finest places to watch the sunset in Yosemite. Its steep western face is a de facto granite playground for everyone from kids (who stick around the gently sloping bottom) to climbers (who rope up and head to the top). Nonclimbers can reach the summit by hiking up the backside (see p94). The dome was named for 19th-century shepherd

Hetch Hetchy

No developed part of Yosemite feels as removed from the rest of the park as Hetch Hetchy. Despite the fact that 'Hetchy's' soaring waterfalls, granite domes and sheer cliffs rival its more glamorous counterparts in Yosemite Valley, Hetch Hetchy receives but a fraction of the visitors that the Valley does. This is mainly because Hetch Hetchy Valley is filled with water – the Hetch Hetchy Reservoir – and because, save for a couple of

Hetch Hetchy

drinking fountains, a parking lot and a backpacker campground, there are practically no visitor services. Hetch Hetchy is a magical place, and is definitely worth the detour north from the much busier Big Oak Flat Entrance.

Hetch Hetchy Valley was filled with water only after a long political and environmental battle that lasted a dozen years during the early 20th century. Despite the best efforts of John Muir, who led the fight against it, the US Congress approved the 1913 *Raker Act,* which allowed the city of San Francisco to construct O'Shaughnessy Dam in the Hetch Hetchy Valley. This blocked the Tuolumne River and created Hetch Hetchy Reservoir. Muir's spirit was crushed, and he died a year later, supposedly of a broken heart.

Today, the reservoir and dam supply water and hydroelectric power to much of the Bay Area, including Silicon Valley. When you turn on a tap in San Francisco, out pours Tuolumne River water from the Hetch Hetchy Reservoir. Some politicians and environmentalists (particularly the Sierra Club) still argue for pulling the cork and draining the valley. And who knows? Stranger things have happened in California.

There's one good thing you can say about the dam: by filling in the valley, it has prevented the overdevelopment that plagues Yosemite Valley. Hetch Hetchy remains a lovely, quiet spot – good for a quick day trip or as a jumping-off point for a serious backcountry experience.

Its low elevation makes Hetch Hetchy an especially suitable hiking destination in spring and fall, when much of the high country is still blanketed by ice and snow. In summer, however, it can be very hot and dry – bring a hat, sunscreen and plenty of water. Tueeulala and Wapama Falls (see p98) are best in spring. The former dries up by late summer.

The 8-mile-long Hetch Hetchy Reservoir stretches behind O'Shaughnessy Dam, the site of the area's trailheads, parking area and backpackers' campground (available only to those with a valid wilderness permit).

Hetch Hetchy is a 40-mile drive from Yosemite Valley. From the park's Big Oak Flat Entrance, drive a mile or two west on Hwy 120 and look for the signed turnoff to Hetch Hetchy along Evergreen Rd; turn right (north), drive 8 miles to Mather and turn right (east) on Hetch Hetchy Rd. The **Hetch Hetchy Entrance Station** (☑209-379-1922; ☺7am-9pm summer, 8am-5pm winter) is just a mile beyond the junction; here backpackers can pick up wilderness permits and rent bear canisters.

From the entrance, it's about 9 miles to the parking lot beside O'Shaughnessy Dam. About 5.7 miles past the entrance, at roadside marker H3, you'll pass an overlook of the reservoir to the east and lovely Poopenaut Valley some 1200ft below.

The road to Hetch Hetchy is open only during daylight hours – approximately 7am to 9pm in summer, 8am to 7pm in spring and fall, and 8am to 5pm in winter. Hours vary year to year and season to season; they're posted on a sign at the Evergreen Rd turnoff. The gate is locked at night, and the road may close in winter due to heavy snows (carry chains). Vehicles over 25ft are not permitted on the narrow, winding road.

The closest convenience supplies and lodging are at Evergreen Lodge (p127), just south of Mather.

DRIVING

Driving is hardly the proper way to see Yosemite Valley (unless you enjoy craning your neck in traffic to see the sights otherwise blocked by your roof), but it's an undeniably superb way to experience the high country – and beyond – via the spectacular Tioga Rd. This is the only road that bisects the park between its eastern and western borders. All park roads, however, are lined with beautiful scenery, so really you can't go wrong. If you're going to drive within Yosemite Valley, try to avoid doing it on weekends.

Yosemite Valley

Map p58 & p60

Duration varies depending on traffic

Distance 12.5-mile round-trip

Start/Finish Yosemite Village

Nearest Town Yosemite Village

Transportation Shuttle or car

Summary The only driving route in Yosemite Valley takes you past the Valley's classic sights and viewpoints, including Bridalveil Fall and Yosemite Falls.

Most of this route is covered by the free Valley and El Capitan shuttles (the latter goes as far west as the El Capitan Bridge), so consider parking the car, freeing up your hands, and doing this by public transportation.

This loop follows the only two roads in and out of Yosemite Valley: Northside Dr and Southside Dr. Each is (mostly) one way and, as their names suggest, they sit on either side of the Merced River. Without traffic, you can easily drive this loop in less than an hour, but budget more time as you'll want to stop frequently. Despite the fact that the park service has tried to limit the number of cars in the Valley, it remains a popular driving tour.

Starting in Yosemite Village, head west on Northside Dr, which leads past Yosemite Falls, the Three Brothers (Lower, Middle and Eagle Peak) and El Capitan to **Valley View** (roadside marker V11), a great viewpoint along the Merced River. To complete the loop, turn left (south) at the Pohono Bridge, just past Valley View, and cross the Merced River. Then head east on Southside Dr back toward Yosemite Village. From that road you get wider views of Yosemite Falls and El Capitan on the north rim and a closer look at south rim features such as Cathedral Rocks, Sentinel Rock and Bridalveil Fall. You also drive by the site of **old Yosemite Village**, near where the chapel now sits. The road dead-ends just past Curry Village, or you can turn at Sentinel Bridge back toward Yosemite Village.

Tioga Road to Mono Lake

Map p54

Duration 2–4 hours

Distance 60-miles one way

Start Crane Flat

Finish Mono Lake

Nearest Junction Crane Flat

Transportation Car

Summary Get ready to ascend over 3500ft as you drive over dizzying Tioga

ROADSIDE KNOWLEDGE

Ever wonder what those little wooden roadside markers are? You know, the ones with the Half Dome symbol and a code like H15 or T32. Well, wonder no longer. They demarcate sights along roadways throughout Yosemite. But in order to decipher the code, you have to carry a copy of the handy little *Yosemite Road Guide* ($3.50), a booklet featuring descriptions that correspond to the codes on the signs. Also packed with some great park history, the booklet is a must-have for any drive through the park. Pick one up at a visitor center or Yosemite Conservancy bookstores anywhere in the park.

Pass (elevation 9945ft) before zigzagging down the steep eastern side to surreal Mono Lake.

Without a doubt, this is one of California's ultimate drives. From Crane Flat, the tour follows Tioga Rd up through the trees to **Olmsted Point**, **Tenaya Lake** and **Tuolumne Meadows**. It then flanks beautiful **Dana Meadows** before crossing the dizzying **Tioga Pass**. You can either turn around here or, if you have enough time, continue down the precipitous eastern side of the Sierra Crest to the town of Lee Vining and beautiful Mono Lake.

The scenery along this route – the spiky peaks of the Cathedral Range, the granite domes around Tuolumne Meadows, the stunted subalpine forests, the meandering creeks and shimmering lakes – will give you whiplash harder than driving into a giant sequoia.

Tioga Rd is open only during summer and fall, usually from late May to early November. From Yosemite Valley, it's only about 1½ hours to Tuolumne Meadows, but that's not including stops for views (Olmsted Point is a must), hikes or lunch at the Tuolumne Meadows Grill. From Tioga Pass, it's another half-hour east to Hwy 395 and Mono Lake. While you could easily make the drive in about two hours, it's best to take all day.

🚗 Wawona Road & Glacier Point Road

Map p66

Duration 2 hours

Distance 52 miles one way

Start Tunnel View

Finish Glacier Point

Nearest Towns Yosemite Village; Wawona Hotel & store

Transportation Car

Summary Some of the best park views are along this route south of Yosemite Valley. The Tunnel View and Glacier Point overlooks give excellent Valley views from different angles.

Start your expedition from the east side of the Wawona Tunnel in the spectacular pull-off point of **Tunnel View**. No, you will not be staring slack-jawed at a dark traffic structure, but at the magnificent landscape to the east. Best in the spring when snowmelt has it gushing, 620ft **Bridalveil Fall** leaps off a plateau. When it thins out in summer, it sways like a string in the wind. The sheer wall of El Capitan rises to the north side of the Valley, and Half Dome pops out in the background past deep green forest.

Buckle up and proceed west through **Wawona Tunnel**, the longest tunnel in the park at almost a mile. Two miles after your return to daylight, you approach **Turtleback Dome**, a slab of exfoliating granite that looks like it's been sliced horizontally into pieces of crumbling bread.

In six more miles you'll come to the Chinquapin junction; turn left onto Glacier Point Rd to begin the forested 16-mile stretch to Glacier Point. In 2 miles is the wide western view of Merced Canyon, which descends 4500ft below you. The **Badger Pass Ski Area** appears in three more miles, though the lifts and lodge will be deserted in warm weather. In winter, the road is closed beyond here. Pass Bridalveil Creek campground, with nearby views of the Clark Range to the east.

The road turns abruptly north near Mono Meadow, reaching **Pothole Meadows**, where strangely small bowls of water collect during wet months. A quarter-mile more lands you at **Sentinel Dome** (8122ft), one of the park's easiest-to-hike granite domes (see p86). Switchbacks descend through red fir forest to **Washburn Point**, which has views *almost* as good as those from Glacier Point. Winding through into **Glacier Point**, the peak of Half Dome parades before you.

Retrace your route back to the Chinquapin junction, and turn left to continue south on the Wawona Rd (Hwy 41). The final 12-mile stretch passes the turnoff for Yosemite West, a private community that's accessible only through the park, and crosses the South Fork of the Merced River before reaching the **Wawona Hotel**, a landmark lodging dating from 1879.

DAY HIKES

There's no better way – and often no other way – to see Yosemite than by hiking into it. It's impossible to say one area of the park is better for hiking than another. Really, it depends on the hiker's ability and interests and the time of year. For example, the vast wilderness surrounding Tuolumne Meadows is a hikers' mecca, but it's accessible only when Tioga Rd is open (usually late May through early November).

Hikes along Tioga Rd are likewise only accessible when the road is open, and when it is, the walking is phenomenal. There are easy hikes and day hikes to splendid lakes – including Harden, Lukens and May Lakes – all sans the heat and crowds of the Valley.

Offering what is likely the park's finest view, Glacier Point is also a good jumping-off point for hikes into the backcountry to the south. The area is also popular for the Valley rim walks along the Pohono Trail.

Yosemite Valley is accessible year-round, but in the height of summer the heat can be brutal and the trails get crowded. Spring is a great time for hiking in the Valley as well as at Hetch Hetchy, another low-elevation area that experiences harsh summer heat. Temperatures in Wawona are similar.

See the hiking chart on p32 for a list of all hikes and p31 for a few organizations offering guided hikes.

Levels of Difficulty
Yosemite Valley offers hikes for all levels. Those seeking gentle strolls can visit Mirror Lake and wander the Valley Loop trails as far as they wish. The rest of the Valley's trails involve significant elevation gains. At the far end of the spectrum is the trek to the summit of Half Dome, perhaps the single most difficult (and popular) day hike in the entire park. Just remember that the altitude can

make you short of breath before you become acclimatized (see p235).

For more on how we rate the hikes, see the boxed text p31.

Yosemite Valley

Many of Yosemite's easiest hikes – some might call them strolls – are along the mostly flat floor of Yosemite Valley. It's a lovely place to wander, especially in the evenings when the day-trippers are gone and Half Dome glows against the sunset. Nearly all day hikes from Yosemite Valley require some ascent. Assuming you can score a wilderness permit, the popular Half Dome hike (see p101) is more relaxed as an overnighter.

🏃 Yosemite Valley Loops

Maps p58 & p60

Duration varies

Distance varies

Difficulty Easy

Start/Finish varies

Nearest Town Yosemite Village

Transportation Shuttle

Summary Generally flat and paved, these easy-to-follow trails are a great way to acquaint yourself with Yosemite Valley and its many historic sites. Plaques along the way explain the Valley's natural and human history.

Whether you want to plot a route from your campsite to the nearest hot shower, or take in the views from the meadows and bridges around the Valley floor, the vaguely defined loop trails are an undeniably great way to get to know Yosemite Valley. Parts are even wheelchair- and stroller-friendly, and they connect the Valley's most important historic and natural features. In some places the trail joins the road, in other places it peters out only to reappear later. Generally, it follows alongside Northside and Southside Drives, and it's nearly impossible to get lost.

For the ambitious, a well-marked path leads up and down the entire Valley, but it's easily broken into segments, making the journey manageable for just about any level of hiker.

You can walk a 2.6-mile loop around the eastern end of the Valley by starting

FINDING SOLITUDE

If you've come to Yosemite looking for peace and solitude, there are plenty of places to find it. Sure, the park gets packed every summer, but with a little effort you can find near-empty trails, quiet riverside hangouts and other hideaways tucked throughout the park. If solitude is a priority, avoid summer (especially August weekends). Winter and spring are both excellent times to visit. A good rule is to hit the trail just after sunrise or late in the day, when the crowds are either sleeping or running off to supper. Yosemite Valley is where most visitors throng, and roads, campgrounds and popular trails (such as that to Vernal Fall) are predictably packed. Even in summer, though, you may find peace and quiet along the Yosemite Valley Loop trails, which few Valley visitors seem to know about.

at **Curry Village**. From here, head east along the edge of the day-use parking area, with the tent cabins on your right. When you hit the shuttle road, turn right and follow the road into and through the trail-head parking area. Southeast of the parking lot, two trails lead to **Happy Isles**: one skirts the shuttle road, and another leads into the trees and across a delicate meadow area known as the **Fen**. After visiting the **Nature Center at Happy Isles**, cross the Merced River and follow the trail alongside the road, veering left when you can to stay along the banks of the river. Just before you reach the stables, head left (southwest) on the road across the river, past the entrances to Lower and Upper Pines Campgrounds. Then look for the sign pointing to Curry Village.

Further removed from the Valley's central commercial district, the 6.5-mile loop on the west end of the Valley passes good swimming spots on the Merced and offers fabulous views of El Capitan and Bridalveil Fall. The trail basically follows Northside and Southside Drives between the base of El Capitan and **Pohono Bridge**, the westernmost bridge over the Merced River.

🚶 Mirror Lake

Map p58

Duration 1 hour

Distance 2-mile round-trip

Difficulty Easy

Start/Finish Mirror Lake Trailhead

Nearest Town Curry Village

Transportation Shuttle stop 17

Summary Shallow Mirror Lake, reflecting Mt Watkins and Half Dome on its tranquil surface, is one of the Valley's most photographed sites. Further

northeast, Tenaya Canyon offers one of the quietest corners of Yosemite Valley.

Formed when a rockfall dammed a section of Tenaya Creek, Mirror Lake has been slowly reverting to 'Mirror Meadow' ever since the park service stopped dredging it in 1971. Only folks who visit in spring and early summer get the splendid sight that Mirror Lake is named for. By mid-summer, it's just Tenaya Creek, and by fall, the creek has sometimes dried up altogether. Spring is also a marvelous time to visit for other reasons: the dogwoods are in full bloom and Tenaya Creek becomes a lively torrent as you venture further up the canyon. The Ahwahneechee called Mirror Lake Ahwiyah, meaning 'quiet water.'

From the Mirror Lake Trailhead, near shuttle stop 17, follow the Mirror Lake road to **Tenaya Bridge**. Cross Tenaya Creek and follow the partially paved trail 0.9 miles to **Mirror Lake**, where interpretive signs explain the area's natural history. From here you can return to the shuttle stop along the Mirror Lake road (for the sake of looping), or journey up Tenaya Canyon for a little solitude.

It was once possible to continue partway up Tenaya Canyon and loop back on the opposite side of Tenaya Creek. But on March 28, 2009, a 115,000-ton rockfall cascaded almost 2000ft from Ahwiyah Point near Half Dome, shaking the ground with the intensity of a 2.4 magnitude earthquake and burying a large section of the trail. It's still possible to continue on the trail to a footbridge over the creek 1.2 miles further, but the trail is closed to hikers soon after. Past Mirror Lake, there are plenty of quiet spots to picnic along **Tenaya Creek**.

🚶 Inspiration Point

Map p66

Duration 1½–2½ hours

Distance 2.6-mile round-trip

Difficulty Moderate–Difficult

Start/Finish Tunnel View parking lot

Nearest Town Yosemite Village

Transportation Car

Summary Some of the best vistas in all Yosemite are granted to those who hike this steep trail to this classic viewpoint.

Sure, Tunnel View offers an amazing look into the Valley. But the view is even more impressive along the steep trail to Inspiration Point. Best of all, you'll leave the crowds behind.

Inspiration Point used to be a viewpoint along an old road into Yosemite Valley. The roadbed still exists, but this hike (actually the western end of the Pohono Trail) is now the only way to reach the point. You'll start by climbing a series of switchbacks from the upper Tunnel View parking lot (which is on Hwy 41 immediately east of the Wawona Tunnel). Almost immediately the view improves, with fewer trees and no bus tourists to battle for camera positions. Short spur trails lead to open viewpoints.

The climb is steep and steady but, thankfully, fairly short. The view from Inspiration Point itself – a large open area – isn't as spectacular as what you get on the way up, but it's a worthy destination nonetheless, quiet and perfect for a picnic. If you've got the energy, continue up the trail 2.5 miles further to **Stanford Point** and even on to **Crocker Point** (7090ft). Both offer epic views. The Inspiration Point trail is often doable in winter.

🚶 Yosemite Falls

Map above

Duration 5–6 hours

Distance 6.8-mile round-trip

Difficulty Difficult

Start/Finish Yosemite Falls Trailhead near Camp 4

Nearest Town Yosemite Village

Transportation Shuttle stop 7

Summary This classic hike along one of the park's oldest trails leads from the Valley

Yosemite Falls

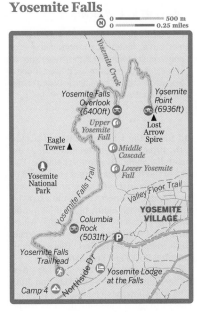

YOSEMITE NATIONAL PARK DAY HIKES

floor to the top of the three-step falls. The stiff ascent (and equivalent descent) make it a real thigh-burning, knee-busting haul.

The heart-stopping views from atop Upper Yosemite Fall will make you quickly forget any pain endured on the hike up. If it seems a bit much, you can always hike just the first mile (and 1000 vertical feet) to **Columbia Rock** (5031ft), a justifiably classic viewpoint.

From the northeastern side of Camp 4, the Yosemite Falls Trail immediately starts in on the four dozen short switchbacks that zigzag up a talus slope through canyon live oaks. After 0.8 miles, the grade eases as the trail follows more switchbacks east to Columbia Rock.

In another 0.4 miles, the trail approaches the top of **Lower Yosemite Fall**, where breezes may shower you with a fine, cooling mist. After admiring the view of Upper Yosemite Fall, brace yourself for the numerous switchbacks that run steadily up a rocky cleft to the Valley rim. The falls once ran down this cleft.

The trail tops out 3.2 miles from the trailhead and bends east. At the junction, the trail going straight leads to **Eagle Peak** (7779ft). Turn right at this junction

WATERFALL WARNING

On a blistering day, the park's waterways are a siren song for sweaty hikers with aching feet. But no matter how inviting, *never* enter rivers or creeks near a waterfall. Pay attention to posted warning signs (they're there because of prior fatalities), and use common sense if there aren't any. All it takes is one slip and within seconds you could be barreling toward a waterfall's precipice. Over a dozen visitors have died at Vernal Fall – please don't increase that statistic.

and follow the trail two-tenths of a mile to the brink of Upper Yosemite Fall at the **Yosemite Falls Overlook** (6400ft). The view of the falls is impressive, but views of El Capitan and Half Dome are obscured. For a wider perspective, go the extra 1.6 miles (and nearly 600ft more in elevation gain) to **Yosemite Point** (6936ft), where you'll get incredible views of Half Dome, North Dome, Clouds Rest, Glacier Point, Cathedral Rocks and Lost Arrow.

Keep in mind that the falls are often dry by midsummer, so late May and June (after the snow has cleared) are the best months to catch the scene in all its frothy glory. When you're done, retrace your steps to the trailhead.

🥾 Four Mile Trail

Map p60

Duration 4–8 hours

Distance 9.2-mile round-trip

Difficulty Difficult

Start/Finish Four Mile Trailhead

Nearest Town Yosemite Village

Transportation Shuttle stop 7; El Capitan Shuttle stop 5

Summary A fulfilling day hike from Yosemite Valley that ascends the Valley's southern wall to Glacier Point, the park's most famous viewpoint. The reward for the grunt is one of the finest vistas in the entire country.

Sure, you can easily get to Glacier Point by car or bus, but there's something supremely rewarding about making the journey on foot. From shuttle stop 7, it's a short walk south along a paved footpath leading across Swinging Bridge to Southside Dr. From here walk parallel to the road a short distance west to the Four Mile Trailhead.

Today the Four Mile Trail actually spans closer to 4.6 miles, having been rerouted since it was first completed in 1872. It was originally intended as a toll pathway, at the time being the quickest way into the Valley.

The trail climbs steadily, passing 2000ft **Sentinel Fall** and **Sentinel Rock** (7038ft). At **Union Point**, 3 miles from the trailhead, you'll first catch a glimpse of Half Dome. Continue climbing until the trail levels out for the final leg to **Glacier Point**. Take in the views and check out that all-important snack bar.

When you're ready, return the way you came. Hardy hikers can turn this into an excellent loop trail (and avoid retracing their steps) by continuing on the Panorama Trail to Nevada Fall, then down to Happy Isles (see p87).

🥾 Vernal & Nevada Falls

Map p101

Duration 4–7 hours

Distance 6.5-mile round-trip

Difficulty Moderate–Difficult

Start/Finish Vernal & Nevada Falls/John Muir Trail trailhead

Nearest Junction Happy Isles

Transportation Shuttle stop 16

Summary Affording views that are unmatched anywhere else in the park, this well-trodden partial loop ascends the so-called Giant Staircase: the route of the Merced River as it plunges over Nevada and Vernal Falls.

If you can only do a single day hike in Yosemite – *and it's springtime* – make this the one. Not only are Vernal and Nevada Falls two of Yosemite's most spectacular waterfalls, but Yosemite Falls and Illilouette Fall both make appearances in the distance from select spots on the trail. If you prefer a shorter excursion, stop at the top of Vernal Fall.

There are two ways to hike this loop: up the **Mist Trail** and down the **John Muir**

Trail (in a clockwise direction) or vice versa. It's easier on the knees to climb rather than descend the plethora of steep granite steps along the Mist Trail, so it's best to go for the clockwise route. Then you can lollygag along the John Muir Trail – which has astounding views of both falls – on the way down. The granite slabs atop Nevada Fall make for a superb lunch spot (as close to the edge as you want), with the granite dome of Liberty Cap (7076ft) towering above.

From the Happy Isles shuttle stop, cross the road bridge over the Merced River, turn right at the trailhead and follow the riverbank upstream. As the trail steepens, watch over your right shoulder for Illilouette Fall (often dry in summer), which peels over a 370ft cliff in the distance. From a lookout, you can gaze west and see Yosemite Falls. After 0.8 miles you arrive at the Vernal Fall footbridge, which offers the first view of 317ft Vernal Fall upstream.

Shortly beyond the Vernal Fall footbridge (just past the water fountain and restrooms), you'll reach the junction of the John Muir and Mist Trails. To do the trail clockwise, hang a left and shortly begin the steep 0.3-mile ascent to the top of Vernal Fall by way of the Mist Trail's granite steps. If it's springtime, prepare to get drenched in spray – wear some waterproof clothing! – and peer behind you as you near the top to see rainbows in the mist.

Above the falls, the Merced whizzes down a long ramp of granite known as the Silver Apron and into the deceptively serene Emerald Pool before plunging over the cliff. No matter how fun the apron looks on a hot day, *don't enter the water:* underwater currents in Emerald Pool have whipped many swimmers over the falls.

From above the apron, it's another 1.3 miles via granite steps and steep switchbacks to the top of the Mist Trail, which meets the John Muir Trail, about 0.2 miles northeast of the falls. From this junction, it's 2.5 miles back to Happy Isles via the Mist Trail or 4 miles via the John Muir Trail.

Shortly after joining the John Muir Trail, you'll cross a footbridge (elevation 5907ft) over the Merced. Beneath it, the river whizzes through a chute before plummeting 594ft over the edge of Nevada Fall. Nevada Fall is the first of the series of steps in the Giant Staircase, a metaphor that becomes clear when viewed from afar at Glacier Point. Plant yourself on a slab of granite for

lunch and views, and be prepared to fend off the ballsy Stellar jays and squirrels that will have your jerky in their jaws in no time, should you let down your guard.

Returning back from Nevada Fall along the John Muir Trail offers a fabulous glimpse of Yosemite Falls. The trail passes the Panorama Trail junction and traverses a cliff, offering awesome views of Nevada Fall as it winds down the canyon. Soon you'll reach Clark Point and a junction that leads down to the Mist Trail. From here it's just over 2 miles downhill, through Douglas firs and canyon live oaks to Happy Isles.

If you choose to do this hike in summertime, be sure to hit the trail early to avoid the crowds and afternoon heat.

Glacier Point & Badger Pass

If you're looking for bird's-eye views of Yosemite Valley, then several Glacier Point Rd hikes will fit the bill perfectly. Dewey Point, Taft Point and the Sentinel Dome hikes all lead to spectacular overlooks of Yosemite Valley. Sentinel Dome hike offers perhaps the widest, finest view of all, and the hike to its summit takes a mere half-hour. Some of the hikes link up with other top-notch trails, such as the Four Mile Trail to Glacier Point and the trail from Wawona Tunnel to Inspiration Point (the westernmost leg of the Pohono Trail). Bask in views as you descend from Glacier Point and ogle some of Yosemite's best waterfalls.

🚶 McGurk Meadow

Map p66

Duration 1 hour

Distance 1.6-mile round-trip

Difficulty Easy

Start/Finish McGurk Meadow Trailhead

Nearest Junction Bridalveil Creek campground

Transportation Car

Summary An effortless and relaxing walk through grassy wildflower meadows, this is a nice choice for families or those who want an easier, less-crowded hike.

For a short stroll with solitude and tranquility, lush, open McGurk Meadow fits the bill. Park at a pullout along Glacier Point Rd just west of the Bridalveil Creek campground entrance; the posted trailhead is about 100yd west of the parking area.

Shaded by lodgepole pines, a level and sun-dappled path meanders through quiet forest. After about a mile, a historic one-room log cabin appears on the left. Kids will love playing in and around this former seasonal shelter for cattle ranchers, and adults will need to double over to enter the low, half-scale doorway.

The meadow sits across a small foot-bridge just beyond the cabin, and its wild-flowers peak in July, erupting in splashes of red, white and yellow. If you wish to continue on, another 3.2 miles takes you to Dewey Point and big, wide views down into the Valley.

Taft Point & The Fissures

Map p66

Duration 1 hour

Distance 2.2-mile round-trip

Difficulty Easy

Start/Finish Sentinel Dome/Taft Point Trailhead

Nearest Junction Glacier Point

Transportation Car

Summary A hike over easy terrain leads to a spectacular overlook and drop-off at the edge of a sheer 3000ft cliff. Sizeable boulders fill a series of enormous granite cracks.

Park in the Sentinel Dome/Taft Point lot on the north side of Glacier Point Rd, about 13 miles from Chinquapin. Note that the main parking area is not that large and often fills up by midmorning; it is less packed in the afternoons.

Taft Point (7503ft) is a fantastic, hair-raising viewpoint at the edge of a sheer 3000ft cliff, with impressive views of El Capitan and Yosemite Valley. On the same promontory are the Fissures, a series of deep, narrow cracks in the granite, many with large boulders wedged inside. Choose your steps carefully, especially when accompanying small children.

After a gentle descent through pleasant forest, you'll emerge on an open, rocky slope dotted with hardy wind-shaped trees. On your right are the Fissures, which drop hundreds of feet along the edge of Profile Cliff. Across Yosemite Valley, you'll see the Three Brothers, with similar yet longer cracks in the rock.

Ahead is Taft Point, guarded only by a short metal railing. Unless you have a profound fear of heights, approach and peer over the edge – the sheer drop is mind-boggling. Look west through binoculars to spot climbers on the southeast face and nose of El Capitan. After soaking up the views, which include a close-up look at Cathedral Spires, return on a gentle uphill climb to the parking lot.

Sentinel Dome

Map p66

Duration 1 hour

Distance 2.2-mile round-trip

Difficulty Easy–Moderate

Start/Finish Sentinel Dome/Taft Point Trailhead

Nearest Junction Glacier Point

Transportation Car

Summary The easiest trail up one of the park's fabled granite domes will reward you with sprawling panoramic vistas of high peaks and falls. Ravaged and surreal trees strain to grow against the wind.

For those unable to visit Half Dome's summit, Sentinel's summit (8122ft) offers an equally outstanding 360-degree perspective of Yosemite's wonders. A visit at sunrise, sunset or during a full moon is spectacular. You can also combine a trip up Sentinel Dome with a walk to Taft Point and the Fissures, an equidistant hike from the same trailhead, or combine the two to form a loop via the solitary Pohono Trail.

Park in the Sentinel Dome/Taft Point lot on the north side of Glacier Point Rd. From the parking lot, take the trail's gently rising right fork. After 20 minutes, it heads north-west across open granite slabs to the dome's base. Skirt the base to an old service road, which leads to the dome's northeast shoulder. From here, head up the gentle granite slope to the top (wear good hiking shoes).

The gnarled, bleached bones of a wind-beaten Jeffrey pine once crowned the top. The photogenic tree died in a drought in the late 1970s, but caused heartbreak to many when it finally fell in 2003.

From the top, the views take in almost the entire park. To the west are Cathedral Rocks and El Capitan, while to the north you'll spot Yosemite Falls and, in the distance, Mt Hoffmann. North Dome, Basket Dome and Mt Watkins line the Valley's northeast side, and Clouds Rest and Half Dome rise dramatically above Tenaya Canyon. In the distance, above Nevada Fall, you'll see the notable peaks of the Cathedral and Ritter Ranges. To the east lie Mt Starr King and the peaks of the Clark Range.

 Panorama Trail

Map p58

Duration 5 hours

Distance 8.5 miles one way

Difficulty Moderate–Difficult

Start Glacier Point

Finish Happy Isles

Nearest Junction Glacier Point

Transportation Glacier Point hikers' bus or car

Summary Picture-postcard views accompany this trail and eye-popping sightlines of Half Dome are a highlight. Visit Nevada Fall as you descend down, down, down to the Valley floor.

Connecting Glacier Point and Nevada Fall, this trail is gorgeous, comprising several miles of Yosemite's most picture-perfect scenery. Hikers seeking a full loop from the Valley must first tackle the steep 3200ft ascent on the Four Mile Trail (see p84). Those starting from Glacier Point and heading down to the Valley must arrange a car shuttle or reserve a seat on the Glacier Point hikers' bus. Or you can simply hike to Nevada Fall and return to Glacier Point the way you came.

At Glacier Point, look for the Panorama Trail signpost near the snack bar. Descend a fire-scarred hillside south toward Illilouette Fall. The route down is largely easy, with magnificent views to your left – including Half Dome, which from here looks like the tip of a giant thumb. If you're lucky, you'll also find blue grouse on the trail, hooting and cooing in gentle, haunting tones. Make sure you bring sunscreen and a hat, as most of the tree cover has burned away.

After about 1.2 miles you'll meet the trail from Mono Meadow. Turn left and take a short series of switchbacks down to Illilouette Creek. The best place to admire 370ft Illilouette Fall is a well-worn viewpoint above the creek on the left.

At the 2-mile mark, a footbridge crosses **Illilouette Creek**, whose shaded banks invite a picnic. The trail leaves the creek and climbs east to **Panorama Point**, then **Panorama Cliff**. This 760ft climb is the only significant elevation gain on the hike. Vantage points high above the Merced River afford amazing views of the Glacier Point apron, Half Dome, Mt Broderick (6706ft), Liberty Cap (7076ft) and Mt Starr King (9092ft).

The trail descends to a junction with the John Muir Trail. Turn right and follow the trail 0.2 miles to the top of **Nevada Fall**, 3.2 miles from Illilouette Creek.

To reach the Valley, descend the Mist Trail via Vernal Fall or take the slightly longer and gentler John Muir Trail. You'll emerge at Happy Isles on the Valley's east end (see the Vernal & Nevada Falls hike, p84).

 Pohono Trail

Map p66

Duration 7–9 hours

Distance 13.8 miles one way

Difficulty Moderate–Difficult

Start Glacier Point

Finish Tunnel View parking lot

Nearest Junction Glacier Point

Transportation Glacier Point hikers' bus or car

Summary A panoramic traverse of the southern Valley rim between Glacier Point and the Wawona Tunnel overlook, this hike descends along a scenic ridge above three waterfalls.

Romantically named Bridalveil Fall was called Pohono by the Ahwahneechee, who thought the fall bewitched. According to Native American legend, an evil spirit who breathed out a fatal wind lived at its base; to sleep near it meant certain death. Some claimed to hear the voices of those who had drowned, warning others to stay away.

As the trailheads are many miles apart, you'll need either two vehicles or to arrange for pickup following your hike. The Glacier Point hikers' bus can take you to Glacier Point from the Valley, but it doesn't stop at the Wawona Tunnel parking area.

It's best to go from east to west, starting at Glacier Point. (The trail descends more than 2800ft, so hiking the opposite direction would involve a strenuous climb.) Though it's generally downhill, the trail does make some noticeable climbs here and there. Highlights include Glacier Point (7214ft), Taft Point, Dewey Point (7385ft), Crocker Point (7090ft), Stanford Point and Inspiration Point. The trail traverses an area high above three waterfalls – Sentinel, Bridalveil and Silver Strand.

Look for the well-marked trailhead near the snack bar at **Glacier Point**. After about a mile, you'll reach the trail junction for **Sentinel Dome**. You can either climb to the top or keep going, skirting just north of the dome along the Valley rim. After about 2 miles, you'll join the trail to **Taft Point**, which leads you across open rock, past the **Fissures** to the point itself. Peer over the railing before resuming your hike.

The trail continues west along the Valley rim, dipping to cross **Bridalveil Creek**. Past the creek, a trail veers left toward McGurk Meadow. Instead, bear right toward **Dewey Point** and another magnificent view (use extreme caution when peering over the edge). Across the Valley, you'll see 1612ft Ribbon Fall – when flowing, the highest single-tier waterfall in North America.

About a half-mile further west is **Crocker Point**, again worth a short detour for the view, which takes in Bridalveil Fall. Another short walk brings you to **Stanford Point**, the last cliff-edge viewpoint on this trail. Once you cross Meadow Brook and Artist Creek, you'll begin the steep, 2.5-mile descent to **Inspiration Point**, an overgrown viewpoint along an old roadbed. The final 1.3-mile leg ends at the Tunnel View parking lot.

Wawona

Mariposa Grove features quite a few lovely hiking trails, and you could easily spend a half-day or more crisscrossing its 250 acres. A trail connects the grove with Wawona, where an easy loop circles Wawona Meadow and a more difficult trail leads to Chilnualna Falls, one of the park's lesser-known waterfalls. From there, long-distance trails head to such remote areas the Buena Vista Crest and the Clark Range.

🚶 Wawona Meadow Loop

Map p70
Duration 1–1½ hours
Distance 3.5-mile round-trip
Difficulty Easy
Start/Finish Wawona Hotel
Nearest Town Wawona Hotel and store
Transportation Car
Summary A relaxed loop on a former stage-coach road, this level hike surveys a pretty meadow, with wildflowers raging in late spring and early summer.

Though you won't huff and puff too much on this gentle, shaded loop around pretty Wawona Meadow, you will have to dodge copious amounts of smelly horse manure plopped and squashed along the entire trail. Horseback riders and stagecoaches use the loop, throwing up lots of dust – another unpleasant element, especially on an already hot summer day.

On the other hand, this short, easy trail is a nice way to spend an hour or two beneath the trees beside the meadow. It's especially lovely when native wildflowers are in bloom. If you're lucky, you might even be alone most of the way – aside from the horses.

From the Wawona Hotel, cross Hwy 41 on a small road through the golf course. The trail starts a short distance down on your left and follows an old dirt road around the meadow perimeter. On the return, you'll cross Hwy 41 again and wind up on the hotel's back lawn. Plunk down in an Adirondack chair and soak up the scene.

🚶 Mariposa Grove to Wawona

Map p70
Duration 2–3 hours
Distance 6.5 miles one way
Difficulty Easy–Moderate
Start Mariposa Grove
Finish Wawona Hotel
Nearest Town Wawona
Transportation Wawona–Mariposa Grove shuttle
Summary Walk through a woodsy and winding downhill trail, sometimes in the company of horses, on this solitary alternative to the shuttle-bus route from Mariposa Grove.

Take the free shuttle bus up to the grove to enjoy this downhill one-way hike. You can actually do several miles' worth of hiking in Mariposa Grove alone, but this trail is a great way to escape the crushing crowds and recover some peace of mind on your way back to Wawona. The trail leaves from the outer loop on the west side of the grove; follow signs from either the museum (if you're in the upper grove) or the parking lot.

🏃 Chilnualna Falls

Map p70

Duration 4–5 hours

Distance 8.6-mile round-trip

Difficulty Moderate–Difficult

Start/Finish Chilnualna Falls Trailhead

Nearest Town Wawona

Transportation Car

Summary Chilnualna Creek tumbles over the north shoulder of forested Wawona Dome in an almost continuous series of cascades. The largest and most impressive of these, Chilnualna Falls, thunders into a deep, narrow chasm.

Unlike its Valley counterparts, this fall is not free-leaping, but its soothing, whitewater rush makes it an attractive day hike without lots of company. Carry lots of water or a filter, as the route can be hot. The top is a nice picnic spot. Like all Yosemite waterfalls, Chilnualna Falls is best between April and June when streams are at their fullest. July and August are often too hot for an afternoon hike, and by September the fall is limited by low water.

The trailhead is at the eastern end of Chilnualna Falls Rd. Follow Hwy 41 (Wawona Rd) a quarter-mile north of the Wawona Hotel and store, and take a right just over the bridge on Chilnualna Falls Rd; follow it for 1.7 miles. The parking area is on the right, and the trailhead is marked.

The trail follows the northwest bank of Chilnualna Creek 0.1 miles to the first series of tumbling cascades, which in spring shower the trail with a cool mist. Ascend several brief sets of granite steps beside the falls. Above, the stock trail joins the footpath along the Yosemite Wilderness boundary, a short but steep 0.2 miles and 600ft above the trailhead.

The trail rises gently yet continually through open, mixed-conifer forest, leveling out as it passes the rushing creek. It then moves away from the creek, taking you on long, sweeping switchbacks. The sheer granite curve of Wawona Dome fills the sky to the east as you rise above forested Wawona Valley. About one to 1½ hours from the trailhead, you'll reach an unobstructed viewpoint from a granite **overlook** (5400ft); it offers the first good view of the fall. To the southwest are the forested Chowchilla Mountains.

The trail climbs several well-graded switchbacks, then a final dynamite-blasted switchback across a granite cliff to the top of Chilnualna Falls (6200ft). While you won't find any better view of the fall, it's worth continuing 15 minutes further to a nice picnic spot along Chilnualna Creek. If you're on an overnight trip, head for the campsites further up both Chilnualna and Deer Creeks.

Retrace your steps 4.3 miles to the trailhead in two hours or so, past a sign that reads '5.6 miles to Wawona' (referring to the Hotel and store, not your trailhead). At a junction 0.2 miles from the trailhead, avoid the tempting, broad horse trail (which comes out at a different trailhead) in favor of the footpath that bears left back down along the creek.

Big Oak Flat Road & Tioga Road

Two of the area's main hikes lead to groves of giant sequoias. Though neither grove is as magnificent as Wawona's Mariposa Grove, the crowds are mercifully thinner.

Day hikes and backcountry excursions are plentiful in Yosemite's subalpine wilderness, which stretches north and south from either side of Tioga Rd. Like Tuolumne Meadows further east, this truly is a hikers' paradise. Several trails from the south side of the road lead to Yosemite Valley, and if you take the hikers' bus up from the Valley, they're more or less downhill all the way – an exquisite and rare treat.

🏃 Tuolumne Grove

Map p71

Duration 1½ hours

Distance 2-mile round-trip

Difficulty Easy–Moderate

Start/Finish Tuolumne Grove Trailhead

Nearest Junction Crane Flat gas station

Transportation Car

Summary Descend into Yosemite's second-most-visited grove of giant sequoias (the walk back up is a bit of a haul). There's even a tree you can walk through.

You can reach this moderately sized grove of sequoias via a short, steep hike down a section of the Old Big Oak Flat Rd (closed to cars). Follow the road and a few switchbacks to the first trees, then meander through the grove and along an interpretive nature trail. The most popular attraction is the **Tunnel Tree** (or 'Dead Giant'), already a stump when a tunnel was cut into it in 1878. Another interesting specimen is the **Leaning Towering Tree**. It fell over in 1983, and now looks like a huge set of cracked vertebrae. At one end, its roots shoot out like flares, and the hollowed-out core makes a fun tunnel for kids to explore.

The only bummer about this hike is the steady uphill climb back to the parking area. When it's hot, you'll be hurting – or panting at the very least. It's not awful though, and hikers of any age should be able to handle it given time and patience.

🏃 Merced Grove

Map p71

Duration 1½–2 hours

Distance 3-mile round-trip

Difficulty Easy–Moderate

Start/Finish Merced Grove Trailhead

Nearest Junction Crane Flat gas station

Transportation Car

Summary This hike leads down to a beautiful sequoia grove, with crowds rarely present to break the solitude. The walk follows a dirt road to a dense cluster of giant trees.

The smallest sequoia grove in the park, Merced is also the quietest, thanks in part to its distance from major park sights. If you seek solitude amid the sequoias, this is for you. You'll start from a small parking lot along Big Oak Flat Rd midway between Crane Flat and the Big Oak Flat gate. The trail follows a dirt road (closed to cars), which remains flat for the first half-mile before dipping downhill into the grove. A handful of the trees surround a small log cabin. Reserve your energy for the hike out.

🏃 Lukens Lake

Map p72

Duration 1 hour

Distance 1.6-mile round-trip

Difficulty Easy

Start/Finish Lukens Lake Trailhead

Nearest Town White Wolf

Transportation Tuolumne Meadows hikers' bus or car

Summary A gentle, quick jaunt to a wildflower meadow and a peaceful lake edged by shaded forest. Even small children can do this walk with ease.

Hike up here early in the morning or late in the afternoon, especially on a weekday, and you just might have the quiet blue lake, green meadow and surrounding sea of colorful wildflowers all to yourself. (Weekends are a different story.) Corn lilies trace the path leading up to the lake, and thousands of orange and black butterflies cluster on the ground in summer. If you hold still and listen, you can hear the low hum of omnipresent bees. Purple and white flowers erupt as you near the lakeshore, forming an exquisitely colored carpet. Revel in the idyllic setting and serenity in the 'golden hour' of early evening light. Even beginners can handle the short jaunt from Tioga Rd.

Start from the marked parking area a couple of miles east of the White Wolf turn-off. Cross the road and begin the trail in the soft woods. Climbing steadily, you'll reach a small ridge, then drop down to Lukens Lake. The trail follows the north shore to the far (west) end, where you'll find plenty of shady spots to rest, picnic or simply sit in quiet contemplation.

An alternative 2.3-mile trail leads to the lake's west side from White Wolf Lodge.

🏃 Tenaya Lake

Map p72

Duration 1 hour

Distance 2-mile round-trip

Difficulty Easy

Start/Finish East Tenaya Lake parking lot

Nearest Town Tuolumne Meadows

Transportation Tuolumne Meadows shuttle stop 9

Summary A back-and-forth stroll along one of Yosemite's prettiest lakes, with no need to head high into the backcountry to reach it. A long sandy beach tempts you into trying the chilly blue water.

A pleasant stroll, this loop trail skirts the south shore of one of the park's biggest natural lakes. Begin from the parking lot on the lake's east end, adjacent to the popular sandy beach. Walk south along the beach, and look for the trail amid the trees just ahead. As the path traces the shore, small spurs lead down to the water. Though the shoreline is rocky, there are several nice spots for a picnic. When you reach the west end (and the Sunrise Trailhead), it's best to either wait for the free shuttle bus back to the parking lot or simply return the way you came.

As part of a large multiyear project, parts of the trail are in the process of being rerouted to avoid sensitive wetland areas, and a boardwalk will be added in one section to minimize damage from thousands of footsteps.

🏃 Harden Lake

Map p72

Duration 2–3 hours

Distance 5.8-mile round-trip

Difficulty Easy–Moderate

Start/Finish White Wolf

Nearest Town White Wolf

Transportation Tuolumne Meadows hikers' bus or car

Summary Tracing sections of the old Tioga Rd, this nicely forested out-and-back route is mostly level. Your reward is a tranquil and pretty lake basin that's good for a swim.

From the White Wolf Lodge parking area, start toward the direction of the White Wolf campground but follow the gravel road to the left of the campground entrance. The road is a section of the old Tioga Rd and closed to public traffic. The roadway passes a mixed forest of lodgepole pine and Jeffrey pine, running parallel to the Middle Fork of the Tuolumne River. A few areas of fire damage are visible just before a discreet sewage-treatment facility appears off to the left. Continue through a stand of tall red firs, and at the 2-mile mark take a right off the road and onto a foot trail. Jittery leaves of quaking aspens flutter in the breeze, and the occasional pinedrops plant can be spotted by its unusual red stalks.

Rejoin the road approximately 0.5 miles from the lake, and after a quarter-mile on the road, follow the junction sign and turn right off the road onto the lake trail. On the path toward the small boulder-littered shore, a meadow erupts with bulbous yellow Bigelow sneezeweed and white sprays of yampa.

Harden Lake is an unusually warm-water lake for these parts, primarily because it evaporates rapidly during the summer. So bring a towel and splash around without feeling like a polar bear. Retrace your steps to the parking lot.

🏃 May Lake & Mt Hoffmann

Map p72

Duration 4–5 hours

Distance 6-mile round-trip

Difficulty Moderate–Difficult

Start/Finish May Lake Trailhead

Nearest Town Tuolumne Meadows

Transportation Tuolumne Meadows hikers' bus or car

Summary May Lake is a relatively easy uphill jaunt to instant backcountry. A new trail to Mt Hoffmann winds up its rocky slope, and the payoff is one of the best viewpoints of the park.

At the park's geographical center, **Mt Hoffmann** (10,850ft) commands outstanding views of Yosemite's entire high country. The broad summit plateau offers a superb perspective, a vista that drew the first California Geological Survey party in 1863. They named the peak after Charles F Hoffmann, the party's topographer and artist. The first peak climbed in Yosemite, Mt Hoffmann remains one of the park's most frequently visited summits.

Alternatively, some hikers go no further than **May Lake** (9350ft), on the High Sierra Camps loop, a pristine mountain lake that cries out for a shoreline picnic. It alone is a satisfying destination, with great views of Half Dome, Cathedral Peak and Mt Clark along the way. The hike takes only about 30 to 40 minutes in each direction, and if you have a wilderness permit you can overnight at the nice backpackers' campground next to the May Lake High Sierra Camp.

Start from the May Lake Trailhead (8846ft), 1.7 miles up a paved section of the old Tioga Rd. The turnoff from Tioga Rd is 2.2 miles west of Olmsted Point and 3.2 miles east of the Porcupine Flat Campground. Be sure to use the bear boxes in the parking lot. (Note that the May Lake stop on the Tuolumne Meadows shuttle is a different trailhead east of Olmsted Point.)

The 1.2-mile stretch to May Lake is fairly easy, although it's a steady 500ft climb. At the lake the trail splits; the right fork leads to May Lake High Sierra Camp, the left traces the lake shore and then ascends to Mt Hoffmann. The Hoffmann trail winds through a talus field, where it's recently been rerouted to one distinct path. Follow a small stream, cross a meadow where the trail turns sharply toward Mt Hoffmann's east summit, and then aim for the higher west summit.

The last bit up involves some basic scrambling. Don't be surprised if some curious marmots pop their heads out of the rocks to check your progress. Be warned: the swarms of marmots living at the summit and in the rocks piles are not shy – they'll come right up to you. If you sit down, keep an eye on your day pack!

Retrace your steps to the May Lake Trailhead.

🚶 Clouds Rest

Map p105

Duration 6–7 hours

Distance 14.4-mile round-trip

Difficulty Difficult

Start/Finish Sunrise Lakes Trailhead

Nearest Town Tuolumne Meadows

Transportation Tuolumne Meadows shuttle stop 10 or car

Summary A fair amount of effort and distance is required for this classic hike, but you'll be amply rewarded with phenomenal 360-degree views from one of the park's best vantage points.

Yosemite's largest granite peak, Clouds Rest (9926ft) rises 4500ft above Tenaya Creek, with spectacular views from the summit and along the trail. More than 1000ft higher than nearby Half Dome, Clouds Rest may well be the park's best panoramic viewpoint. The hike involves a strenuous ascent and equally significant descent (make sure you have a cold drink waiting for you!), but getting here is definitely worth the effort. This hike forms part of the Tenaya Lake to Yosemite Valley hike.

Start from the Sunrise Lakes Trailhead at the west end of Tenaya Lake. Trailhead parking is limited, and the lot fills early. If you're staying in Tuolumne Meadows, it's easier to take the free shuttle bus to the trailhead.

Follow the trail along **Tenaya Creek** for your first glimpse of Clouds Rest and Tenaya Canyon's shining granite walls. As the trail climbs steadily up well-constructed switchbacks, the view expands to include prominent Mt Hoffmann (10,850ft) to the northwest and Tuolumne Peak (10,845ft) to the north. After a steady 30-minute ascent, the grade eases atop soft earth amid large red firs. Continue straight past the Sunrise Lakes junction and descend southwest. As Yosemite Valley and Sentinel Dome come into view, the trail reaches the level floor west of Sunrise Mountain (9974ft). Paintbrushes, lupines and wandering daisies bloom here, alongside mats of pink heather and bushes of poisonous white-flowered Labrador tea. Fifteen minutes past a shallow pond you'll reach a creek that's the last water source en route to the summit – so fill up here (and filter it).

At approximately 5 miles you'll reach the Forsyth Trail junction, although it's not labeled as such on the sign. Bear southwest and ascend the ridgeline that culminates in **Clouds Rest**. To the southeast are fabulous views of wedge-shaped Mt Clark (11,522ft), the Cascade Cliffs and Bunnell Point in Merced Canyon. The granite swell of Mt Starr King (9092ft) rises to the southwest. The trail soon passes over a low rise and through a slight but obvious saddle. At a large white pine 20 minutes beyond the saddle, a small unmarked trail forks left; this is recommended for those not willing or able to hike the more exposed summit path.

A sign reading 'Clouds Rest Foot Trail' directs you along the granite ridge, which narrows rather thrillingly in one place. Never less than 5ft wide, the narrowest section might look intimidating but takes only five to 10 seconds to cross. The summit itself offers breathtaking views of Half Dome and the Valley. The view stretches from the Sawtooth Ridge and Matterhorn Peak along the park's north border to Mt Ritter and Banner Peak, standing dark and prominent to the southeast. Mts Conness and Dana on the Sierra Crest and the closer Cathedral Range are all outstanding. This is one of the Sierra Nevada's most inspiring viewpoints – savor the sights before retracing your steps to the trailhead.

You can extend your hike by continuing down to Yosemite Valley (see the Tenaya Lake to Yosemite Valley hike, p104).

🚶 North Dome

Map p72

Duration 4½–5 hours

Distance 8.5-mile round-trip

Difficulty Moderate

Start/Finish Porcupine Creek Trailhead

Nearest Town White Wolf

Transportation Tuolumne Meadows hikers' bus or car

Summary Perhaps the best vantage point along the Valley rim, this trail sees relatively few hikers. It's a downhill trek outbound, so you'll be doing the ascent on the return.

The trail descends 1000ft and rises 422ft on the way there, so be ready for a climb on the return trip. A side trip to the natural arch on Indian Ridge adds another 240ft climb.

From Tioga Rd, start at the Porcupine Creek Trailhead (8120ft), 1.3 miles east of Porcupine Flat Campground. To reach the trailhead from the campground, walk to the southern side of the highway from the camp entrance and follow the footpath that parallels the road.

An abandoned road leads beneath red firs until the pavement ends and the trail crosses Porcupine Creek via a log. After an easy 30-minute ascent into the forest, you'll reach a sign for the Snow Creek Trail to the Valley. Continue straight another 50ft to a second trail junction and take the left fork toward North Dome.

The trail climbs gently up Indian Ridge for 10 minutes to an inviting view across the Valley to Sentinel Dome and Taft Point. The trail soon turns sharply and ascends steadily for another 10 minutes, leading to the marked Indian Rock trail junction.

A worthwhile but optional 30-minute side trip leads to **Indian Rock** (8360ft), Yosemite's only visible natural arch. Follow the short, steep spur trail to the arch. From the trail you can see the arch from all sorts of angles, and the arch affords good views of Clouds Rest, the Clark Range, Mt Starr King and Sentinel Dome. Clamber onto the rock for a view of Half Dome framed by the arch.

At the Indian Rock trail junction, the main trail continues south, leading to a spectacular viewpoint at the end of the ridge: front and center is Half Dome, and across the Valley is hard-to-see Illilouette Fall. North Dome lies directly below to the south, and Basket Dome's rounded peak (7612ft) lies to the southeast. This is a fantastic spot to camp; if you do decide to spend the night here (or on North Dome), you'll need to bring water, as none is available nearby.

The trail drops south off the ridgeline in the direction of Half Dome and descends on switchbacks across open granite. Cairns lead to the marked North Dome Trail junction. Turn east for the final half-mile stretch. The rough trail descends steeply before a short final ascent to the **summit**. West are the Sentinels, Cathedrals, El Capitan, the Three Brothers and Yosemite Point (Yosemite Falls lie hidden). To the northeast are Basket Dome, Mt Watkins and the distant peaks of the Cathedral Range. Horse Ridge rims the horizon to the south, while dominating the scene is the sheer north face of Half Dome – surely one of Yosemite's most impressive sights. Clouds Rest rises on the far side of granite-walled Tenaya Canyon.

It will take about two hours to retrace your steps along Indian Ridge and return to the trailhead.

You can extend the hike by descending to the Valley on either the Snow Creek Trail (which heads down to Tenaya Canyon and Mirror Lake) or on the trail west to Yosemite Point and Yosemite Falls Overlook. From the latter, take the Yosemite Falls Trail down to Camp 4.

Use the hikers' bus from the Valley to reach the North Dome Trailhead in the morning. You can also start hiking from the Valley and visit North Dome on a very demanding round-trip of eight to 10 hours. For an especially vigorous day hike, traverse the Valley's north rim via North Dome by ascending the Snow Creek Trail's 100-plus switchbacks and returning via the Yosemite Falls Trail.

Tuolumne Meadows

The many day hikes out of Tuolumne Meadows are some of the finest in all of Yosemite, especially in July, when colorful wildflowers – poking up wherever they can – bring the high country to life. If you don't need to return to the Valley the same day using public transportation, all of these hikes are reachable via the Tuolumne Meadows hikers' bus or the YARTS Hwy 120 bus.

🚶 Lembert Dome

Map p76

Duration 2–3 hours

Distance 2.4-mile round-trip

Difficulty Moderate

Start/Finish Dog Lake parking lot

Nearest Town Tuolumne Meadows

Transportation Tuolumne Meadows shuttle stop 2

Summary The short hike (and scramble) to the top of Tuolumne's most iconic dome offers fun on granite and fantastic views in all directions, especially at sunset.

Lembert Dome (9450ft) rises from the meadows' east end, opposite the campground. Scrambling around the base of the dome's steep southwest face is a favorite Tuolumne pastime, but the real pleasure is hiking up the backside and standing atop the summit, where the views are staggering. Mt Dana, the Cathedral Range, Tuolumne Meadows, Pothole Dome, Fairview Dome and the Lyell Fork Tuolumne are all visible from the top. To the east, the Sierra Crest stretches from Mt Conness to the Kuna Crest. It's magical just before sunset.

This hike is doable for most walkers, but reaching the summit requires scrambling up the granite at the end – not recommended for the slippery-footed or faint at heart. Once you're on top, however, you can picnic upon a ledge or walk the ridge, scramble down some rock and cross a tree-filled saddle to the section of Lembert Dome that's so prominent from the road below.

Two similarly named trails lead to Lembert Dome. The one from the Lembert Dome parking lot, at the very base of the dome, is a steep, borderline unpleasant trail that's been damaged by storms. To reach the preferred Dog Lake Trail by car, drive east from the Tuolumne Meadows campground and turn right onto the road leading to Tuolumne Meadows Lodge. Park in the Dog Lake parking lot, about a half-mile up this road. From the north side of the lot, follow the signed Dog Lake/Young Lakes trail up and across Tioga Rd.

This trail, almost entirely shaded in pine forest, is the quickest way up the backside of the dome. From the top of the trail, you can scramble up the granite to the dome's summit.

🚶 Dog Lake

Map p76

Duration 2 hours

Distance 2.8-mile round-trip

Difficulty Easy–Moderate

Start/Finish Dog Lake or Lembert Dome parking lots

Nearest Town Tuolumne Meadows

Transportation Tuolumne Meadows hikers' bus; Tuolumne Meadows shuttle stop 2

Summary This short hike skirts the base of Lembert Dome and climbs gently through lodgepole pine forest to scenic Dog Lake, a great spot for an afternoon picnic and, if you can take it, a chilly dip.

Pine tree–ringed Dog Lake (9170ft) is accessible via the same trails that head to Lembert Dome. The better one leaves from the appropriately named Dog Lake parking lot, near Tuolumne Meadows Lodge. Follow this trail to the base of Lembert Dome. When you reach the turnoff for the summit, continue straight. A half-mile or so up the fairly flat trail is another junction; turn right toward Dog Lake (left is a steep downhill to the Lembert Dome parking lot). It's about another half-mile to the lake. Although most topo maps don't show it, a trail circles the lake, allowing you to hike around it before heading home.

Be prepared to share this subalpine gem with fellow hikers – on weekends it may resemble your local reservoir, as people lug abundant picnic supplies and even inflatable rafts up to the lake's forested shores.

🚶 Elizabeth Lake

Map p76

Duration 2½–4 hours

Distance 5.2-mile round-trip

Difficulty Moderate

Start/Finish Elizabeth Lake Trailhead, Tuolumne Meadows Campground

Nearest Town Tuolumne Meadows

Transportation Tuolumne Meadows hikers' bus; Tuolumne Meadows shuttle stop 5

Summary At the foot of jagged Unicorn Peak, this easily reached alpine lake offers spectacular views and plenty of opportunity for exploration beyond the lake itself.

Any time is a good time for a hike to this beautiful lake, but it's a particularly good choice if you've just rolled into the Tuolumne Meadows area and need a short acclimatization hike before sunset. Because it's fairly short, the trail gets busy, but heading up in the late afternoon means you'll encounter fewer people. That said, you could easily stretch a day out of this hike by exploring the saddles and ridges around the lake or, if you're experienced, by attempting the summit of **Unicorn Peak** (10,823ft), a class 3-4 climb.

The trailhead lies in the upper 'B' section of Tuolumne Meadows Campground. When you pull in, ask the ranger on duty for a campground map, or follow the sign to Elizabeth Lake. Once you're on the trail, the climbing kicks in immediately, and most of the elevation gain is out of the way within the first mile or so. Most of this section is shaded by lodgepole pines. The first real treat is the trail's encounter with **Unicorn Creek**, which drains into **Elizabeth Lake**. After that, the trail widens and levels off, and finally meets a fork at the northeast end of the lake. Turn right, and you'll hit the water. Otherwise, you'll follow Unicorn Creek into a meadow (a reward in itself), where several side trails also lead to the lakeshore. Climbing the slopes on the south side of the lake affords views of Lembert Dome and, far beyond, 12,649ft Mt Conness. To return to the trailhead, retrace your steps.

If you choose to come earlier in the day, Elizabeth Lake makes a nice spot for a picnic lunch.

🏃 Cathedral Lakes

Map p96

Duration 4-7 hours

Distance 8-mile round-trip (upper lake)

Difficulty Moderate

Start/Finish Cathedral Lakes Trailhead

Nearest Town Tuolumne Meadows

Transportation Tuolumne Meadows hikers' bus; Tuolumne Meadows shuttle stop 7

Summary Easily one of Yosemite's most spectacular hikes, this steady climb through mixed conifer forest ends with glorious views of Cathedral Peak from the shores of two shimmering alpine lakes.

If you can only manage one hike in Tuolumne, this should probably be it. **Cathedral Lake** (9588ft), the lower of the two lakes, sits within a mind-blowing glacial cirque, a perfect amphitheater of granite capped by the iconic spire of nearby **Cathedral Peak** (10,911ft). From the lake's southwest side, granite drops steeply away, affording views as far as Tenaya Lake, whose blue waters shimmer in the distance. Although it's only about two hours to this lower lake, you could easily spend an entire day exploring the granite slopes, meadows and peaks surrounding it. Continuing to the **upper lake** (9585ft) adds less than an hour to the hike and puts the round-trip walk at 8 miles, including the stop at Cathedral Lake. Admittedly, the upper lake is less spectacular when measured against the lower lake, but by all other standards it's utterly sublime.

Parking for the Cathedral Lake Trailhead is along the shoulder of Tioga Rd, 0.5 miles west of Tuolumne Visitor Center. Due to the popularity of this hike, parking spaces fill up fast, so arrive early or take the free shuttle. Camping is allowed at the lower lake (despite what some maps show), but be absolutely certain you're 100ft from the water *and* the trail, and that you choose an already impacted site to prevent further damage. Better yet, camp somewhere near the upper lake or off the pass.

From the Cathedral Lake Trailhead on Tioga Rd, the hike heads southwest along the John Muir Trail. Almost immediately, it begins to climb through forest of lodgepole pine, mountain hemlock and the occasional whitebark pine. After ascending over 400ft, the trail levels out and a massive slab of granite – the northern flank of Cathedral Peak – slopes up from the left side of the trail. Soon you'll see Fairview Dome (9731ft) through the trees to your right.

Before long, the trail begins its second ascent, climbing nearly 600ft before leveling off and affording outstanding views of Cathedral Peak. Three miles from the trailhead, you'll hit the junction that leads 0.5 miles southwest to Cathedral Lake. This trail crosses a stunning **meadow** (turn around as you cross it for the head-on view of Cathedral Peak) before arriving at the granite shores of the lake. Be sure to follow the trail around the lake and take in the views from the southwest side.

To visit the upper lake, backtrack to the main trail, turn right (southeast) and, after

Cathedral Lakes

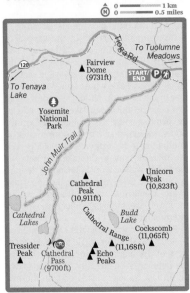

about 0.5 miles, you'll hit the lake. If you wish to stretch the hike out even further, you can continue past the upper lake to **Cathedral Pass** (9700ft), where you'll be rewarded with a stellar side-view of Cathedral Peak and Eichorn Pinnacle (Cathedral's fin-like west peak). This side trip adds about 0.6 miles to the trip.

🏃 Glen Aulin

Map p108

Duration 6–8 hours

Distance 11-mile round-trip

Difficulty Moderate

Start/Finish Glen Aulin Trailhead near Lembert Dome parking lot

Nearest Town Tuolumne Meadows

Transportation Tuolumne Meadows shuttle stop 4

Summary The first leg of the multiday hike through the Grand Canyon of the Tuolumne makes for a great day hike, offering stunning views of the Cathedral Range before reaching Glen Aulin High Sierra Camp.

Except for the dip in the final stretch, most of the elevation change along this hike is

gradual. It's an uphill return, so save energy for the climb home. The hike follows a section of the Pacific Crest Trail (PCT), the same stretch that horse packers use to supply the High Sierra Camp. It's a beautiful walk, but it's well worn and there's plenty of aromatic horse dung along the way.

The trailhead lies behind the Lembert Dome parking lot, which is immediately east of the Tuolumne Meadows campground and bridge. Follow the dirt road northwest toward the stables. When you reach the gate, swing west (left) toward Soda Springs, watching for the Glen Aulin Trail signs to the right of Parsons Lodge.

The trail leads through open lodgepole pine forest, crosses shallow **Delaney Creek**, then continues to a signed junction with the Young Lakes Trail, 1.3 miles from Soda Springs. Take the left fork, heading northwest through lodgepole pines. You'll emerge on riverside meadows with outstanding views of Fairview Dome (9731ft), Cathedral Peak (10,911ft) and Unicorn Peak (10,823ft).

Thirty minutes on, the level, cairn-dotted trail crosses a vast, glacially polished granite slab over which the **Tuolumne River** flows. The river's roar signals the end of Tuolumne Meadows and the start of a series of cascades that tumble toward the Grand Canyon of the Tuolumne.

The trail climbs briefly over a granite rib, affording distant views of Matterhorn Peak (12,264ft) and Virginia Peak (12,001ft) on Yosemite's north border and a first view of the huge, orange-tinged granite cliff above Glen Aulin. Descend through forest to a two-part wooden footbridge spanning the river, 2.3 miles from the Young Lakes Trail junction.

The trail descends steadily, alternating between forest and riverside before reaching **Tuolumne Falls**. Continue along the plunging river to a signed junction with the May Lake Trail and then a steel girder footbridge spanning the river. Cross it and you'll reach two trail junctions in close succession. To the right is the Glen Aulin High Sierra Camp. At the second junction, the PCT continues north (straight) to a backpackers' campground and on to Cold and Virginia Canyons.

You can hang out here, or turn west (toward Waterwheel Falls) and continue a short distance into Glen Aulin itself – a long, level forested valley where the river flows green and tranquil beneath a massive water-stained granite wall.

To extend this into an overnight excursion, see the Waterwheel Falls hike (p111).

🚶 Gaylor Lakes

Map p106

Duration 2–3 hours

Distance 3-mile round-trip

Difficulty Moderate

Start/Finish Gaylor Lakes Trailhead and parking lot

Nearest Town Tuolumne Meadows

Transportation Tuolumne Meadows–Tioga Pass shuttle

Summary This spectacular and popular trail climbs gently up to Gaylor Lakes, set in pristine alpine territory just inside the park boundary near Tioga Pass.

The hike to Gaylor Lakes is a high-altitude hike, so prior acclimatization (such as a day in Tuolumne) is a good idea. There can be snow any time of the year. Sound good? It is.

The trail begins from the parking lot, immediately west of Tioga Pass Entrance, and wastes no time in starting its steep ascent. At the crest, **Lower Gaylor Lake** (10,334ft) lies in a basin below you, with great views everywhere you turn. The trail skirts the lower lake and then climbs to **Upper Gaylor Lake** (10,510ft).

For an extra bonus, head past the lake and climb again to the site of the old **Great Sierra Mine**, where the views are even wider and more stunning. All told, the alpine countryside here is knockout beautiful, so budget some time for poking around.

🚶 Mono Pass

Map p106

Duration 4 hours

Distance 7.4-mile round-trip

Difficulty Moderate–Difficult

Start/Finish Mono Pass Trailhead

Nearest Town Tuolumne Meadows

Transportation Tuolumne Meadows–Tioga Pass shuttle

Summary This outrageously scenic, high-altitude hike from Dana Meadows starts at 9689ft and follows an ancient Native American trail past meadows and through open forest to the vast, lake-crowned Mono Pass.

A saddle on the Sierra Crest between the rounded summits of Mts Gibbs (12,764ft)

and Lewis (12,296ft), Mono Pass was the highest point on an ancient Native American trade route that linked the Mono Lake area with Tuolumne and continued to Yosemite Valley via Cathedral Pass. Remnants of late-19th-century log buildings – relics of the mining years – remain along the trail among subalpine meadows and lakes. It's a fantastic walk through some of the highest of Tuolumne's readily accessible high country.

The Mono Pass Trailhead and parking lot is at road marker T37, 1.4 miles south of Tioga Pass. The trail leads southeast through open forest within the shadow of 13,057ft Mt Dana to the northeast. After an easy half-mile hike alongside **Dana Meadows**, the trail crosses the Dana Fork of the Tuolumne River, then crosses two small ridges before passing beneath lodgepole pines beside several small, buttercup-filled meadows. Emerging from the pines, the trail makes a gentle ascent along **Parker Pass Creek**, with the reddish bulk of Mt Gibbs above and to the east.

When you reach the signed Spillway Lake trail junction, follow the left fork toward Mono and Parker Passes. The trail passes the remains of a log cabin and opens onto a large meadow beside a small creek, with impressive views of Kuna Crest and Mammoth Peak (12,117ft). Thirty minutes (1.4 miles) past the Spillway Lake junction, a small trail branches right toward Parker Pass. Keep going straight, however, past twisted white-bark pines and two small lakes to **Mono Pass** (10,604ft).

Tiny Summit Lake lies to the west, while east of the pass are Upper and Lower Sardine Lakes. Further down, Walker Lake lies in an area known as Bloody Canyon. Tree frogs chirp from the banks of Summit Lake in early summer. Flourishing in meadows along its north side are scrub willows, Sierra onions and yellow potentillas. At the south end of the pass sit three historic log cabins.

Retrace your steps to the trailhead. To make this an overnight trip, camp at Upper Sardine Lake east of Mono Pass, just outside the park in the Ansel Adams Wilderness.

🚶 Mt Dana

Map p106

Duration 6–7 hours

Distance 5.8-mile round-trip

Difficulty Difficult

Start/Finish Unmarked trailhead immediately east of Tioga Pass Entrance

Nearest Town Tuolumne Meadows

Transportation Tuolumne Meadows–Tioga Pass shuttle or car

Summary Starting at 9945ft, this strenuous hike is a leg-working, lung-busting climb to the top of Yosemite's second-highest peak, which, at 13,057ft, offers stunning views in every direction.

Mt Dana, which takes its name from American geologist James Dwight Dana, offers unrivaled views of Mono Lake, the Grand Canyon of the Tuolumne and the rest of the Yosemite high country from its summit. Remember, though, that this is a steep, high-altitude hike which *starts* at nearly 10,000ft. Prior acclimatization will ease your struggle.

The hiking season runs from July to mid-September, though snow may block the trail in early summer. Don't even start the hike if a storm threatens.

Parking for the trailhead is available on either side of the Tioga Pass Entrance. From Tioga Pass the trail heads east, passing between two broad, shallow pools before the ascent begins. The trail passes through flower-filled meadows on the 1700ft climb to a west-descending ridge, marked by a large, loose cairn, 1.8 miles from Tioga Pass.

From this cairn, several indistinct paths head up the rocky west slope to the summit. Shun the leftmost path through difficult talus in favor of paths to the right, which offer easier footing. The views from the summit of Mt Dana are outstanding enough to invite lingering, but no camping is permitted. From the summit, retrace your steps downhill to the trailhead.

Hetch Hetchy

Hetch Hetchy offers some outstanding hiking, but day hikers are essentially limited to the Wapama Falls Trail, which traces the reservoir's scenic north shore, a fairly easy hike for just about anyone.

🚶 Tueeulala & Wapama Falls

Map p78

Duration 2½–3 hours

Distance 5.4-mile round-trip

Difficulty Easy–Moderate

Start/Finish Rancheria Falls Trailhead, O'Shaughnessy Dam

Nearest Junction Evergreen Lodge

Transportation Car

Summary This hike along the north shore of Hetch Hetchy Reservoir leads to the base of two neighboring falls: the free-leaping, seasonal Tueeulala Falls and the enormous triple cascades of year-round Wapama Falls.

Few – if any – trails in Yosemite bring you as close to the shower and roar of a giant waterfall as this one does to Wapama Falls. In springtime, after a good snowmelt, the falls can rage so mightily that the National Park Service (NPS) occasionally has to close the trail itself as water rolls over the bridges. On your way, you'll pass the wispy Tueeulala Falls (*twee*-la-la), which spring spectacularly from the cliffs from more than 1000ft above the trail. All the while, Hetch Hetchy Dome (6197ft), on the north shore, and the mighty Kolana Rock (5772ft), on the south shore, loom over the entire scene. You can capture both falls and adjacent Hetch Hetchy Dome in a single striking photo. Kolana Rock's vertical north face provides nesting sites for peregrine falcons, once close to extinction but now present in healthier numbers.

The gentle north shore trail is fairly flat, but does have a few ups and downs that will challenge unfit hikers in the summer heat. Plan the hike for mid- to late spring, when temperatures are cooler, butterflies are abundant, wildflowers are in bloom and the falls are full.

From the parking lot (3813ft), cross O'Shaughnessy Dam and pass through the tunnel on its far side. The broad, oak-shaded trail then heads northeast, above and parallel to the north shore of Hetch Hetchy Reservoir. In just over a mile, after rising gradually past several small seasonal streams, you'll reach a signed trail junction (4050ft).

Take the right (east) fork, following the sign reading '1.6 miles to Wapama Falls.' The trail descends gently, then bears left onto broad granite slabs before reaching Tueeulala Falls. Most of the falls end up flowing beneath the footbridge, but in spring a small section of the trail can fill with runoff. By June, the falls are usually dry.

The trail continues 10 minutes down a staircase that switchbacks gently to the base of thundering **Wapama Falls** (3900ft), where wooden footbridges span Falls Creek. In spring, water cascades over the trail beyond the first footbridge and almost covers the second. When the water is high, crossing is dangerous (two hikers were swept to their deaths in 2011), but at other times the flow is ankle-deep. The frothy, gushing torrents create billowing clouds of mist that drench the entire area and make for a cool bath on a warm afternoon.

Return to the trailhead via the same route.

🏃 Carlon Falls

Off Map p78

Duration 2 hours

Distance 2.4-mile round-trip

Difficulty Easy–Moderate

Start/Finish Carlon Day Use area

Nearest Junction Evergreen Lodge

Transportation Car

Summary This short but sweet hike follows the South Fork Tuolumne River up to Carlon Falls, which cascade down granite slabs into perfect swimming holes.

Most people blow right by Carlon Falls on their way to Hetch Hetchy, but a quick stop for this short venture is well worthwhile. The hike is especially satisfying on a hot day, when the swimming holes beneath the falls are paradisiacal. Folks who stay at Evergreen Lodge and Camp Mather frequent the falls, so arrive early to have the place to yourself. The only thing making this hike 'moderate' is a section of washed-out trail that requires surefootedness.

To get to the trailhead, drive northwest on Evergreen Rd, which departs Hwy 120 about 1 mile before the Big Oak Flat Entrance. About 1 mile after turning off, you'll see the

Carlon Day Use Area at a bridge across the river. Park in the pullout on the far (north) side of the bridge and hike upstream from there. Although the trailhead is outside the Yosemite park boundary, you enter the park after about 0.1 miles.

Shaded by ponderosa pines, incense-cedars and the occasional dogwood, the trail winds along the north bank of the river, through patches of fragrant kitkitdizze (an exceptionally pungent shrub also known as Sierran Mountain Misery) and finally arrives at **Carlon Falls**. Better described as a cascade, the falls tumble nearly 40ft across moss- and fern-draped granite into two separate **swimming holes**. There's plenty of granite around for sunning, so be sure to bring lunch.

OVERNIGHT HIKES

Backcountry hiking and sleeping beneath the stars is one of Yosemite's finest adventures. The vast majority of the almost four million people who visit Yosemite every year never leave the Valley floor, meaning the park's 1101 sq miles of wilderness is, for the most part, empty. There are a few painless bureaucratic hurdles to jump before heading out, however, but a little planning will make your trek a triumph.

For information on wilderness centers, see p132. For information on the John Muir and Pacific Crest Trails, see p34. See the hiking chart on p32 for a list of all hikes.

Wilderness Permits

Wilderness permits are required for all overnight backcountry trips (not for day hikes). To stem overuse of the backcountry, a quota system is in effect for each trailhead. You must spend your first night in the area noted on your permit – from there, you're free to roam.

BACKPACKERS' CAMPGROUNDS

If you're like most backpackers heading into the Yosemite wilderness, you probably didn't reserve a campsite for the night before (or night after) your backcountry trip. Worry not. To accommodate backpackers heading into or out of the wilderness, the park offers walk-in backpackers' campgrounds in Yosemite Valley (Map p60), Tuolumne Meadows (Map p76), White Wolf (Map p72) and Hetch Hetchy (Map p78). If you hold a valid wilderness permit, you may spend the night before and the night after your trip in one of these campgrounds. The cost is $5 per person per night, and reservations are unnecessary.

Long-distance cyclists may also use these campgrounds for one-night stays.

Permits are available either in advance (between 24 weeks and two days ahead) or on a first-come, first-served basis from the nearest wilderness center. The park reserves 40% of its wilderness permits for walk-ups; these become available at 11am one day before the hike-in date. If you show up early the day before your hike, you should have no problem getting a permit. For popular hikes (such as Little Yosemite Valley, Cathedral Lakes or the High Sierra Camp routes), you should show up and get in line before the permit offices open the day before you hike. Always have a backup plan, as some spots fill very quickly. Hikers who turn up at the wilderness center nearest the trailhead get priority over someone at another wilderness center. For example, if there is one permit left for Lyell Canyon, the Yosemite Valley Wilderness Center will call the Tuolumne Meadows Wilderness Center to make sure that no one breezing in to the Tuolumne office wants it before giving it to someone who has been waiting overnight in the Valley.

Reserving a **permit** (☎209-372-0740; fax 209-372-0739; www.nps.gov/yose/planyourvisit/wpres.htm; advance reservation fee $5, plus $5 per person; ☺8:30am-4:30pm Mon-Fri late Nov–Oct) is the best way to ensure you get one, and you can do so by fax, phone or through the mail. Faxes received between 5pm (the previous day) and 7:30am (the first morning you can reserve) get first priority. Reservations are not available from October to April, but you'll still need to get a permit.

In winter, wilderness permits are available at the Yosemite Valley Visitor Center, the Hetch Hetchy Entrance Station and the seasonal ranger station at the Badger Pass A-frame building. Self-registration permits are available 24 hours a day outside the Wawona and Big Oak Flat Information Stations and the Tuolumne Meadows Ranger Station. See www.nps.gov/yose/planyourvisit/permitstations.htm for more information.

Study your maps, read your guidebooks and decide where you want to go before registering for a permit. Rangers can offer guidance about starting points and trail conditions, but they will not recommend one area over another because they don't know hikers' skills. See the National Park Service (NPS) website for **updated trail conditions** (www.nps.gov/yose/planyourvisit/wildcond.htm) or contact the wilderness centers.

ⓘ ALTERNATIVE HALF DOME ROUTES

As an alternative to the hugely popular route from Happy Isles, consider approaching Half Dome from other points in the park. Beginning from higher elevation also saves you the initial climb. Just about anywhere works, depending on how long you want to spend on the trail (overnighting requires a wilderness permit, and you get a Half Dome permit automatically). Good starting points include Tenaya Lake and Glacier Point, the latter leading you along the gorgeous Panorama Trail.

Wilderness Regulations

For the sake of the bears more than your food, approved bear-resistant food canisters are required for all overnight hikes in the park. When you pick up your wilderness permit, you'll have to rent a bear canister or show that you have one. They're also sold at stores throughout the park. These canisters weigh just under 3lb each and, when carefully packed, can store three to five days' worth of food for one or two people. As with the lockers, keep the canisters closed when cooking.

Campfires are forbidden above 9600ft. Where available, use pre-existing campsites to reduce your impact, and camp at least 100ft from water sources and trails. Never put soap in the water, even 'biodegradable' types. Properly filter all drinking water or boil it for three to five minutes, and don't burn trash. Pack out everything you bring, including toilet paper.

Wilderness camping is prohibited within four trail-miles of Yosemite Valley, Tuolumne Meadows, Glacier Point, Hetch Hetchy and Wawona, and you must be at least one 'air mile' from any road. No one is actually going to bust out the measuring tape – the idea is to keep people from simply wandering into the trees and camping when they can't find open campsites in the park.

Yosemite Valley

Most hikes within and around Yosemite Valley proper are day hikes. Most overnight hikes from the Valley will take you out of its confines entirely. The hike to the top of Half Dome, Yosemite's most famous trek, is one major exception.

🚶 Half Dome

Map below

Duration 10–12 hours

Distance 17-mile round-trip

Difficulty Difficult

Start/Finish Vernal & Nevada Falls/John Muir Trailhead near Happy Isles

Nearest Junction Happy Isles

Transportation Shuttle stop 16

Summary Ideally done over two days, but doable as a grueling day hike, the demanding trek to the top of Yosemite's signature peak offers views (and crowds and sore muscles) like you wouldn't believe.

For many visitors, this is the ultimate Yosemite hike, an achievement to boast about to the grandkids some day. The stand-alone summit of this glacier-carved chunk of granite offers awesome 360-degree views, and peering down its sheer 2000ft north face offers a thrill you'll remember the rest of your life. But, unless you get a crack-of-dawn start, you'll have people aplenty to deal with. Most importantly, advance permits are now required for day hikers, making a Half Dome summit even harder to arrange; see Mandatory Half Dome Permits, p63).

Ideally, Half Dome is best tackled in two days, allowing you more time to rest up and enjoy the gorgeous surroundings. But since it's so popular, you'll have a hard time getting a wilderness permit to sleep overnight at the limited legal camping areas on the route (the most popular being Little Yosemite Valley). If you do attempt this hike in a single day (and many people do), and have a coveted permit, be ready for some serious exertion. Get an early start (like 6am – though the shuttle doesn't start until 7am), pack lots of water and bring a flashlight, because you may wind up hiking home in the dark.

Climbing gear is unnecessary. Instead, hikers haul themselves up the final 650ft to the summit between two steel cables. Climbing this stretch is only allowed when the **cable route** is open, usually late May to mid-October, depending on snow conditions. If planning an early-season or late-season trip, confirm ahead that the cables are in place.

Start at Happy Isles and ascend to the top of **Nevada Fall** on either the John Muir or Mist Trails (see p84). Continue over a low rise to level **Little Yosemite Valley**, which boasts views of Half Dome's south side. You'll also find solar composting toilets, bear boxes and a seasonal ranger station, all

Half Dome and Vernal & Nevada Falls

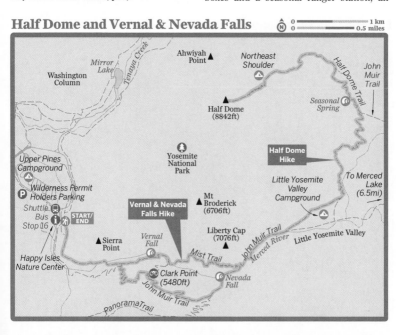

welcome features at the well-used campground, which is one of the park's most heavily visited areas.

From the west end of Little Yosemite Valley, the Merced Lake Trail heads east along the river to the Merced Lake High Sierra Camp. Stay on the John Muir Trail, which turns north and climbs steeply from forest 1.3 miles to the Half Dome Trail junction, just 2 miles from the summit.

Take the left fork onto the Half Dome Trail. Ten minutes above the junction on the left is a hard-to-spot seasonal spring – the last source of water en route (filter or treat it). Continue for 30 minutes, first through forest and then up switchbacks to the northeast shoulder (7600ft), an alternative camping spot with spectacular views. Visit the summit at sunset and sunrise for exquisite solitude.

From here, a rocky 20- to 30-minute trail snakes 650ft up two dozen switchbacks to a notch at the base of the cables. The twin steel cables are draped from posts bolted into the granite on the final 600ft ascent up an exposed 45-degree rock face. There are gloves available to protect your hands, and intermittent wooden cross-boards provide footholds. A trip in light crowds takes only 15 minutes, but on crowded cables (or if you're jittery), expect it to take much longer. 'Sharing the road' will be your biggest challenge.

A word of caution: do *not* ascend the cables if there's any chance of a storm. The exposed summit is no place to be when lightning strikes (should you have any doubts, read Bob Madgic's *Shattered Air,* 2005), nor do you want to get stuck halfway up with your hands wrapped around virtual lightning rods.

The **summit** is fairly flat and about 5 acres in size. From here, enjoy amazing views of Yosemite Valley, Mt Starr King, Clouds Rest, the Cathedral Range and the Sierra Crest. Camping on the summit is prohibited, and as tempting as it is to linger, watch the time carefully to avoid a hazardous descent in darkness.

Glacier Point & Badger Pass

Trails from the south and east side of Glacier Point Rd wind into some of Yosemite's largest wilderness tracts. Serious backpackers interested in longer hauls can explore such rugged areas as the Merced headwaters or the Clark Range, along the park's southeast border.

Ostrander Lake

Map p66
Duration 2 days
Distance 12.4-mile round-trip

Old Big Oak Flat Road to Yosemite Falls

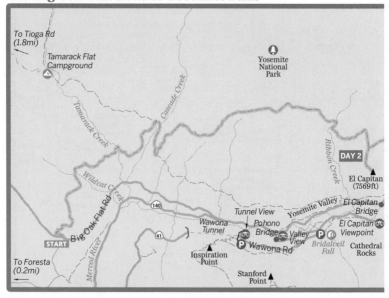

Difficulty Moderate–Difficult

Start/Finish Ostrander Lake Trailhead

Nearest Junction Bridalveil Creek campground

Transportation Car

Summary A deservedly popular out-and-back trek to an atmospheric stone ski hut. A gorgeous granite-bowl lake cuts into the forest, with water perfect for a brisk dip.

Sure this trail is doable as a day hike, but what's the rush? Doing the trek over two days gives you the chance to check out regenerating forest, enjoy wildflowers and spy some wild strawberries.

Park at the Ostrander Lake Trailhead lot (just over a mile east of Bridalveil campground road) and use the bear boxes to stockpile any food that you're not packing in. You soon cross over a footbridge and the level trail starts through a swath of burned-through **lodgepole forest**. The trail, remaining level, fords through purple, yellow and white banks of waisthigh wildflowers, ecstatic bees and ground-hugging wild strawberries.

The hiking path that you're following was once a jeep road, but it is now also a winter route to the Ostrander Ski Hut, and yellow and orange cross-country ski markings are posted on trees the whole way there.

At almost 2 miles, bear left at a signed junction. Another junction comes within a mile, and once again bear left, following the trail sign to Ostrander Lake. The right-hand side trail goes to Wawona, among other places. A climb gears up slowly, and Horizon Ridge appears to your left (east) through the skeletons of burned-out trees and the dainty little puffs of young fir trees. The climb becomes steeper, but a clearing just past the ridge offers energizing views, just when you need the extra encouragement. The jagged Clark Range perches to the northeast, and you can spy on Basket Dome, North Dome and Half Dome as well. In approximately a half-mile, the pitched roof of the handcrafted stone **Ostrander Ski Hut** (see the boxed text, p119) comes into view, framed by **Ostrander Lake** with a slope of rock boulders tumbling down its far shore from Horse Ridge.

You can trace the lake's western bank to find established campsites, and then cool off with a refreshing dip in the lake. When you're ready, you can return following the same trail.

Big Oak Flat Road & Tioga Road

Sometimes the best way to appreciate the beauty of Yosemite Valley is to sneak up on it from above. The Old Big Oak Flat Rd to Yosemite Falls hike skirts the Valley's northern perimeter, while the Tenaya Lake to Yosemite Valley hike drops down from Tioga Rd.

Old Big Oak Flat Road to Yosemite Falls

Map opposite

Duration 2 days

Distance 18.8 miles one way

Difficulty Difficult

Start Old Big Oak Flat Trailhead

Finish Yosemite Falls Trailhead

Nearest Junction Crane Flat gas station

Transportation Tuolumne Meadows hikers' bus

Summary Climb up to bird's-eye views of Yosemite Valley, Half Dome and the Clark Range on a trail that never gets crowded.

Spend the night on top of El Capitan before descending Yosemite Falls.

When planning for this hike, note that some creeks along the way can be difficult to cross during peak spring runoff (Tamarack is the hardest), but run dry in summer. Unless you don't mind carrying in *all* your water, this is best done as a late-spring trip. Ask at the Yosemite Valley or Big Oak Flat wilderness office about the status of water sources and creek levels en route.

DAY 1: OLD BIG OAK FLAT ROAD TRAILHEAD TO EL CAPITAN
7–8 HOURS, 10.1 MILES

From Yosemite Valley, get the Tuolumne Meadows hikers' bus to drop you a quarter-mile west of Foresta turnoff on Big Oak Flat Rd, in the 'Old Big Oak Flat Rd' parking lot. The trailhead (across the street) begins with switchbacks, climbing through an area charred first by the 1990 Foresta fire and then retorched for good measure by the 2009 Big Meadow fire.

Over 4 miles, cross Wildcat Creek and then Tamarack Creek (a more challenging crossing with heavy runoff) before coming to a junction at a footbridge. To the left, it's just over 2 miles to Tamarack Flat campground via the Old Big Oak Flat Rd. Instead continue right (southeast), crossing the footbridge over Cascade Creek. The path is forested with red fir, Jeffrey pine and canyon live oak. Pass through **Ribbon Meadow**, with corn lilies and, in wet years, many mosquitoes. Cross Ribbon Creek and veer a quarter-mile south off the trail to camp on the sandy top of **El Capitan** (at just over 10 miles). Camp at an existing site to avoid trampling the undergrowth. At eye level, the surrounding peaks look like frothy waves, with the iconic Half Dome to the east. It's a stunning viewpoint to see the evening alpenglow.

DAY 2: EL CAPITAN TO YOSEMITE FALLS
6–7 HOURS, 8.7 MILES

Rejoin the trail and continue east for 1.7 miles to the **Three Brothers**. A half-mile jut takes you to **Eagle Peak** (7779ft), the upper of the trio, with more awesome and dizzying views of the Valley and the Clark Range. Continue northeast and, at the junction of the Yosemite Creek Trail, turn south to reach the top of **Yosemite Falls** in about a half-mile. It's 3.6 miles down more than a hundred switchbacks and 2700ft of knee-knocking descent to the Valley floor.

🥾 Tenaya Lake to Yosemite Valley

Map p105

Duration 2 days

Distance 17.1 miles one way

Difficulty Difficult

Start Sunrise Lakes Trailhead

Finish Happy Isles

Nearest Town Tuolumne Meadows

Transportation Tuolumne Meadows hikers' bus; Tuolumne Meadows shuttle stop 10; YARTS Hwy 120 bus

Summary Instead of driving between Tioga Rd and Yosemite Valley, why not hike it? The Tenaya Lake to Yosemite Valley hike is one of the classics, allowing you an up-close look at the major landscape changes.

The most spectacular trail from Tioga Rd to Yosemite Valley traverses the summit of **Clouds Rest** (9926ft), arguably Yosemite's finest panoramic viewpoint. An easier variation bypasses Clouds Rest completely and follows Sunrise Creek. Both hikes descend through Little Yosemite Valley and pass world-renowned Nevada and Vernal Falls to Happy Isles. Hearty hikers can also include a side trip to the top of Half Dome. On stormy days, steer clear of both Half Dome and Clouds Rest.

The trailheads are almost 50 miles apart by road. Unless you plan to shuttle two vehicles, use public transportation for the uphill leg.

DAY 1: TENAYA LAKE TO LITTLE YOSEMITE VALLEY
8–10 HOURS, 12.3 MILES

Start from the well-marked Sunrise Lakes Trailhead, at the west end of Tenaya Lake off Tioga Rd. Trailhead parking is limited, and the lot fills early. Those leaving from Tuolumne Meadows can instead use the free Tuolumne to Olmsted Point shuttle bus, which stops at the trailhead.

See the Clouds Rest hike (p92) for the trail to the summit. From there, head down steps off the south side to the ridge below. In 0.6 miles there's a signed junction with a bypass trail for horses. Continue straight, down through pines, chinquapins and manzanitas, for 20 minutes. Pass beneath granite domes and continue the descent on switchbacks for another hour. Near the bottom of the 2726ft descent, the trail enters shady forest.

Two hours (3.8 miles) from the summit of Clouds Rest, you'll reach the marked junction with the John Muir Trail (7200ft). Nearby **Sunrise Creek** offers several forested campsites and provides the first water since well before Clouds Rest. Turn west onto the John Muir Trail and descend a half-mile to the signed junction with the heavily traveled Half Dome Trail. Go south 1.3 miles to the established and busy campsites in **Little Yosemite Valley** (6100ft) along the Merced River. Beware: both Sunrise Creek and Little Yosemite Valley experience chronic problems with bears.

ALTERNATIVE ROUTE: TENAYA LAKE TO LITTLE YOSEMITE VALLEY VIA FORSYTH & JOHN MUIR TRAILS

7–9 HOURS, 10.9 MILES

Those not inclined to visit the Clouds Rest summit can follow an easier, forested alternative trail along Sunrise Creek, which eventually meets the trail from Clouds Rest and descends to Little Yosemite Valley.

To begin, follow the Day 1 description above for 2.5 hours (4.7 miles) to the signed junction (9100ft) with the Clouds Rest and Forsyth Trails. Bear southeast and follow the Forsyth Trail across a meadow into the pine and granite landscape. The trail leads down a slope of red firs, offering good views of the Clark Range, Merced Canyon and Mt Starr King. Follow Sunrise Creek until a slight ascent takes you to the marked junction (8000ft) with the John Muir Trail, also known here as the Sunrise Trail. Go southwest on the John Muir Trail 0.1 miles to another junction, where a trail to Merced Lake heads east. Stay on the John Muir Trail, heading west along Sunrise Creek, then descend switchbacks to the junction (7200ft) with the Clouds Rest Trail. Continue a half-mile to the busy Half Dome Trail, then turn south and descend the John Muir Trail to Little Yosemite Valley.

DAY 2: LITTLE YOSEMITE VALLEY TO HAPPY ISLES VIA THE JOHN MUIR TRAIL

2–3 HOURS, 4.8 MILES

Today you can follow either the Mist Trail or the John Muir Trail some 1065ft down to Happy Isles in Yosemite Valley. We recommend the John Muir Trail because the granite steps on the Mist Trail tend to pound your knees on the descent. If you do take the Mist Trail, it's 3.9 miles to Happy Isles.

Tenaya Lake to Yosemite Valley

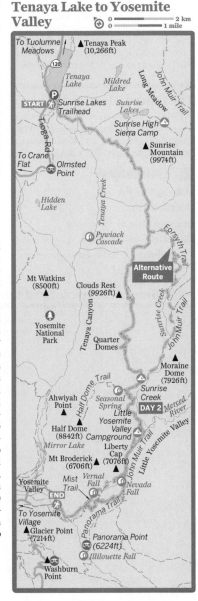

From Little Yosemite Valley, follow the John Muir Trail for 0.5 miles, where it traces the Merced River and then contours to the south of Liberty Cap. At 1.1 miles, meet the Mist Trail (and follow it to the right, if you wish). Continue southwest along the John

Muir Trail, fording the footbridge over the rushing Merced at **Nevada Fall**. Pass the junction with the Panorama Trail and, at approximately 4 miles, cross the river again. From here it's less than a mile to the trailhead, walking along the eastern riverbank.

Tuolumne Meadows

In addition to the following multiday hikes, several of the day hikes can be extended into overnight excursions, including Cathedral Lakes, Mt Dana, and Glen Aulin.

🥾 Lyell Canyon

Maps pp76 & 106

Duration 2 days

Distance 17.6-mile round-trip

Difficulty Easy–Moderate

Start/Finish Lyell Canyon Trailhead at Dog Lake parking lot

Nearest Town Tuolumne Meadows

Transportation Tuolumne Meadows hikers' bus; Tuolumne Meadows shuttle stop 1 or 3; YARTS Hwy 120 bus

Summary This flat section of the John Muir Trail meanders deep into Lyell Canyon to the base of Mt Lyell, the park's highest peak. Fishing, relaxing, views and side trips are all excellent.

If destinations like Cathedral Lake and Nevada Fall slap you in the face with their shockingly good looks, Lyell Canyon gently rolls its beauty over you like a blanket on a cool day. The Lyell Canyon trail takes you through a special place, along a section of the John Muir Trail as it follows the Lyell Fork of the Tuolumne River through a gorgeous subalpine meadow hemmed in by tree-covered granite peaks. The final reward is the view of 13,114ft Lyell Peak and its eponymous glacier, towering over the meadow

High Sierra Camps & Lyell Canyon

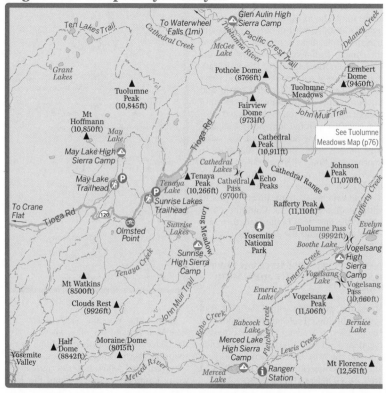

beyond Donohue Pass. This is also a great choice for those who loathe uphill climbs.

The best place to park is the Dog Lake parking lot, off the road to Tuolumne Lodge. If that's full, park in the wilderness center parking lot, further west on the same road. From the latter, look for a hidden trail sign reading 'John Muir Trail' and walk southeast, paralleling the road. After about 0.2 miles, you'll pass the trail that comes down from the Dog Lake lot. Soon, you'll cross the Dana Fork (Tuolumne River) by bearing right at a junction (continuing straight would take you to the lodge) and crossing the footbridge over the river. Soon you'll hit another junction; veer right toward Donohue Pass (hint: always head toward Donohue Pass). About 0.5 miles further, you'll cross the Lyell Fork over two footbridges and come to yet another junction. This time, bear left.

Another 0.5 miles on, the trail passes the Vogelsang/Yosemite Valley junction and

crosses Rafferty Creek. Finally it turns southeast into **Lyell Canyon**, and you can start paying attention to the scenery rather than the trail junctions. After 4.2 miles you'll pass the turnoff to Ireland and Evelyn Lakes, cross Ireland Creek and pass beneath the inverted cone of Potter Point (10,732ft).

If you wish to camp in Lyell Canyon – a highlight of any Yosemite trip – you'll find several sites alongside the river; just make sure you're at least 4 miles from the trailhead. Basically, anything south of Ireland Creek is fine. Some of the best sites are about 0.5 miles before the head of the canyon, where you can see Mt Lyell (13,114ft) looming over the southeast end of the meadow. There are sites on both sides of the river and above the trail. Once you start heading up the 'staircase' at the head of the canyon, campsites are few until you reach Lyell Base Camp, a busy climbers' camp below Donohue Pass.

You can take a day-long side trip to the summit of **Mt Lyell**, but only experienced climbers should attempt it. The ascent alone gains over 4000ft, and the difficult route traverses a glacier, involves steep and complex climbs, and requires safety ropes. Another option is setting up your own base camp in the canyon and continuing another few miles up the John Muir Trail to **Donohue Pass** (a 2000ft climb), admiring the impressive peaks and glaciers along the way.

On your second day, the task is simple: follow the John Muir Trail along the Lyell Fork back to the trailhead.

🏃 Young Lakes

Map p108

Duration 2 days

Distance 13-mile round-trip

Difficulty Moderate

Start/Finish Dog Lake Trailhead near Lembert Dome parking lot

Nearest Town Tuolumne Meadows

Transportation Tuolumne Meadows hikers' bus; Tuolumne Meadows shuttle stop 4; YARTS Hwy 120 bus

Summary After climbing through forests of lodgepole pines, this trail opens up to offer sweeping views of the Cathedral Range before reaching shimmering Young Lakes, at the base of gnarly Ragged Peak.

Map showing: 0 – 5 km / 0 – 2.5 miles scale. Gaylor Lakes, Tioga Pass Entrance Station, Tioga Pass (9945ft), Mono Pass Trailhead, Mt Dana (13,057ft), Tioga Rd, 120, Mt Gibbs (12,764ft), Pacific Crest Trail/John Muir Trail, Mammoth Peak (12,117ft), Kuna Crest, Mono Pass (10,604ft), Parker Pass (11,102ft), To Mt Lewis (1mi), Potter Point (10,732ft), Lyell Canyon, Tuolumne River, Ireland Creek, Ireland Lake, Donohue Peak (12,023ft), Amelia Earhart Peak (11,974ft), Cathedral Range, Lyell Base Camp, Donahue Pass (11,056ft), Mt Lyell (13,114ft), Lyell Glacier, Pacific Crest Trail/John Muir Trail.

Young Lakes & Glen Aulin

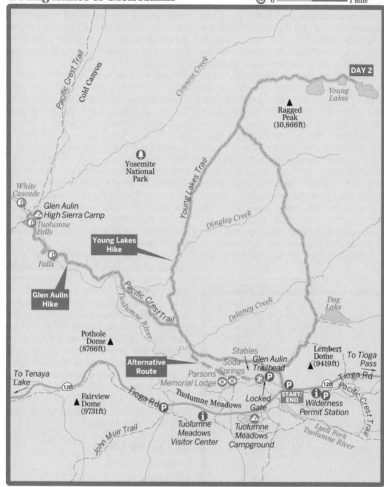

DAY 1: TRAILHEAD TO YOUNG LAKES
3–4 HOURS, 6.2 MILES

Set at elevations between 9950ft and 10,050ft, the three Young Lakes make for a vigorous day hike but offer much more – particularly at sunrise and sunset – to those who make an overnight journey out of it. If the permit quota for Cathedral Lakes is full, this is a good alternative. Some walkers knock this off their favorite-hikes list because much of it is through pine forest, meaning fewer vistas. But the rewards at the lakes above make up for this tenfold.

Day hikers can park at the Lembert Dome parking lot; overnighters must park along the dirt road leading from the lot to the stables. From the parking lot, follow the Dog Lake trail into the trees, with Lembert Dome on your right. After 1.3 miles you'll pass the trail to Lembert Dome. After another 0.3 miles, you'll hit the junction to 9240ft **Dog Lake**, good for a quick detour and snack stop.

Back on the Young Lakes trail, you'll ascend gradually to about 9400ft before descending to **Delaney Creek**, which burbles along the edge of a lovely meadow.

Cross Delaney Creek and follow the trail across the meadow and around the western side of a granite peak. Shortly thereafter, the trail meanders into a clearing and you'll see snarled Ragged Peak to the north. After entering a gently sloping meadow spotted with wildflowers and stunted whitebark pines, you're presented with a magnificent view to the south: the entire Cathedral Range and all its major peaks, including Cathedral Peak, Unicorn Peak and Echo Peaks (with Cockscomb just behind Unicorn). To the far left stands Mt Lyell (13,114ft), Yosemite's highest peak.

Cross **Dingley Creek** (a good spot to fill up the water bottles), and follow the trail over a small crest, with Ragged Peak on your right. The trail winds down through the pines and boulders to meet a junction (the return route). Keep to your right and continue around the northwest shoulder of Ragged Peak until, after 1.5 miles from the junction, you arrive at the lowest of the **Young Lakes**. There are numerous places to camp along the northwest shore, and trees offer shade and shelter from any wind that might pick up. The lake itself sits within a sort of granite amphitheater formed by the northern flanks of Ragged Peak, which takes on a fiery golden glow at sunset, lighting up the lake with its reflection in the water.

From the northeast side of the lake, a trail leads up to **middle Young Lake**. From the middle lake's eastern shore, a vaguely defined, steep trail climbs alongside a pretty waterfall before reaching a meadow and gently sloping down to the third, **upper Young Lake**. It's a truly stunning alpine setting boasting marvelous views in every direction. There are a couple of campsites eked out above the northwestern shore.

DAY 2: YOUNG LAKES TO TRAILHEAD
3–4 HOURS, 6.8 MILES

To return from the lower lake, follow the same trail out until, after 1.5 miles from Young Lake, you reach the junction you passed on the way up. Stay to your right. The views are less impressive along the return trail, but it makes for variation. After 3.7 miles of mostly downhill walking you'll join the Pacific Crest Trail. After crossing Delaney Creek, the trail becomes extremely worn, sandy and mule-trodden. At a junction you can either stay to your left to reach the stables and the road where you parked, or head to your right to visit Soda Springs.

🏃 Vogelsang

Map p110
Duration 3 days
Distance 27-mile round-trip
Difficulty Moderate–Difficult
Start/Finish Lyell Canyon Trailhead from Dog Lake parking lot
Nearest Town Tuolumne Meadows
Transportation Tuolumne Meadows hikers' bus; Tuolumne Meadows shuttle stop 1 or 3

Summary This exquisite but very popular semi-loop crosses Tuolumne and Vogelsang Passes through Yosemite's Cathedral Range, offering a remarkable circuit through John Muir's 'Range of Light.'

The sloping subalpine meadows and streams on either side of gentle Tuolumne Pass (9992ft) provide a scenic backdrop for some of the Sierra Nevada's most delightful hiking. The trail takes in multiple cascades and sweeping views of distant peaks in several mountain ranges, including the hard-to-see Clark Range. Camping at Vogelsang Lake and crossing the alpine Vogelsang Pass (10,660ft) rank among the highlights of this journey around Vogelsang Peak.

Vogelsang Peak, Lake and Pass, and High Sierra Camp, all take their name from the Vogelsang brothers, who headed the California Fish and Game Board from 1896 to 1910. The name itself translates aptly from German as 'a meadow where birds sing.'

DAY 1: LYELL CANYON TRAILHEAD TO VOGELSANG LAKE
4–6 HOURS, 7.2 MILES

On Day 1, follow the Lyell Canyon hike (p106) to the Pacific Crest/John Muir Trail. After 0.8 miles, at Rafferty Creek, turn south, leaving the John Muir Trail; the 2½-hour, 4.9-mile ascent along Rafferty Creek begins with a rugged uphill climb. Gouged out by the steel-shod hooves of packhorses and mules that supply the Vogelsang High Sierra Camp, the trail clambers over granite steps and cobblestones through forest for some 20 to 30 minutes before it eases and nears Rafferty Creek's left bank. To the north you'll see Mt Conness and White Mountain, while the Lyell Fork Meadows spread out some 500ft below to the east.

With the steepest part of the trail now behind you, you'll gradually ascend an

Vogelsang

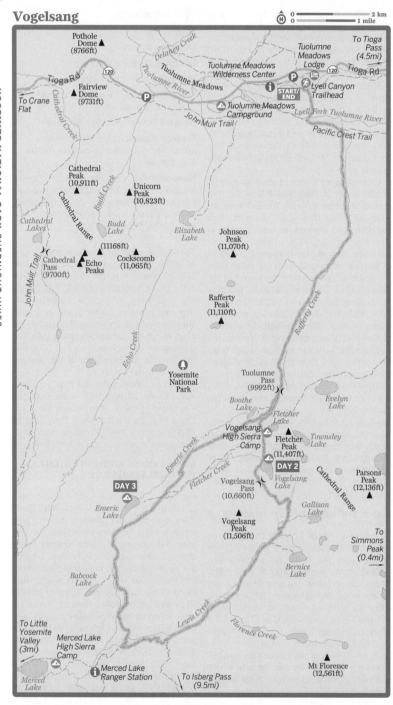

attractive little valley, following the west bank of Rafferty Creek. The forested trail gently climbs another 30 to 40 minutes, then enters a small open meadow. Passing beneath lodgepole pines and crossing several smaller streams, the well-worn trail finally emerges into a lovely meadow along Rafferty Creek. Finally, 6.1 miles from the trailhead, you'll arrive at gentle **Tuolumne Pass** (9992ft).

At the signed Tuolumne Pass junction, take the left fork and head southeast. The trail offers enticing views of Boothe Lake and the granite ridge above it as it travels 0.8 miles to Vogelsang High Sierra Camp (10,130ft). At a signed junction, a backpackers' campground lies to the left (east), while the trail to the right (west) descends to Merced Lake High Sierra Camp. Instead, continue straight (south) toward Vogelsang Pass. About 0.5 miles beyond the High Sierra Camp you'll reach large **Vogelsang Lake** (10,341ft), set in a picture-perfect cirque beneath Fletcher and Vogelsang Peaks. Above the northeast shore are campsites set among whitebark pines.

DAY 2: VOGELSANG LAKE TO EMERIC LAKE
5–7 HOURS, 10.2 MILES

The trail ascends above the southwest end of Vogelsang Lake, eventually crossing a large, cold stream just below its spring-fed source. The view of the lake below and Cathedral Range beyond is sublime. Five minutes further you'll reach **Vogelsang Pass** (10,660ft), in the serrated granite ridge that descends from Vogelsang Peak (11,506ft).

From here the trail rises a bit and provides a long view of the upper Lewis Creek Basin. Lovely **Gallison Lake**, surrounded by meadow, issues forth a cascading stream. Large **Bernice Lake** spreads out at the base of a massive granite ridge beneath Mt Florence (12,561ft). Half a dozen more lakes lie hidden in a chain above Gallison Lake, fed by permanent snow from the slopes of Simmons Peak (12,503ft) at the valley's head. To the southwest is the more distant Clark Range, sweeping from the west to the southeast.

Descend the switchbacks that follow the course of a small stream. At the base, enter a forest along the level valley floor. Streams course across the meadow, involving a few crossings. Continue straight past the Bernice Lake junction, heading downstream along Lewis Creek as the descent grows steeper.

Three miles from Bernice Lake trail junction, you'll pass the Isberg Pass trail junction. Continue on 1 mile through a dramatic canyon for a view of distant Half Dome before passing the signed Merced Lake trail junction (8160ft). Turn north at the junction and follow the trail up Fletcher Creek. After crossing a footbridge, the trail climbs beside the creek, crosses several side streams and climbs high above the left bank of Fletcher Creek. The trail levels out about one hour past the footbridge, offering a fabulous vista over Merced Canyon and the Clark Range.

Leaving the views behind, head beneath lodgepole pines past the signed Babcock Lake trail junction. After 25 minutes, trail emerges in a lovely meadow and finally hits a four-way trail junction. Turn northwest and head 0.4 miles to the large **Emeric Lake** (9338ft). Cross its inlet to reach good campsites above the northwest shore.

DAY 3: EMERIC LAKE TO LYELL CANYON TRAILHEAD
4½–5 HOURS, 9.1 MILES

On Day 3, retrace your steps to the four-way junction. Turn north on the route to **Boothe Lake** (rather than the heavily used trail to Vogelsang High Sierra Camp). This lovely lake, which lies 2.7 miles from the junction, was the original site of the High Sierra Camp before the camp was moved and renamed Vogelsang. The trail stays well above the lake, where camping is prohibited. Arrive once again at **Tuolumne Pass**, 0.4 miles beyond Boothe Lake. From here, retrace your steps: 4.9 miles down Rafferty Creek to the John Muir Trail and 1.1 miles to the Lyell Canyon Trailhead.

Waterwheel Falls

Maps p72 & p76

Duration 2 days

Distance 18-mile round-trip

Difficulty Difficult

Start/Finish Glen Aulin Trailhead near Lembert Dome parking lot

Nearest Town Tuolumne Meadows

Transportation Tuolumne Meadows hikers' bus; Tuolumne Meadows shuttle stop 4; YARTS Hwy 120 bus

Summary Follow this hike along the Grand Canyon of the Tuolumne River to Waterwheel Falls. It's the last and most impressive of six cascades along the river, before it plunges into the canyon on its descent toward Hetch Hetchy Reservoir.

For the first several miles of the hike, follow the Pacific Crest Trail (PCT) to Glen Aulin (p96). About 0.2 miles after **Tuolumne Falls**, head northwest along the trail to Waterwheel Falls, which is 3.3 miles downstream from where you leave the PCT. The trail meanders through ghost forest to the river's edge, inviting a dip in the placid waters, then crosses an area made marshy by a stream that descends from Cold Mountain to the north.

After a 40-minute stroll, you'll reach the far end of the peaceful glen, where the river flows briskly to the brink of the first in a series of near continual cascades. The trail, too, plunges along the river, dropping over gorgeous orange-tinted granite. Ahead, the **Grand Canyon of the Tuolumne** stretches as far as the eye can see. The trail continues between the sheer, polished granite walls of **Wildcat Point** (9455ft) to the north and the 8000ft granite wall of **Falls Ridge** on the opposite bank. **California Falls** and **LeConte Falls** are the most prominent cascades in this section; most are unnamed. If you have to ask yourself, 'Is this Waterwheel Falls?' keep going – you'll know it when you see it.

About an hour after leaving the glen, you'll reach a small unsigned junction where a hard-to-see spur trail branches southwest (left) to a viewpoint of **Waterwheel Falls**. The obvious roar tells you this is the spot, although the falls remain hidden from view. From the main trail, walk two minutes to the edge of the massive falls, named for the distinctive 15ft- to 20ft-high plumes of water that curl into the air like a wheel midway down the more than 600ft-long falls.

After admiring the cascade, return to the main trail, turn west (left), and descend another 10 minutes. As you approach the scattered junipers beside an obvious dark granite rib perpendicular to the trail, turn south (left) and head down a sandy slope through manzanita, following a trail that parallels the rocky rib. It leads to a large, forested campsite (6440ft) that's partly visible from the main trail above. Camp beneath big ponderosa pines and incense cedars, about 0.3 miles below Waterwheel Falls, with the green and tranquil Tuolumne River about 200ft away.

On day two, retrace your steps 9 miles to the trailhead.

Hetch Hetchy

Hetch Hetchy offers some excellent backpacking opportunities, as well as access to some of the park's most remote areas, north of the reservoir. Summers can be brutally hot, which is why the trails out here are busiest in spring and fall.

🥾 Rancheria Falls

Map p78

Duration 7 hours–2 days

Distance 13-mile round-trip

Difficulty Moderate–Difficult

Start/Finish Rancheria Falls Trailhead, O'Shaughnessy Dam

Nearest Junction Evergreen Lodge

Transportation Car

Summary This classic Hetch Hetchy hike passes the spectacular Tueeulala and Wapama Falls, then takes you to the gentler Rancheria Falls, where swimming holes abound and the scenery is outrageous.

Rancheria Falls is doable as a day hike, but it's best enjoyed as an overnighter, allowing you to experience sunset over Rancheria Creek and Hetch Hetchy Reservoir. This part of Yosemite can be brutally hot in summer and, like the Tueeulala and Wapama Falls hike, is best in the spring. Still, it can be rewarding in July and even August, despite the heat, thanks to fewer people and the excellent swimming holes near the falls. Watch out for poison oak along the trail.

Follow the hike to **Wapama Falls** (p98). After the falls, the trail climbs into the shade of black oaks and laurels, offering relief from the sun. It then ascends a series of switchbacks and skirts around the base of **Hetch Hetchy Dome** (6197ft), passing two epic viewpoints over the reservoir on the way. Alternately climbing and falling through shaded oak forest and hot, exposed stretches, the trail finally arrives at two footbridges over **Tiltill Creek**, which mark the end of the no-camping zone.

After climbing up from Tiltill Creek, you'll begin to notice the charred manzanita and fire-scarred trees from the 2003 Tiltill Valley Fire, started by an arsonist who shot himself after setting the forest ablaze. Soon, you'll get your first glimpse of **Rancheria Falls** as they shoot down a granite apron into the reservoir below. Camping below the falls looks inviting but, because the area has become so impacted, it's best to continue 0.25 miles further to the established Rancheria Falls campground.

After chucking your sack and pitching your tent, walk further up the trail, past the Tiltill Valley junction (stay to your right) to the footbridge over **Rancheria Creek**. During summer, when the water levels are low, there are two superb emerald-green swimming holes set in a chasm of granite, both with rock- and bridge-jumping opportunities for the adventurous. The views of Rancheria Creek and the reservoir from here are sublime.

To return on day two, retrace your steps.

BIKING

Bikes are prohibited from all hiking trails within Yosemite, so you'll need to stick to roads and bike paths. Moderate-level bike rides within Yosemite, which is dominated by steep grades except in Yosemite Valley, are few and far between. Generally it's either easy (ie the Valley) or difficult (everywhere else).

Many people bicycle along formidable **Tioga Rd**, though it's not a route for the casual cyclist. If you succumb to the temptation, keep in mind that this winding, climbing route has many blind spots and often fields a lot of traffic. It's a tough, relentless grind, so start riding early in the morning and keep well hydrated. From Crane Flat, it's just under 100 miles to Tioga Pass and back. In late spring, before plowing is complete at Olmsted Point, the road on either side of it is usually open to cyclists for a week or so before the road reopens to cars.

Glacier Point Rd, a 32-mile round-trip from the Chinquapin junction, is another option for a longer ride. The pavement's smooth, the traffic is usually not too heavy and the vistas at Glacier Point are worth the climbs.

Bicycle Rentals

If you can't bring your own bike, stands at Yosemite Lodge and Curry Village rent single-speed beach cruisers (per hour/day $10/28) or bikes with an attached child trailer (per hour/day $16.50/54) You're required to leave either a driver's license or credit card for collateral. Neither location accepts reservations, but you should be fine if you arrive before 11am or so.

᪣ Yosemite Valley Loops

Map p60
Duration 1-3 hours
Distance Up to 12 miles round-trip
Difficulty Easy
Start/Finish Yosemite Lodge
Nearest Town Yosemite Village
Transportation Shuttle stop 8
Summary Whether done in segments or in its entirety, this easy pedal around the floor of Yosemite Valley is as relaxing as it gets – and the views are amazing.

Twelve miles of paved, mostly flat bicycle paths run up and down the length of Yosemite Valley, making for some very relaxed and superbly enjoyable peddling, whether you're solo or a family of five. The free hiking map provided at the visitor center shows the bike route in detail, and it's easy to whip out while riding.

You can pick up the bike path near just about anywhere you're staying in the Valley. Most people start where they rent bikes at either Curry Village or Yosemite Lodge. From the latter, follow the path down to the riverside, past the lodge buildings, across a meadow and west to **Swinging Bridge** (which actually doesn't swing at all). Cross over the Merced River, veer east along Southside Dr, take in the magnificent view of Yosemite Falls, then Half Dome. Soon you'll pass Curry Village, the Royal Arches will appear on your left and you'll finally hit the road to Happy Isles. Pass the **Nature Center at Happy Isles** and continue along the road to loop around to North Pines Campground. Cross the Merced again, then cut north to Northside Dr, which you can follow back to Yosemite Lodge.

If you only have time for one section, the route from Yosemite Village to the Mirror Lake road is especially serene after it splits from Northside Dr. Widening, it passes through thick woods and travels over the Merced, out of sight of any traffic and most people.

᪣ Carlon to Hetch Hetchy

Map p78
Duration 3-4 hours
Distance 34-mile round-trip

Difficulty Moderate

Start/Finish Carlon Falls Day Use Area

Nearest Junction Evergreen Lodge

Transportation Car

Summary With a gentle ascent to the Hetch Hetchy Entrance Station and an adrenaline-spiking descent to the reservoir, this ride offers fabulous views and a spectacular destination.

With relatively little traffic, this ride to Hetch Hetchy Reservoir offers a splendid way to take in the scenery along the northwest boundary of the park. Fuel up with a good picnic lunch at the reservoir: the return climb is much more strenuous than the exciting drop on the way there. In summer, it can get extremely hot out here, so get an early start. In spring, it's divine.

To get to the starting point, drive northwest on Evergreen Rd, which departs Hwy 120 about 1 mile west of the Big Oak Flat Entrance. About 1 mile after turning off, you'll see the **Carlon Day Use Area** at a bridge across the South Fork Tuolumne River. Park in the parking lot and ride out to Evergreen Rd, cross the bridge and you're off. The first 9.5 miles rise and fall fairly gently with a modest overall elevation gain of about 550ft. About 1.5 miles after the park entrance (which lies about 7 miles from Carlon), you'll hit the crest of the ride (topping out around 5000ft) and begin the 1205ft descent to the reservoir. The views over the Poopenaut Valley are outstanding – be sure to stop for a breather at one of the viewpoints.

After you reach the reservoir, gobble down your energy bars, take a deep breath and slog your way back to the car.

OTHER ACTIVITIES

Rock Climbing & Bouldering

When it comes to rock climbing, Yosemite reigns supreme. While covering Yosemite's climbing routes is beyond the scope of this book (try something by Don Reid), at least we can point the first-time climber or visitor in the right direction. If you're new to climbing, consider taking a class at the Yosemite Mountaineering School. For more information on climbing within the park, see www.nps.gov/yose/planyourvisit/climbing.htm.

YOSEMITE VALLEY

First, know this: all ropes lead to Camp 4. Most of the Valley's climbing activity revolves around this walk-in campground and historic hangout for climbing's most legendary figures. Camp 4 is where you go when you want to stop reading and start asking real people questions about where to climb, what to carry and what to expect. It's also where you find climbing partners, pick up used gear (among other things) and find the car keys you left sitting at the base of the climb.

For many climbers, reaching the summit of El Capitan is a lifetime achievement, and hopefuls from around the world arrive to tackle its fabled routes.

As for bouldering, the possibilities are limitless. Popular areas include the west end of Camp 4, Sentinel Rock, the Four Mile Trail Trailhead, and the rocks near Housekeeping Camp and around Mirror Lake, to name only a few.

BIG OAK FLAT ROAD & TIOGA ROAD

The big draw in these parts is Polly Dome, right next to Tenaya Lake. Stately Pleasure Dome, on the side of Polly adjacent to the lake, is the most popular spot, offering a good mix of easy and moderate routes. The granite rocks in this part of the park are well suited for slab and friction climbing, and both are well represented here.

For more difficult climbing, try the backside of Pywiack and Medlicott Domes, both just northeast of the lake toward Tuolumne Meadows. The beach at the east end of Tenaya Lake is an ideal spot for watching climbers.

For good bouldering, head to the Knobs, just over a mile north of Tenaya Lake on the west side of the road. Beginners will find excellent climbing on nearby Low-Profile Dome, particularly along the Golfer's Route.

TUOLUMNE MEADOWS

Come summertime, when temperatures in the Valley regularly top 90°F (30°C), climbers head to Tuolumne Meadows where the cool, high-country air is much more conducive to climbing. Thanks to the altitude, the air is also thinner, so climbing here requires at least a day's acclimatization for most people.

Cathedral Peak and its fin-shaped west peak, the frightening Eichorn Pinnacle, are both epic and extremely popular climbs. It's fun watching climbers tackle these peaks from the Cathedral Lakes trail. The Northwest Books route on Lembert Dome is one

YOSEMITE MOUNTAINEERING SCHOOL

Since 1969 **Yosemite Mountaineering School** (Map p60; ☎209-372-8344; www .yosemitemountaineering.com) has been teaching and guiding rock climbers, mountaineers and back-country skiers of all levels. While you can learn everything from basic backpacking skills to building a snow cave, the school's specialty is teaching folks how to move their bodies up slabs of granite. Whether you're a 12-year-old who wants to learn the basics of climbing, belaying and rappeling or a sport climber who wants to learn the art of big walls, you'll find this school a gold mine of opportunity. Beginners over the age of 10 can sign up for the Go Climb a Rock seminar ($148 per person), which is pretty much guaranteed to inspire participants to go on for more. For parents, it's a great and constructive way to turn the kids loose for a day.

Other class offerings include anchoring, leading/multipitch climbing, self-rescue/aid and crack climbing, for which Yosemite, of course, is famous. You can even create your own custom climbing trip or hire guides to take you climbing.

The school is based out of the Curry Village Mountain Shop from April through November; it relocates to Badger Pass in winter. From late June through early September (when Tioga Rd is open) it also maintains a branch at the Tuolumne Meadows Sport Shop. At all locations, the friendly and knowledgeable staff will offer suggestions based on your skill level and objectives.

For more on climbing, see p36.

of the most popular climbs on that iconic dome. Mt Conness, on the park's eastern border, is a challenging all-day climb.

Horseback Riding
Guided Trail Rides

There's ample opportunity to ride in Yosemite, but unless you bring your own horse you'll probably be on the back of a mule. For kids, it's a great way to take in the scenery, breathe some dust and have a little fun. Guided mule rides are offered at three stables within the park from roughly spring through fall.

For guided rides throughout the park, no experience is necessary, but riders must be at least seven years old and 44in tall and weigh less than 225lb. Don't sign on for a full-day trip unless you're in good physical shape – you'll regret it. Prices at all three park-operated stables are the same: $64 for two hours, $85 for a half-day trip and $128 for a full-day trip. The season runs from May to October, although this varies slightly by location. During the popular summer months, you should make a reservation, particularly for the longer rides, by calling the stable directly.

Yosemite Valley Stables   HORSEBACK RIDING
(Map p60; ☎209-372-8348) Located near North Pines Campground, with rides to Mirror Lake and Clark's Point (for views of Vernal Fall).

Tuolumne Meadows Stables   HORSEBACK RIDING
(Map p76; ☎209-372-8427) Has some of the park's most scenic riding trips, including part of the Young Lakes trail and along the Tuolumne River.

Wawona Stables   HORSEBACK RIDING
(Map p70; ☎209-375-6502) Located behind the Pioneer Center, offers rides around Wawona Meadow and to Chilnualna Falls.

Yosemite Trails Pack Station   HORSEBACK RIDING
(Map p70; ☎559-683-7611; www.yosemitetrails .com) Just outside the park's South Entrance, offers rides to the Mariposa Grove of big trees ($140 per person for half-day), and sleigh rides (adult/child $30/20) in winter.

High Sierra Camps
Yosemite High Sierra Camps Saddle Trips   HORSEBACK RIDING
(☎801-559-4909, freight 209-372-8427; trip per person adult/child from $1018/856) These are far and away the most popular (though definitely not the cheapest) way to see the park from a saddle, with mules schlepping you and all the supplies. These four- to six-day trips include all meals and depart from the Tuolumne Stables for the spectacular High Sierra Camps circuit (see p128). They fill up months in advance; for availability, navigate to the Pack & Saddle Trips section of the **DNC website** (www.yosemitepark.com). If you

COFFEE WITH A RANGER

Rise and shine and schmooze with a perky park ranger at one of the morning Coffee with a Ranger sessions held at campgrounds throughout the park. A chance to get some quality time with the best sources of park information, you can solicit suggestions for your day's adventures while getting a complimentary caffeine fix. Check the *Yosemite Guide* for locations and times, and don't forget to bring a mug!

just want to carry your own weight and have mules carry your gear, it'll cost you $5 per pound. You can also hire mules for custom trips to carry you and/or your gear to a destination of your choosing.

Stock Camps

If you're bringing your own pack animals, you can use the stock camps at Tuolumne Meadows, Wawona and Bridalveil Creek campgrounds. Each site accommodates six people and six animals. You can reserve sites up to five months in advance by phone only through **Recreation.gov** (☏877-444-6777; www.recreation.gov). Stock are allowed on all Yosemite trails except those posted on the **Stock Closure list** (www.nps.gov/yose/plan yourvisit/stock.htm). For more information on traveling with your own animals, see p47.

Rafting & Kayaking

Bad news first: there are no rapids to ride within the park – you'll have to head outside Yosemite for that (see p39). The good news is that the Merced River flows lazily through Yosemite Valley, offering rafters and kayakers a marvelous way to take in the scenery on a hot summer day. That said, you do have to share the water with a plethora of other boats, but with the right sense of humor and a little Merced River water running down your face, it's undeniably fun.

Rafts, kayaks, air mattresses and inner tubes (or whatever strange, nonmotorized flotation device you're using) are allowed only along the 3-mile stretch between Stoneman Bridge (near Curry Village) and Sentinel Beach. The waters are gentle enough for children, and **raft rentals** (Map p60; ☏209-372-4386; per adult/child over 50lbs $26/16; ☺approx late May–Jul) for the 3-mile trip are

available at Curry Village. Rates include all equipment and a return shuttle to the rental kiosk. No permit is required to use your own raft, canoe or kayak on the Merced. Shuttles depart every 30 minutes and cost $5 for those bringing their own flotation devices.

Whenever you disembark, be sure to do so only on sand or gravel bars – *not* vegetated riparian areas which cannot handle the human impact.

Rafting is also fun in Wawona on the South Fork of the Merced, between the campground and Swinging Bridge. On Tioga Rd, near Tuolumne Meadows, Tenaya Lake is a great place for a float and especially good for kayaking.

Swimming

River swimming throughout Yosemite is best mid- to late summer, when the water levels are low and the current gentler. The Merced River is Yosemite's biggest killer, so never swim where you're not certain the current is safe.

YOSEMITE VALLEY

On a hot summer day in Yosemite Valley, nothing beats the heat like lounging in the gentle Merced River. Provided you don't trample the riparian life on your way, you can jump in just about anywhere, but there are several locations proving particularly good: at the beach just behind Housekeeping Camp; on the stretch behind Yosemite Lodge; and at the Cathedral Beach and Devil's Elbow areas opposite the El Capitan Picnic Area. The beach immediately below Swinging Bridge is hugely popular and, thanks to calm waters, great for families. Tenaya Creek offers good swimming as well, especially near the bridge leading toward Mirror Lake.

Skin too thin? Curry Village and Yosemite Lodge provide public outdoor **swimming pools** (Map p60; admission adult/child $5/4). The price includes towels and showers.

WAWONA

You'll find nice swimming holes near the campground and by Swinging Bridge. The latter is reached via a 2-mile drive east along Forest Dr, which parallels the south bank of the Merced River. Park in a lot beyond private Camp Wawona and walk the short distance to the river.

BIG OAK FLAT ROAD & TIOGA ROAD

If you can handle cold water, Tenaya Lake offers some of the most enjoyable swimming in the park. It's hard to resist this glistening lake that beckons with sapphire waters. A sandy half-moon beach wraps around the east end. Sunbathers and picnickers are also drawn to the rocks that rim its north and west sides.

Want to work a little for that dip? May Lake is an easy hike and gorgeous, if a bit chilly. You can swim anywhere except a signed section of the western side where the May Lake High Camp draws its drinking water. Further west, Harden Lake is unusually warm compared with other nearby lakes because much of its volume evaporates in summer. A late- or even mid-season swim is practically balmy.

TUOLUMNE MEADOWS

The Tuolumne River is an excellent choice for high-country swimming, with many easy-to-reach sandy-bottomed pools and slightly warmer temperatures than other High Sierra rivers. From the pullout at the west end of Tuolumne Meadows, follow the trail along Pothole Dome and the river for about a mile to a gorgeous waterfall and hidden swimming spot.

You'll also find a couple of small but good swimming holes at the twin bridges crossing the chipper Lyell Fork Tuolumne; to get there, head out on the trail to Lyell Canyon. If you don't mind hiking a bit further, the Lyell Fork also has some great (albeit shallow) swimming areas. Elizabeth Lake can be a bit bone-chilling, but on a hot summer day, plenty of people take the plunge and love it.

Fishing

Yosemite may not be the sort of place you go to catch whopping trophy trout, but the setting is fabulous, and wettin' a line, so to say, in the Merced or Tuolumne River is pretty darn satisfying. Stream and river fishing is permitted only from the last Saturday in April until mid-November; lake fishing is okay year-round. In Wawona the South Fork of the Merced offers some of the best stream fishing in the park. In and around the park you can fish the Merced River between Happy Isles and the Forest Bridge in El Portal, although if you catch a rainbow trout, you'll have to throw it back. In Yosemite Valley, you're allowed only five brown trout per day, and bait is prohibited (artificial lures or barbless flies only).

The park's most satisfying fishing, especially for fly casters, is undoubtedly in Tuolumne Meadows. Although the fish aren't big, they're still out there, and the setting is unbeatable. The Dana Fork Tuolumne and especially the Lyell Fork Tuolumne are good, with easy access from shore and no wading required. As for lakes, Elizabeth Lake is the most easily accessible. If you're heading up to Young Lakes, bring a pole. Some of the best lake fishing is on Saddlebag Lake, just outside the park, east of the Tioga Pass entrance, off Hwy 120.

Hetch Hetchy Reservoir is said to house a trove of very large trout; casting is permitted from the shore only, though no live bait is allowed. Above the reservoir, the Tuolumne River is supposedly very good.

You can pick up tackle and supplies at the Yosemite Village Sport Shop and the stores in Tuolumne Meadows, Wawona and Crane Flat. For more information on fishing in the park, see www.nps.gov/yose/planyourvisit /fishing.htm.

Hang Gliding

You can actually hang glide from Glacier Point for a mere $5, provided you're an active member of the **US Hang Gliding & Paragliding Association** (USHPA; ☎719-632-8300; www.ushpa.aero), have a level 4 (advanced standing) certification, and you preregister online with the **Yosemite Hang Gliding Association** (YHGA; www.yhga.org). On weekend mornings from late May to early September, weather permitting, qualified hang gliders can launch from the overlook between 8am and 9am, well before any thermal activity rolls in, and float down to Leidig Meadow, just west of Yosemite Lodge. One of the best free shows in the park is watching the colorful gliders sprint off the edge and soar over the Valley like tiny paper airplanes.

Boating

Motorless boats of any kind can use beautiful and easy-to-access Tenaya Lake – hands down the best place to boat in the park. Lounging at the foot of John Muir's beloved Mt Hoffmann is tranquil May Lake, a lovely place to paddle an inflatable; that is, unless you want to hoof anything heavier for the 1.2 miles from the trailhead along Tioga Rd.

Golf

If you find the need to smack the ol' tiny white ball around, head to Yosemite's nine-hole, par-35 **Wawona Golf Course** (☎209-375-6572; www.yosemitepark.com; green fees for 9/18 holes from $21.50/36), which was built in 1917. The course hails itself as one of the country's few 'organic' golf courses, meaning no pesticides are used on the lawn and everything is irrigated with gray water. Cart and club rentals are available.

Campfire & Public Programs

There's something almost universally enjoyable about group campfire programs. Pull a bench around a roaring bonfire, with stars above, big trees behind you and lots of friendly folks all around, and it's as if you've left the world's troubles behind.

During the summer, free campfire programs are held at the following Yosemite campgrounds: Tuolumne Meadows, Wawona, Bridalveil Creek, Crane Flat, White Wolf and Lower Pines. Check the *Yosemite Guide* for the week's programs and times. Rangers, naturalists and other park staff lead the programs, and topics include the history, ecology and geology of the local region, a few tips on dealing with bears, and maybe some stories and songs. They're geared toward families and people of all ages.

Similar evening programs are also held at amphitheaters behind Yosemite Lodge and Curry Village – even in the absence of an actual campfire, the mood remains the same. These programs include general talks about the area, with occasional slide shows and films.

The Sierra Club's LeConte Memorial also hosts programs each week. A little more in-depth than the average campfire talk, these cover such topics as the founding of the John Muir Trail and the history of Hetch Hetchy.

Glacier Point rangers lead weekly programs at a lovely stone amphitheater near the snack bar, and sometimes offer sunset talks along the railing overlooking the Valley. Over at Tuolumne Meadows, talks take place at Parsons Memorial Lodge, reachable via an easy half-mile hike.

The busiest time is, of course, during the summer, usually June to September. Limited programs are offered in the low season, and they're held during cold weather at indoor locations such as Yosemite Lodge and the Ahwahnee Hotel.

WINTER ACTIVITIES

The white coat of winter opens up a different set of things to do, as the Valley becomes a quiet, frosty world of snow-draped evergreens, ice-coated lakes and vivid vistas of gleaming white mountains sparkling against blue skies. Winter tends to arrive in full force by mid-November and whimper out in early April.

Cross-Country Skiing

GLACIER POINT & BADGER PASS
Cross-Country Skiing

Twenty-five miles of groomed track and 90 miles of marked trails fan out from Badger Pass. From here, you can schuss out to the Clark Range Vista and Glacier Point, an invigorating 21-mile round-trip. Pick up a trail map or download one from the Yosemite website (www.nps.gov/yose).

The **Yosemite Cross-Country Ski Center** (☎209-372-8444) offers learn-to-ski packages ($46), guided tours (from $102 per person), telemark instruction ($49), private lessons (starting at $37) and equipment rental ($23 for skis, boots and poles). It also leads very popular overnight trips to the Glacier Point Ski Hut.

WAWONA

Mariposa Grove contains a series of well-marked cross-country skiing trails, including an 8-mile loop trail from the South Entrance. Trail maps can be purchased at the park or printed from the park website. The trails also connect to marked Sierra National Forest trails just south of the park in Goat Meadow and along Beasore Rd.

BIG OAK FLAT ROAD & TIOGA ROAD

You'll find good marked cross-country skiing and snowshoeing trails in the Crane Flat area, including Old Big Oak Flat Rd, which leads to Tuolumne Grove and Hodgdon Meadow. Trail maps are available at the park and on the park website. When Tioga Rd is closed in winter, it becomes a popular, though ungroomed, ski route.

Downhill Skiing & Snowboarding

California's oldest ski slope, **Badger Pass Ski Area** (Map p60; ☎209-372-8430; www .badgerpass.com; adult/child/youth lift tickets $42/23/37; ⊙mid-Dec–early Apr; ⚑) sits at 7300ft on Glacier Point Rd, about 22 miles from the Valley. Known as a family-friendly mountain geared toward beginners and intermediates, it features an 800ft vertical drop, nine runs, two terrain parks, five lifts, a full-service lodge and equipment rental ($31 for a full set of gear). For great money-saving deals, check out the stay-and-ski packages at

WINTER SKI HUTS

When the park is hushed and white, three classic ski huts are open for overnight guests who make the trek on snowshoes or cross-country skis. The journeys aren't easy, but certainly worth the work. Make sure to self-register for a wilderness permit before you head out.

In winter, the concession stand at Glacier Point fills with bunk beds and becomes the **Glacier Point Ski Hut** (Map p60; ☏209-372-8444; www.yosemitepark.com). It's operated by the park concessionaire and reached by a 10.5-mile trip on an intermediate trail. Guided trips are led by the Cross-Country Ski Center; one-night trips cost $350 per person, two nights run $550. These tariffs include meals, wine, accommodations and guides. Or you can get there without a guide (reservation required) and pay $120 per day for meals and lodging.

The handcrafted stone **Ostrander Lake Ski Hut** (off Map p66; www.yosemite conservancy.org; bunk weekday/weekend $32/52), operated by the Yosemite Conservancy, can accommodate up to 25 skiers in a gorgeous lakeside spot beneath Horse Ridge. Cooking facilities are provided, but you must ski in with all of your supplies. The 10-mile trip requires experience and a high fitness level. Staffed throughout the winter, the hut is open to backcountry skiers and snowshoers, and a drawing is held for reservations in November.

Are you up to a 16-mile trek from the eastern side of the park, summiting Tioga Pass? In winter, the Tuolumne Meadows campground reservation office reinvents itself as the free **Tuolumne Meadows Ski Hut** (Map p76). It has a wood-burning stove, sleeps 10, and is first come, first served. If you're hesitant to try this on your own, the Cross-Country Ski Center runs infrequent six-day tours for $876 per person. It's a slightly easier journey when the Tioga Pass Resort (p143) is open to break up the trip; it's located one mile east of Tioga Pass. A stone building facing Tioga Rd, just west of the bridge across the Tuolumne River, it's right at the entrance to the campground.

the Wawona Hotel, Yosemite Lodge and Ahwahnee Hotel, and note that lift-ticket prices drop considerably during midweek. They also rent tubes for snow tubing.

The excellent on-site Yosemite Ski School is highly regarded for its top-notch instruction, particularly for beginners. Group lessons are $35, private lessons start at $65 per hour and the 'Guaranteed Learn to Ski/Snowboard' package costs $74 to $84. Badger's gentle slopes are well suited for first-time snowboarders.

In winter, a free daily shuttle runs from the Valley to Badger Pass in the morning, returning to the Valley in the afternoon. There's also a new **Oakhurst shuttle** (www .yosemitepark.com) that runs between that gateway town and the resort on Saturdays, Sundays and holidays; it's $10 round-trip including park admission.

Snowshoeing

It wouldn't be difficult to argue that Yosemite Valley is at its very best just after a fresh snowfall. Snowshoeing around the Valley, past icy monoliths, frozen waterfalls and meadows blanketed in snow, is a truly magical activity. The John Muir Trail, which begins at Happy Isles, is a popular destination.

You can rent snowshoes ($18.50/22.50 per half-/full day) at Badger Pass (and sometimes at the Curry Village Ice Rink), where rangers lead two-hour naturalist treks that are informative, fun and almost free ($5). Check the *Yosemite Guide* for schedules. From January to March, rangers offer two-hour 'Full Moon Snowshoe Walks' ($18.50 with equipment rental; $5 without) on nights of, and leading up to, a full moon. Sign up at the Yosemite Lodge Tour Desk or by calling ☏209-372-1240.

Ice-Skating

A delightful way to spend a winter's afternoon is twirling about on the large outdoor **Curry Village Ice Rink** (Map p60; 2½hr session adult/child $8/6, skate rental $3; ☉Nov-Mar). Daily sessions begin at 3:30pm and 7pm, with additional sessions at 8:30am and noon on weekends and holidays.

Snow Camping

Off-limits in summer, Wawona's peaceful and protected Mariposa Grove is open for snow camping from December to mid-April. You'll need a wilderness permit (see p99 for where to get them in wintertime), and you must set up your tent uphill from Clothespin Tree. The Wawona campground also stays open for winter camping on a first-come, first-served basis.

The **Yosemite Cross-Country Ski Center** (☏209-372-8444) offers an overnight trip at Badger Pass ($292 per person, including meals), with instruction in snow-camping fundamentals and survival skills.

Sledding & Tubing

If tubing down a hill is more your fancy, there's a snow-play area located in Crane Flat. Badger Pass also has a tubing area for younger kids, with two-hour sessions ($15) starting at 11:30am and 2pm, tubes included.

SLEEPING

One of the biggest questions facing Yosemite visitors is where to spend the night. More than four million people visit Yosemite each year, many as day visitors but many also vying for one of the 1504 campsites or 1386 rooms and tent cabins available in the park. During the height of summer, visitors fill open reservations faster than blue jays descend on a picnic. Newcomers with visions of sleeping soundly under the stars often find that campsites and rooms are full, having been reserved months in advance.

Most lodges and campgrounds both inside and outside the park open and close at slightly different times each year, depending on weather. Always check before you go. If you're stuck without a place to sleep inside the park, look outside its borders.

Those hoping to get in touch with nature may find they're more in touch with their neighbors, who are often clanging pans, slurping beer by the fire or snoring in their tents just 10ft or 20ft away. It gets especially crowded in Yosemite Valley. Overnighters looking for a quieter, more rugged experience are better off in spots like Bridalveil Creek, Yosemite Creek and Porcupine Flat.

Campgrounds in Yosemite range from primitive tent-only sites to developed ones that can accommodate large RVs. Most have flush toilets and potable water. The exceptions are the park's three primitive sites (Tamarack Flat, Yosemite Creek and Porcupine Flat) and the Yosemite Valley backpackers' campground, which have vault (pit) toilets and require you to bring your own water or a means of purifying water from nearby streams. None of the campgrounds have showers (see the boxed text p126).

Campground elevations are important to consider. For instance, the campgrounds along Tioga Rd and in Tuolumne Meadows, some of which sit above 8000ft, may boast warm weather during the day, but come nightfall you'll be wishing you'd packed that wool sweater.

Yosemite has four campgrounds open all year: Upper Pines, Camp 4, Wawona and Hodgdon Meadow. The rest are open seasonally. For a list of the park backpackers' camps, see p99.

Yosemite Valley

While Yosemite Valley campgrounds are convenient to many of the park's major sights and activities, they're also very crowded, often noisy and definitely lacking in privacy. Don't camp here expecting to get away from it all – for solitude, you're better off in less-visited areas of the park.

Yosemite Valley's three Pines campgrounds (North Pines, Upper Pines and Lower Pines) are all located east of Yosemite Village at the far end of the Valley and are open to both RVs and tent campers.

Camping

Upper Pines CAMPGROUND $
(Map p60; campsites $20; ☺year-round; ☻) With 238 sites spread under a forest of pine, Yosemite's second-largest campground is close-quarters camping at its finest. It sits along the bus and pedestrian road to the Nature Center at Happy Isles and trailhead, only a short walk away from Curry Village.

Lower Pines CAMPGROUND $
(Map p60; campsites $20; ☺Mar-Oct; ☻) Directly west of North Pines, Lower Pines is smaller but almost identical to Upper Pines, set amid the trees on the south shore of the Merced River. It has 60 sites.

North Pines CAMPGROUND $
(Map p60; campsites $20; ☺Apr-Sep; ☻) Across the Merced River from Lower Pines, the 81-site North Pines campground is probably the quietest of the Valley's campgrounds.

HOW TO SCORE A CAMPSITE IN YOSEMITE

If you're one of those folks who can't bear the thought of driving four hours or more without knowing whether there's a campsite waiting for you, then you'd better make a reservation if you want to camp in Yosemite. It's the only way to ensure you'll have a place to lay your head. However, if you'd rather chance it – or if you couldn't get (or never got around to making) a reservation before you came – there are options.

Reservations

Reservations for all campgrounds within the park are handled by **Recreation.gov** (☑877-444-6777, 518-885-3639; www.recreation.gov; ⊗7am-7pm Nov-Feb, to 9pm Mar-Oct). See the chart on p122 for a list of which campgrounds require reservations. Campsites can be reserved up to five months in advance. Reservations become available on the 15th of every month in one-month blocks. Be sure to act quickly (preferably online), as most dates in summer fill up the first day reservations become available – usually within minutes!

If you still have questions regarding the whole process or simply wish to speak with a human being in Yosemite, call the **Yosemite Valley Campground Office** (☑information only 209-372-8502). Also, check the website of **Yosemite National Park** (www.nps.gov /yose). Unaffiliated with the park, **Yosemitesites.com** (www.yosemitesites.com) is a good place to conduct initial research; you can see exactly what's available before reserving a site through Recreation.gov.

If you already have a reservation, proceed directly to the campground gate to check in. If you're going to be more than 24 hours late, call the campground office; otherwise you may lose your reservation.

Trying Your Luck

If you arrive at Yosemite without reservations, there are several options. Practically every day, reservation-only campsites become available due to cancellations or early departures, and these are sold on a first-come, first-served basis from the reservation offices. If nothing's available when they open, you can put your name on a waiting list and return at the prescribed time (usually 3pm) to find out if you've gotten one.

YOSEMITE VALLEY

If you want to stay in Yosemite Valley, you have two options, though in summer you'll need to be there before opening time for either. Option one is the first-come, first-served, walk-in campground at **Camp 4**. A lawn chair line starts forming by 6:30am for summer weekends, and the benefit of getting a site here is that you can stay for up to seven nights.

Option two is the **Yosemite Valley Campground Reservation Office** (Map p60; ☑information only 209-372-8502; ⊗8am-5pm) in the day-use parking lot near Camp Curry. It rarely has multiple-night cancellations, but it has more potential sites available than Camp 4.

OTHER PARK AREAS

Outside the Valley, the first-come, first-served campgrounds are Bridalveil Creek, Tamarack Flat, White Wolf, Yosemite Creek, Porcupine Flat and half the sites at Tuolumne Meadows (see p223 for more details on how to get first-come, first-served sites). Or you can stop by one of the other reservation offices:

Wawona (Map p70; ☑209-375-9535; ⊗8am-5pm late May–early Oct) On Chilnualna Falls Rd.

Big Oak Flat (Map p71; ☑209-379-2123; ⊗8am-5pm mid-Apr–mid-Oct) Next to the Big Oak Information Station; no waiting list so be here when it opens to scoop up cancellations.

Tuolumne Meadows (Map p76; ☑209-372-4025; ⊗8am-5pm Jul-Sep) Near the campground entrance.

YOSEMITE NATIONAL PARK CAMPGROUNDS

CAMPGROUND	LOCATION	DESCRIPTION	NO OF SITES	ELEVATION
Hodgdon Meadow	Big Oak Flat Rd	Close to park entrance; utilitarian, can be crowded & noisy; easy drive to Yosemite Valley	105	4872ft
Crane Flat	Crane Flat	Large family campground across five loops; varied sites; easy drive to Yosemite Valley	166	6192ft
Bridalveil Creek	Glacier Point Rd	Near Glacier Point; some attractive sites; removed from Valley crowds	110	7200ft
Porcupine Flat	Tioga Rd	Primitive, close to road but relatively quiet; RV access front half only	52	8100ft
Tamarack Flat	Tioga Rd	Quiet, secluded, primitive; accessed via rough 3-mile road; tent only	52	6315ft
White Wolf	Tioga Rd	Only nonprimitive campground in area; walking distance to store and restaurant	74	8000ft
Yosemite Creek	Tioga Rd	Park's most secluded, quiet, primitive campground; accessed via rough 4.5-mile road; tent only	75	7659ft
Tuolumne Meadows	Tuolumne Meadows	Park's biggest campground, many sites well dispersed over large, forested area	304	8600ft
Wawona	Wawona	Located along river; nicer sites in back section (open summer only); short drive to store	93	4000ft
Camp 4	Yosemite Valley	Walk-in campground, popular with climbers; fee is per person; campers share sites; tent-only	35	4000ft
Lower Pines	Yosemite Valley	Smaller Valley campground; minimum privacy	60	4000ft
North Pines	Yosemite Valley	Smaller Valley campground; pleasant sites, slightly removed from development; adjacent to stables	81	4000ft
Upper Pines	Yosemite Valley	Largest Valley campground, expect little privacy, especially in summer; close to Happy Isles	238	4000ft

All campgrounds have: bear-proof boxes, parking, picnic tables, fire pits and trash cans.

 Drinking Water   *Flush Toilets*   *Ranger Station Nearby*   *Wheelchair Accessible*

Although most of its sites are similar to those at the other Pines, it boasts a handful of riverside sites that are comparatively outstanding.

Camp 4
CAMPGROUND **$**

(Map p60; tent sites person $5; ☉year-round) Formerly known as Sunnyside, legendary Camp 4 is Yosemite's only first-come, first-served campground and, for over half a century, has been hub and home for Valley climbers. Outside climbing season, however, you'll find as many families (who couldn't get into the Pines campgrounds) as you will rock jocks. Each of the 35 sites holds six tents, so be ready to share your table, your campfire and the night's conversation with others. It's a fun, low-key place. It's also a walk-in campground; cars must be left in an adjacent parking lot, and sites are for tent campers only. The check-in kiosk opens at 8:30am; from Thursday through Saturday in summer, be in line by 6:30am.

Backpackers' Campground
CAMPGROUND **$**

(tent sites per person $5; ☉Apr–mid-Oct) The 20 quiet, wooded sites at Yosemite Valley's backpackers' campground are open only to backpackers holding valid wilderness permits. It's a walk-in, self-registration campground, reached via a bridge over Tenaya Creek from the west end of North Pines campground. It has vault toilets, but no potable water.

Lodging

Yosemite Valley offers a fair range of accommodations, from simple tent cabins to standard motel units to luxurious

OPEN (APPROX)	RESERVATION REQUIRED?	DAILY FEE	FACILITIES	PAGE
year-round	mid-Apr–mid-Oct	$14-20		126
Jun-Sep	yes	$20		126
Jul–early Sep	no	$14		124
Jul-Sep	no	$10		126
Jul-Sep	no	$10		126
Jul–early Sep	no	$14		126
Jul–mid Sep	no	$10		126
Jul-Sep	half reserved	$20		127
year-round	Apr-Sep	$20		125
year-round	no	$5 per person		122
Mar-Oct	yes	$20		120
Apr-Sep	yes	$20		120
year-round	mid-Mar–Nov	$20		120

 Dogs Allowed (On Leash)   Grocery Store Nearby   Restaurant Nearby   Payphone   RV Dump Station

accommodations at the historic Ahwahnee. Tent cabins at Curry Village and Housekeeping Camp are great for families who wish to avoid both exorbitant hotel costs and the labor of setting up camp.

Ahwahnee Hotel HISTORIC HOTEL **$$$**
(Map p60; ☎209-372-1407; r from $449; ✳@✥🖵) A National Historic Landmark, the Ahwahnee has been offering its guests the royal treatment since 1927. A stunning work of architecture, the hotel is by far the most luxurious place in the park. The 99 rooms, all tastefully decorated with Native American touches, boast great views and supremely comfortable beds. Other options include 24 cottages out back and a handful of suites. Tucked away in its own quiet, secluded corner of the Valley, the Ahwahnee

is worth a visit even if you're not staying overnight. The hotel features an upscale restaurant, a café and friendly bar, a swimming pool, occasional evening programs and an amazing series of public common rooms.

Yosemite Lodge at the Falls MOTEL **$$**
(Map p60; ☎209-372-1274; r $191-218; @✥🖵) Located a short walk from the base of Yosemite Falls, the modest and meandering Yosemite Lodge makes for great family accommodations, thanks to its giant swimming pool, an array of hosted activities, tours, bike rentals, a small amphitheater, a store and 226 spacious 'lodge' rooms and a few bigger 'family' rooms. Its 19 'standard' rooms are comfy for couples but about as exciting as a Motel 6 in Barstow, California. There are also restaurants and a bar on the premises.

LODGING RESERVATIONS IN YOSEMITE

Nearly all the lodging in Yosemite National Park, from tent cabins and High Sierra Camps to the Ahwahnee Hotel, is managed by **DNC Parks & Resorts** (☎801-559-4884; www .yosemitepark.com). The only accommodations DNC doesn't manage are the Ostrander Ski Hut and the homes and cabins in Foresta (a private vacation settlement south of Big Oak Flat Rd), Yosemite West and the Redwoods in Yosemite.

Reservations are available through DNC 366 days in advance of your arrival date. Places get snapped up early for summer months, especially on weekends and holidays, but if you're flexible, there's often some space available on short notice, especially midweek. You can go on the website and easily view everything that's available.

If you roll into the park without a reservation, the Yosemite Valley Visitor Center and all the lodging front desks have courtesy phones so you can inquire about room availability throughout the park. That said, it's important to remember that rooms *rarely* become available midsummer.

Despite the number of rooms, the place fills up a year in advance (so plan ahead).

Housekeeping Camp   TENT CABINS $
(Map p60; 4-person tent cabin $93; ☉Apr-Oct) A 10-minute walk from Yosemite Village, Housekeeping Camp is a conglomeration of 266 tent cabins grouped tightly together on the southern shore of the Merced River. Each cabin has concrete walls, a canvas roof, an electrical outlet, cots, an enclosed outdoor table and a fire pit. The complex can feel pretty cramped, especially with all the cars parked around the cabins, but they're pleasant nonetheless. One guest offered a friendly tip: bring a space heater if it's cold. Our tip – expect noise and bring your sense of humor. The cabins along the riverbank are excellent. Housekeeping Camp offers the only lodging facilities that allow cooking. There's a small store (where you can get newspapers), hot showers ($5 for nonguests) and laundry facilities (from 7am to 10pm). Bring your own linens and pillows or rent bedding from the front desk (about $2.50 per item per person).

Curry Village   CABINS, MOTEL $$
(Map p60; tent cabins $112-120, cabins without/ with bath $127/168, r $191; ☀) Resembling a cross between a summer camp and a labor camp, the vast, crowded and historic Curry Village offers several types of accommodations. The 319 canvas tent cabins sleep up to five people each and include linens but lack heating, electrical outlets and fire pits. Cars must park outside the cabin area, however, which cuts down on the noise. Some tents have propane heaters that can be used during winter. The wooden cabins are a bit nicer: some share central bathroom units and have propane heaters but are still crowded together;

and some boast private baths, electric heat and outlets, plus more spacious and cozy quarters. Its Stoneman House also contains 18 straightforward motel-style rooms (including a loft suite sleeping up to six) without televisions or phones.

Glacier Point & Badger Pass

Camping

Bridalveil Creek   CAMPGROUND $
(Map p66; Glacier Point Rd; campsites $14; ☉Jul-early Sep; ☀) If the Valley's stewing through a summer heat wave, remember that the altitude here (7200ft) keeps things much cooler. Tucked 25 miles (a mere 40 minutes) away from the Valley buzz, this 110-site campground is the only developed place to stay in the Glacier Point Rd area. Sites are well spaced beneath pretty pine forest, and the ones near the amphitheater front a long granite outcropping that's perfect for watching the sunset in solitude. Located 8 miles up from Hwy 41, it's first-come, first-served, has drinking water and flush toilets, and there's a horse camp at the back.

Lodging

Yosemite West   ACCOMMODATIONS SERVICES $$-$$$
(Map p66; www.yosemitewest.com; accommodations $100-300) This private development rents contemporary homes, cabins, rooms and apartments in a community just west of Hwy 41. Although it is outside the park proper, Yosemite West is accessible only from inside the park. Look for the turnoff about half a mile south of the intersection with Glacier Point Rd. Drive about a mile

and you'll reach a sign, where there are maps and phone numbers of the local establishments. Rates are for double occupancy, but larger units are available; prices rise with the size of the group.

Inside the Yosemite West development are also a few B&Bs, including the following:

Yosemite Peregrine (☎209-372-8517, 800-396-3639; www.yosemiteperegrine.com; 7509 Henness Circle; r $195-290; ⓦ)

Yosemite West High Sierra (☎209-372-4808; www.yosemitehighsierra.com; 7460 Henness Ridge Rd; r $225-290)

Wawona

Camping

Wawona CAMPGROUND $

(Map p70; campsites $20; ⏱year-round; 🐾) The south fork of the Merced River cuts through this southernmost section of Yosemite, and this campground includes some sites situated right alongside its banks. It's a pleasant place to set up your tent or RV, though some of the nicer 93 spots are in the back section and are open only during summer (approximately May to September), when the whole campground goes on the reservation system. The rest of the year it's first-come, first-served. Horse sites are available.

Lodging

Wawona Hotel HISTORIC HOTEL $$

(Map p70; ☎209-375-6556; r without/with bath incl breakfast $147/217; ⏱mid-Mar–Dec; ⓦ🏊👪) This National Historic Landmark, dating from 1879, is a collection of six graceful, New England–style buildings, each painted white and lined with wide porches. The 104 rooms come with Victorian furniture and other period items, and most open up onto a verandah. About half the rooms share baths, and nice robes are provided for the walk there. Rooms with private facilities are a bit larger, and most rooms can be configured to connect to others, which is handy for families. None has a TV or phone. The grounds are lovely, with a tennis court and a spacious lawn dotted with Adirondack chairs. There's an excellent restaurant in the main building, as well as bar service nightly in the lobby lounge or out on the porch.

Redwoods in Yosemite ACCOMMODATIONS SERVICES $$$

(Map p70; ☎209-375-6666, 877-753-8566; www.redwoodsinyosemite.com; 8038 Chilnualna Falls Rd; homes per night $250-800; ⓦ🐾) This private enterprise rents some 130 fully furnished accommodations of various sizes and levels of comfort, from rustic log cabins to spacious six-bedroom vacation homes. (Hot tub, anyone?) There's a three-night minimum stay in summer and during holidays; two nights otherwise. The main office (where there is free coffee and tantalizing fresh popcorn) is 2 miles east of Hwy 41 on Chilnualna Falls Rd; look for the junction just north of the Wawona Store.

> **CAMPSITE SCALPING**
>
> After years of complaints, in 2011 the park began cracking down on the resale of campsites. At check-in, the person listed on the reservation is now required to be present and show identification, and it is no longer possible to change the name on a camping reservation without canceling it.

Big Oak Flat Road & Tioga Road

Camping

If you're in the mood for some solitude and crisper evening air, you'll find a number of options along Tioga Rd (Hwy 120) as it heads east from Crane Flat to Tuolumne Meadows. When it's been a light snow season, early birds may get the place all to themselves. The four campgrounds along Tioga Rd operate on a first-come, first-served basis, and two of them are the most rugged, quiet and beautiful in the park. White Wolf offers flush toilets and running water, while the other three are primitive, with only vault toilets and no water tap, so be sure to bring your own water or be prepared to purify it from adjacent streams.

Next door to the Big Oak Flat Information Station, the staff at the small **Campground Reservation Office** (Map p71 ☎209-379-2123; ⏱8am-5pm, closed mid-Oct–mid-Apr) offers advice on camping options and posts information on site availability at the first-come, first-served campgrounds at Tamarack, Yosemite Creek, Porcupine Flat and White Wolf, though they don't assign sites. Come in at 8am to see if there are any cancellations at Hodgdon Meadow or Crane Flat campgrounds.

Hodgdon Meadow
CAMPGROUND $

(Map p71; campsites $14-20; ⊙year-round; 🐾) Just east of the Big Oak Flat Entrance, this popular campground has 105 decent sites; a few of the nicer ones are walk-ins, though you won't have to go more than 20yd. All campsites here must be reserved mid-April to mid-October but are first-come, first-served the rest of the year.

Crane Flat
CAMPGROUND $

(Map p71; campsites $20; ⊙Jun-Sep; 🐾) Around 8 miles east of the Big Oak Flat Entrance is this campground, which sits near the Crane Flat store and the junction with Tioga Rd. Sites lie along five different loops, most in the trees and some very nicely dispersed (there's 166 in total). The central location is great for those wanting to split their time between Tuolumne Meadows and Yosemite Valley. Reservations are required year-round; it can open late during high snow years.

Tamarack Flat
CAMPGROUND $

(Map p72; tent sites $10; ⊙Jul-Sep) One of the most serene and spacious places in the park to set up your tent is 3 miles down a rough, barely paved road that's as steep and narrow as it is woodsy and beautiful. Expect about a 15-minute drive off Tioga Rd; RVs and trailers aren't recommended. The 52 tent-only sites are well dispersed among trees, with some near a creek – which lends the campground a very open feel, with lots of sun and sky. The parts of the park accessible by road are rarely this quiet.

White Wolf
CAMPGROUND $

(Map p72; campsites $14; ⊙Jul–early Sep; 🐾) Don't feel like cooking over the ol' Coleman every night but don't want to deal with Valley throngs? Located north of Tioga Rd on a mile-long spur road, this 74-site campground, adjacent to the White Wolf Lodge and store, enjoys a relaxed setting among pine trees and granite boulders beside a lazy stream. It's an attractive and convenient alternative to the food options available to Valley campers without forsaking *all* the creature comforts of civilization. There's also a backpackers' campground.

Yosemite Creek
CAMPGROUND $

(Map p72; tent sites $10; ⊙Jul–mid-Sep; 🐾) Halfway down this rutted road, you may ask yourself if it's really worth it. Don't fret, it is. Drive 4.5 miles (about 20 minutes) down a stretch of the old Tioga Rd – a narrow, winding and very chopped-up piece of roadway that's no good for RVs or trailers – and you find yourself in the most secluded, spacious and serene car-accessible campground in the park. The 75 sites are surprisingly well dispersed: some in the trees, others in the open. A trail from here leads to the top of Yosemite Falls.

Porcupine Flat
CAMPGROUND $

(Map p72; campsites $10; ⊙Jul-Sep) If you want easy access to Tioga Rd and don't mind treating or bringing your own water, try this 52-site campground, which sits about halfway between Crane Flat and Tuolumne Meadows, the latter only a 20-minute drive away. The sites up front can handle RVs and campers, but the quieter and more rustic back half is for tents only. There's some road noise in the daytime, but it dissipates after dark. At 8100ft, it's the second-highest developed campground in the park, and a good place to spend the night acclimatizing before hitting the high country.

SHOWERING IN & AROUND YOSEMITE

Yosemite campers have one thing in common: they all need a wash. No campgrounds in the park have showers. Should you feel the need to remove that four-day layer of grime or wash your hair, head to the public showers at Curry Village or Housekeeping Camp. Both places have hot showers and charge about $5 for nonguests. No public shower facilities exist at Wawona or Tuolumne Meadows.

The following are some handy pay showers outside the park:

Mono Vista RV Park (☎760-647-6401; Hwy 395, Lee Vining; showers $2.50; ⊙9am-6pm Apr-Oct)

Indian Flat RV Park (☎209-379-2339, www.indianflatrvpark.com; 9988 Hwy 140, El Portal; showers $3; ⊙9am-9pm year-round)

High Sierra RV Park (☎559-683-7662; 40389 Hwy 41, Oakhurst; showers $4; ⊙8am-7pm year-round)

Lodging

White Wolf Lodge
CABINS $$

(Map p72; tent cabins $99, cabins with bath $120; ☺Jul–mid-Sep) This complex enjoys its own little world a mile up a spur road, away from the hubbub and traffic of Hwy 120 and the Valley. It also features nice hiking trails to Lukens and Harden Lakes. There are 24 spartan tent cabins and four very in-demand hard-walled cabins housed in two duplex buildings. There's also a dining room and a tiny counter-service store. The four-bedded tent cabins include linens, candles and wood stoves with wood, but have no electricity; they share central baths. A step up are the hard-walled cabins, which have the feel of a rustic motel room. Each unit contains a private bath, two double beds, a porch and propane heat. The generator cuts out at 11pm, so you'll need a flashlight until early morning.

Tuolumne Meadows

Camping

Tuolumne Meadows
CAMPGROUND $

(Map p76; campsites $20; ☺Jul-Sep; 🐾) This is the largest campground in the park, with 304 sites for tents or RVs (35ft limit). Despite its size, many of the sites are tucked into the trees, making the place feel far less crowded than other park campgrounds. Some of the sites in the 'E' and 'F' sections are delightfully peaceful, and 'A' is adjacent to the Tuolumne River. At 8600ft, it also includes a horse camp, group camp and walk-in backpackers' campground for those with wilderness permits. Half the sites here are on the reservation system, while the other half are kept first-come, first-served.

Lodging

Tuolumne Meadows Lodge
TENT CABINS $$

(Map p76; ☑information 209-372-8413; tent cabins $107; ☺mid-Jun–mid-Sep) Don't let the name confuse you. This 'lodge' consists of 69 wood-framed, canvas-covered tent cabins, each set on a cement floor and boasting a prehistoric wood-burning stove, card table, roll-up canvas window and candles (no electricity). The lodge complex – which is part of the original High Sierra Camp loop – also includes a dining hall serving great breakfasts, box lunches and dinner. Baths and showers are shared, and each cabin has four twin beds or two twins and a double. Linens

are included, but bring your sleeping bag if you want to be extra warm. Cooking is prohibited. To guarantee you get a room, book 366 days in advance.

Hetch Hetchy

Camping

The only place to stay in this area is the **backpackers' campground** (Map p78; tent sites per person $5), which is one of the park's nicest. But it's brutally hot in summer and available only to holders of valid wilderness permits for Hetch Hetchy.

Once you leave the park, you can drive down any of the dirt Forest Service roads and camp for free wherever you wish. The nearest official campground is the pleasant **Dimond O Campground** (Map p78; ☑877-444-6777; www.recreation.gov; Evergreen Rd; sites $21; ☺May–mid-Sep), which lies 6 miles north of Hwy 120 on Evergreen Rd, in the Stanislaus National Forest. Some sites can be reserved; others are first-come, first-served.

Lodging

There is no park lodging in Hetch Hetchy. The nearest accommodations are at the lovely **Evergreen Lodge** (Map p78; ☑209-379-2606, 800-935-6343; www.evergreenlodge.com; 33160 Evergreen Rd; tents $75-110, cabins $175-350; ☺closed Jan; @🛜🋊), about 1.5 miles outside the park border, just south of Camp Mather (a summer camp open to San Francisco residents by lottery). The resort was completely renovated in 2009, and consists of a series of lovingly decorated and comfy cabins (each with its own cache of board games) spread out among the trees. The place has just about everything you could ask for, including a bar (complete with pool table), a general store, a restaurant, live music, horseshoes, ping-pong and all sorts of guided hikes and activities.

EATING & DRINKING

With the exception of dining at the Mountain Room Restaurant or the Wawona and Ahwahnee Hotels, Yosemite is hardly defined by its culinary wonders – except, of course, when setting comes into play. As for the food, content yourself with reliably prepared, fill-the-stomach type meals that are slightly overpriced but certainly do the trick after a good hike. Some places, such

HIGH SIERRA CAMPS

In the exquisite backcountry near Tuolumne Meadows, the exceptionally popular High Sierra Camps (Map p106) provide shelter and sustenance to hikers who'd rather not carry food or a tent. The camps – called **Vogelsang**, **Merced Lake**, **Sunrise**, **May Lake** and **Glen Aulin** – are set 6 miles to 10 miles apart along a loop trail. They consist of dormitory-style canvas tent cabins with beds, blankets or comforters, plus showers (at three camps) and a central dining tent. Guests bring their own sheets and towels. The rate is $151 per adult ($91 for children aged seven to 12), per night, including breakfast and dinner. Organized hiking or saddle trips led by ranger naturalists are also available (from $901).

A short season (roughly late June to September) and high demand require a lottery for reservations. **Applications** (☎801-559-4909; www.yosemitepark.com) are currently accepted in September and October only. If you don't have a reservation, call in February to check for cancellations. Dates vary year to year, so check the website for updates.

While the camp lodgings are only for reserved guests, each has an adjacent backpackers' campsite available to anyone with a wilderness permit. The backpackers' campsites come complete with bear boxes, toilets and potable water taps. It's also possible to reserve meals at a High Sierra Camp, which can ease the burden of carrying your own food. Meals-only spaces are limited to six per camp; use the above lottery application to reserve.

as the Tuolumne Meadows Grill (where the French fries are undoubtedly phenomenal) or the Wawona Hotel (for brunch), do have a sort of cult following among visitors in the know. Whether you're looking for a sit-down meal or a sandwich for the road, the following listings will guide you to just about every option available in Yosemite.

All Yosemite restaurants in the park are run by the park concessionaire, and everything (except dinner at the Ahwahnee) is child-friendly.

Yosemite Valley

Yosemite Village and Curry Village are the best options for relatively cheap eats and to-go items.

YOSEMITE VILLAGE

Frankly, the restaurant choices in Yosemite Village won't set the gourmands among you salivating. But, like they say, hunger's best sauce.

Village Store   SUPERMARKET $
(Map p60; ☺8am-8pm, to 10pm summer) The biggest and best grocery store in the park is located smack in the center of Yosemite Village. Whether you're after last-minute items or full-fledged dinners, there's no denying the place comes in handy. The store carries decent produce, fresh meat and fish, and even some surprising items like tofu

hotdogs, hummus, udon noodles and polenta. You'll also find a small section of camping supplies along with plenty of souvenirs.

Degnan's Deli   DELI $
(Map p60; sandwiches $6-8; ☺7am-5pm; 🖶) Likely the best of the bunch in the Yosemite Village complex, this store-cum-deli whips up fresh sandwiches, soups and lots of snacks and beverages. Good for sandwiches to go.

Degnan's Cafe   CAFE $
(Map p60; sandwiches & salads $5-10; ☺11am-6pm Apr-Sep; 🖶) Beside the deli, Degnan's Cafe serves espresso drinks, smoothies and pastries, which you can guzzle down over a newspaper purchased at one of the stands outside.

Degnan's Loft   PIZZERIA $
(Map p60; mains $8-10; ☺5-9pm Apr-Oct; 🖶) Upstairs from the café, this no-frills pizza parlor has a totally unadorned, ski-lodge feel. Despite the lack of atmosphere, it's a great spot for pizza (or veggie lasagna, chicken wings or salad) and cold beer.

Village Grill   FAST FOOD $
(Map p60; burgers $5.25-7; ☺11am-5pm Apr-Oct; 🖶) A few buildings south of the Degnan's empire, the Village Grill is a standard fast-food counter with patio seating and subpar burgers, chicken sandwiches and the like. At least the fries are good.

CURRY VILLAGE

Curry Village's dining choices are hardly exciting, but they're convenient if you're staying in one of the Curry tent cabins or returning hungry from a grueling hike via the nearby Happy Isles Trailhead.

Curry Village Taqueria
MEXICAN $

(Map p60; mains $4.50-10; ⊙11am-5pm mid-Apr-Oct; 🍴) Although it's a far cry from a proper California taqueria, this walk-up taco stand does the trick if you're craving something even vaguely Mexican. Think fast-food Mexican food. Portions are substantial.

Pizza Patio
PIZZERIA $

(Map p60; pizzas from $8; ⊙noon-10pm, shorter winter hrs; 🍴) Also called the Pizza Deck, this popular joint serves mediocre pizzas (which, after a long hike, taste amazing with a pint of beer from the bar next door), chili dogs and 'veggie bowls.' The sunny outdoor patio gets packed on summer evenings.

Curry Village Dining Pavilion
CAFETERIA $$

(Map p60; breakfast adult/child $11.50/7.75, dinner adult/child $15.25/8.25; ⊙7-10am & 5:30-8pm Apr-Oct; 🍴) All-you-can-eat breakfasts and dinners draw ravenous families to Curry Village's giant cafeteria. The breakfast is a great way to fill up before a hike, but to enjoy dinner you'll have to toss your sense of taste and summon your sense of humor. But, hey, carrying vast quantities of warm chicken and pasta, decent salads, standard soup and – if you're a kid – platefuls of jiggling green Jell-O back to the table is an experience everyone should share at least once.

Coffee Corner
CAFE $

(Map p60; pastries $2-4; ⊙6am-10pm, shorter winter hrs; 🍴) Fill up on pastries, ice cream and espresso drinks at this small cafe inside the Curry Village Dining Pavilion.

Curry Village Store
MARKET $

(Map p60; ⊙8am-10pm summer, 9am-7pm rest of year; 🍴) The Curry Village store is undoubtedly handy if you're in the neighborhood and need snacks, sodas, gifts or beer.

Curry Village Bar
BAR $

(Map p60; ⊙noon-10pm; 🍴) Directly beside the Pizza Patio window, this tiny bar pulls a couple of decent microbrews and pours a full range of cocktails.

AHWAHNEE HOTEL

🖊 Ahwahnee Dining Room
CALIFORNIAN $$$

(Map p60; 🖊209-372-1489; breakfast $7-16, lunch $16-23, dinner $26-46; ⊙7-10:30am, 11:30am-3pm & 5:30-9pm) Sit by candlelight beneath the 34ft-high beamed ceiling and lose yourself in the incredible scenery, viewed through massive picture windows – it's nothing less than spectacular. The food is excellent, though compared with the surroundings may come in second. There's a dress code at dinner, but you can wear shorts and sneakers at breakfast and lunch. The outrageously decadent Sunday brunch ($39.50) is a classic Yosemite experience. Reservations highly recommended for brunch and dinner.

Ahwahnee Bar
BAR $$

(Map p60; mains $9.50-23; ⊙11:30am-11pm) Pinching pennies? Worry not – you can still experience the Ahwahnee's charms at the casual Ahwahnee bar. Drinks aren't exactly cheap, but the atmosphere on the patio is splendid. The food (salads, wraps, sandwiches, cheese-and-fruit plates and the like) is affordable and quite good, making it an excellent choice for a light dinner.

Ahwahnee Coffee Bar
CAFE $

(pastries $4; ⊙7-10:30am; 🍴) In the morning, the bar transforms into a cafe serving espresso drinks, pastries and continental breakfast items.

YOSEMITE LODGE AT THE FALLS

Near the base of Yosemite Falls, this 'lodge' is not a single rustic building but rather a cluster of contemporary condo-type hotel units, gift shops and restaurants.

🔝TOP CHOICE Mountain Room Restaurant
NEW AMERICAN $$

(Map p60; mains $17-35; ⊙5:30-9:30pm, shorter winter hrs; 🍴) Dig into a plate of Southwestern chicken, seafood pasta, halibut, mahi-mahi or one of several cuts of deliciously grilled beef at the lodge's classy yet casual restaurant. Views of Yosemite Falls compete with the food – arguably the best in the park – for diners' attention. Great cocktails, and no reservations unless your group has eight or more.

Yosemite Lodge Food Court
CAFETERIA $

(Map p60; mains $7-12; ⊙6:30am-8:30pm Sun-Thu, to 9pm Fri & Sat; 🍴) The lodge's cheapest option is this self-service cafeteria, just behind the hotel's main lobby.

YOSEMITE NATIONAL PARK EATING & DRINKING

Sauntering over from Camp 4 for breakfast and coffee before the climb is a Valley tradition. Dinner choices include burgers, pizza, salads and pasta, with vegetarian and gluten-free options available.

Mountain Room Lounge BAR $
(Map p60; ☉4:30-11pm Mon-Fri, noon-11pm Sat & Sun; ☻) Across the courtyard from the restaurant, the Mountain Room Lounge is an undeniably fine place to knock back a couple of cocktails, thanks to the spacious interior and big windows. In winter, order a s'mores kit (graham crackers, chocolate squares and marshmallows) to roast in the open-pit fireplace. Kids welcome until 9pm.

Glacier Point & Badger Pass

When the road is open, the unexciting **snack bar** (Map p66; ☉9am-5pm) at Glacier Point is your only food option.

In the wintertime (until 4pm), Badger Pass runs a **fast food grill** (mains $3-8) serving pizza, burgers, nachos and chicken strips. On weekends and holidays, the **Snowflake Room** (mains under $10; ☉11am-4pm) has a cozy wood-beamed room offering sandwiches and salads, a bar and a view of the lifts. Its walls are covered with cool old ski photos and pieces of vintage ski equipment.

Wawona

The Wawona General Store (Map p70), a short walk from the Wawona Hotel, offers a few picnic and camping items but focuses more on snacks and gifts.

Wawona Hotel Dining Room AMERICAN $$
(Map p70; ☎209-375-1425; breakfast & lunch $11-15, dinner $19-30; ☉7:30-10am, 11:30am-1:30pm, 5:30-9pm Easter-Dec; ☝☻) Inside the historic 1879 Wawona Hotel, this old-fashioned white-tablecloth dining room is lit by beautiful painted lamps, and the Victorian detail makes it an enchanting place to have an upscale (though somewhat overpriced) meal. 'Tasteful, casual attire' is the rule for dinner dress. Seating is first-come, first-served, though reservations are required for parties of six or more. The restaurant is open during the Thanksgiving and Christmas seasons, and it puts on a barbecue on the lawn every Saturday

during summer. The Wawona's wide, white porch makes a snazzy destination for evening cocktails, served from 5pm to 9:30pm. In the hotel's lobby – which doubles as its lounge – listen for pianist Tom Bopp, who's been running through his repertoire of Yosemite-themed chestnuts since 1983.

Pine Tree Market MARKET $
(Map p70; 7995 Chilnualna Falls Rd; ☉8am-8pm summer, 8:30am-6:30pm rest of year) This tiny and superfriendly market sells groceries and bags of divine locally roasted coffee (take a deep breath in the aisles), and in summer it sells flats of seasonal fruit grown by regional farmers. It's located a mile east of Hwy 41 amid the redwoods in Yosemite; turn east off Chilnualna Falls Rd, which is just north of the Pioneer History Center.

Big Oak Flat Road & Tioga Road

A mile north of Tioga Rd, the White Wolf Lodge area (Map p72) has a miniscule store that sells snacks, ice-cream bars and coffee. At lunchtime, it has prepared sandwiches available, and there's always a vegetarian option available. The small, rustic **dining room** (☎209-372-8416; breakfast $10.75, dinner $24; ☉7:30-9:30am & 6-8pm) is open for a buffet breakfast and in the evening for family-style dinners inside or on the front porch. Reservations are highly advised for dinner, with four seating times available.

Tuolumne Meadows

As with everything else along Tioga Rd, the eating establishments in Tuolumne Meadows are open roughly late June to mid-September only. Exact dates depend on snowfall.

Tuolumne Meadows Store MARKET $
(Map p76; ☉8am-8pm; ☻) Browse the busy aisles of the Tuolumne Meadows Store, which stocks just about every necessity item you could have possibly forgotten: wine, beer, chips, dehydrated backpacking food, a smattering of produce, tofu dogs, dorky hats, camp cups, firewood, candy bars, fishing tackle and camping supplies, all at marked-up prices.

TOP CHOICE ⟩ **Tuolumne Meadows Grill** FAST FOOD $
(Map p76; mains $4-9; ☉8am-5pm; ☻) You can hardly say you've visited Tuolumne without smacking down a burger and a basket

of fries in the parking lot in front of the Tuolumne Grill. The soft-serve ice-cream cones and hearty breakfasts – not to mention the people-watching – are equally mandatory.

Tuolumne Meadows Lodge　AMERICAN $$
(Map p76; ☑209-372-8413; breakfast $7-12.50, dinner $10-$26; ⊘7-9am & 5:45-8pm; ⊛) For yet another classic Yosemite experience, make a dinner reservation (for breakfast, just show up) at the Tuolumne Meadows Lodge. The place is as basic-looking as they come, but the breakfasts are hearty and the dinners are good. Best of all, good company is pretty much guaranteed (or at least required): tables are shared. Snacks and cold drinks are sold all day at the lodge lobby.

Hetch Hetchy

There are no eating establishments or stores in Hetch Hetchy, just one excellent place a mile outside the park border.

TOP **Evergreen Lodge**　CALIFORNIAN $$
CHOICE
(Map p78; ☑209-379-2606; www.evergreenlodge .com; 33160 Evergreen Rd; breakfast & lunch mains $10-14, dinner mains $18-28; ⊘7-10:30am & noon-3pm, plus 5:30-10:30pm May-Oct & 5-9pm Nov-Apr; ⚐⊛) Creative and satisfying, the Evergreen's restaurant serves some of the best meals around, with big and delicious breakfasts, three types of burgers (Black Angus beef, buffalo and veggie) and dinner choices including dishes like rib-eye steak, grilled venison and braised seitan. The homey wooden tavern is a perennial favorite for evening cocktails, beers on tap over a game of pool and live music on select weekends. A general store fills the gaps with to-go sandwiches, snacks and dreamy gelato.

INFORMATION

Bookstores

Almost every park store, from the gift shop at Yosemite Lodge to the convenience stores at Wawona and Crane Flat, offers a variety of books and park maps. For the best selection of information about the park and Sierra Nevada region, visit the **Yosemite Conservancy Bookstore** (www.yosemiteconservancystore.com), adjacent to the Yosemite Valley Visitor Center. The store is operated by the nonprofit Yosemite Conservancy, and proceeds benefit the park.

Hiking maps and guides can be found in all the park's sports shops, visitor centers and wilderness centers.

The Ansel Adams Gallery in Yosemite Village also carries a great selection of books, including fine-art and photography volumes.

Internet Access

Bassett Memorial Library (Map p70; Chilnualna Falls Rd; ⊘1-6pm Mon-Fri, 10am-3pm Sat, shorter hrs fall-spring) Free internet terminals in Wawona.

Camp Curry Lounge (Curry Village) Behind the registration office; free wi-fi.

Degnan's Cafe (Map p60; Yosemite Village; per min 25¢) Pay terminals in this café adjacent to Degnan's Deli.

Mariposa County Public Library (Girls Club Bldg, 58 Cedar Ct, Yosemite Valley; ⊘8:30am-11:30am Mon, 2-5pm Tue, 8:30am-12:30pm Wed, 4-7pm Thu) Free internet terminals available.

Yosemite Lodge at the Falls (Map p60; Yosemite Valley; per min 25¢) Pay terminals are in the lobby. Wi-fi costs $6 per day for non-guests.

Internet Resources

Though it's hard to tell who's at the helm, the regularly updated **Yosemite Forum** (www .yosemite.ca.us/forum) features discussion boards on a wide range of subjects, from trip planning to rock climbing. The **Yosemite Blog** (www.yosemiteblog.com) always makes for an interesting browse. For more useful websites (including park service sites), see p19.

Media

For newspapers in Yosemite Valley, hit the coin-operated boxes outside Degnan's Deli, in front of the stores at Curry Village and at Housekeeping Camp. In Tuolumne Meadows, they're sold in front of the store and at the Tuolumne Meadows Lodge.

Money

Stores in Yosemite Village, Curry Village and Wawona all have ATMs, as does the Ahwahnee Hotel and Yosemite Lodge.

Post

Tuolumne Meadows (Map p76; ⊘9am-5pm Mon-Fri, to 1pm Sat, closed mid-Sep–mid-Jun) Inside the Tuolumne Meadows Store.

Wawona (Map p70; ⊘9am-5pm Mon-Fri, to noon Sat) At Wawona Store.

Yosemite Lodge (Map p60; ⊘12:30-2:45pm Mon-Fri) Next to the pool.

Yosemite Village Post Office (Map p60; ⊙8:30am-5pm Mon-Fri, 10am-noon Sat) To the right (east) of the Wilderness Center.

Telephone

There are pay phones at every developed location throughout the park. Cell-phone reception is sketchy, depending on your location, and AT&T, Verizon and Sprint have the best coverage.

Visitor Centers

Rangers staff the park visitor centers and smaller information stations, and can answer questions and suggest suitable hiking trails, activities and sights. The visitor centers offer excellent displays on park history and the local environment, as well as a range of maps, hiking and climbing guides, geology and ecology books, and gift items. The information stations, while less elaborate than the visitor centers, are still good places to ask questions, get your bearings and purchase useful books and maps.

Big Oak Flat Information Station (Map p71; ☑209-379-1899; ⊙8am-5pm May-Sep) See also p71.

Tuolumne Meadows Visitor Center (Map p76; ☑209-372-0263; ⊙9am-6pm late spring-early fall) See also p75.

Wawona Information Station (Map p70; ☑209-375-9531; ⊙8:30am-5pm May-Sep) Located inside the Hill's Studio building next to the Wawona Hotel; see also p68.

Yosemite Valley Visitor Center (Map p60; ☑209-372-0299; ⊙9am-7:30pm in summer, shorter hrs rest of year) The park's main visitor center; also see p58.

Wilderness Centers

Yosemite's two main wilderness centers are in Yosemite Valley and Tuolumne Meadows. At both, hikers can buy maps and guidebooks, check current weather and trail conditions, get helpful tips on planning and packing, and – most importantly – obtain wilderness permits. You can also rent the all-important bear-proof food canisters ($5 per week; see p242).

Advance reservations for wilderness permits cannot be made through the wilderness centers themselves. For information on reserving wilderness permits, as well as where to get them in wintertime, see p99.

Yosemite Valley Wilderness Center (Map p60; ☑209-372-0745; ⊙7:30am-5pm summer, 8am-5pm fall & spring, closed winter)

Tuolumne Meadows Wilderness Center (Map p76; ☑209-372-0309; ⊙approx 8am-4:30pm Jun & Sep, 7:30am-5pm Jul-Aug) See also p75.

Big Oak Flat Wilderness Center (Map p71; ☑209-379-1967) Inside the Big Oak Flat Information Station.

Wawona Information Station (Map p70; ☑209-375-9531; ⊙8:30am-5pm May-Sep)

Hetch Hetchy Entrance Station (Map p78; ☑209-379-1922; ⊙7am-9pm summer, 8am-5pm winter)

GETTING AROUND

For information on public transit into and out of the park, see Getting There & Away (p230). For information on tours within the park, see p227.

Bicycle

Twelve miles of mostly flat, paved bicycle trails run up and down Yosemite Valley, making biking a fantastic way to get around. If you've ever sat in Valley traffic on a summer day, you know the merits of strapping a couple of bikes to the car. Since the Valley is flat, single-speed bikes are great. For a good two-wheeled tour of the Valley, see p113.

Car & Motorcycle

The park speed limit is 35mph, except in Yosemite Valley and by Tenaya Lake, where it drops to 25mph. The truth is that you'll mostly be driving slower than that due to traffic.

You'll find gas stations in Crane Flat, Wawona and (in summer) Tuolumne Meadows. The stations generally close after dark, but you can gas up anytime by paying at the pump with a credit card. Gas is not available in Yosemite Valley; the closest gas station to the Valley is in El Portal.

If you're in Yosemite and happen upon the unfortunate need for automotive repairs, you can call the **Village Garage** (☑209-372-8320; ⊙8am-5pm), which is across the street from the Village Store. It also offers 24-hour roadside service.

Most trailheads have free parking areas where you can leave your vehicle for several days. Make sure to put all food and scented items in a bear box. In Yosemite Valley, backpackers must park in the hikers' parking area between Curry Village and Happy Isles. Day-use visitors can use the day-use parking lots either at Curry Village or near Yosemite Village, and take the free shuttle bus around the Valley.

Overnight parking is not permitted on Tioga or Glacier Point Rds after October 15.

Free Shuttles

Yosemite offers good public transportation within Yosemite Valley and minimal service along Tioga Rd to Tuolumne Meadows. For information, schedules and departure points, check the *Yosemite Guide* or the park's website at www.nps.gov/yose/planyourvisit/bus.htm.

YOSEMITE VALLEY

The free Yosemite Valley Visitor Shuttle stops year-round at 21 numbered locations, from Happy Isles and Mirror Lake in the east (both inaccessible by car) to Yosemite Lodge in the west, with stops at all popular sites. This excellent, easy-to-use, hybrid-fuel bus service operates 7am to 10pm daily at 10- to 20-minute intervals. Small, fold-up route maps are available free at most stores and lobby desks throughout the park.

EL CAPITAN

From mid-June through early September, this free bus runs a western Valley loop from Yosemite Village to El Capitan Bridge, with stops including Camp 4 and the Four Mile Trailhead. Service is from 9am to 6pm, at 30-minute intervals.

YOSEMITE–BADGER PASS

From approximately mid-December through March (when the Badger Pass Ski Area is open), a free Badger Pass shuttle bus runs daily from Yosemite Valley in the morning, returning from the Badger Pass ski area in the afternoon at 2pm and 4:30pm.

WAWONA–YOSEMITE VALLEY

A free shuttle bus between Wawona and Yosemite Valley departs every morning from Memorial Day until sometime in October. It leaves from the Wawona Hotel at 8:30am and departs from Yosemite Lodge for its return leg at 3:30pm.

WAWONA–MARIPOSA GROVE

Between about April and October, the free Wawona–Mariposa Grove Shuttle loops between the Wawona Store, the South Entrance and Mariposa Grove from 9am until 6pm (the last bus back from Mariposa Grove) daily. Taking the bus is not only a good idea, but sometimes it's your only option for visiting the grove. The small parking lot fills up quickly, and the shuttle guarantees that you can get in even when it's full.

TUOLUMNE MEADOWS

TUOLUMNE MEADOWS–OLMSTED POINT The free Tuolumne Meadows shuttle bus plies part of Tioga Rd daily from about mid-June to mid-September (the exact schedule varies annually). The shuttle travels between Tuolumne Meadows Lodge and Olmsted Point, starting at the lodge at 7am and operating at roughly 30-minute intervals until 7pm. The last eastbound shuttle usually departs Olmsted Point at 6pm.

TUOLUMNE MEADOWS–TIOGA PASS A free shuttle travels between Tuolumne Meadows Lodge and Tioga Pass, departing the lodge at 9am, noon, 3pm and 5pm; returns depart from Tioga Pass at 9:15am, 12:15pm, 3:15pm and 5:15pm.

Hikers' Buses

YOSEMITE VALLEY–GLACIER POINT

From about mid-June to mid-September, the **Glacier Point Sightseeing Bus** (☏209-372-4386; adult/senior/child $41/35/26) loops from Yosemite Valley to Glacier Point and back, stopping at various points along the way and taking about four hours for the whole trip. It runs three times daily from about June to October. Hikers can pay for a one-way journey (adult/senior/child $25/23/15) and return to the Valley under their own steam. This is a very popular bus, so reservations must be made a day or two in advance.

YOSEMITE VALLEY–TUOLUMNE MEADOWS

TUOLUMNE MEADOWS TOUR & HIKERS' BUS Departing daily from approximately July through September, this **bus** (☏209-372-4386; www.yosemitepark.com) leaves from Curry Village at 8am, from Yosemite Village at 8:05am and from Yosemite Lodge at 8:20am, stopping at Crane Flat, White Wolf, May Lake Junction, Olmsted Point and Tenaya Lake. It arrives at the Tuolumne Meadows Store about 10:25am and Tuolumne Meadows Lodge at 10:35am.

On the return trip, the bus leaves Tuolumne Meadows Lodge at 2:05pm and arrives at Curry Village at 4:15pm, making all the same stops in between. You can also flag the bus for pickup from any trailhead or ask the driver to drop you at a trailhead along the way.

Reservations are strongly recommended. They can be made up to one week in advance, or stop by the tour desk at Yosemite Lodge. Fares vary according to your trip. From Yosemite Valley, a one-way adult ticket to Tuolumne Meadows costs $14.50; children (aged five to 12) ride for half price.

YARTS To get from the Valley to Tuolumne and other points along Tioga Rd, you can also ride the **YARTS** (www.yarts.com) buses heading to Mammoth Lakes (see p148). The 5pm YARTS bus is the only eastbound evening service from the Valley to Tuolumne.

Around Yosemite

Includes »

Why Go?

Though many consider Yosemite the crème de la crème of the Sierras, you may just find you prefer the flavor of other regions around it. You'll find many who'd argue the unbeatable merits of the Eastern Sierra, which is home to sights such as Mono Lake, Mammoth Lakes, hidden hot springs, shimmering alpine lakes and some of the state's most dramatic mountain scenery.

Heading to Yosemite by car or bus, you'll travel along one of four primary approaches. To the west, Hwys 120 and 140 provide the main access routes, with wonderful little gold-rush-era towns and groovy old-time saloons. To the south, Hwy 41 passes through pastoral fishing lakes and mountain roads, and the eastern route over Tioga Pass is the highest auto pass in California.

Best Places to Eat

» Narrow Gauge Inn (p142)

» Lakefront Restaurant (p151)

» Yosemite Bug Rustic Mountain Resort (p137)

» Savoury's (p136)

» Whoa Nellie Deli (p145)

Best Places to Stay

» River Rock Inn (p136)

» Groveland Hotel (p139)

» Narrow Gauge Inn (p142)

» Sierra Sky Ranch (p140)

When to Go
Mammoth Lakes

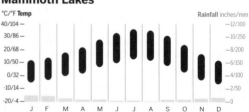

Dec–Mar
Take a wintertime romp through snowy forests.

Jul & Aug
Head for the mountains for wilderness adventures and high-altitude sunshine.

Sep & Oct
Brilliant fall foliage lights up the woods and canyons.

ⓘ Information

Roadside Heritage (www.roadsideheritage .org) Free audio downloads about the history and sights along Hwy 395; excellent for road trips.

Sierra Web (www.thesierraweb.com) Area events and links to local visitor information in the Eastern Sierra.

US Forest Service (www.fs.fed.us/r5/forests .shtml) Comprehensive portal for national forests in California.

ⓘ Getting Around

Hwys 120 and 108 both lead over the Sierras to Hwy 395, the main north–south artery through the Eastern Sierra. Due to heavy snowfall, both are only open roughly May or June through

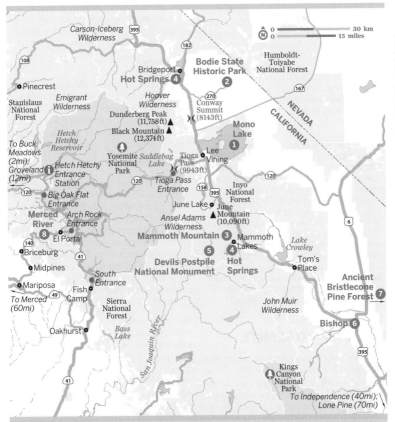

Around Yosemite Highlights

❶ Marvel at the tufa formations at **Mono Lake** (p145) against the backdrop of the Eastern Sierra

❷ Amble around the evocative ghost town of **Bodie** (p146)

❸ Shred a path through fresh powder from the dizzying peak of **Mammoth Mountain** (p149)

❹ Soak in an Eastern Sierra **hot spring** under a glittering night sky near Bridgeport or Mammoth (p150)

❺ Shuttle out to the bizarre volcanic formation of **Devils Postpile** (p152)

❻ Go bouldering in the dramatic landscape near **Bishop** (p152) at the

Buttermilks or Volcanic Tablelands

❼ Detour to the high-altitude groves of the ethereal **Ancient Bristlecone Pine Forest** (p155)

❽ Raft the **Merced River** (p136) in the swift white-water near El Portal

September. The **Yosemite Area Regional Transportation System** (YARTS; ☑877-989-2787; www.yarts.com) provides bus service to/from Yosemite; see p230 for more details.

HWY 140 A year-round YARTS route stops at all the towns west of the park between Merced and Yosemite Valley. See individual towns for details.

HWY 120 YARTS runs buses from Yosemite Valley east over Tioga Pass (Hwy 120/Tioga Rd) and south to Mammoth Lakes via Crane Flat, White Wolf, Tuolumne Meadows, Lee Vining and June Lake, stopping on demand so you can get off (but not on) at any trailhead or campground along Tioga Rd. This route runs during summer only, with daily buses in July and August, but only Saturday and Sunday service during June (after Tioga Pass opens) and September. The Mammoth-bound bus leaves the Valley Visitor Center at 5pm; it departs from Mammoth at 8am. Confirm the schedule, as it can change year-to-year.

HWY 395 Buses operated by **Eastern Sierra Transit Authority** (☑760-872-1901, 800-922-1930; www.easternsierratransitauthority.com) make round-trips between Lone Pine (the eastern gateway to Mt Whitney) and Reno (east of Lake Tahoe) on Monday, Tuesday, Thursday and Friday ($54, six hours), and between Lancaster (an Amtrak stop between LA and southern Hwy 395) and Mammoth ($40, five hours) on Monday, Wednesday and Friday, with both routes stopping at all Hwy 395 towns in between. Fares depend on distance, and reservations are recommended. There's also an express bus between Mammoth and Bishop ($6.50, one hour) that operates three times daily Monday through Friday.

WEST OF YOSEMITE

The two most important arteries into Yosemite – Hwy 140 and Hwy 120 – lie to the west. Aside from offering easy access to the national park, the highways are home to some marvelous little historic towns resting along their dusty shoulders.

Highway 140

The approach to Yosemite via Hwy 140, which parallels the bed of the long-defunct Yosemite Valley Railroad, is one of the most scenic, especially the section that meanders through Merced River Canyon. The springtime runoff makes this a spectacular spot for **river rafting**, with many miles of class III and IV rapids. See p39 for a list of outfitters.

A major transportation hub, Merced is the end of the line for Amtrak train and Greyhound bus passengers. From here, passengers can take the Yosemite Area Regional Transportation System (YARTS) bus along Hwy 140 into the park, making this route the easiest option for travelers without cars.

A 2006 rockslide buried a section of the road about 8 miles west of El Portal, and the continuing one-way traffic controls bypassing it will give you a few extra minutes to admire the scenery.

MARIPOSA
POP 2200 / ELEV 2000FT

About halfway between Merced and Yosemite Valley, at the junction of Hwys 140 and 49, Mariposa (Spanish for 'butterfly') is the largest and most interesting town near the park. It was established as a mining and railroad settlement during the gold rush.

🛏 Sleeping

River Rock Inn MOTEL $$
(☑209-966-5793; www.riverrockncafe.com; 4993 7th St; r incl breakfast $109-159; ❋🕸🐾) A bold splash of psychedelic purple and dusty orange paint spruces up what claims to be the oldest motel in town. Rooms done up in artsy earth tones have TVs but no phones, and calming ceiling fans resemble lily pads. On a quiet side street, it features a small courtyard deck and deli café serving beer and wine.

Mariposa Lodge MOTEL $$
(☑209-966-3607, 800-966-8819; www.mariposalodge.com; 5052 Hwy 140; r $119-159; ❋🕸🐾🐾) The simple, well-kept Mariposa sports clean, quiet rooms (with TVs and phones) and friendly staff. It earns pluses for its good-sized rooms and the blooming flowers that border the grounds.

Mariposa Historic Hotel HISTORIC HOTEL $$
(☑209-966-7500; www.mariposahotelinn.com; 5029 Hwy 140; r incl breakfast $122-159; ❋@🕸) This creaky 1901 building has six king or queen rooms with old-time quilts and fussy flocked wallpaper, and a corridor crammed with old town photos and newspaper clippings.

✕ Eating

Savoury's NEW AMERICAN $$
(☑209-966-7677; www.savouryrestaurant.com; 5034 Hwy 140; mains $15-30; ☺5-9pm Thu-Tue; 🖋) Now in a roomier location, upscale yet

casual Savoury's is still the best restaurant in town. Black lacquered tables and contemporary art create a tranquil window dressing for dishes like apricot- and miso-glazed pork chops, hearty pastas and steak Diane.

Happy Burger   DINER $
(www.happyburgerdiner.com; Hwy 140 at 12th St; mains $6-10; ⏰5:30am-9pm; 🛜🚲👶) Boasting the largest menu in the Sierra, this buzzing roadside joint decorated with old album covers serves the cheapest meals in Mariposa. Its all-American cuisine means burgers, sandwiches, Mexican food and a ton of sinful ice-cream desserts.

Pioneer Market   SUPERMARKET $
(5034 Coakley Circle; ⏰7am-10pm Mon-Sat, 8am-9pm Sun summer, shorter hrs winter) A good medium-sized supermarket; about a mile east of downtown on Hwy 140, turn left (north) on Coakley Circle, just past the Burger King.

❶ Information

Mariposa County Visitor Center (📞209-966-7081, 866-425-3366; www.homeofyosemite.com; 5158 N Hwy 140; ⏰8am-8pm mid-May–mid-Oct, 8am-5pm mid-Oct–mid-May) Towards the north end of town; loads of brochures on both Yosemite and the region.

❶ Getting There & Away

YARTS (📞877-989-2787; www.yarts.com) buses run year-round into Yosemite Valley (1¾ hours one way, adult/child $12/8 round-trip), from the Mariposa visitor center. Price includes park admission. See p230 for more details and information on buses from Merced to Mariposa.

MIDPINES
POP 1200 / ELEV 2400FT

There's not much to see or do in Midpines, a rural community about 25 miles west of Yosemite's Arch Rock Entrance. The highlight of this almost nonexistent town is the folksy Yosemite Bug Rustic Mountain Resort.

The small **Midpines Country Store** (6428 Hwy 140; ⏰8am-6pm winter, until 7pm summer) marks the center of 'town,' which is actually spread thin over several miles along Hwy 140. Run by the current owners for over 30 years, the store has a gas station and a pay phone.

From Midpines, Hwy 140 drops down into the beautiful Merced River Canyon.

🛏 Sleeping & Eating

🏕 **Yosemite Bug Rustic Mountain Resort**   RESORT $
(📞209-966-6666, 866-826-7108; www.yosemitebug.com; dm $25, tent cabins $45-75, r $75-155, cabins with shared bath $65-100; @🛜🏊) Tucked away on a forested hillside, this place is more like a convivial mountain retreat than a hostel. At night, a united nations of friendly folks of all ages share stories, music and excellent meals in the woodsy **café** (mains $8.50-18; ⏰7am-9pm, drinks until 11pm; 🚲) before retreating to whatever bed their money can buy – a dorm bunk, a tent cabin, a private room with shared facilities or a uniquely decorated cabin with private bathroom. Dorm dwellers have access to a communal kitchen, and the resort has a spa with a hot tub, yoga lessons and massages available. Tasty meals always include awesome vegan and vegetarian options, and filling dinners include smoked pork, trout or pasta. The resort's Bug Bus tours (see p227) offer a range of hiking trips (including overnights) to Yosemite.

KOA Campground   CAMPGROUND $
(📞209-966-2201, 800-562-9391; www.koa.com/campgrounds/yosemite-west; campsite $40-50, cabins $68-155; ⏰Mar-Oct; 🛜🏊👶🐾) Mostly crammed with RVs, the KOA has pseudo-log cabins that can sleep four to six people, and a small store.

CAMPING OUTSIDE YOSEMITE

You'll find more camping options outside Yosemite than within the park itself – both US Forest Service (USFS) campgrounds and dispersed camping, which is allowed in most national forests. Dispersed camping is a great way to go if you crave solitude (no nearby campers) and affordability (it's free) – but remember, you're entirely on your own, which means no toilets or potable water (bring your own or come with a means to filter or purify stream water). If you're going to build a fire, you'll also need a fire permit, which you can pick up at one of the local USFS ranger stations for free. Ranger stations also sell detailed USFS maps, which are helpful for navigating the maze of dirt roads. Finally, note that some areas (along Tioga Rd east of the park, for instance) don't allow dispersed camping; watch for signs.

❶ Getting There & Away

YARTS (☎877-989-2787; www.yarts.com) buses run year-round into Yosemite Valley (1¾ hours one way, adult/child $12/8 round-trip), stopping at the KOA and the Yosemite Bug driveway. Price includes park admission. See p230.

BRICEBURG
ELEV 1200FT

Some 20 miles outside the park, right where the Merced River meets Hwy 140, Briceburg consists of a **visitor center** (☎209-379-9414; www.blm.gov/ca/st/en/fo/folsom/mercedriverrec .html; ⏷1-5pm Fri, 9am-5pm Sat & Sun late April-early Sep) and three primitive Bureau of Land Management (BLM) campgrounds ($10) with a to-die-for location right on the river. To reach them, you cross a beautiful 1920s wooden suspension bridge; long trailers and large RVs are not recommended.

EL PORTAL
POP 470 / ELEV 2100FT

Once the terminus of the Yosemite Valley Railroad, El Portal is now home to a collection of gateway services (including a pricey gas station), housing for park staff and park administrative offices. Just west of the Arch Rock Entrance and about 14 miles west of Yosemite Village, the town stretches 7 miles alongside the Merced River.

🛏 Sleeping & Eating

Restaurants have shorter hours in winter.

Yosemite View Lodge   LODGE $$$
(☎209-379-2681, 888-742-4371; www.stayyosemite viewlodge.com; 11136 Hwy 140; r $164-254, ste $304-714; ✳🛜🏊🏊) Less than 2 miles from the park entrance is this big, modern complex with hot tubs and four pools. All the 336 rooms feature kitchenettes, some have gas fireplaces and views of the Merced River, and the ground-floor rooms have big patios. The souped-up 'majestic suites' are massive, with crazy-opulent bathrooms featuring waterfall showers and plasma TV entertainment centers. There's an on-site **pizzeria** (pizzas & sandwiches from $8; ⏷5-9:30pm Apr-Nov), plus a **restaurant** (dinner mains $14-23; ⏷7-11am & 5:30-10pm; 🅿) offering pasta, seafood dishes and meaty mains.

Cedar Lodge   LODGE $$
(☎209-379-2612, 888-742-4371; www.stayyosemite cedarlodge.com; 9966 Hwy 140; r $119-200; ✳🛜🏊) Approximately 9 miles west of the Arch Rock Entrance, the Cedar is a sprawling establishment with more than 200 adequate rooms, an indoor pool and a seasonal outdoor pool. There are a couple of restaurants: the **grill** (mains $10-13; ⏷11am-10pm; 🍴) offers food and cocktails in a room that looks like an overeager cross between a sports bar and a 1950s diner, while steaks, pasta and chicken are on hand in the adjacent **restaurant** (breakfast buffet $11, dinner mains $14-24; ⏷7-11am & 5:30-10pm).

Indian Flat RV Park   CAMPGROUND, CABINS $
(☎209-379-2339, www.indianflatrvpark.com; 9988 Hwy 140; tent sites $25, RV sites $37-42, tent cabins $59, cottages $109; ⏷year-round; ✳🏊) This private campground has a number of interesting housing options, including two pretty stone cabin cottages with air-conditioning. Guests can use the pool and wi-fi at the Cedar Lodge next door, and nonguests can pay to shower.

USFS Campgrounds   CAMPGROUND $
(☎877-444-6777; www.recreation.gov; Incline Rd; tent sites $21; 🏊) Dry Gulch and Dirt Flat are small but reservable tent-only campgrounds on the north shore of the Merced River.

El Portal Market   MARKET $
(⏷7am-9pm summer, 8am-7pm winter) In a new location next to the gas station, everyone stops at this midsized market for groceries, booze and prepared wraps.

Sal's Taco Truck   MEXICAN $
(mains under $10; ⏷approx 5-9pm, every other Thu) The local's favorite food spot, Sal's biweekly arrival conveniently coincides with payday for government employees. Look for the line next to the post office.

❶ Information

YARTS (☎877-989-2787; www.yarts.com) buses run from Cedar Lodge and Yosemite View Lodge to Yosemite Valley (one hour, adult/child round-trip $7/5). See p230.

Highway 120 (West)

Most folks visiting from the San Francisco Bay area take Hwy 120 into the park, entering Yosemite at the Big Oak Flat Entrance. This is also the main route to Hetch Hetchy; instead of entering at Big Oak Flat, you head north on Evergreen Rd, just before entering the park.

GROVELAND
POP 600 / ELEV 2800FT

There's no missing Groveland – it's as if Hwy 120 rolls right into a Spaghetti Western, taking you with it. As the road slows to a crawl, it passes two blocks of exceptionally well-preserved gold-rush-era buildings.

COMING FROM SAN FRANCISCO

From San Francisco, it's a straightforward drive to Yosemite, taking about four hours to reach Yosemite Valley or Hetch Hetchy. Take the Bay Bridge to I-580 E, jog briefly onto I-205 E near Tracy and then continue on Hwy 120 E towards Manteca. Continue east to Oakdale – the self-proclaimed 'Cowboy Capital of the World' – and consider a stop for cheap gas and a midtrip leg stretch.

After crossing the flat San Joaquin Valley, Hwy 120 bears east (you turn right), slowly entering the foothills and finally facing the precipitous Priest Grade, which climbs some 1500ft over two miles. You can choose the modern, circuitous Hwy 120, or – if you're a daredevil with a strong transmission and trustworthy brakes – opt for vertiginous Old Priest Grade Rd, a much steeper and narrower though somewhat shorter drive to the top. The old road is a *bad* idea for RVs or trailers.

The highway then meanders through the historic towns of Big Oak Flat (not to be confused with the entrance station) and cute Groveland, which has the best hotels and restaurants along this route. It then passes Evergreen Rd and finally enters the park.

About 25 miles west of Yosemite's Big Oak Flat Entrance, Groveland is a picture-perfect old mining town that, together with nearby Big Oak Flat, was originally called Savage's Diggings, after James Savage, who found gold here in 1848. Groveland boomed again with the damming of nearby Hetch Hetchy Valley, drawing loads of workers into town to work on the dam and water project.

🛏 Sleeping

In addition to the following, there are B&Bs and rental properties further east along the highway.

TOP CHOICE **Groveland Hotel**　　　HISTORIC HOTEL $$$
(☑209-962-4000, 800-273-3314; www.groveland .com; 18767 Main St; r incl breakfast $135-349; ✷@☎☀) Built in 1850, this stately historic property now houses an upscale restaurant, a small bar and 17 quaint, lovingly decorated rooms. With teddy bears adorning the beds, it definitely qualifies as cute.

Hotel Charlotte　　　HISTORIC HOTEL $$
(☑209-962-6455; www.hotelcharlotte.com; 18736 Main St; r incl breakfast $129-225; ✷@☎☀) Since Italian immigrant Charlotte DeFerrari opened this historic hotel in 1918 a few things have changed: now it has flowery wallpaper and patchwork quilts, carpet on the floor, private bathrooms and, thankfully, air-conditioning. It's a splendid little place, with friendly owners and a great restaurant.

🍴 Eating & Drinking

TOP CHOICE **Mountain Sage**　　　CAFE $
(18653 Main St; snacks $4-5; ☺7am-6pm Mon-Thu, to 7pm Fri & Sat, 8am-5pm Sun, closed Mon &

Tue winter; @☎☀) Play soccer with the border collie at this popular café, store, nursery and live-music venue all rolled into one. The place stocks fair trade and organic products (including clothes and coffee), maps, books and artistic souvenirs. It also holds an excellent summer concertseries (www.mountainsagemusic.org).

Cellar Door　　　CALIFORNIAN $$
(☑209-962-4000; www.groveland.com; 18767 Main St; mains $14-27; ☺7:30-10am & 6-10pm) The most elegant meal option in town is the Victorian dining room at the historic Groveland Hotel. The menu, which changes regularly, includes items like buffalo meatloaf and local trout, and the 550-label wine list is renowned. Reservations recommended.

Iron Door Grill & Saloon　　　AMERICAN $$
(www.iron-door-saloon.com; 18761 Main St; mains $8-21; ☺11am-late; ☑) Claiming to be the oldest bar in the state, the Iron Door is a dusty, atmospheric old place, with big swinging doors, a giant bar, high ceilings, mounted animal heads and hundreds of dollar bills tacked to the ceiling. The adjacent, more contemporary, dining room (open until 9pm or 10pm) serves good burgers, steaks and pasta dishes, and there's live music every weekend night.

Mar Val Market　　　MARKET $
(Hwy 120 at Ferretti Rd; ☺7am-9pm summer, 8am-8pm winter) On the east end of town just north of the highway, with a good stock of produce and groceries.

ℹ Information

Information station (☺8am-4:30pm Jun-Aug) Staffed by Yosemite rangers, this new station is inside the Mountain Sage café, with park brochures and printed information available in numerous languages.

USFS Groveland Ranger Station (209-962-7825; www.fs.usda.gov/stanislaus; 24545 Hwy 120; 8am-4:30pm Mon-Sat Jun-Aug, reduced hr Sep-May) About 8 miles east of Groveland, offers recreation information for the surrounding Stanislaus National Forest and nearby Tuolumne Wild and Scenic River Area. A big national forest map posted outside lists the location of local campgrounds.

BUCK MEADOWS & AROUND
POP 30 / ELEV 3200FT

A former stagecoach stop en route to Yosemite, Buck Meadows is only 20 minutes' drive from the park entrance, and a good alternative to staying inside the park.

🛏 Sleeping & Eating

Yosemite Westgate Lodge   LODGE $$$
(209-962-5281, 800-253-9673; www.yosemite westgate.com; 7633 Hwy 120; r $189-299; 🏵@ 🛜🐾🛗) In Buck Meadows proper, this generic lodge features better-than-average motel rooms with modern amenities overlooking a large parking lot and a small pool.

Blackberry Inn Bed & Breakfast   B&B $$$
(209-962-4663, 888-867-5001; www.blackberry -inn.com; 7567 Hamilton Station Loop; r $195-215; 🏵@🛜) Owned by a local Yosemite expert, this stunningly converted house, in town, offers three rooms, *big* breakfasts and plenty of visiting hummingbirds.

Stanislaus National Forest   CAMPGROUNDS $
(209-962-7825; www.fs.usda.gov/stanislaus) A number of first-come, first-served campgrounds can be found in this nearby forest: The Pines (campsites $16; 🐾), LostClaim (209-962-7825; tent sites $16; May-early Sep; 🐾), and Sweetwater (campsites $19; May-early Sep; 🐾).

Buck Meadows Restaurant   RESTAURANT $$
(www.buckmeadowsrestaurant.com; 7647 Hwy 120; mains $9-23; 6am-10pm summer, shorter hrs otherwise) After a long day at the park, the half-pound 49er burgers (or more manageable third-pounders) and the big pasta dishes at hit the spot.

SOUTH OF YOSEMITE (HIGHWAY 41)

If you're heading up from Los Angeles or other Southern California points, this is the highway you'll likely wind up driving.

Hwy 41 is generally open year-round. Public transportation is limited to infrequent intercounty buses that don't go to the park.

Oakhurst
POP 2800 / ELEV 2400FT

At the junction of Hwys 41 and 49, about 15 miles south of the park entrance, Oakhurst functions primarily as a service town. This is your last chance to stock up on reasonably priced groceries, camping supplies, gasoline and bug spray.

Miller's Mountain Sports (559-683-7946; 40343 Hwy 41) has a good selection of sporting goods and is the departure point for the new shuttle that runs to Badger Pass Ski Area (see p119).

🛏 Sleeping

TOP CHOICE Sierra Sky Ranch   LODGE $$
(559-683-8040; www.sierraskyranch.com; 50552 Rd 632; r incl breakfast $145-225; 🏵🛜🐾🐕) A sprawling former ranch dating back to 1875, its homespun rooms have oversized wooden headboards and double doors that open onto shady verandahs. The beautiful old lodge features a **restaurant** (dinner mains $12-41) and a rustic saloon, and has loads of comfortable lounging areas. It counts a storied history including periods as a TB hospital and a bordello, and guests including Marilyn Monroe and John Wayne – many swear that it's cheerfully haunted by former residents.

Château du Sureau   BOUTIQUE HOTEL $$$
(559-683-6860; www.chateaudusureau.com; r incl breakfast $385-585, villa $2950; 🏵@🛜🐾) Never in a billion years would you expect to find this in Oakhurst. A luxe and discreet full-service, European-style hotel and world-class spa, this serene property boasts an exceptional level of service and is prepared to pamper you.

Hounds Tooth Inn   B&B $$
(559-642-6600; www.houndstoothinn.com; 42071 Hwy 41; r incl breakfast $95-179; 🏵🛜) A few miles north of Oakhurst, this gorgeous garden B&B is swimming in rosebushes and Victorianesque charm. Its 12 airy rooms, some with spas and fireplaces, feel a bit like an English manor house. Complimentary wine and hot drinks are available in the afternoon.

Oakhurst Lodge   MOTEL $$
(559-683-4417, 800-655-6343; www.oakhurst lodge.com; 40302 Hwy 41; r $145-160; 🏵🛜🐾)

COMING FROM LOS ANGELES

From the LA area, it's about a six-hour trip to Yosemite. Drive north on I-5 (or I-405 to I-5) to Hwy 99, passing through Bakersfield. Continue north to Fresno, the biggest city in the blazing hot San Joaquin Valley and about two-thirds of the way to the park. From Fresno, Hwy 180 E winds towards Kings Canyon National Park.

Continuing north from Fresno on Hwy 41, the busy foothills town of Oakhurst is your best bet for car and tummy refueling, as it's the last sizeable commercial area along this route. The popular boating and fishing resort of Bass Lake sits 10 miles east of town, and the Sierra National Forest fills in the 100-mile gap between southern Yosemite to Kings Canyon. North Fork, a small community about 18 miles southeast of Oakhurst, is the main service and information center for points in the Sierra National Forest.

The highway slaloms through stretches of deep pine forest as it nears the park, passing the small town of Fish Camp just 2 miles before reaching the park's South Entrance Station near Wawona.

Right in the center of town, this 58-unit motel presents a fine no-frills budget option, with quiet, clean rooms, some with kitchenettes.

✖ Eating

El Cid MEXICAN $$
(41939 Hwy 41; mains $9-18; ⊙10am-10pm Mon-Thu, 10am-10:30pm Fri & Sat, 9am-10pm Sun; ✦) The hometown favorite, this midrange Mexican place on the north side of town is usually packed with hungry patrons tucking in to huge portions laced with chili sauce. Snag a seat on the open back patio overlooking the cactus garden swarming with finches.

Erna's Elderberry House CALIFORNIAN, FRENCH $$$
(✦559-683-6800; prix-fixe dinner $95, Sun brunch $58; ⊙dinner daily, plus 11am-1pm Sun; ✦) Got a stack of extra cash or an expense account to burn up? Then definitely make a reservation at Erna's. It offers a renowned Californian-French dining experience in humble Oakhurst, at the super-swank Château du Sureau hotel. Look for it about a mile south of town on the west side of Hwy 41.

Bean CAFE $
(40120 Hwy 41; pastries $1-4; ⊙6:30am-6pm Mon-Fri, 7am-3pm Sat; ⊙) Park your laptop on the wisteria-draped patio and nibble on a breakfast sandwich or sweet treat at this friendly café serving organic, shade-grown and fair trade coffee.

❶ Information

Forest Service desk (✦559-658-7588; www.fs.usda.gov/sierra; ⊙variable hr & days Apr-Sep) Issues wilderness permits.

Yosemite Sierra Visitors Bureau (✦559-683-4636; www.yosemitethisyear.com; 40637 Hwy 41; ⊙8:30am-5pm Mon-Sat summer, 9am-4:30pm winter, plus 9am-1pm Sun year-round) A half-mile north of the Hwy 41/Hwy 49 intersection; free direct-dial lodgings phone.

Sierra National Forest

The Sierra National Forest blankets the area between the Merced and Kings Rivers and brushes Yosemite from the south. You'll find lots of camping, much of it rather rustic, as well as excellent fishing, hiking and swimming.

Besides the Summerdale Campground in Fish Camp, more than 60 developed campgrounds dot the forest. Reserve sites online at www.recreation.gov or by calling ✦877-444-6777. Dispersed camping is also allowed.

North Fork, a small community about 18 miles southeast of Oakhurst, is the main service and information center for points in the Sierra National Forest. The **USFS Bass Lake Ranger Station** (✦559-877-2218; www.fs.usda.gov/sierra; ⊙8am-4:30pm Mon-Sat), offers information on campgrounds, hikes and sights in the forest. The office issues free fire permits, which are required if you want to build a campfire. You can also obtain wilderness permits here for overnight trips in the nearby Ansel Adams Wilderness.

Fish Camp

POP 60 / ELEV 4300FT

Fish Camp is practically just a bend in the road; a tiny, pretty place with a small general store, a post office, and a handful of lodges and worthwhile B&Bs. It's only 2 miles from

Yosemite's southernmost entrance, so it makes a good base for visiting the park.

At the south end of Fish Camp next to the Narrow Gauge Inn, **Yosemite Mountain Sugar Pine Railroad** (☎559-683-7273; www .yosemitesteamtrains.com; ☺Mar-Oct & 3rd weekend of Nov; ⊕) is by far the biggest and boldest attraction in town. Tours on either the old **'Logger' steam train** (adult/child $18/9; wheelchair accessible) or the **Jenny railcar** (adult/child $14.50/7.25) take place several times daily. Call for reservations or just show up. The **Moonlight Special** (adult/child $49/24), on selected Saturday and Wednesday nights, includes a steak dinner and live music; reservations are essential.

🛏 Sleeping

TOP CHOICE **Narrow Gauge Inn** INN $$
(☎559-683-7720, 888-644-9050; www.narrow gaugeinn.com; 48571 Hwy 41; r incl breakfast Nov-Mar $79-109, Apr-Oct $120-220; ✿❂❅❆) Adjacent to the popular Sugar Pine Railroad, this beautiful, friendly and supremely comfortable 26-room inn has a hot tub, small bar and one of the finest restaurants around. Each tastefully appointed room features unique decor and a pleasant deck facing the trees and mountains, and all have flat-screen TVs.

Big Creek Inn B&B B&B $$$
(☎559-641-2828; www.bigcreekinn.com; 1221 Hwy 41; r incl full breakfast $219-259; @❂) Each of the three white-palette rooms has peaceful creek views and a private balcony, and two have gas fireplaces. From the comfortable rooms or the bubbling hot tub, you can often spot deer and beavers, or hummingbirds lining up at the patio feeder. Amenities include in-room DVD players and a large movie library and kitchenette use.

Summerdale Campground CAMPGROUND $
(Map p70; ☎877-444-6777; www.recreation.gov; campsites $21; ☺May-Sep; ❅) The closest campground to the park, it's a pleasant spot down along Big Creek, with 28 well-dispersed sites in an area of grassy meadow and trees.

Tenaya Lodge HOTEL $$$
(☎559-683-6555, 888-514-2167; www.tenayalodge .com; 1122 Hwy 41; r from $305; ✿❂@❂❆) A hulking, modern hotel and conference center just 2 miles from Yosemite's south entrance, this 244-room resort and full spa feels like a convention hotel.

White Chief Mountain Lodge MOTEL $$
(☎559-683-5444; www.whitechiefmountainlodge .com; 7776 White Chief Mountain Rd; r $125-190; ☺Apr-Oct) The cheapest and most basic option in town is this 1950s-era motel with simple kitchenette rooms. It's located a few hundred yards east of Hwy 41, up a wooded country road.

✕ Eating

TOP CHOICE **Narrow Gauge Inn** NEW AMERICAN $$$
(☎559-683-6446; dinner mains $19-37; ☺5:30-9pm Wed-Sun Apr-Oct) Excellent food coupled with knockout views make the dining experience at the Narrow Gauge Inn one of the finest in the Yosemite region. The dinners are creatively prepared, the lodge-like atmosphere is casual but elegant, and windows look out on lush mountain vistas. Cozy up to the fireplace on colder evenings or warm yourself up at the small Buffalo Bar, perfect for a cocktail or glass of chardonnay. Reservations recommended.

Fish Camp General Store MARKET $
(1191 Hwy 41; sandwiches $5.50; ☺7am-8pm summer, to 7pm rest of year) This small place pretty much defines the 'center of town,' and it's been open since the 1920s. Open 365 days a year, it sells sandwiches and boxed lunches, a limited amount of groceries, snow chains and (not surprisingly) fishing supplies. ATM on site.

EASTERN SIERRA

Compared with the western side, the Eastern Sierra is another world. While rolling oak-covered foothills grace the Western Sierra and impede views of the mountains from a distance, a sweeping, nearly treeless desert basin abuts the steep eastern slopes. The result? Views – whether from the basin floor or from high in the mountains – like you wouldn't believe. Within this dramatic setting, National Forest roads lead to marvelously uncrowded campgrounds, hiking areas and undeveloped hot springs.

Tioga Pass to Mono Lake

The stretch of Hwy 120 between Tioga Pass and Lee Vining is the most epic route into or out of Yosemite National Park – and one of the most stunning anywhere in California. The roadbed is scratched into the side of steep, dramatic Lee Vining Canyon, with sheer drop-offs, rugged rock walls and sweeping views. It's incredible to witness how quickly and significantly the scenery changes from one side of Tioga Pass to the other. Once you cross the pass heading east and start downhill, you'll leave behind the lush grasses and tall pines of Tuolumne and Dana Meadows for the dry, sagebrush-coated landscape of the Great Basin Desert. At the end of Hwy 120 lies Mono Lake, a massive expanse of saltwater at the edge of the Great Basin Desert.

Several excellent first-come, first-served campgrounds are found along Tioga Rd, most run by **Inyo National Forest** (☑760-647-3044; www.fs.usda.gov/inyo).

TIOGA PASS

The campground closest to Tioga Pass is at **Tioga Lake** (Hwy 120; sites $19; 🖾), which has a handful of sunny, exposed sites right on the lake but visible from the road.

Founded in 1914, **Tioga Pass Resort** (tiogapassresortllc@gmail.com; r $125, cabin $160-240) justifiably attracts a loyal clientele with its 10 rustic cabins tucked into the rocks and trees beside Lee Vining Creek, just 2 miles east of Tioga Pass. The cabins are basic but cozy, and each includes a kitchen, a porch, a bathroom and linens. Book via email; there are discounts available for multinight stays. Although the attached **diner** (breakfast & lunch $8-9, dinner $15; ⊘7am-9pm) has only a small counter and two tables, the intimate, old-time character makes for a superb setting. The lodge is open roughly from late May through September, depending on snow. In some winters the lodge serves as a base camp for backcountry skiing forays into the surrounding wilderness. Winter visitors approach from Lee Vining and park their cars along Hwy 120. From there, they ski more than 6 miles to the resort. Email in advance to see whether the resort will open for the winter season and to get updated wintertime prices.

In September, check out the **Tioga Pass Run** (www.tiogapassrun.com), a footrace from Lee Vining to Tioga Pass: 12.4 miles – and only one (3100ft) hill!

SADDLEBAG LAKE & AROUND

Reflecting its bleak, high-alpine surroundings at an elevation of 10,087ft, Saddlebag Lake (actually a reservoir) lies at the end of a 2.5-mile dirt road that branches north from Hwy 120, about 2 miles east of Yosemite's Tioga Pass Entrance. The dam here was built in 1919 to help power Lee Vining before the water was diverted to LA. A favorite haunt for anglers, Saddlebag itself pales in comparison to the scenery surrounding it. With countless lakes and stunning views of North Peak (12,242ft) and Mt Conness (12,590ft) on the Yosemite border and pointy Tioga Peak (11,526ft) to the southeast, the area is utterly spectacular. Saddlebag Lake is California's highest car-accessible lake.

The Saddlebag Lake Resort operates a **water taxi** (adult/child/senior round-trip $11/6/10, one way $7/5/6), rents **fishing boats** (2/5/10hr $30/60/90) and sells fishing licenses.

Hiking

From Saddlebag Lake, one of the most popular hikes is a loop of the high altitude **20 Lakes Basin**. Never dropping below 10,000ft, this mostly level trail meanders past some of the most breathtaking scenery in the entire Yosemite region. If you backpack (overnight) here, you can pick up a wilderness permit from either the Tuolumne Meadows Wilderness Center (p74) or the Mono Basin Scenic Area Visitor Center (p146). Overnight camping is prohibited within the Monroe Hall Research Area, west of Saddlebag Lake.

From Junction Campground (at the Saddlebag Lake turnoff from Hwy 120), a mile-long trail leads to the former site of **Bennettville**, a one-time mining town. About a mile north on Saddlebag Lake Rd you'll find a trailhead for **Gardisky Lake**, an oft-overlooked gem tucked beneath 11,526ft Tioga Peak. The hike is short but steep, with an elevation gain of almost 800ft in about a mile.

🛏 Sleeping

The **Inyo National Forest** (☑760-647-3044; www.fs.usda.gov/inyo) runs three small, primitive campgrounds in this area. Due to their size, large RVs and trailers are effectively prohibited, making for extremely pleasant tent camping:

Junction CAMPGROUND $
(cnr Hwy 120 & Saddlebag Lake Rd; campsites $14; 🖾) Named for its location at the intersection of Hwy 120 and the Saddlebag Lake road, this 13-site campground offers sunny sites near Lee Vining Creek.

Sawmill Walk-in CAMPGROUND $
(Saddlebag Lake Rd; tent sites $14; 🖾) One of the most scenic established campgrounds in the entire Sierra Nevada, Sawmill offers 12 sites

TWIN LAKES

These exquisite lakes are shadowed by the jagged Sawtooth Ridge, which includes 12,279ft Matterhorn Peak. Primarily a **fishing** resort revered for its trout and Kokanee salmon, Twin Lakes (elevation 7081ft to 7092ft) is another good access point into Hoover and Yosemite's lake-riddled eastern reaches. Several trails fan out from the west end of Barney Lake. The main trailhead is at the end of Twin Lakes Rd just past Annett's Mono Village; weekly overnight parking is $10 per vehicle.

The road to Twin Lakes intersects Hwy 395 at the north end of Bridgeport and crosses rolling pastures and foothills, passing five good forest service campgrounds on Robinson Creek. The route has little traffic, a smooth surface and few serious hills, making it an excellent 12-mile scenic biking excursion.

Also check out **Buckeye Hot Spring**, where piping hot water emerges from atop a steep hillside and cools as it trickles down into several rock pools right by the side of lively Buckeye Creek. Clothing is optional. To get here, turn right at Doc & Al's Resort (7 miles from Hwy 395), and drive 3 miles on a graded dirt road. Cross the bridge at Buckeye Creek (2.5 miles on), and bear right at the y-junction, following signs to the hot spring. Go uphill a half mile until you see a flat-ish parking area on your right. Follow the hillside trail down to the pools.

on the edge of the beautiful Monroe Hall Research Area. It's an approximately 0.25-mile walk to the campground.

Saddlebag Lake CAMPGROUND $
(Saddlebag Lake; campsites $19; 🐾) Perched atop a hill overlooking the reservoir, this is a favorite with anglers. All sites are small and well kept and some have splendid views over the lake.

✗ Eating

Saddlebag Lake Resort DINER $
(www.saddlebaglakeresort.com; Saddlebag Lake; mains $2-8; ⊙7am-7pm Jul-Sep) On the southeast shore of Saddlebag Lake, this diner-cum-general store (no lodging) serves up egg and pancake breakfasts, burgers, sandwiches and homemade pie.

Lee Vining

POP 220 / ELEV 6781FT

Hwy 395 skirts the western bank of Mono Lake, rolling into this gateway town where you can eat, sleep, gas up (for a pretty penny) and catch Hwy 120 to Yosemite National Park when the road's open. A superb base for exploring Mono Lake, Lee Vining is only 12 miles (about a 30-minute drive) from Yosemite's East Entrance.

Lee Vining Canyon is a popular location for ice climbing. Bishop-based **Sierra Mountain Guides** (www.sierramtnguides.com) and **Sierra Mountain Center** (www.sierra mountaincenter.com) offer classes and guides

to lead you up the dazzling frozen waterfalls both here and at June Lake.

Before you leave town, take a quick look at the **Upside-Down House**, a kooky tourist attraction created by silent film actress Nellie Bly O'Bryan. Originally situated along Tioga Rd, it now resides in a park in front of the tiny **Mono Basin Historical Society Museum** (www.monobasinhs.org; suggested donation $2; ⊙10am-4pm Thu-Mon, noon-4pm Sun, mid-May–early Oct). To find it, turn east on 1st St and go one block to Mattley Ave.

🛏 Sleeping

All of Lee Vining's modest, family-run motels are along Hwy 395. Rates drop when Tioga Pass is closed.

El Mono Motel MOTEL $
(☑760-647-6310; www.elmonomotel.com; 51 Hwy 395; r $69-99; ⊙May-Oct; 🛜) Grab a board game or soak up some mountain sunshine in this friendly, flower-ringed place attached to an excellent café serving organic coffee, espresso drinks and muffins. In operation since 1927, and often booked solid, each of its 11 simple rooms (a few share bathrooms) is unique, decorated with vibrant and colorful art and fabrics.

Yosemite Gateway Motel MOTEL $$
(☑760-647-6467; www.yosemitegatewaymotel.com; Hwy 395; r $169; 🛜) Think vistas. This is the only motel on the east side of the highway, and the views from some of the rooms are phenomenal.

Murphey's Motel — MOTEL $$

(☑760-647-6316, 800-334-6316; www.murpheys yosemite.com; Hwy 395; r $88-123; 🛎🐾) At the north end of town, this large and friendly motel offers comfy rooms with all mod cons.

Lee Vining Motel — MOTEL $

(☑760-647-6440; Hwy 395; r $60-96) If you didn't make a reservation and everything else is booked, try this first-come, first-served hostel-like motel. Reception opens at 4pm.

✕ Eating & Drinking

Whoa Nellie Deli — DELI $$

(www.whoanelliedeli.com; near junction of Hwys 120 & 395, mains $8-19; ⊙7am-9pm mid-Apr–Oct) Great food in a gas station? Come on… No, really, you gotta try this amazing kitchen where chef Matt 'Tioga' Toomey feeds delicious fish tacos, wild buffalo meatloaf and other tasty morsels to locals and clued-in passersby. Portions are huge, the prices are fair and the views from the outdoor patio are as great as the food.

Historic Mono Inn — CALIFORNIAN $$$

(☑760-647-6581; www.monoinn.com; 55620 Hwy 395; dinner mains $8-25; ⊙11am-9pm May-Dec) A restored 1922 lodge owned by the family of photographer Ansel Adams, it's now an elegant lakefront restaurant with outstanding California comfort food, fabulous wine and views to match it all. Browse the 1000-volume cookbook collection upstairs, and stop in for music on the creekside terrace. It's located about 5 miles north of Lee Vining. Reservations recommended.

Mono Market — MARKET $

(⊙7am-9pm Sun-Thu & 7am-10pm Fri & Sat summer, shorter hrs in winter; ☑) Stock up on quality groceries at the local market, whose diverse selection seems more like that of a big city grocery store. The deli out back serves delicious breakfast burritos, pastries and coffee, all to go.

❶ Information

Gas is outrageously expensive. There are ATMs at the Mono Market and the Mobil gas station at the corner of Hwys 395 and 120. The Mobil station also has a pay phone and a free courtesy phone for contacting local accommodations.

Bell's Sporting Goods (Hwy 395; ⊙7am-7pm Apr-Nov) carries camping and fishing supplies and **Mono Vista RV Park** (☑760-647-6401; Hwy 395; showers $2.50; ⊙9am-6pm Apr-Oct) has pay showers.

See p146 for area visitor information.

Mono Lake
ELEV 6379FT

North America's second-oldest lake is a quiet and mysterious expanse of deep blue water whose glassy surface reflects jagged Sierra peaks, young volcanic cones and the unearthly tufa (too-fah) towers that make Mono Lake so distinctive. Jutting from the water like drip sand castles, the tufas form when calcium bubbles up from subterranean springs and combines with carbonate in the alkaline lake waters.

In *Roughing It,* Mark Twain described Mono Lake as California's 'dead sea.' Hardly. The brackish water teems with buzzing alkali flies and brine shrimp, both considered delicacies by dozens of migratory bird species that return here year after year. So do about 85% of the state's nesting population of California gulls, which take over the lake's volcanic islands from April to August. Like the Owens Valley, Mono Lake has also been a political football in the state's historical battle over water rights.

❖ Sights & Activities

South Tufa Reserve — NATURE RESERVE

(☑760-647-6331; adult/child $3/free) Tufa spires ring the lake, but the biggest grove is on the south rim with a mile-long interpretive trail. Ask about ranger-led tours at the visitor center. To get to the reserve, head south from Lee Vining on Hwy 395 for 6 miles, then east on Hwy 120 for 5 miles to the dirt road leading to a parking lot.

Navy Beach — BEACH

The best place for swimming is at Navy Beach, just east of the reserve. It's also the best place to put in canoes or kayaks. From late June to early September, the Mono Lake Committee operates one-hour **canoe tours** (☑760-647-6595; www.monolake.org/visit/canoe; tours $25; ⊙8am, 9:30am & 11am Sat & Sun) around the tufas. Half-day kayak tours along the shore or out to Paoha Island are also offered by **Caldera Kayaks** (☑760-934-1691; www.calderakayak.com; tours $75; ⊙mid-May–mid-Oct). Both places require reservations.

Panum Crater — NATURAL FEATURE

Rising above the south shore, Panum Crater is the youngest (about 640 years old), smallest and most accessible of the craters that string south toward Mammoth Mountain. A panoramic trail circles the crater rim (about 30 to 45 minutes), and a short but

LONG LIVE MONO LAKE

In 1941 the City of Los Angeles Department of Water and Power (DWP) bought vast tracts of land throughout the Mono Basin and diverted four of the five streams that feed Mono Lake to the California Aqueduct to provide water to Los Angeles. Over time, the lake dropped 40ft and doubled in salinity.

Aside from its beauty, Mono Lake is of major importance to California gulls, which use the lake for breeding and nesting. Roughly 85% of California's 'seagulls' are born at Mono Lake. Historically, the lake's islands, which had no natural predators for the gulls, were the primary nesting grounds. But as lake levels dropped, land bridges emerged, giving coyotes and other predators access to the islands and the nests. For the gull population, the result was disastrous.

In 1976 environmental activist David Gaines began to study the effects of the diversion and projected that the lake would dry up within about 20 years. Because of Mono Lake's importance for gulls, along with eared grebes and red-necked phalaropes, its potential demise posed a major ecological threat. Gaines formed the Mono Lake Committee in 1979 and, through numerous campaigns and court battles, managed to win water back from Los Angeles.

A fluke of nature aided the struggle. In 1989 heavy snows caused dams to overflow into previously dry spillways, rejuvenating streams that had not seen water for 10 years. When fish were found in the streams, the courts ruled that although the DWP technically owned the water rights, the department could not allow the fish to die and, thus, was obliged to maintain the streams at life-sustaining levels.

In 1994 the courts required that the lake level return to 6392ft above sea level (estimated to take 10 more years) before the DWP can take water from the lake or its tributaries. Bumper stickers and T-shirts bearing the 'Save Mono Lake' slogan changed to 'Restore Mono Lake.' Mono is indeed rebounding, and faster than expected. Although still far below its highest historic levels, the lake is only about 8ft from the target level. Today, the lake is widely considered healthy, and bumper stickers now read 'Long Live Mono Lake.'

steep 'plug trail' puts you at the crater's core. A dirt road leads to the trailhead from Hwy 120, about 3 miles east of the junction with Hwy 395.

Black Point Fissures   NATURAL FEATURE
On the north shore are these narrow crags that opened when lava mass cooled and contracted about 13,000 years ago. Access is from three places: east of Mono Lake County Park, from the west shore off Hwy 395, or south of Hwy 167. Check at the visitor center for specific directions.

ℹ Information

Mono Basin Scenic Area Visitor Center
(☎760-647-3044; www.fs.usda.gov/inyo; Hwy 395, ☺usually 8am-5pm mid-Apr–Nov) Half a mile north of Lee Vining. Maps, interpretive displays, wilderness permits, bear-canister rentals, a bookstore and a 20-minute movie about Mono Lake.

Mono Lake Committee Information Center
(☎760-647-6595; www.monolake.org; cnr Hwy 395 & 3rd St, Lee Vining; ☺9am-5pm late Oct–mid-Jun, 8am-9pm mid-Jun–Sep) Internet access (per 15 minutes $2), maps, books, free 30-minute video about Mono Lake and passionate, preservation-minded staff. Public restroom too.

Bodie State Historic Park
ELEV 8375FT

For a time warp back to the gold-rush era, swing by **Bodie** (☎760-647-6445; www.parks.ca.gov/?page_id=509; Hwy 270; adult/child $7/5; ☺9am-6pm Jun-Aug, 9am-3pm Sep-May), one of the West's most authentic and best-preserved ghost towns. Gold was first discovered here in 1859, and within 20 years the place grew from a rough mining camp to an even rougher boomtown with a population of 10,000 and a reputation for unbridled lawlessness. Fights and murders took place almost daily, the violence no doubt fueled by liquor dispensed in the town's 65 saloons, some of which did double duty as brothels, gambling halls or opium dens. The hills disgorged some $35 million worth of gold and silver in the 1870s and '80s, but when production plummeted, so did the population and eventually the town was abandoned to the elements.

About 200 weather-beaten buildings still sit frozen in time in this cold, barren and windswept valley heaped with tailing piles. Peering through dusty windows you'll see stocked stores, furnished homes, a schoolhouse with desks and books, and workshops filled with tools. The jail is still there, as are the fire station, churches, a bank vault and many other buildings. The former Miners' Union Hall now houses a **museum and visitor center**, which is open from 9am to one hour before the park closes. Rangers conduct free general **tours**. In summertime, they also offer tours of the landscape and the cemetery; call for details.

Bodie is about 13 miles east of Hwy 395 via Rte 270; the last 3 miles are unpaved. Although the park is open year-round, the road is usually closed in winter and early spring, so you'd have to don snowshoes or cross-country skis to get there.

Virginia Lakes

South of Bridgeport, Hwy 395 gradually arrives at its highest point, **Conway Summit** (8148ft), where you'll be whipping out your camera to capture the awe-inspiring panorama of Mono Lake, backed by the Mono Craters, backed by June and Mammoth Mountains.

Also at the top is the turnout for Virginia Lakes Rd, which parallels Virginia Creek for about 6 miles to Virginia Lakes, a cluster of lakes flanked by Dunderberg Peak (12,374ft) and Black Mountain (11,797ft). A trailhead at the end of the road gives access to the **Hoover Wilderness** and the **Pacific Crest Trail**. The trail continues down Cold Canyon through to Yosemite National Park. Check with the folks at the 1923 **Virginia Lakes Resort** (☎760-647-6484; www.virginialakesresort.com; cabins from $107; ⊙usually mid-May–mid-Oct; 🐾) for maps and tips about specific trails. The resort itself has snug cabins, a café and a general store. Cabins sleep two to 12 people, and usually have a minimum stay.

There's also the option of camping at **Trumbull Lake Campground** (☎800-444-7275; www.recreation.gov; campsites $17; ⊙mid-Jun–mid-Oct). The shady sites here are located among lodgepole pines. Nearby, **Virginia**

Lakes Pack Station (☎760-937-0326; www.virginialakes.com) offers horseback trips.

Lundy Lake

After Conway Summit, Hwy 395 twists down steeply into the Mono Basin. Before reaching Mono Lake, Lundy Lake Rd meanders west of the highway for about 5 miles to Lundy Lake. This is a gorgeous spot, especially in spring when wildflowers carpet the canyon along Mill Creek, or in fall when it is brightened by colorful foliage. Before reaching the lake, the road skirts first-come, first-served **Lundy Canyon Campground** (campsites $12; ⊙mid-April–mid-Nov), with vault toilets but no water. At the end of the lake, there's a ramshackle resort on the site of an 1880s mining town, plus a small store and boat rentals.

Past the resort, a dirt road leads into Lundy Canyon where in 2 miles it dead-ends at the trailhead for Hoover Wilderness. A moderate 1.5-mile hike follows Mill Creek to the 200ft-high Lundy Falls. Ambitious types can continue on via Lundy Pass to Saddlebag Lake.

June Lake Loop

Under the shadow of massive Carson Peak (10,909ft), the stunning 14-mile June Lake Loop meanders through a picture-perfect horseshoe canyon past the relaxed resort town of June Lake and four sparkling, fish-rich lakes: Grant, Silver, Gull and June. It's especially scenic in fall when the basin is ablaze with golden aspens. Catch the loop (Hwy 158) a few miles south of Lee Vining.

🏃 Activities

Hiking

June Lake is backed by the Ansel Adams Wilderness, which runs into Yosemite National Park. Rush Creek Trailhead has a day-use parking lot, posted maps and self-registration permits. Gem and Agnew Lakes make spectacular day hikes, while Thousand Island and Emerald Lake (both on the Pacific Crest/John Muir Trail) are stunning overnight destinations.

Other Activities

Cyclists can zip around the entire loop, a moderate 22-mile circle including a section of Hwy 395. Boat and tackle rentals, as well as fishing licenses, are available at five marinas.

AROUND YOSEMITE VIRGINIA LAKES

In wintertime, ice climbers flock to the area's frozen waterfalls. See Lee Vining, p144, for local outfitters.

June Mountain Ski Area
SKIING

(☑24hr snow info 760-934-2224, 888-586-3686; www.junemountain.com; lift tickets adult/child $69/35) Winter fun concentrates in this area, which is smaller and less crowded than nearby Mammoth Mountain and perfect for beginner and intermediate skiers. Some 35 trails crisscross 500 acres of terrain served by seven lifts, including two high-speed quads. Boarders can get their adrenaline flowing at three terrain parks with a kick-ass superpipe.

Ernie's Tackle & Ski Shop
OUTDOOR EQUIPMENT

(☑760-648-7756; www.erniestackleandski.com; 2604 Hwy 158) One of the most established outfitters in June Lake village.

Frontier Pack Train
HORSEBACK RIDING

(☑760-648-7701; www.frontierpacktrain.com; Silver Lake; one hr/half-day/full-day rides $30/70/105; ⊗Jun-Sep) Area and backcountry horseback rides.

🍴 Sleeping & Eating

Double Eagle Resort & Spa
RESORT $$$

(☑760-648-7004; www.doubleeagleresort.com; 5587 Hwy 158; r incl breakfast $199, cabins $349; 🔊🏊🐾) A mighty swanky spot for these parts, the resort specializes in pampering and proximity to outdoor activities. The sleek two-bedroom log cabins and balconied hotel rooms here lack no comfort, while worries disappear at the elegant spa. The restaurant (dinner mains $15-30; ⊗8am-9pm) exudes rustic elegance, with cozy booths, a high ceiling and a huge fireplace.

June Lake Motel
MOTEL $$

(☑760-648-7547, www.junelakemotel.com; 2716 Hwy 158; r with/without kitchen $115/105; @🐾) Enormous rooms – most with full kitchens – catch mountain breezes and sport attractive light-wood furniture. There's a fish cleaning sink and BBQs, plus a good book library and a friendly resident Newfoundland dog.

USFS Campgrounds
CAMPGROUNDS $

(☑800-444-7275; www.recreation.gov; campsites $20; ⊗mid-Apr–Oct; 🐾) Of June Lake, Oh! Ridge, Silver Lake, Gull Lake and Reversed Creek, the first three accept reservations; Silver Lake has gorgeous mountain views.

Carson Peak Inn
AMERICAN $$

(☑760-648-7575; Hwy 158 btwn Gull & Silver Lakes; meals $19.50-34; ⊗5-10pm, shorter hrs winter) Inside a cozy house with fireplace, this well-regarded restaurant is much beloved for its tasty old-time indulgences, such as beef brochette, pan-fried trout and chopped sirloin steak. Portion sizes can be ordered for regular or 'hearty' appetites.

Tiger Bar
AMERICAN $$

(www.thetigerbarcafe.com; 2620 Hwy 158; mains $8-17; ⊗8am-10pm) After a day on slopes or trails, people gather at the long bar or around the pool table of this no-nonsense, no-attitude place. The kitchen feeds all appetites with burgers, salads, tacos and other tasty grub, including homemade fries.

eastsierra.net
CAFE $

(2775 Hwy 158, June Lake; ⊗6am-5pm; 🔊) Internet café with organic coffee and teas.

Mammoth Lakes
POP 8200 / ELEV 7800FT

Mammoth Lakes is a small mountain-resort town endowed with larger-than-life scenery. The Eastern Sierra's commercial hub and a four-season resort, it's backed by a ridgeline of jutting peaks, ringed by clusters of crystal-line alpine lakes and enshrouded by the dense Inyo National Forest. Active, outdoorsy folk worship at the base of the dizzying 11,053ft Mammoth Mountain, its slopes covered in white powder from winter through to late spring. When the snow finally fades, the area is a wonderland of mountain-bike trails, excellent fishing, endless alpine hiking and blissful, hidden spots for hot-spring soaking.

Orientation

Mammoth Lakes is 3 miles off Hwy 395 via Hwy 203, which turns into Main St after the first traffic light. At the second light it turns right and continues as Minaret Rd, going past the Village at Mammoth and gaining elevation on the way to the Mammoth Mountain Ski Area and the shuttle bus to Reds Meadow/Devils Postpile. Continue straight at the second light for Mammoth Lakes Basin via Lake Mary Rd (closed in winter).

⊙ Sights

Earthquake Fault
TOP CHOICE / NATURAL FEATURE

On Minaret Rd about 1 mile west of the Mammoth Scenic Loop, detour to gape at Earthquake Fault, a sinuous fissure half a mile long and gouging a crevice up to 20ft deep into the earth. Ice and snow often linger at the bottom until late summer, and Native Americans and early settlers used it to store perishable food.

Mammoth Museum   MUSEUM
(⚐760-934-6918; 5489 Sherwin Creek Rd; suggested donation $3; ⊙10am-6pm mid-May–Sep) For a walk down memory lane, stop by this little museum inside a historic log cabin.

🏃 Activities

Skiing & Snowboarding
Main Lodge and Canyon Lodge have ski schools and state-of-the-art equipment rental.

Mammoth Mountain   SKIING
(⚐760-934-2571, 800-626-6684, 24hr snow report 888-766-9778; www.mammothmountain.com; lift tickets adult/senior & child $92/46) A skier's and snowboarder's dream resort, where sunny skies, a reliably long season (usually from November to June) and over 3500 acres of fantastic tree-line and open-bowl skiing prove to be a potent cocktail. At the top you'll be dealing with some gnarly, nearly vertical chutes. The other stats are just as impressive: 3100 vertical feet, 150 trails, 29 lifts (including 10 quads). Boarders, meanwhile, will find world-class challenges in nine terrain parks with three intense super-pipes and urban-style jibs.

Cross-Country Skiing
There's free cross-country skiing along the 19 miles of nongroomed trails of the Blue Diamond Trails System, which winds through several patches of scenic forest around town. Pick up a map at the welcome center or check out www.mammothnordic.com.

Tamarack Cross-Country Ski Center SKIING
(⚐760-934-2442; Lake Mary Rd; all-day trail pass adult/child/senior $27/15/21; ⊙8:30am-5pm) Let the town shuttle take you to the Tamarack Lodge, which has almost 20 miles of meticulously groomed track around Twin Lakes and the lakes basin. The terrain is also great for snowshoeing. Rentals and lessons are available.

Biking
Stop at the welcome center for a free map with route descriptions and updated trail conditions.

A local recreational umbrella group has been developing a fantastic new system of bike paths (www.mammothtrails.org). One completed segment is the 5.3-mile Lakes Basin Path, which begins at the southwest corner of Lake Mary and Minaret Rds and heads uphill (at a 5% to 10% grade) to Horseshoe Lake, skirting lovely lakes and breathtaking mountain views.

Mammoth Mountain   MOUNTAIN BIKING
(⚐800-626-6684; www.mammothmountain.com; day pass adult/child $43/22; ⊙9am-4:30pm) Come summer, Mammoth Mountain morphs into the massive Mammoth Mountain Bike Park with more than 80 miles of well-kept single-track trails. Several other trails traverse surrounding forest. In general, Mammoth-style riding translates into plenty of hills and soft, sandy shoulders, which are best navigated with big knobby tires.

When the park's open, it runs a free bike shuttle (⊙9am-5:30pm late Jun-Sep) from the Village area to the Main Lodge. Shuttles depart every 30 minutes, and bikers with paid mountain passes get priority over pedestrians.

But you don't need wheels (or a medic) to ride the vertiginous gondola (adult/senior $23/12; ⊙year-round) to the apex of the mountain, where there's a café and an interpretive center with scopes pointing towards the nearby peaks. And for kids 13 and under, there's a fun zip line (1st zip $12, additional $7, ⊙summer) behind the Adventure Center at the base of the gondola.

Hiking
Mammoth Lakes rubs up against the Ansel Adams Wilderness and John Muir Wilderness, both laced with fabulous trails leading to shimmering lakes, rugged peaks and hidden canyons. Major trailheads leave from the Mammoth Lakes Basin, Reds Meadow and Agnew Meadows; the latter two are accessible only by shuttle. Shadow Lake is a stunning 7-mile day hike from Agnew Meadows that can also be part of a back-country trip to the base of the Ritter Range (see Thousand Island Lake hike, p153).

Fishing & Boating
Starting on the last Saturday in April, the dozens of lakes that give the town its name lure in fly and trout fishers from near and far. California fishing licenses and equipment are available at sporting goods stores throughout town, including **Troutfitter** (⚐760-934-2517; cnr Hwy 203 & Old Mammoth Rd) and **Rick's Sports Center** (⚐760-934-3416; Main St at Center St).

HOT SPRINGS HEAVEN

If you live to soak, the Eastern Sierra will fulfill your every hot-spring fantasy. Thanks to its volcanic past and wealth of underground mountain-fed springs, the stretch of Hwy 395 from just north of Bridgeport south to Lone Pine is sprinkled with secluded spots for simmering. Over the years, first shepherds, then locals, have crafted actual drainable tubs, with rubber hosing used to divert the springs. Many are well known and thus can get crowded on weekends, so if you're after seclusion, it's best to spring-hop in midweek or off-season.

Nestled between the White Mountains and the Sierra Range near Mammoth is a tantalizing slew of natural pools with snowcapped panoramic views. When the high-altitude summer nights turn chilly and you can hear the coyotes cry, you'll never want to dry off. About 9 miles south of town, Benton Crossing Rd juts east off of Hwy 395, accessing a trove of hot springs. Locals call this 'Green Church Rd,' because of the road's unmistakable marker.

For a soaking to-do list with detailed directions and maps, pick up the bible – Matt Bischoff's excellent *Touring California and Nevada Hot Springs*. And keep in mind these three golden rules: no glass, no additives to the water and, if you can, no bathing suit.

The **Pokonobe Store and Marina** (☎760-934-2437; www.pokonoberesort.com), on the north end of Lake Mary, rents motor boats ($20 per hour), rowboats ($10), canoes ($16) and kayaks ($16 to $20). **Caldera Kayaks** (☎760-935-1691; www.calderakayak.com) has single ($30 for a half-day) and double kayaks ($50) for use on Crowley Lake.

Sleeping

Mammoth Creek Inn INN $$
(☎760-934-6162, 800-466-7000; www.mammothcreekinn.com; 663 Old Mammoth Rd; r $190-235, with kitchen $277-356; @📶) It's amenities galore at this pretty inn at the end of a commercial strip, with down comforters and fluffy terry robes, as well as a sauna, a hot tub and a fun pool table loft. The best rooms overlook the majestic Sherwin Mountains; some have full kitchens and can sleep up to six.

Tamarack Lodge & Resort RESORT $$
(☎760-934-2442, 800-626-6684; www.tamaracklodge.com; lodge r $99-169, cabins $169-599; @📶🐾) Kind people run this charming year-round resort on the shore of Lower Twin Lake. In business since 1924, the cozy lodge includes a fireplace, a bar, an excellent restaurant, 11 rustic rooms and 35 cabins. The cabins range from very simple to simply deluxe, and come with full kitchen, telephone, private bathroom, porch and wood-burning stove.

Cinnamon Bear Inn B&B $$
(☎760-934-2873, 800-845-2873; www.cinnamonbearinn.com; 133 Center St; r incl breakfast $79-179; @📶) At this down-to-earth inn you'll sleep like a log in four-poster beds, and most rooms have cozy gas fireplaces. Swap stories about the day's adventures with other guests over homemade refreshments in the afternoon, or soak away soreness in the small outdoor Jacuzzi.

Davison Street Guest House HOSTEL $
(☎760-924-2188, reservations 858-755-8648; www.mammoth-guest.com; 19 Davison St; dm $35-49, d $75-120; 📶) A cute five-room A-frame chalet hostel on a quiet residential street, it has a stocked kitchen, plus mountain views from the living room with fireplace or sun deck. There's self-registration when the manager isn't around.

USFS Campgrounds CAMPGROUNDS $
(☎877-444-6777; www.recreation.gov; campsites $20-21; 🐾; ⏲approx mid-Jun–mid-Sep) About 15 USFS campgrounds are scattered in and around Mammoth Lakes, all with flush toilets but no showers. Many sites are available on a first-come, first-served basis, but some are reservable. Note that nights get chilly at these elevations, even in July. Stop by the Mammoth Lakes Welcome Center or check its website for a full list of campgrounds and public shower locations.

Some of the nicest campgrounds are in the lakes basin around Twin Lakes, Lake Mary and Lake George, with well-spaced sites in a pine forest and along crackling creeks. Less picturesque but close to town, New Shady Rest and Old Shady Rest are two sprawling options right behind the welcome center/ranger station.

You can also camp for free on National Forest land unless posted otherwise. The welcome center/ranger station has a map showing which areas are closed to dispersed camping, and also issues free but mandatory fire permits.

✕ Eating

Lakefront Restaurant   CALIFORNIAN, FRENCH $$$
(☑760-934-3534; www.tamaracklodge.com/lakefront-restaurant; Lakes Loop Rd, Twin Lakes; mains $28-38; ☺5-9:30pm year-round, plus 11am-2pm summer, closed Tue & Wed in fall & spring) For a splurge, the Tamarack Lodge has an intimate and romantic dining room overlooking Twin Lakes. The chef crafts Californian-French specialties like elk medallions au poivre and heirloom tomatoes with Basque cheese, and the staff are superbly friendly. Reservations recommended.

**Petra's Bistro
& Wine Bar**   CALIFORNIAN, FRENCH $$$
(☑760-934-3500; www.petrasbistro.com; 6080 Minaret Rd; mains $19-34; ☺5-9:30pm Tue-Sun) Settle in here for seasonal cuisine and wines recommended by the three staff sommeliers. In wintertime, the best seats in the house are the cozy fireside couches. Start the evening with a cheese course and choose from 28 wines available by the glass or 250 vintages by the bottle. Reservations recommended.

Good Life Café   CALIFORNIAN $
(www.mammothgoodlifecafe.com; Mammoth Mall, 126 Old Mammoth Rd; mains $8-10; ☺6:30am-3pm; ☑) Healthy food, generously filled veggie wraps and big bowls of salad make this a perennially popular place. The front patio area is blissful for a long brunch on a warm day.

Stellar Brew   CAFE $
(www.stellarbrewnaturalcafe.com; 3280b Main St; salads & sandwiches $5.50; ☺5:30am-8pm; ☑☎) Proudly locavore and mostly organic, settle into a comfy sofa here for your daily dose of locally roasted coffee, homemade granola and scrumptious vegan (and some gluten-free) pastries.

Stove   RESTAURANT $
(www.thestoverestaurant.com; 644 Old Mammoth Rd; breakfast mains $6-10; ☺6:30am-2pm & 5-9pm) Good for breakfast, with great coffee and carbs – try the French toast made with cinnamon bread.

Sierra Sundance Whole Foods   HEALTH FOOD $
(26 Old Mammoth Rd; ☑) Self-catering vegetarians can stock up on organic produce, bulk foods and tofu at this handy store and deli.

🍷 Drinking

Clocktower Cellar   PUB
(www.clocktowercellar.com; 6080 Minaret Rd) In the winter especially, locals throng this half-hidden basement of the Alpenhof Lodge. The ceiling is tiled with a swirl of bottle caps, and it stocks 31 beers on tap – especially German brews – as well as about 50 bottled varieties.

FREE **Mammoth Brewing
Company Tasting Room**   BREWERY
(☑760-934-7141; www.mammothbrewingco.com; 94 Berner St; ☺10am-6pm) Free samples anyone? Try some of the dozen brews on tap, then buy some IPA 395 or Double Nut Brown to go.

ℹ Information

The **Mammoth Lakes Welcome Center** (☑760-934-2712, 888-466-2666; www.visitmammoth.com; ☺8am-5pm) and the **Mammoth Lakes Ranger Station** (☑760-924-5500; www.fs.fed.us/r5/inyo; ☺8am-5pm) share a building on the north side of Hwy 203. This one-stop information center issues wilderness permits, helps find accommodations and campgrounds, and provides road and trail condition updates. From May through October, when trail quotas are in effect, walk-in wilderness permits are released at 11am the day before; permits are self-issue the rest of the year.

Mammoth Hospital (☑760-934-3311; 85 Sierra Park Rd; ☺24hr) Emergency room.

Mammoth Mountaineering Supply (☑760-934-4191; www.mammothgear.com; 3189 Main St) Offers friendly advice, topo maps and all-season equipment rentals.

ℹ Getting There & Around

Mammoth's updated airport (Mammoth Yosemite; MMH) has a daily winter–spring nonstop to/from San Francisco on **United** (www.united.com). **Horizon Air** (www.alaskaair.com) runs a similar seasonal (and cheaper) flight to/from San Jose and a year-round Los Angeles service. All flights are about an hour. Taxis meet incoming flights, and some lodgings provide free transfers. **Mammoth Taxi** (☑760-934-8294; www.mammoth-taxi.com) does airport runs as well as hiker shuttles throughout the Sierra.

Mammoth is a snap to get to/from by public transportation year-round. See p136 for details on traveling to Yosemite along the Hwy 395 corridor. Within Mammoth, a year-round system of free and frequent bus shuttles connects the whole town with the Mammoth Mountain lodges; in summer, routes with bike trailers service the Lakes Basin and Mammoth Mountain Bike Park.

Reds Meadow

West of the Mammoth Mountain resort, Reds Meadow Valley is one of the beautiful and varied landscapes nearby Mammoth. Drive about 1 mile up from the ski area on Hwy 203 to Minaret Vista for eye-popping views of the Ritter Range, the serrated Minarets and the remote reaches of Yosemite National Park. At dusk, the lacy granite spires of the Minarets seem to come alive in the rosy alpenglow.

A handful of nice first-come, first-served campgrounds are sprinkled about the valley road. Some, like Minaret Falls, are right on the Middle Fork of the San Joaquin River, and are very popular with anglers. The kiosk at the road entrance lists which campgrounds are full. Even if you don't stay overnight there, you can use the free hot-springs showers at the Reds Meadow campground

---

ⓘ REDS MEADOW/DEVILS POSTPILE SHUTTLE

The road to Reds Meadow and Devils Postpile is generally open (free of snow) from June until September. When open, between 7am and 7pm you can only get there by hiking or biking or aboard a shuttle (adult/child 3–15 years $7/4). The shuttle leaves from a lot in front of the Adventure Center at the base of Mammoth Mountain's gondola approximately every 30 minutes between 7:30am and 7pm (last bus out leaves Reds Meadow at 7:45pm), and you must buy tickets inside the Adventure Center before joining the queue. There are also a half dozen direct departures from the Village (on Canyon Blvd, under the gondola) in the morning.

You can drive in if you are camping in one of the six valley campgrounds, have reservations at the Reds Meadow Resort, or are a person with a disability (all incur a $10 vehicle fee).

(not the resort), a decadent treat after a long hike.

Devils Postpile National Monument

Like a stack of warped organ pipes, the Devils Postpile National Monument is one of the strangest rock formations you might ever see. The 60ft, multisided columns of blue-gray basalt are the most conspicuous and interesting evidence of the area's volcanic activity. The accordion-like columns first took shape about 10,000 years ago, when lava, which flowed through Mammoth Pass, cooled and fractured vertically. A glacier came through later, giving them their cracked, shiny surface and causing several to snap off, forming the pile of broken posts at the base. Don't miss the view from above, where the distinct hexagonal honeycomb design is particularly visible, and the pattern could be mistaken for garden paving stones.

Carved from the Ansel Adam Wilderness, the monument is 10 miles west past the Mammoth Mountain ski area. The shuttle stops at campgrounds, viewpoints and the Devils Postpile Ranger Station (☎760-934-2289; www.nps.gov/depo; ◷9am-5pm). From here, hike a half mile to the columns or 2.5 miles through fire-ravaged forest to the true-to-its-title Rainbow Falls, a 101ft sheet cascade and prism of mist formed by the Middle Fork of the San Joaquin River. Free, daily ranger-guided walks to the columns leave from the station at 11am.

Bishop

POP 3900 / ELEV 4140FT

The second-largest town in the Eastern Sierra, Bishop is about two hours from Yosemite's east gate. A major recreation hub, Bishop offers access to excellent fishing in nearby lakes, climbing in the Buttermilks just west of town, and hiking in the John Muir Wilderness via Bishop Creek Canyon and the Rock Creek drainage. The area is especially lovely in fall when dropping temperatures cloak aspen, willow and cottonwood in myriad glowing shades.

The earliest inhabitants of the Owens Valley were Paiute and Shoshone Native Americans, who today live on four reservations; the largest is the Bishop Indian Reservation. White settlers came on the

THOUSAND ISLAND LAKE HIKE

Duration 3 days

Distance 24 miles round-trip

Difficulty Moderate–difficult

Start/Finish Agnew Meadows Trailhead

Transportation Reds Meadow Shuttle

Summary A glorious high-country loop via sections of both the John Muir Trail (JMT) and the Pacific Crest Trail (PCT), this hike visits a bevy of alpine lakes and brings you up close to dramatic snow-dipped Sierra peaks.

Day 1: Agnew Meadows to Ediza Lake

(3–4 hours, 6.9 miles) From the second trailhead parking area at Agnew Meadows (8340ft), cross a creek and walk 1 mile northeast, descending briefly via the joint River/Shadow Trail. Continue for 0.8 level miles, past the shallow and reed-lined **Olaine Lake**, until you come to a junction where the two trails split. Bear left (west) on the Shadow Lake Trail, soon climbing about 700ft to the outflow of gorgeous **Shadow Lake** (no camping permitted here), meeting the JMT at 1.9 miles. Tracing the north shore of Shadow Creek, split west from the JMT after 0.9 miles, continuing another 2.3 miles to 9300ft **Ediza Lake**. The lake is spectacularly framed by the snow-topped Ritter Range, Banner Peak and Mt Ritter. Camping is not permitted on the south side of the lake or in the westside meadows.

Day 2: Ediza Lake to Thousand Island Lake

(4–5 hours, 7.4 miles) Retrace your steps back to the JMT, and prepare to follow it north through a string of jewel-named lakes, also reaching the highest point of the hike. From 9000ft, ascend steadily through forest cover until the trail emerges on a granite ridgetop overlooking dreamy Garnet Lake, with sweeping views of Mt Ritter, Banner Peak and Mt Davis. Descend to Garnet Lake, where the trail briefly follows the north shore and then turns north and zigzags up the very rocky slope to the ridgetop above (10,160ft). The trail drops down, passing along the east shore of Ruby Lake and then the west shore of Emerald Lake. The island-speckled **Thousand Island Lake** soon comes into sight below, and this viewpoint is perhaps the best perch to survey its beauty. Descend to the lake, crossing a footbridge over its outlet and intersecting with the PCT. Turn left (west) at this point, tracing the far (north) side of the lake for approximately half a mile to find a campsite. You must camp at least a quarter mile from the outflow area.

Day 3: Thousand Island Lake to Agnew Meadows

(4–5 hours, 9.7 miles) Return to the junction of the JMT and the PCT, and follow the PCT (also known as the High Trail here) along the outlet (the headwaters of the Middle Fork of the San Joaquin River). Ascend briefly along a granite outcrop to a junction with the River Trail, and stay on the PCT as it passes the shallow grassy Badger Lakes and then two trails leading to Agnew Pass. At the second pass trail, you're now 2.6 miles from the day's starting point, and at 9720ft, the highest point of the day. For the next 6.6 miles, the PCT traverses the west side of a ridge, with spectacular sightlines of Shadow Lake to the west, and the unmistakable Two Teats formation marking the eastern ridge. With a final 560ft descent via tight switchbacks, the trail returns to Agnew Meadows, about a half-mile east of the parking lot where you began.

scene in the 1860s and began raising cattle to sell to nearby mining settlements.

Bishop also serves as the northernmost gateway to the Owens Valley, a once fertile agricultural region reduced to a desertlike wasteland. Since the early 20th century, water from the Owens River has been siphoned off by the Los Angeles Aqueduct. The 100-sq-mile Owens Lake was sapped dry, leading to decades of toxic dust storms and the loss of important wetlands for migratory birds. Some environmental mitigation and restoration is now in place, but the area is still in recovery mode.

◉ Sights

TOP CHOICE **Laws Railroad Museum** MUSEUM
(☎760-873-5950; www.lawsmuseum.org; suggested donation $5; ☺10am-4pm; 🔞) Railroad and Old West aficionados should make the 6-mile detour north on Hwy 6 to this museum. It recreates the village of Laws, an important stop on the route of the *Slim Princess,* a narrow-gauge train that hauled freight and passengers across the Owens Valley for nearly 80 years. The original 1883 train depot is here, as are a post office, a schoolhouse and other rickety old buildings with funky and eclectic displays from the pioneer days.

FREE **Mountain Light Gallery** GALLERY
(☎760-873-7700; 106 S Main St; ☺10am-6pm) To see the Sierra on display in all its majesty, pop into this gallery, which features stunning outdoor images by the late Galen Rowell. His work bursts with color, and the High Sierra photographs are some of the best in existence.

FREE **Owens Valley Paiute Shoshone Cultural Center** CULTURAL BUILDING
(☎760-873-3584; www.bishoppaiutetribe.com/cul turalcenter.html; 2300 W Line St; ☺9am-5pm) A mile west of Hwy 395, this tribal cultural center includes exhibits on basketry and the use of medicinal herbs.

🏃 Activities

Bishop is prime bouldering and rock climbing territory with terrain to match any level of fitness, experience and climbing style. The main areas are the granite Buttermilk Country west of town on Buttermilk Rd, and the stark Volcanic Tablelands and Owens River Valley to the north. For details, consult with the staff at **Wilson's Eastside Sports** (☎760-873-7520; 224 N Main St), which rents equipment and sells maps and guidebooks. Another excellent resource is **Mammoth Mountaineering Supply** (☎760-873-4300; 298 N Main St), which also sells used gear, including shoes. Keep a look out for Native American petroglyphs in the tablelands too.

Hikers will want to head to the high country by following Line St (Hwy 168) west along Bishop Creek Canyon past Buttermilk Country and on to several lakes, including Lake Sabrina and South Lake. Trailheads lead into the John Muir Wilderness and on into Kings Canyon National Park. Check with the White Mountain Ranger Station for suggestions, maps and wilderness permits for overnight stays. Fishing is good in all lakes, but North Lake is the least crowded.

Keough's Hot Springs SWIMMING
(☎760-872-4670; www.keoughshotsprings.com; 800 Keough Hot Springs Rd; adult/concession $8/6; ☺11am-7pm Wed-Fri & Mon, 9am-8pm Sat & Sun, longer hrs summer) About 8 miles south of Bishop, this historic institutional-green outdoor pool (dating from 1919) is filled with bath-warm water from local mineral springs and doused with spray at one end. A smaller and sheltered 104°F (40°C) soaking pool sits beside it. Camping and tent cabins are also available.

🛏 Sleeping

Joseph House Inn Bed & Breakfast B&B $$
(☎760-872-3389; www.josephhouseinn.com; 376 W Yaney St; r incl full breakfast $143-178; 🅿❄🛜🐾) A beautiful, restored ranch-style home that has a patio overlooking a tranquil 3-acre garden, and six nicely furnished rooms, some with fireplaces, all with TV and VCR. Guests enjoy a complimentary gourmet breakfast and afternoon wine and snacks.

Chalfant House B&B $$
(☎760-872-1790, 800-641-2996; www.chalfant house.com; 213 Academy; d incl breakfast $80-110; ❄🛜🐾). Lace curtains and Victorian accents swirl through the six rooms of this restored historic home. Originally built by the editor and publisher of Owens Valley's first newspaper, some of the rooms are named after Chalfant family members.

USFS campgrounds CAMPGROUNDS $
(campsites $21; ☺May-Sep) For a scenic night, stretch out your sleeping bag beneath the stars. The closest USFS campgrounds, all but one first-come, first-served, are between 9 miles and 15 miles west of town on Bishop Creek along Hwy 168, at elevations between 7500ft and 9000ft.

🍴 Eating & Drinking

Raymond's Deli DELI $
(www.raymondsdeli.com; 206 N Main St; sandwiches $7-9; ☺10am-6pm; 🚲) A sassy den of kitsch, pinball and Pac-man, it serves heaping sandwiches with names like 'When Pigs

Fly, 'Flaming Farm' and 'Soy U Like Tofu.' Kick back with a Lobotomy Bock and watch your food order get flung to the cook along a mini-zipline.

Erick Schat's Bakerÿ   BAKERY $
(www.erickschatsbakery.com; 763 N Main St; sandwiches $5-8.50; ⊙6am-6pm Sun-Thu, to 8pm Fri) A much-hyped tourist mecca filled to the rafters with racks of fresh bread, this bakery has been making the signature shepherd bread and other baked goodies since 1938. It also features a popular sandwich bar.

Whiskey Creek   AMERICAN $$
(www.whiskeycreekbishop.com; 524 N Main St; mains $11-29; ⊙11am-9pm, to 10:30pm Fri & Sat) This country dining room has comfort food like meatloaf and chicken pot pie, and a smattering of seafood and pastas.

❶ Information

Public showers are available in town at **Wash Tub** (☎760-873-6627; 236 Warren St; ⊙approx 5pm & 8-10pm), and near South Lake at **Bishop Creek Lodge** (☎760-873-4484; www.bishop creekresort.com; 2100 South Lake Rd; ⊙May-Oct) and **Parchers Resort** (☎760-873-4177; www.parchersresort.net; 5001 South Lake Rd; ⊙late May–mid-Oct).

Bishop Area Visitors Bureau (☎760-873-8405; www.bishopvisitor.com; 690 N Main St; ⊙10am-5pm Mon-Fri, to 4pm Sat & Sun)

Inyo County Free Library (☎760-873-5115; 210 Academy) Free computers with internet access.

Spellbinder Books (☎760-873-4511; 124 S Main St; ⊛) Great indie bookstore with attached café.

White Mountain Ranger Station (☎760-873-2500; www.fs.usda.gov/inyo; 798 N Main St; ⊙8am-5pm Mon-Fri Nov-Apr, daily May-Oct) Wilderness permits, trail and campground information for the entire area.

Ancient Bristlecone Pine Forest

For encounters with some of the earth's oldest living things, plan at least a half-day trip to the **Ancient Bristlecone Pine Forest** (admission per vehicle $5). These gnarled, other-worldly trees thrive above 10,000ft on the slopes of the seemingly inhospitable White Mountains, a parched and stark range that once stood even higher than the Sierra. The oldest tree – called Methuselah – is estimated to be over 4700 years, beating even the Great Sphinx of Giza by about two centuries.

To reach the groves, take Hwy 168 east 12 miles from Big Pine, just south of Bishop, to White Mountain Rd, then turn left (north) and climb the curvy road 10 miles to **Schulman Grove**, named for the scientist who first discovered the trees' biblical age in the 1950s. The entire trip takes about one hour. There's access to **self-guided trails**, and a new solar-powered **visitor center** (☎760-873-2500; www.fs.usda .gov/inyo; ⊙late May-Oct). White Mountain Rd is usually closed from November to April. It's nicest in August when wildflowers sneak out through the rough soil.

A second grove, the **Patriarch Grove**, is dramatically set within an open bowl and reached via a 12-mile graded dirt road. Four miles further on you'll find a locked gate, which is the departure point for day hikes to **White Mountain Peak** – at 14,246ft it's the third-highest mountain in California. The round-trip is about 14 miles via an abandoned road, soon passing through the Barcroft High Altitude Research Station; some ride the route on mountain bikes. The easiest 14er in California, the nontechnical and marmot-laden route winds above the tree line, though naturally, high elevation makes the going tough. Allow plenty of time and bring at least two quarts of water per person. For maps and details, stop at the White Mountain Ranger Station in Bishop.

For altitude adjustment or some good star-gazing, spend a night at the **Grandview Campground** (suggested donation $5) at 8600ft. About half way up to the visitor center, it has awesome views, tables and vault toilets, but no water.

Sequoia & Kings Canyon National Parks

Best Hikes

» General Sherman Tree to Moro Rock (p171)

» Tokopah Falls (p171)

» Monarch Lakes (p173)

» Zumwalt Meadow Loop (p174)

» Rae Lakes Loop (p176)

Best Places to Stay

» Lodgepole Campground (p181)

» Sheep Creek Campground (p186)

» Sequoia High Sierra Camp (p184)

» Silver City Mountain Resort (p184)

» Sequoia Village Inn (p191)

Why Go?

With a cleft deeper than the Grand Canyon and forests harboring the world's largest trees, Sequoia and Kings Canyon National Parks dazzle visitors with superlatives. Throw in opportunities for spelunking, rock climbing, splashing in swimming holes or backcountry hiking through granite-carved Sierra Nevada landscapes, and you have all the ingredients for an unforgettable national-parks experience.

Although larger than Yosemite, Sequoia and Kings Canyon National Parks receive fewer than half as many visitors as their more iconic neighbor to the north. Luckily, that makes these southern Sierra Nevada parks almost effortless places to find solitude, even with five-star geological highlights, hulking giant sequoias and wildflower meadows all within easy reach.

The two contiguous parks are administered together as one unit, with a section of the Giant Sequoia National Monument gouging into them like a bite out of a cookie.

When to Go
Sequoia National Park

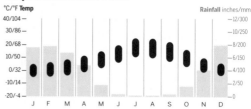

Feb
Go snowshoeing, cross-country skiing or play in the snow beside giant sequoias.

May & Jun
Beat the crowds before or after the Memorial Day holiday weekend.

Sep
Summer vacation crowds melt away after Labor Day, but all park roads are still open.

Entrances

Both national parks are only accessible by car from the west, and no roads cross the Sierra Nevada mountain range, only trails. Furthest south, Sequoia National Park's main entrance is at Ash Mountain in the Sierra Nevada foothills. Furthest north, Big Stump is the only entrance to Kings Canyon National Park.

All park entrances are open 24 hours a day year-round, although some roads (eg from Three Rivers to Mineral King in Sequoia National Park, Hwy 180 past the Hume Lake turn-off to Cedar Grove in Kings Canyon National Park, and Big Meadows Rd in the Sequoia National Forest off the Generals Hwy) are closed during winter. Exact opening and closing dates vary by area of the park and on the weather from year to year, but sometimes the most remote and hazardous roads are inaccessible from autumn's first snowfall until the snow melts in late spring or early summer.

DON'T MISS

Although there's a lot to see just inside both of these national parks, the neighboring Sequoia National Forest also harbors some amazingly scenic spots, from ancient sequoia groves to alpine lakes. In fact, to drive between the national parks on the Generals Hwy, or from Grant Grove to Cedar Grove via the Kings Canyon Scenic Byway, you'll pass right through the Sequoia National Forest and its Giant Sequoia National Monument anyway, making it easy to stop off and see the sights, score a campsite or hike less-trammeled trails into the wilderness.

When You Arrive

» Although administered as a single unit by the National Park Service (NPS), Sequoia and Kings Canyon National Parks are actually two national parks.

» The two parks together are commonly referred to as 'SEKI.' The phrase 'Kings Canyon' may refer the national park or may just mean the eponymous canyon itself.

» The $20 vehicle entrance fee covers both national parks and also the Hume Lake Recreation Area in the nearby Sequoia National Forest.

» The national parks' free seasonal newspaper *The Guide* is loaded with information on activities, campgrounds, lodging, shuttles, visitor services and more.

» All telephone numbers within the parks have the same area code (☎559) and prefix (☎565). Locals often give telephone numbers by their last four digits only (eg '4436' means ☎559-565-4436).

PLANNING TIPS

For 24hr recorded information, including winter road conditions and summer road-construction updates, call ☎559-565-3341.

The comprehensive **NPS website** (www.nps .gov/seki) offers free downloads of the park newspaper and helpful trip-planning tips.

Fast Facts

» Total area: 1353 sq miles (865,734 acres)

» Foothills (Sequoia) elevation: 1700ft

» Grant Grove (Kings Canyon) elevation: 6600ft

Reservations

Delaware North Companies (☎801-559-4948, 866-807-3598; www .visitsequoia.com) Sequoia National Park lodgings.

NPS & USFS Campgrounds (☎518-885-3639, 877-444-6777; www .recreation.gov)

Sequoia-Kings Canyon Park Services Company (☎559-335-5500, 866-522-6966; www.sequoia-kings canyon.com) Kings Canyon and some Sequoia National Forest lodgings.

Resources

NPS website (www.nps .gov/seki/planyourvisit/lodging outsideparks.htm) Lists even more area lodgings.

Sequoia National Forest (www.fs.fed.us/r5 /sequoia/gsnm.html) All about the Giant Sequoia National Monument.

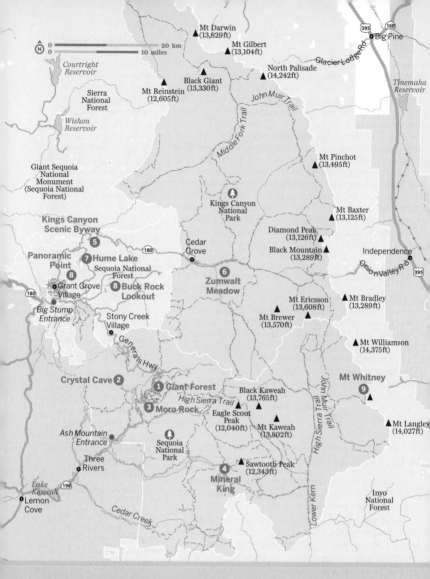

Sequoia & Kings Canyon National Parks Highlights

1 Throw your arms around the world's largest tree in the **Giant Forest** (p159)

2 Duck through a maze of toothy stalactites at **Crystal Cave** (p164)

3 Hoof it up the precipitous granite dome of **Moro Rock** (p163)

4 Backpack through the marmot-guarded alpine lakes of **Mineral King** (p165)

5 Gaze down into North America's deepest canyon along the hair-raising **Kings Canyon Scenic Byway** (p167)

6 Spy on black bears and bird-watch from the boardwalk at **Zumwalt Meadow** (p167)

7 Laze away an afternoon on the shore of **Hume Lake** (p168)

8 Stargaze from Grant Grove's **Panoramic Point** (p167) or historic **Buck Rock Lookout** (p166) in Sequoia National Forest

9 Summit the highest peak on continental USA, **Mt Whitney** (p194)

Orientation

Sequoia and Kings Canyon National Parks lie about 125 miles southeast of Yosemite National Park, although it takes at least three hours to make the drive. Most of the star attractions are off the Generals Hwy, the main road that starts in the Foothills area and continues north to Grant Grove, traversing both parks and parts of the Giant Sequoia National Monument in the Sequoia National Forest.

Visitor activity in Sequoia National Park concentrates in the Giant Forest area and Lodgepole Village, which has the most tourist facilities. Just outside the gateway town of Three Rivers, south of Sequoia's Ash Mountain Entrance, the windy road to remote Mineral King Valley veers east of Hwy 198.

Further north in Kings Canyon, Hwy 180 passes Big Stump Entrance before reaching Grant Grove Village, the main tourist hub. Continuing northeast, the Kings Canyon Scenic Byway winds through a section of the Giant Sequoia National Monument, then descends to Cedar Grove, where it dead ends at aptly named Road's End.

Park Rules & Regulations

It probably won't come as a surprise that the parks don't let visitors climb giant sequoias. Hitchhiking is allowed, as long as it's done safely. Pets are allowed only in developed areas (eg picnic areas, campgrounds), but not on any trails (see p46). Never feed any wildlife, no matter how cute or tame it seems – it's illegal, and food handouts teach wild animals to act aggressively towards humans.

Bear boxes must be used in developed areas. In day-use areas where they aren't provided, all food and scented items (eg trash, empty recyclables, toiletries, coolers) must be stored inside your vehicle's trunk or at least placed as low as possible inside, and completely covered up so they aren't visible. See p235 for more safety tips about bear encounters.

Overnight backcountry camping requires a wilderness permit, which may be subject to trail quotas (see p176). Park-approved bear canisters (p245) must be used in the backcountry, unless a food-storage locker is available (which is rare, and can't be relied upon being available).

Campfires using existing fire rings are allowed only in park campgrounds or in parts of the backcountry, with some exceptions. In Kings Canyon, no fires are permitted above

10,000ft or in Granite Basin or Redwood Canyon. Sequoia prohibits fires in many parts of the Kaweah, Kern and Tule River drainages, especially above 9000ft. Ask about current fire restrictions at park campgrounds, visitor centers and wilderness permit stations.

SIGHTS

Giant sequoia groves, underground marble caves, sculpted granite domes, jagged high-altitude peaks and wildflower meadows where mule deer and black bears graze are just a small taste of what you'll see in both national parks and nearby national forest lands. When the weather won't cooperate, a modest museum, educational displays and orientation movies at park visitor centers, and a seasonal kids' activity center are welcome indoor diversions.

Sequoia National Park

LODGEPOLE VILLAGE & WUKSACHI

Lodgepole Village is Sequoia's main hub. The visitor center, market, deli, snack bar, showers and coin-op laundromat are usually open from mid-April until mid-October. Lodgepole's busy campground and tiny post office operate year-round. Two miles further north, Wuksachi boasts the park's highest-end hotel, restaurant and bar, all of which stay open year-round.

Lodgepole Visitor Center   VISITOR CENTER
(☑559-565-4436; ☺9am-4:30pm mid-Apr–mid-May, 8am-4:30pm mid-May–late Jun & early Sep–mid-Oct, 7am-6pm late Jun-early Sep) Exhibits on park history cover buffalo soldiers (see boxed text, p206), competing land uses from Native American dominion until the present, and environmental challenges such as air pollution and wildfires. There's an especially thought-provoking mural about the interdependence of species. Entertaining and educational, the short movie *Bears of the Sierra* is screened upon request, or check out the video booth at the back to learn about the human history of the Giant Forest.

GIANT FOREST

During his travels in the Sierra Nevada, peripatetic conservationist John Muir wandered into this cathedral-like grove of giant sequoias in 1875, baptizing it the 'Giant Forest.' Having escaped being logged in the late 19th century, today the Giant Forest

Sequoia & Kings Canyon National Parks

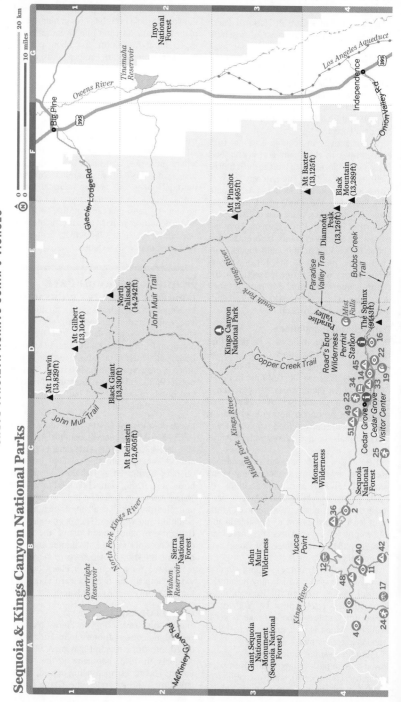

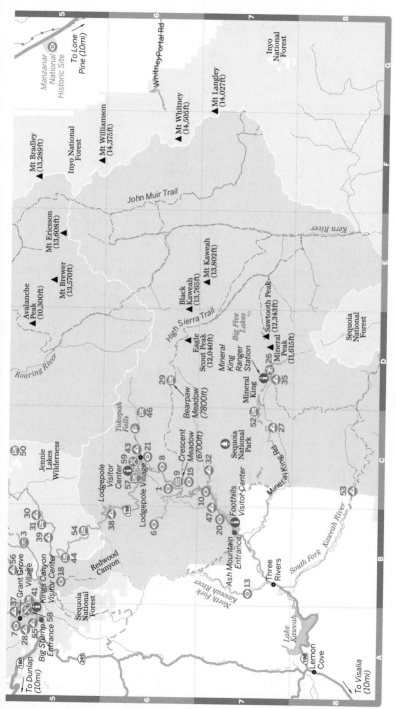

Sequoia & Kings Canyon National Parks

encompasses an amazing concentration of ancient sequoias, where the happy shouts of kids and native birdsong echo through the misty groves.

By the late 20th century, over 300 buildings, including campgrounds and a lodge, that had been built in the Giant Forest encroached upon the giant sequoias' delicate root systems, as did traffic jams. Tourist development had also made it necessary to suppress all wildfires, without which giant sequoias can't reproduce naturally.

Recognizing these adverse impacts, in 1997 the national park began to remove structures, relocate visitor services further north and resite parking lots. The park also introduced a convenient, free visitor shuttle, significantly cutting traffic congestion and reducing the potential harm to these majestic trees.

General Sherman Tree
NATURAL FEATURE

By volume the largest living tree on earth, the massive General Sherman Tree rockets

275ft into the sky and *waaay* out of the camera frame. Pay your respects to this giant, which measures over 100ft around its base, via a half-mile descent from the upper parking lot off Wolverton Rd, about 1.5 miles south of Lodgepole Village.

Or join the Congress Trail, a paved 2-mile pathway that takes in General Sherman and other notable named sequoias, including the fallen Telescope Tree. To lose the crowds, set off on the 6-mile Trail of the Sequoias, which takes you into the heart of the forest, or follow our one-way shuttle hike (see p171) to Moro Rock.

FREE **Giant Forest Museum** MUSEUM
(☎559-565-4480; ⏰9am-5pm mid-May–late May & mid-Aug–mid-Oct, 9am-6pm late May-late Jun, 9am-7pm late Jun–mid-Aug, sometimes also 9am-4pm mid-Oct–mid-May) For a primer on the intriguing ecology and history of giant sequoias, this pint-sized museum will entertain both kids and adults. Hands-on exhibits teach about the life stages of these big trees, which can live for over 3000 years, and the fire cycle that releases their seeds and allows them to sprout on bare soil. Don't miss the diorama of all of the parks' giant sequoia groves, or the touch tables for kids. The museum itself is housed in a 1920s historic building designed by Gilbert Stanley Underwood, famed architect of Yosemite's Ahwahnee Hotel.

Outside the museum, a ruler embedded in the sidewalk lets you virtually walk the whopping length of an actual sequoia tree, making it easy to appreciate its mammoth stature. To see giant sequoia ecology in action, stroll the nearby Big Trees Trail (see p170). The museum is just over 4 miles south of Lodgepole Village.

FREE **Beetle Rock Education Center** ACTIVITY CENTER
(☎559-565-4480; ⏰usually 1-4pm late Jun–mid-Aug; ♿) Bugs, bones and artificial animal scat are just some of the cool things kids get to play with here. A bright and cheerful cabin with activity stations galore, it's run by the Sequoia Natural History Association and is appropriate for ages three to 12 (all children must have a parent or adult to supervise them). Inquisitive kiddos can touch a taxidermied bobcat, scan bugs with digital microscopes, put on puppet shows and paint ecology posters. There are binoculars out back for spotting animals in the forest

outside. To visit the center, take the short trail uphill from the parking lot across the road from the Giant Forest Museum.

Moro Rock NATURAL FEATURE
Although not nearly as mammoth as Yosemite's Half Dome, Sequoia's iconic granite dome is nonetheless impressive. A staircase climbs over 300ft to the top for mind-boggling views of the Great Western Divide, running north to south through the center of the park and splitting the watersheds of the Kaweah River to the west and the Kern River to the east.

Due to pollution drifting up from the Central Valley, this spectacular vantage point may be obscured by thick haze on some days, especially during summer. Historical photos at the trailhead show the rock's original rickety wooden staircase, erected in 1917. You'll be grateful that the current staircase, built in 1931 by the Civilian Conservation Corps (CCC), is solidly carved into the granite and has sturdy handrails for gripping.

From the Giant Forest Museum, the trailhead is 2 miles up narrow, twisty Moro Rock–Crescent Meadow Rd; the free seasonal visitor shuttle stops at the small parking lot, which is often full.

Crescent Meadow NATURAL FEATURE
A lush meadow buffered by a forest of firs and giant sequoia, Crescent Meadow was allegedly once described by John Muir as the 'gem of the Sierra.' High grass and striking summer wildflowers are good excuses for a leisurely loop hike (see p171), as is watching black bears snacking on berries and ripping apart logs to feast on the insects crawling around beneath the bark.

The meadow environment is fragile, so always stay on established trails and don't go tramping willy-nilly across it, tempting though it may be. Several short hikes surround the meadow, including spur trails to

SEQUOIA & KINGS CANYON NATIONAL PARKS SIGHTS

ⓘ SHUTTLE SHORTCUT

If the idea of the steep walk back uphill from the General Sherman Tree doesn't thrill you, catch the seasonal park shuttle bus from the lower parking lot (disabled permit required) and shuttle stop, then ride back north to the upper (main) parking lot.

DON'T MISS

CRYSTAL CAVE

Accidentally discovered in 1918 by two parks employees going fishing, this unique marble cave was carved by an underground river, and has formations estimated to be 10,000 years old. Stalactites hang like daggers from the ceiling, and milky white marble formations take the shape of ethereal curtains, domes, columns and shields. The cave is also a unique biodiverse habitat for spiders, bats and tiny aquatic insects that are found nowhere else on earth.

To see the **cave** (☎559-565-3759; www.sequoiahistory.org; Crystal Cave Rd; tours adult/child 5-12yr/senior from $13/7/12; ☺regular tours 10:30am-4:30pm mid-May–late Oct), you must buy a ticket for a 45-minute guided tour. Beyond the historic Spider Gate at the entrance, underground passageways wind for over 3 miles. Teens and adults can take more in-depth 'Discovery Tours,' go on lantern-lit cave explorations or sign up for full-day spelunking adventures.

Tour tickets are *only* sold at the Lodgepole and Foothills visitor centers, *not* at the cave itself. Tours fill up quickly, especially on weekends, so buy them early in the day or a day or so in advance. Wheelchairs, baby backpacks, strollers, tripods and walking sticks are prohibited inside the cave. Bring along a light jacket, as chilly cave temperatures average only 50°F (10°C).

From the Lodgepole or Foothills areas, allow at least 90 minutes to get to the cave, which is a half-mile walk from the parking lot at the end of a twisty 6.5-mile-long paved road. Look for the signed turnoff for Crystal Cave Rd about 2 miles south of the Giant Forest Museum.

Tharp's Log, where the area's first white settler, Hale Tharp, spent summers in a fallen sequoia, and **Squatters Cabin**, an 1880s log cabin that's a ghostly remnant of the failed utopian-socialist Kaweah Colony (see the boxed text, p190).

The meadow is almost 3 miles down Moro Rock–Crescent Meadow Rd, best accessed by the free seasonal visitor shuttle. The road closes to all traffic after the first snowfall and doesn't reopen until spring, but you can still snowshoe or cross-country ski along it.

FOOTHILLS

From the Ash Mountain Entrance outside Three Rivers, the Generals Hwy ascends steeply through the southern section of Sequoia National Park. With an average elevation of less than 2500ft, the Foothills are much drier and warmer than the rest of the park. Hiking here is best in spring, when the air is still cool and wildflowers peak for a colorful show. Summers are buggy and muggy, but fall again brings moderate temperatures and colorful foliage. The visitor center is open year-round.

Foothills Visitor Center   VISITOR CENTER
(☎559-565-3135; ☺8am-4:30pm, to 6pm late May-early Sep) A mile north of the park's Ash Mountain Entrance, this tiny visitor center has educational exhibits on the park's human history and ecology, with a focus on Sierra Nevada wildlife across different life zones, as well as Native American heritage and 19th-century pioneers and conservationists.

Tunnel Rock   LANDMARK
Here's proof that in the 1930s, no one anticipated the development of monster SUVs. About 1.5 miles north of the Foothills Visitor Center via the Generals Hwy, a flat granite boulder on the west side of the road caps a tunnel dug by the CCC. Until the highway was finally widened in 1997, this narrow passageway was the only route through. It's closed to modern-day vehicles, which would have a tough time squeezing through side by side, but pedestrians can stroll under its constricted arch.

Hospital Rock   ARCHAEOLOGICAL SITE
The Potwisha people, a band of Monache (also known as Western Mono), originally lived here. When the first white man, Hale Tharp, arrived in 1858, this site was home to about 500 villagers and had been inhabited for five centuries.

Diseases introduced by white settlers from Three Rivers nearby soon killed many of the Native Americans, and within a decade the village had been abandoned. Pictographs (rock paintings) and grinding holes used by tribeswomen to make acorn meal can still be seen at the picnic area, about 5 miles north of the visitor center.

In 1873 pioneer James Everton shot his own leg by getting it caught in his own bear trap; he lay down here to recuperate from his injury, hence the rock's name. A word to the wise: shooting firearms is prohibited in the park today.

MINERAL KING

Perched at 7500ft, this giant, gorgeous and glacially sculpted valley ringed by massive mountains, including jagged Sawtooth Peak (12,343ft), is a supremely good place to find solitude.

For two decades starting in the 1870s, Mineral King witnessed heavy silver mining and lumber activity. There are still remnants of old shafts and stamp mills around, though it takes some exploring to find them. The **Mineral King Preservation Society** website (www.mineralking.org) has all kinds of information on the area, including historic mining cabins. After mining turned out to be a bust, Mineral King became a cool mountain retreat for families escaping the Central Valley's summer heat. A contentious proposal by the Walt Disney Company to develop the area into a ski resort was thwarted when Congress annexed it to the Sequoia National Park in 1978.

Hiking anywhere from here involves a steep climb out of the valley along strenuous trails, so be aware of the high altitude, even on short hikes. Beautiful day hikes or overnight backpacking trips head up to Crystal, Monarch (see p173), Mosquito, Eagle, Franklin, Little Five and Big Five Lakes. If you're not up for the tough stuff, take a serene mile-long ramble along the nature trail from Cold Springs Campground to the Eagle/Mosquito trailhead parking area.

The valley is reached via narrow, twisting 25-mile Mineral King Rd (see p169), which heads east from Hwy 198 south of the park's Ash Mountain Entrance. The road is usually open only from late May through late October. Scattered along the last 6 miles of road are two first-come, first-served park campgrounds, a ranger station and the private Silver City Mountain Resort (p184), offering lodging, a restaurant and a tiny market.

GENERALS HIGHWAY

As it winds for almost 11 miles through the Sequoia National Forest, the Generals Hwy bridges the gap between Sequoia and Kings Canyon National Parks. A few campgrounds, lodging and tourist services are right off the highway, while paved Big Meadows Rd (Forest Service road 14S11) burrows east into the Giant Sequoia National Monument near the Jennie Lakes Wilderness, a popular backpacking area.

A seasonal outpost, Stony Creek has a gas station (pumps available 24 hours with credit cards), ATM, pay phones, coin-op laundry and showers, a small lodge (see p185), a small market and pizzeria, and nearby campgrounds. Everything closes from mid-October until late April or early May, including the gas station. Four miles north, Montecito Sequoia Lodge (see p184) is an active year-round lodge and summer family camp set around

MARMOT ALERT!

You've locked the doors and rolled up the windows. All food and scented stuff has been removed to deter bear break-ins. So why is your car still at risk? Mineral King is swarming with hungry yellow-bellied marmots (see p214), and what's under your hood might be what's for dinner.

In late spring and early to mid-summer, many of Mineral King's curious marmots come out of hibernation and anxiously await parked cars at trailheads. Besides such epicurean items as sweaty boots, backpack straps and hiking pole grips, these rodents also love to feast on radiator hoses, belts and wiring of vehicles to get the salt they crave. They can chew through brake lines and completely disable your car.

Marmot-proofing one's vehicle has become a local art form. Some folks swear by wrapping the engine block in chicken wire (which can be rented from Silver City Mountain Resort, p184), while others swaddle the entire undercarriage with an enormous tarp (like a vehicular diaper).

Always check under the hood before you drive off. Some marmots have ended up hitching as far as southern California before they were finally discovered, still munching away.

a small private lake, with groomed cross-country ski trails (see p180) and other snow sports in winter.

FREE **Buck Rock Lookout** LOOKOUT
(www.buckrock.org; ⊙usually 9:30am-6pm Jul-Oct) Built in 1923, this active fire lookout is one of the finest restored watchtowers you could ever hope to visit. Staffed during the wildfire season, 172 stairs lead to a dollhouse-sized wooden cab on a dramatic 8500ft granite rise. To get here from the Generals Hwy, go a mile north of the Montecito Sequoia Lodge, then turn east onto Big Meadows Rd (Forest Service road 14S11). At approximately 2.5 miles, turn north on the signed dirt road (Forest Service road 13S04) and drive another 3 miles to the lookout parking area. Opening hours vary, so check online before you make the trek.

Kings Canyon National Park

GRANT GROVE

Year-round Grant Grove Village is the park's main tourist hub. In addition to lodge and cabin accommodations and two restaurants, there's a decent-sized market, small post office and free wi-fi. ATMs are located inside the lodge lobby and at the market, with a few payphones found outside. The closest gas is at Hume Lake (see p168).

Kings Canyon Visitor Center VISITOR CENTER
(☎559-565-4307; ⊙9am-5pm Mar-late May, 8am-6pm late May-early Jul & late Aug-early Sep, 8am-7pm early Jul-late Aug, 8am-5pm early Sep-late Nov, 9am-4:30pm late Nov-Feb) About 3 miles northeast of the park's Big Stump Entrance, Grant Grove's busy visitor center has interesting exhibits on nature conservation, wildlife habitats and environmental issues, and also screens a movie introduction to Kings Canyon – all titled in both English and Spanish. Families can head toward the 'Discovery Room' at the back, which has independent nature-themed activities to entertain younger kids.

General Grant Grove FOREST
The magnificence of this ancient sequoia grove was nationally recognized in 1890 when Congress designated it General Grant National Park. It took another half century for this tiny parcel to be absorbed into much bigger Kings Canyon National Park, estab-

lished in 1940 to prevent damming of the fierce Kings River.

Today, the paved half-mile General Grant Tree Trail (see p174) is an interpretive walk that visits a number of mature sequoias, including the 27-story **General Grant Tree**. This giant holds triple honors: it's the world's third-largest living tree; a national shrine to US soldiers killed in war; and the country's official Christmas tree since 1926. The nearby **Fallen Monarch**, a massive, fire-hollowed trunk that you can walk through, once served as a hotel, a saloon, and a stables for US Cavalry horses (though not all at the same time). The 19th-century pioneer Gamlin Cabin was later utilized as the national park's first ranger station.

To escape the bustling crowds, follow the more secluded 1½-mile North Grove Loop, which passes wildflower patches and bubbling creeks as it gently winds underneath a canopy of stately sequoias, evergreen pines and aromatic incense cedars.

Redwood Mountain Grove FOREST
Over 15,000 sequoias cluster in Redwood Canyon, making it one of the world's largest groves of these giant trees. In an almost-forgotten corner of the park, this secluded forest lets you revel in the majesty of the trees away from the crowds while hiking moderate-to-strenuous trails. What you won't find here, however, are any coast redwood trees. That's what early pioneers mistook these giant sequoias for, hence the erroneous name.

The trailhead is at the end of a 2-mile bumpy dirt road (closed in winter) that starts across from the Hume Lake/Quail Flat signed intersection on the Generals Hwy, just over 5 miles southeast of Grant Grove Village.

CEDAR GROVE

At the bottom of Kings Canyon, the commercial area of Cedar Grove Village consists of a market, ATM, restaurant, lodge, showers, coin-op laundry and a small visitor center. Tourist services here are available from mid-May until mid-October. The road to Cedar Grove closes completely during winter, usually from mid-November through mid-April.

Six miles east of the village, Road's End is just that, with a seasonal ranger station that issues wilderness permits and rents bear canisters. Hikes starting from Road's End head out to all points of the Sierra; it's also the closest park trailhead to both the Pacific

WORTH A TRIP

PANORAMIC POINT

For a breathtaking view of Kings Canyon, head 2.3 miles up narrow, steep and winding Panoramic Point Rd (trailers and RVs aren't recommended). Follow a short paved trail uphill from the parking lot to the viewpoint, where precipitous canyons and the snow-capped peaks of the Great Western Divide unfold below you. Snow closes the road to vehicles during winter, when it becomes a cross-country ski and snowshoe route. From Grant Grove's visitor center, follow the paved side road east, turning left after 0.1 miles, then right at the John Muir Lodge.

Crest National Scenic Trail and the John Muir Trail (see p34).

All of the following sights are between Cedar Grove and Road's End. For sights in the Sequoia National Forest along the Kings Canyon Scenic Byway between Grant Grove and Cedar Grove, see right.

Knapp's Cabin   HISTORIC BUILDING
During the 1920s, wealthy Santa Barbara businessman George Knapp built this simple wood-shingled cabin to store gear during his extravagant fishing and camping excursions into Kings Canyon. From a signed roadside pullout, about 2 miles east of the village, a short trail leads to this hidden building, the oldest in Cedar Grove. Come around dusk, when the views of the glacier-carved canyon are glorious.

Roaring River Falls   WATERFALL
One of the park's most accessible waterfalls, a five-minute walk on a paved trail leads to a 40ft chute that gushes into a granite bowl. In late spring and early summer, the strength of this cascade won't disappoint. Look for the parking lot and trailhead on the south side of the road, about 3 miles east of the village, slightly closer to Road's End.

Zumwalt Meadow   NATURAL FEATURE
This verdant meadow bordered by the Kings River and soaring granite canyon walls offers phenomenal views. In the early morning, the air hums with birdsong, the sun's rays light up the canyon walls, and mule deer and black bears can often be spotted foraging among the long grasses, wildflowers and berry bushes in the meadow. Taking the partly shaded nature loop trail (see p174) gives you a quick snapshot of the canyon's beauty.

Muir Rock   NATURAL FEATURE
On excursions to Kings Canyon, John Muir would allegedly give talks on this large flat river boulder, a short walk from the Road's

End parking lot and a mile past Zumwalt Meadow. A sandy river beach here is taken over by gleeful swimmers in midsummer. Don't jump in when raging waters, swollen with snowmelt, are dangerous. Ask at the Road's End ranger station if conditions are calm enough for a dip.

KINGS CANYON SCENIC BYWAY

The park's two main visitor areas, Grant Grove and Cedar Grove, are linked by narrow, twisting Hwy 180, which makes a dramatic descent into Kings Canyon, carved by glaciers and the mighty Kings River. The canyon itself, plunging over 8000ft when measured from the tip of Spanish Peak, is North America's deepest.

Expect spectacular views along this outstandingly scenic drive (see p169), where rugged peaks, sheer granite cliffs and a roaring river jostle for your attention. Hwy 180 all the way down to Cedar Grove is closed during winter (usually from mid-November until mid-April), but the stretch from Grant Grove to Hume Lake Rd is open year-round.

Converse Basin Grove   FOREST
Tragically, the Converse Basin Grove once contained the world's largest grove of mature sequoias, but it's now an unsettling cemetery for tree stumps. In the late 19th and early 20th centuries, the entire privately owned grove was felled by lumber companies. A financial boondoggle, in part because of high transportation costs, the trees ravaged in this grove were not even suitable for lumber, and many shattered when they hit the ground. Most of the salvageable wood ended up as fence posts and matches.

The only survivor left is a colossus called the **Boole Tree**. The sixth-largest known giant sequoia, it's ironically named for the lumber mill's foreman, and for reasons unknown it was left to live. A 2.5-mile loop hike reaches it from the dirt access road to the trailhead; bring plenty of water and insect repellant. On the way in, stop at **Stump Meadow** to see the oversized remains of 19th-century logging.

Off another dirt road further south, the 20ft-high **Chicago Stump** is all that's left of the once-mighty 3200-year-old General Noble tree. The 285ft giant was cut into sections and transported to the 1893 World's Columbian Exposition in Chicago to demonstrate the unbelievable scale of the newly discovered giant sequoia trees. Dubious viewers soon nicknamed it the 'California hoax'!

The roads to the Boole Tree and the Chicago Stump are unpaved, and the turnoff signs are hard to spot. The Chicago Stump turnoff is next to a stone marker at a four-way intersection off Hwy 180, about 3 miles north of Grant Grove Village; from there, it's another 2 miles to the trailhead, then an easy half-mile loop walk. The last quarter-mile of road is somewhat steep; consider parking in the turnout just before the descent if it's muddy or you don't have 4WD. The turnoff for the Boole Tree road is 1.2 miles further north along Hwy 180; the trailhead is another 2.5 miles in.

Hume Lake Recreation Area   LAKE
(☑559-338-2251; www.fs.fed.us/r5/sequoia; Hume Lake Rd) When it was originally dammed in 1908, this 87-acre artificial lake powered a huge log flume that whisked sequoias harvested in Converse Basin to a mill more than 70 miles away. Today, a popular USFS campground and sandy coves and beaches line the lakeshore. Privately operated Hume Lake Christian Camps runs a snack bar for burgers and milkshakes, a small market for groceries and camping sundries, gas pumps (available 24 hours with credit cards) and beachside canoe and boat rentals.

Boyden Cavern   CAVE
(☑888-965-8243; www.boydencavern.com; Hwy 180; tours adult/child from $13/8; ☉10am-5pm late May-Sep, 11am-4pm late Apr-late May & Oct-mid-Nov) Walk up a steep paved grade to the entrance of this cave for a tour of fantastical underground formations. While the rooms are smaller and the interiors less eye-popping than Sequoia's Crystal Cave, they are beautiful and, unlike the very-visited Crystal Cave, you can show up for a basic 45-minute tour without making advance reservations. Book ahead for thrilling canyoneering and rappelling tours for all skills levels, or to go group camping inside the cave overnight.

DRIVING

Experience the park on four wheels via an exciting ascent to Mineral King, a descent into Kings Canyon or a shuttle ride through some of the Giant Forest's top attractions.

🚗 Moro Rock–Crescent Meadow Road

Duration 1 hour

Distance 6 miles

Start/Finish Giant Forest Museum

Nearest Town Lodgepole Village

Transportation Shuttle, car (RVs over 22ft long and trailers prohibited)

Summary A narrow, windy and sometimes pockmarked road leads to a number of the Giant Forest's most popular attractions. Moro Rock and Crescent Meadow demand detours, and interesting giant sequoias line the way.

This road is closed to private vehicles on summer weekends and holidays. But why fight traffic anyway? Instead, take the free seasonal park shuttle (see p189)! Note that land closes to all traffic in winter, but you can still cross-country ski or snowshoe along it.

From the **Giant Forest Museum**, Moro Rock–Crescent Meadow Rd swoops into the southwestern section of the Giant Forest. Less than a mile in is the **Auto Log**, a hefty sequoia that fell in 1917. For early park visitors, a flat section was carved onto its top and the tree was actually used as part of the road. You can't drive on it anymore, but you can walk on it and imagine.

After almost another mile, turn into the small parking area (we told you to take the shuttle!) to gawk at the pale dome of **Moro Rock**. Continuing on a half-mile further, the mesmerizing flamelike roots of the 2300-year-old collapsed **Buttress Tree** face the road. On the opposite side of the road just a bit further along is the **Parker Group**, named for the eight-person family of US Cavalry Captain James Parker, who served as the park's superintendent in 1893.

In days gone by, the renown of Yosemite's Wawona Tunnel Tree often prompted visitors to inquire about Sequoia's drive-through tree, but it didn't have one. So when a 275ft sequoia bit the dust and went splat across the road in 1937, the park took advantage of this gift and promptly cut a passageway for cars.

This **Tunnel Log** has an 8ft-wide opening, which larger vehicles (ahem, SUVs and RVs) can skirt using an adjacent bypass. From here, it's another mile to the road's end at verdant **Crescent Meadow**.

Return as you arrived, bypassing the side trip to Moro Rock.

🚗 Mineral King Road

Duration 1.5 hours

Distance 25 miles one way

Start Hwy 198

Finish Eagle/Mosquito trailhead parking area

Nearest Town Three Rivers

Transportation Car (RVs over 22ft long and trailers prohibited)

Summary Steel your nerves and take your time, because this madcap road will test your mettle. Skirting the canyon of the Kaweah River's East Fork, the road makes almost 700 sharp turns while ascending to 7500ft.

Usually only open from the Friday of Memorial Day weekend through late October, this is a twisting 25-mile road that you will not soon forget. Some sections are hair-raisingly narrow and unpaved, but the grade is never too difficult – just remember that uphill vehicles have the right of way. On the return trip, downshift into lower gear to save your vehicle's brakes.

In the town of Three Rivers (last chance for gas), 2 miles south of the national park's Ash Mountain Entrance, take a deep breath and turn off Hwy 198 onto well-signed Mineral King Rd. On the right you'll start to see long sections of **water flume** cutting a sharp line across the hillside. The metal flume you see now replaced the original sequoia-wood structure dating from 1899, which brought hydroelectric power to this remote region before the road was paved. To get a closer look, stop at the 1923 **Kaweah River Bridge**, around 6.5 miles from the start of the road.

Approximately 9 miles in, you'll pass a **waterfall** with natural pools carved into the smooth granite surface next to the road. The park boundary resumes another half-mile further along, and another mile further you'll reach the self-pay **park entrance fee kiosk**, where there are pullovers and canyon views. Occasionally you'll see water troughs to the side of the road, built for horses pulling

stagecoaches – the original users of this road in the late 19th century. Just over 16 miles from its start, the road passes a shady picnic area in a petite grove of giant sequoias.

Another 3 miles up the road, in a grassy clearing opposite the Atwell Mill ranger residence, is a large **steam engine**, a remnant of a lumber mill once used by the Kaweah colonists (see p190) after they lost their Giant Forest land claims. **Silver City Mountain Resort** is 2 miles further along. Your final destination is just over a mile past the **Mineral King ranger station**, where the valley unfolds all of its hidden beauty, and the high country beckons with granite peaks and alpine lakes.

🚗 Kings Canyon Scenic Byway

Duration 1.5 hours

Distance 35 miles one way

Start Grant Grove

Finish Road's End

Nearest Towns Grant Grove Village, Cedar Grove Village

Transportation Car

Summary Among the Sierra Nevada's most jaw-dropping scenic drives, this 35-mile rollercoaster descends into North America's deepest canyon, traversing the forested Giant Sequoia National Monument and shadowing the Kings River all the way to Road's End.

John Muir called Kings Canyon 'a rival of the Yosemite.' You can test out his theory for yourself by taking this scenic byway. Fewer than 3 miles from Grant Grove, pull over to drink in the mountain panorama at **McGee Vista Point**. Then keep winding downhill through the Sequoia National Forest to **Converse Basin**, a lonely testament to the 19th-century logging of giant sequoias. Pay your respects to its sole local survivor, the **Boole Tree**, then hop back on the byway.

About 6 miles from Grant Grove appears a detour to **Hume Lake**, which offers sandy beaches and coves for summer swims. Otherwise, keep heading downhill, ever deeper into the canyon. The road serpentines past chiseled rock walls, some tinged by green moss and red iron minerals, others laced by waterfalls. Roadside turnouts provide superb views, notably at **Junction View**, about 11 miles from Grant Grove, and beyond **Yucca Point**, another 3 miles further along.

After countless ear-popping curves, the road bottoms out and runs parallel to the Kings River, its thunderous roar ricocheting off granite cliffs soaring thousands of feet high above. Marbled **Boyden Cavern** offers guided tours that will delight kids. It's another 5 miles to **Grizzly Falls**, often a torrent in late spring and early summer.

The scenic byway re-enters Kings Canyon National Park 3 miles further, quickly passing the **Lewis Creek** bridge and a riverside beach. It's another mile to **Cedar Grove Village**, where you can stop in at the visitor center and grab snacks, drinks or ice cream at the village market before pushing on. Over the next 6 miles, don't miss **Roaring River Falls** and pretty **Zumwalt Meadow**. More hiking trails and swimming holes await at honestly named **Road's End** – the only way to keep going across the Sierra Nevada from there is on foot!

DAY HIKES

Leave your car behind to ramble around wildflower meadows and serene groves of giant sequoias, or hoof it to rushing waterfalls and up polished granite domes for epic views of Sierra Nevada peaks. To pick the perfect hike, check our chart on p36. For a key to our hike difficulty ratings, see p31. For safety tips, see p238.

The nonprofit **Sequoia Natural History Association** (www.sequoiahistory.org) publishes an excellent series of fold-out trail map brochures covering the Cedar Grove, Grant Grove, Giant Forest, Lodgepole and Mineral King areas ($3.50 each). Hiking maps and books are sold at visitor centers and the Giant Forest Museum bookstore. For more recommended hiking maps, books, online resources and group hikes, see p31.

Sequoia National Park

These gentle to moderate day hikes feature pretty waterfalls, subalpine meadows, granite domes and, of course, some fine giant sequoias. The Giant Forest area has the biggest network of hiking routes, with a few wheelchair-accessible paved trails. More waterfall and riverside hikes begin in the Foothills, while the high-elevation valley of Mineral King steps you into the Sierra Nevada backcountry.

 Moro Rock

Duration 40 minutes

Distance 0.5 miles

Difficulty Easy

Start/Finish Moro Rock parking lot/ shuttle stop

Nearest Town Lodgepole Village

Transportation Shuttle, car

Summary After a quick ascent to the tippy-top of a famous granite dome, the panoramic views are worth every ounce of effort. On clear days, feast your eyes on skyscraping peaks and the foothills ever-so-far below.

Built by the CCC in the 1930s, this trail features almost 400 steps, which shoot up over a quarter-mile to a railed-in viewpoint corridor atop Sequoia's iconic granite dome. Warning – you do *not* want to be anywhere on this trail during a lightning storm. From the summit, stare down at the Middle Fork of the Kaweah River, across to Sawtooth Peak south in the Mineral King region, and toward the peaks of the Great Western Divide to the east, including the spike of Black Kaweah. Near dusk, the monolith-like crags of Castle Rocks cast dramatic shadows over the dizzyingly deep river canyon. On hazy days (which are most common in summer), air pollution may obscure the views.

Big Trees Trail

Duration 45 minutes

Distance 1.2 miles

Difficulty Easy

Start/Finish Giant Forest Museum

Nearest Town Lodgepole Village

Transportation Shuttle, car

Summary On a paved trail circling a petite meadow embraced by giant sequoias, this family-friendly walk shows off some of the park's signature flora, all growing within one small area.

Starting from the 'Trail Center' outside the Giant Forest Museum, follow a well-marked path that loops pretty Round Meadow. Giant sequoias edge the meadow, while interpretive panels give the lowdown on sequoia ecology, explaining how the western Sierra Nevada ecosystem supports these monster trees' growth. Wildflowers peak in early summer, giving the meadow kaleidoscopic bursts of color. This is one of the park's only fully wheelchair-accessible trails; starting from the disabled parking lot (permit required) off the Generals Hwy shortens the total distance to half a mile.

🏃 Crescent Meadow Loop

Duration 1 hour

Distance 1.6 miles

Difficulty Easy

Start/Finish Crescent Meadow parking lot/shuttle stop

Nearest Town Lodgepole Village

Transportation Shuttle, car

Summary At this beautiful and easily reached subalpine meadow, ringed by a canopy of firs and sequoias, early summer wildflowers turn up the color, and bears often forage nearby.

From the trailhead, stroll in either direction around the peaceful, shady meadow loop. Downed logs make handy steps for peering over the high grass, but don't let your footfalls crunch and compact the fragile meadow itself. If you're quiet and stealthy, you may spy black bears ripping apart logs as they look for insects trapped in the bark underneath. Around the meadow's northeast corner, poke your head inside and look up the hollow fire-scarred **Chimney Tree**. It's a 0.3-mile detour east toward Log Meadow to inspect **Tharp's Log**, a fallen giant sequoia that a 19th-century settler converted into a rustic cabin.

🏃 Tokopah Falls

Duration 2 hours

Distance 3.5 miles

Difficulty Easy

Start/Finish Lodgepole Campground

Nearest Town Lodgepole Village

Transportation Shuttle, car

Summary This riverside stroll reaches one of the parks' most scenic waterfalls, tumbling down a boulder-lined canyon. Starting from the campground, it's a popular hike for families with kids.

From the parking area just inside the Lodgepole Campground entrance station, cross the bridge to the opposite side of the Kaweah River's **Marble Fork**. The entire hike runs alongside the river, with exceptional views of the glacier-carved canyon and opportunities to watch pika, marmots and mule deer.

As you near the falls, the severe 1800ft granite face of the **Watchtower** looms to the south. At 1200ft high, **Tokopah Falls** doesn't free fall but rather bounces off the granite canyon cliffs with all the sound and passion it can muster, especially when the snowmelt gushes in late spring and early summer. When you're ready, return along the same route.

🏃 General Sherman Tree to Moro Rock

Duration 2½–4 hours

Distance 6 miles one way

Difficulty Moderate

Start Upper Sherman Tree parking lot/shuttle stop

Finish Moro Rock parking lot/shuttle stop

Nearest Town Lodgepole Village

Transportation Shuttle, car

Summary A deviation from the popular Congress Trail, this rolling one-way hike takes in huge sequoias, gorgeous green meadows and the pinnacle of Moro Rock. Expect stretches of blissful solitude and potential black bear sightings.

Keep in mind that hiking this route one way is possible only when the free seasonal park shuttles are running, usually from late May until late September (see p189).

From the upper (main) parking lot and shuttle stop for the General Sherman Tree, a paved trail quickly descends through towering sequoias. From an overlook on the way down, you'll get the best view of the **General Sherman Tree**. After walking up to the giant's trunk, turn around and walk downhill on the western branch of the Congress Trail loop. (If you end up on the eastern branch by mistake, jog right then left at two minor trail junctions that appear about 0.5 miles from the General Sherman Tree.)

At a five-way junction by the **McKinley Tree**, continue straight on the dirt trail towards **Cattle Cabin**. Pass the hollow-bottom **Room Tree** and the pretty cluster of the **Founders Group**, walking through tufts of ferns and corn lilies. Approaching the bright green strip of 'C'-shaped **Circle Meadow**, there are no more crowds, and all you can hear is the wind and the birds. Trace

General Sherman Tree to Moro Rock

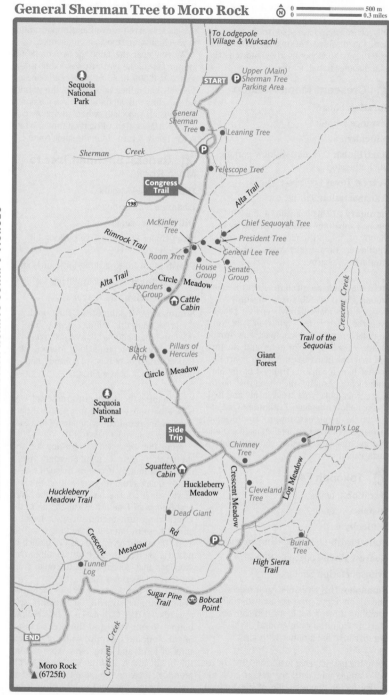

the western edge of the meadow and you'll come to another well-named tree group, the **Pillars of Hercules**. Stand between them and look up for a heroic view. The trail then goes through the huge charred maw of the **Black Arch** tree.

Continue south, veering slightly right and then left at the next two trail junctions. At a three-way intersection, lush Crescent Meadow finally comes into view. Go straight at this junction and the next one to continue, or make a 0.6-mile round-trip detour to the **Squatters Cabin** by going right on the trail marked 'Huckleberry Meadow.' On the north side of Crescent Meadow stands the hollow-bodied **Chimney Tree**. Continue east to visit the tree house of **Tharp's Log**, then turn right (south) along **Log Meadow**, walking its length on a paved trail.

Before reaching the Crescent Meadow parking lot, jog left then right onto the signed High Sierra Trail, heading west for more marvelous ridge views. Stop at the **Bobcat Point** overlook to take in the Great Western Divide and Kaweah Canyon. In 0.2 miles, cross Crescent Creek on a log to join the Sugar Pine Trail above. Go left (west) and follow it for 0.9 miles to **Moro Rock**. Climb your final prize for some of the best views in the park, then return to your starting point via shuttle buses.

Marble Falls

Duration 3–4 hours

Distance 7 miles

Difficulty Moderate

Start/Finish Potwisha Campground

Nearest Town Three Rivers

Transportation Car

Summary Climb over 1500ft as you follow the curves of chaparral-blanketed hills and parallel a river canyon to reach a thundering cascade. Prime time is March through May, when wildflowers bloom and the heat is less intense.

Because of the extreme heat in the low-elevation Foothills, get an early-morning start. Turn right near campsite number 14 and follow the dirt road uphill, parking off to the side of the metal-chain gate, where a bear box is provided. Start walking on the dirt road, heading uphill and across a concrete ditch. Look for a sign for the trail, which starts steeply to the right.

The beginning of this trail is the most challenging, with a quick ascent via switchbacks. Watch out for rattlesnakes, ticks and poison oak (see the boxed text, p40). Past the switchbacks, shady tree cover gives way to scrubby chaparral and the trail continues north along the eastern side of **Deep Canyon**, with views of the Kaweah River's Marble Fork. The path crosses several streams and ducks into the woods, then veers towards the river and the booming falls, dead-ending in a heap of boulders.

Retrace your steps to return.

Monarch Lakes

Duration 4–6 hours

Distance 8.5 miles

Difficulty Difficult

Start/Finish Sawtooth/Monarch trailhead parking area

Nearest Town Silver City

Transportation Car

Summary A marmot-lover's paradise! This scenic out-and-back high-country route reaches two alpine lakes at the base of jagged Sawtooth Peak. Novice backpackers will appreciate that it's not very long, although it can be breathtakingly steep.

Steep stairs kick off this higher-altitude trek. At the Timber Gap Trail junction a half-mile in, you can see the end of Mineral King Rd back below and snow-brushed peaks looking south. Turn right, following the marker for Sawtooth Pass. Corn lilies and paintbrush speckle **Groundhog Meadow**, named for the prolific whistling marmots that seem to scramble everywhere you look during this hike.

Just before leaving the meadow to cross Monarch Creek, glance up to the left to appreciate a small burbling waterfall. On the far bank of the creek, a shady wooded spot is the perfect place for a picnic lunch. From there, begin ascending a stretch of loose and lazy switchbacks with goose-bump views. It's a slow, steady climb through red fir forest that won't leave you too winded, though you'll feel the altitude the higher you climb. Occasionally blue grouse are spotted on the hillsides.

At about 2.5 miles there's a signed junction for the Crystal Lake Trail, which takes a hard and steep right. Bear left and continue straight up toward Sawtooth Pass instead.

After flipping to the opposite side of the ridgeline, the trail crosses into the **Chihuahua Bowl**, an avalanche-prone granite basin named after a Mexican mining region. The tree line wavers and fades away, opening up gorgeous views of Monarch Creek canyon, Timber Gap and the peaks of the Great Western Divide.

The distinctive pitch of Sawtooth Peak (12,343ft) is visible ahead. A walk through a large talus field and some stream crossings bring you to **Lower Monarch Lake** (10,400ft), where round-topped **Mineral Peak** (11,615ft) points up directly south. The maintained trail stops here, but **Upper Monarch Lake** can be reached by a steep trail heading further up the hillside. You'll find established backpacker campsites by Lower Monarch Lake. For overnight camping, a wilderness permit is required (see p176).

When you're ready, retrace your steps to return. If you're looking for challenging cross-country treks with some steep drop-offs and rock scrambling required, detour up scree-covered **Sawtooth Pass** or make an alternate return route via **Crystal Lake**. But ask for route advice and safety tips at the Mineral King ranger station first.

Kings Canyon National Park

Towering stands of giant sequoias await in Grant Grove. Deep inside Kings Canyon, a meditative meadow walk and a day hike to a waterfall start in Cedar Grove and near Road's End.

🏃 General Grant Tree Trail

Duration 30 minutes

Distance 0.5 miles

Difficulty Easy

Start/Finish General Grant Grove parking lot

Nearest Town Grant Grove Village

Transportation Car

Summary On a short, paved, self-guided interpretive loop through one of the parks' most extraordinary giant sequoia groves, meet the General Grant Tree, the third-largest living tree in the world.

At the east end of the parking lot, you can see the cheerfully named tree cluster of **Happy Family**. At the eastern fenced trailhead, bear right and begin a counter-clockwise loop.

Most of the monster sequoias in this grove are named for US states, and the first you come across is the **Pennsylvania Tree**. Beyond stands the **Robert E Lee Tree**, which, like the grove itself, is another Civil War namesake. What looks like submerged logs in front are actually its exposed roots – the accumulated damage from more than a century of visitors' footsteps.

Further along is the **Fallen Monarch**, a toppled log so big that its hollow core has been used as housing, a hotel and saloon, and then as horse stables. Walk through a mix of young sequoias and other conifers, including sugar pine and white fir, until you reach the impressive **General Grant Tree** (see p166).

Further on is the one-room **Gamlin Pioneer Cabin**, built from sugar pine in 1872 by the first white settlers in this area. To see another good view of the Grant Tree, detour right here from the main loop and bear up and around to the left. The path leads to a peaceful overlook called **North Grant View** and, unlike the rest of the trail, there's rarely anyone here to share the scenery.

The **California Tree** has had good luck. Struck by lightning in 1967, the top incinerated and fire burned inside until rangers grew concerned that burning branches would hurt visitors. A nimble park employee strung a rope between two adjacent trees and extinguished the blaze with a hose.

Amble on until you reach the parking lot.

🏃 Zumwalt Meadow Loop

Duration 1 hour

Distance 1.5 miles

Difficulty Easy

Start/Finish Zumwalt Meadow parking lot

Nearest Town Cedar Grove Village

Transportation Car

Summary An extremely scenic, mostly flat loop around a gorgeous meadow, this is a fun nature walk with kids. The trail traces a section of the Kings River and flaunts knockout canyon wall views.

A mile west of Road's End, **Zumwalt Meadow** is best in the early morning, when mist floats above the meadow and birdsong echoes off the canyon's soaring granite walls. Buy the self-guided hike brochure ($1.50) at the visitor center in Cedar Grove Village before driving out to the trailhead.

From the parking lot, walk parallel to the river then across a suspension footbridge spanning the Kings River's South Fork. Behind you to the north is a view of **North Dome**, with a sheer cliff drop of over 3600ft, higher than Yosemite's El Capitan. At the next junction, go left along the River Trail, then keep straight ahead to begin a counter-clockwise loop through a forest of cottonwood, willow, black oak, white fir and ponderosa pine trees.

Looking ahead, the granite cliffs of **Grand Sentinel** cast shadows from over a half mile above the canyon floor. The trail ascends and continues over a talus slope with great views of canyon cliffs and the lush meadow. At the next signed junction, turn left and follow the Kings River bank through ferns and a carpet of soft pine needles, stepping across boardwalks to close the loop. Turn right and retrace your steps across the footbridge to the parking lot.

🏃 Mist Falls

Duration 3–5 hours

Distance 8 miles

Difficulty Moderate

Start/Finish Road's End

Nearest Town Cedar Grove Village

Transportation Car

Summary A satisfying long walk along the riverside and up a natural granite staircase highlights the beauty of Kings Canyon. The waterfall is most thunderous in late spring and early summer.

Bring plenty of water and sunscreen on this hike and get an early morning start, because the return trip can be brutally hot on summer afternoons.

The trail begins just past the **Road's End** wilderness permit station, crossing a small footbridge over **Copper Creek**. Walk along a sandy trail through sparse cedar and pine forest, where boulders rolled by avalanches are scattered on the canyon floor. Keep an eye out for black bears.

Eventually the trail enters cooler, shady and low-lying areas of ferns and reeds before reaching a well-marked three-way junction with the Woods Creek Trail, just shy of 2 miles from Road's End. Turn left (north) toward Paradise Valley and begin a gradual climb of 300ft that runs parallel to powerful cataracts in the boulder-saturated Kings River. Stone-framed stairs lead to a granite knob overlook, with wide southern views of **Avalanche Peak** and the oddly pointed **Sphinx**, another mountain peak, behind you.

Follow cairns up the rock face and continue briefly through shady forest to reach **Mist Falls**, one of the parks' largest waterfalls. Warning – don't wade above the waterfall or swim below it, due to the danger of rockfall and swiftwater currents, especially during snowmelt runoff. In late summer, the river downstream from the falls may be tame enough for a dip – use your own best judgment, however.

Retrace your steps for just less than 2 miles to the three-way trail junction. Instead of returning directly to Road's End, bear left and cross the bridge over the Kings River, briefly joining the Bubbs Creek Trail. After less than a quarter-mile, turn right onto the untrammeled Kanawyer Loop Trail, which is mostly flat. After crossing Avalanche Creek on a makeshift log bridge, the tree canopy opens up to show off sprawling talus slopes along the Kings Canyon's southern walls.

The **Muir Rock swimming hole** comes into view across the river before you make a short climb to the River Trail junction. Turn right and walk across the red footbridge, below which is another favorite late-summer swimming hole, then follow the path back to the paved highway, turning right to get back to the Road's End parking lot.

OVERNIGHT HIKES

Over 850 miles of maintained trails await your footsteps in both national parks. From sun-bleached granite peaks soaring above alpine lakes, to wildflower-strewn meadows and gushing waterfalls, it's backpacking heaven. Mineral King, Lodgepole and Cedar Grove offer the best backcountry trail access, while the Jennie Lakes Wilderness in the Sequoia National Forest boasts pristine meadows and lakes at lower elevations.

Park-approved bear-proof food canisters are always recommended, and may be mandatory in some places (eg Rae Lakes Loop). Bear canisters may be rented at park visitor centers and trailhead ranger stations (from $5 per trip) or at the Lodgepole, Grant Grove and Cedar Grove Village markets (price varies, but typically more expensive).

Sequoia Natural History Association (SNHA; www.sequoiahistory.org) sells topographic maps at park visitor centers and wilderness permit stations. Highly recommended are SNHA's *Rae Lakes Loop Trail Map* ($8.95) and the Tom Harrison Maps series, all printed on waterproof, tear-resistant paper. For more information about maps, online resources, hiking guides and group hikes, see p31.

Permits & Fees

Wilderness permits are required for all overnight trips (not day hikes) in the national parks and are available at visitor centers and trailhead ranger stations. Overnight trips on USFS lands require only campfire permits (free).

For national park trips, there's a $15 wilderness permit fee during the quota season (late May until late September). Outside that period, obtain free self-issue permits at the visitor center or ranger station closest to the trailhead.

About 25% of all available national-park wilderness permits are set aside for first-come, first-served walk-ups starting at 1pm *the day before* your trip. It's not unusual for permits for the most popular trails to sell out immediately.

Wilderness-permit reservations are held until 9am on the day of your trip, after which no-show vacancies may be made available to walk-up visitors.

To reserve your wilderness permit ahead of time during the quota season, requests must be received two weeks in advance of your trip date, beginning on March 1 of that year. Permit applications can be downloaded from the parks' website (www.nps.gov/seki /planyourvisit/wilderness_permits.htm).

Sequoia National Park

Shoulder your backpack and head for alpine lakes and meadows. The park's busiest trailheads cluster around Lodgepole and the Giant Forest. Beware of very hungry marmots (see the boxed text, p165) if you're starting out from the park's remote Mineral King Valley, where sculpted granite peaks and glacial cirques await.

🏃 High Sierra Trail to Bearpaw Meadow

Duration 2 days

Distance 22 miles

Difficulty Difficult

Start/Finish Crescent Meadow parking lot/shuttle stop

Nearest Town Lodgepole Village

Transportation Shuttle, car

Summary Ascending from Crescent Meadow in the Giant Forest, this popular overnight backpacking trip gives you a small taste of a long-distance trail that continues across the Sierras, with wonderful views of the Great Western Divide.

From Crescent Meadow (6700ft), the High Sierra Trail commences an undulating traverse high along the forested north side of the canyon of the Kaweah River's Middle Fork. Trimmed by summer wildflowers, the path passes in and out of mixed-conifer forest as it unfolds a rolling panorama of the Kaweah Basin and the high granite peaks of the Great Western Divide. Emerging from the forest, the first handful of miles are exposed and hot, so get an early-morning start.

Just under a mile from the trailhead, Eagle View lookout is an excellent vantage point from which to see Moro Rock, to the west, and Castle Rocks, across the deep river canyon. The trail passes over Panther Creek after 3 miles, offering the first campsites. Soon after crossing Mehrten Creek, about 5.5 miles in, you'll pass a spur trail leading north to the Alta Trail before crossing over Buck Creek.

The trails then ascends via switchbacks to Bearpaw Meadow (7800ft), where backpacker campsites are signed south of the trail in the forest. A seasonal ranger station and the Bearpaw High Sierra Camp (see p183) are on either side of the trail about a quarter-mile ahead.

Several good day hikes continue past Bearpaw Meadow (for example, to Hamilton Lakes), or you can keep going another 50-plus miles all the way to Mt Whitney (see p194). Otherwise, return along the same route to Crescent Meadow.

Kings Canyon National Park

Myriad backcountry routes leading to granite peaks, alpine lakes and high-country meadows depart from Road's End, deep inside Kings Canyon, about 6 miles east of Cedar Grove Village.

🏃 Rae Lakes Loop

Duration 5 days

Distance 40 miles

Difficulty Difficult

Start/Finish Road's End

Nearest Town Cedar Grove Village

Transportation Car

Summary The best backpacking loop in Kings Canyon tours sun-dappled forests and meadows, crosses one mind-bending pass and skirts a chain of jewel-like lakes beneath the Sierra crest, joining the famous John Muir Trail partway along.

DAY 1: ROAD'S END TO MIDDLE PARADISE VALLEY
4-6 HOURS, 7 MILES

The Rae Lakes Loop kicks off with a 4-mile hike along the Woods Creek Trail from **Road's End** (5045ft) to **Mist Falls** (see p175). A series of short switchbacks takes you to the top of the waterfall and, beyond, a larger and longer set of rocky switchbacks leads you up into the shadier forest above the river.

The trail levels out as it enters **Paradise Valley**, less than 2 miles north of the falls. The Kings River's South Fork flows through forested meadows, inviting you to linger at the first backpacker campsites in **Lower Paradise Valley** (6600ft). Continue up the beautiful valley along river beaches and through mixed-conifer forest just over a mile further to **Middle Paradise Valley** (6700ft), with more open views and typically less crowded campsites.

DAY 2: MIDDLE PARADISE VALLEY TO WOODS CREEK
4-6 HOURS, 7 MILES

Passing ponderosa pines and white firs, the trail ascends gradually, passing alongside a grassy meadow before dropping back down along the river to **Upper Paradise Valley** (6800ft). Forested campsites appear just before the confluence of the Kings River's South Fork and Woods Creek, about 1.5 miles from Middle Paradise Valley.

After crossing a footbridge, the trail steady ascends switchbacks that dart into and out of the shade while climbing through a forested valley above Woods Creek. Less than five miles from the river crossing, the trail rolls into **Castle Dome Meadow** (8200ft) beneath the spectacular, polished white-granite Castle Domes.

The views of Castle Domes get better and better as the trail continues meandering across the meadow and re-enters pine forest. At the signposted John Muir Trail junction (8500ft), turn right and cross Woods Creek on the wooden planks of a steel-cable suspension bridge. Two backpacker camping areas lie just south of the bridge, one near the trail and the other a short distance downstream.

DAY 3: WOODS CREEK TO MIDDLE RAE LAKE
3½-5 HOURS, 6.5 MILES

Heading south, the John Muir Trail rolls easily on open slopes along the west side of Woods Creek's South Fork, with good views of the granite high country above the confluence. Crossing a small side stream, the trail continues upvalley and rises on rocky terrain to reach a small meadow. At the next crossing, a bigger stream cascades over a cleft in the rock as it drains Sixty Lake Basin to the southwest.

Beyond the stream, foxtail pines dot the dry slope above the trail as it continues up to **Dollar Lake** (10,220ft), about 3.5 miles from the Woods Creek crossing. Near the north end of Dollar Lake (camping prohibited), a faint trail branches east toward **Baxter Pass** (12,270ft). The striking view of **Fin Dome** (11,693ft) above Dollar Lake sets the theme of mountain splendor that typifies Rae Lakes.

Skirting Dollar Lake's west shore, continue up and arrive at larger **Arrowhead Lake** (10,300ft). The trail ascends more gradually to enchanting **Lower Rae Lake** (10,535ft). The trail rolls gently through, crossing several small side streams and passing the spur trail to the seasonal Rae Lakes ranger station. Continue to the signed turnoff for campsites above the eastern shore of **Middle Rae Lake** (10,540ft).

DAY 4: MIDDLE RAE LAKE TO JUNCTION MEADOW
5-7 HOURS, 9 MILES

Get up very early and eat a big breakfast, because this is the big game day. Return to the John Muir Trail and turn right (south). Walk along the northern shore of **Upper Rae Lake** (10,545ft). Cross the connector stream between the lakes and come to a signed trail junction, where a faint trail to Sixty Lake Basin heads off northwest. Keep straight ahead on the John Muir Trail, which continues south up well-graded switchbacks above the west side of Upper Rae Lake.

Heading higher, more switchbacks take you up a talus slope to a tarn-filled basin, from where Glen Pass is visible ahead on the dark, rocky ridgeline. The trail passes many small mountain lakes, which glisten in the barren cirque to the west. Then it

Rae Lakes Loop

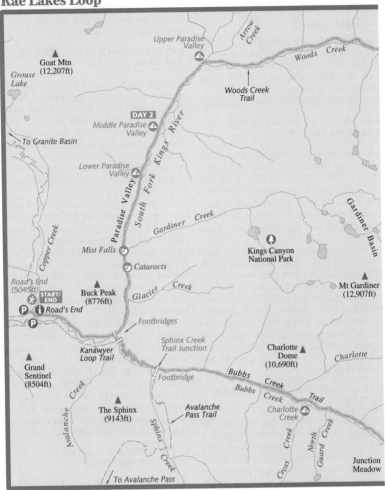

rises on a series of switchbacks up talus to the very narrow and rocky saddle of **Glen Pass** (11,978ft), almost 3 miles from Middle Rae Lakes.

From the pass, visible in the distance to the southwest are massive Mt Brewer (13,576ft), with its snowy northeast face, and other peaks along the Great Western Divide and Kings-Kern Divide. Mt Bago (11,868ft) is that distinctive reddish peak in the foreground. Gravelly but well-graded switchbacks take you down from Glen Pass on a steep scree slope toward a pothole tarn at the tree line. Stop to filter water here,

since the next reliable water is not until the Bullfrog Lake outlets a few miles ahead.

Head down the narrow canyon, passing above a snow-fed, talus-lined pool until the trail swings south, then contours high above Charlotte Lake. A connector trail to Kearsarge Pass appears about 2.5 miles from Glen Pass, after which you'll soon reach a sandy four-way junction with the main Charlotte Lake (northwest) and Kearsarge Pass (northeast) trails. Continuing straight (south), you catch a glimpse of distant Forester Pass (13,180ft), the highest point on the John Muir Trail. At the head of Bubbs Creek, you'll cross a low

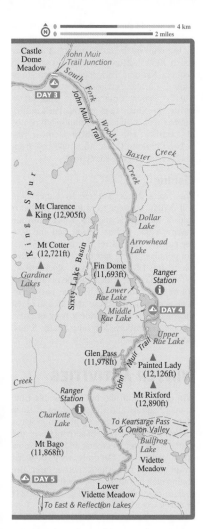

continuing to aspen-filled **Junction Meadow** (8500ft). Past the signed junction with the East and Reflection Lakes Trails you'll find grassy campsites.

DAY 5: JUNCTION MEADOW TO ROAD'S END
5-7 HOURS, 10.5 MILES

From the west end of Junction Meadow, the Bubbs Creek Trail continues meandering downvalley. Granite walls tower on both sides as you descend to Charlotte Creek, about 3.5 miles from Junction Meadow. Crossing the creek, the creekside trail continues downhill for 3 miles to meet the Sphinx Creek Trail Junction (6240ft), where a trail heading off left (south) toward Avalanche Pass crosses the creek on a wooden footbridge.

Continuing straight ahead, the Bubbs Creek Trail descends steeply on hot, open switchbacks, providing sweeping views into **Kings Canyon** and of the granite pinnacle of the **Sphinx** (9143ft) towering above you. At last reaching the canyon floor, the trail crosses braided Bubbs Creek over several wooden footbridges in quick succession. Just beyond the steel **Bailey Bridge**, which spans the Kings River's South Fork, is the junction with the Paradise Valley Trail. Turn left (west) and retrace your steps from Day 1 over mostly level ground for less than 2 miles back to **Road's End**.

OTHER ACTIVITIES

Swimming, Canoeing & Boating

Swimming holes abound along the Marble Fork of the Kaweah River in the Foothills area of Sequoia National Park, especially near Potwisha Campground and Hospital Rock. In Kings Canyon, **Muir Rock** and the **Red Bridge** by Road's End are favorite swimming holes, as is **Lewis Creek** west of Cedar Grove Village. In the Sequoia National Forest, **Hume Lake** is dreamy on a hot summer day, and you can rent canoes and boats by the beach at Hume Lake Christian Camps. You may find swimming holes in the Kings River along the Kings Canyon Scenic Byway east of Boyden Cavern, but never go in if you see white water.

Horseback Riding & Pack Trips

Cedar Grove Pack Station   TOURS
(📞summer 559-565-3464, winter 559-337-2314; Cedar Grove Village; ⏾mid-May–Oct) In Kings Canyon, this family-owned outfit offers day

rise and begin to descend, passing a junction with the trail heading northeast to Bullfrog Lake and Kearsarge Lakes.

The scenic descent twice crosses the outlet from **Bullfrog Lake** to reach **Lower Vidette Meadow** (9480ft). Leaving the John Muir Trail, turn right (southwest) and follow the trail down Bubbs Creek past campsites along the forested edge of the meadow. Descending west along the tumbling creekside, the trail crosses several side streams and a large rockslide, then finds shade beneath firs. Beneath soaring granite walls on either side of the canyon, the trail drops steadily down to the now narrow, rushing Bubbs Creek,

ⓘ WARNING!

Drownings in the Kings and Kaweah Rivers are the leading cause of death in the parks. Swift currents can be deadly, especially when rivers are swollen with snowmelt runoff in late spring and early summer. When in doubt, stay out! Ask for advice about current swimming conditions at park visitor centers and ranger stations.

rides until its backcountry pack-trip business gets busy in July. Half-day rides are $75, all-day rambles are $125 and backcountry trips start at $90 per person per day.

Grant Grove Stables   TOURS
(☑summer 559-335-9292, winter 559-799-7242; ☺early Jun–mid-Sep) Just north of the General Grant Tree Grove, this pint-sized operation offers one- and two-hour trail rides for $40 to $60.

Horse Corral Pack Station   TOURS
(☑summer 559-565-3404, winter 209-564-6429; www.highsierrapackers.org; ☺mid-May–Oct) At Big Meadows in the Giant Sequoia National Monument, a rustic corral offers half-day ($45) and full-day ($75) trail rides, and overnight and multiday backcountry pack trips.

Caving

The caves in Sequoia and Kings Canyon are so extensive that the parks could have been designated on the basis of the cave systems alone. Of all the California caves more than a mile long, half of them are found here, as well as Lilburn Cave – at 17 surveyed miles it's the longest known cave in the state. New caves are still being discovered, like Sequoia National Park's Ursa Minor in 2006. So are new species of troglobites (animals that live in dark caves), like those recently identified in Sequoia's **Crystal Cave** (see the boxed text, p164), which include eyeless insects and a tiny pseudoscorpion. Currently, Crystal Cave and **Boyden Cavern** (p168), off the Kings Canyon Scenic Byway, are the only caves open for public tours.

Rock Climbing

Both parks have tons of rock-climbing spots, though many of the best require a long backcountry hike before you even *start* to climb. The most spectacular climb is an 1800ft granite wall in the Valhalla Cirque called **Angel Wings**, nicknamed 'an alpine El Capitan' by the renowned climber and photographer Galen Rowell. More accessible locations in Sequoia National Park include **Moro Rock** (closed during peregrine nesting season, usually March through July) and **Little Baldy**. In Kings Canyon, the backcountry Bubbs Creek Trail leads to multipitch climbs at **Charlito and Charlotte Domes**, just before Charlotte Creek, an 8-mile trek from Road's End, east of Cedar Grove.

Fishing

The rivers, lakes and creeks found here will delight amateur trout anglers. Tackle is sold at most park markets. Kings Canyon's **Lewis Creek**, **Bubbs Creek** and the **Motor Nature Trail** (River Rd in Cedar Grove) are popular fishing spots, as is **Hume Lake**, where the US Forest Service stocks trout. A fishing license, which can be obtained at Hume Lake and possibly some park markets, is required for those aged 16 and older. Visitor centers can provide a copy of park-specific regulations (eg lures, daily limits, catch-and-release).

WINTER ACTIVITIES

Winter is an unusual but memorable time to visit Sequoia and Kings Canyon. A thick blanket of snow drapes giant sequoia trees and meadows, the pace of activity slows and a hush falls over the roads and trails. Snow often closes the Generals Hwy between Grant Grove and Giant Forest, and tire chains may be required at any time. For up-to-date road conditions call ☑559-565-3341 or check www.nps.gov/seki.

Snowshoeing and **cross-country skiing** are hugely popular activities, with 50 miles of ungroomed trails criss-crossing the Grant Grove and Giant Forest areas (trail maps sold at visitor centers). There are more tree-marked, but groomed, trails in the Giant Sequoia National Monument, along with 30 miles of groomed terrain maintained by the private Montecito Sequoia Lodge (see p184). Winter road closures also make for excellent cross-country skiing and snowshoeing on Sequoia's Moro Rock–Crescent Meadow Rd, Kings Canyons' Panoramic Point Rd and the Sequoia National Forest's Big Meadows Rd. You'll find **snow-play areas** at Wolverton Meadow in Sequoia's Giant Forest; Big

Stump and Columbine in Kings Canyon's Grant Grove; and Big Meadows, Quail Flat and Cherry Gap in the Sequoia National Forest nearby.

Cross-country ski and snowshoe rentals are available at Grant Grove Village, Wuksachi Lodge and the Montecito Sequoia Lodge, all of which also sell limited winter clothing and snow-play gear. In winter, park rangers lead two-hour **snowshoe walks** (free snowshoe use included) around the Giant Forest and Grant Grove. These walks fill up fast, so reserve a spot in advance at park visitor centers or by calling ☎559-565-4480 (Giant Forest) or ☎559-565-4307 (Grant Grove).

Backcountry experts who aren't intimidated by a steep 6-mile cross-country ski or snowshoe trek can enter the lottery to bunk down overnight at Sequoia's rustic Pear Lake Ski Hut (see p183).

SLEEPING

Sequoia National Park

Camping

For campground amenities and elevations, consult the chart on p182.

LODGEPOLE VILLAGE & WUKSACHI

The park's only reservable **campsites** (☎518-885-3639, 877-444-6777; www.recreation.gov; ☻reservations accepted for summer) are here. Pay showers are available at Lodgepole Village Market, usually from mid-April through mid-October.

Lodgepole Campground　　　CAMPGROUND $
(Lodgepole Village, Generals Hwy; campsites $10-20; ☻year-round; 🖧) On the Kaweah River, this is the park's biggest and busiest campground, with over 200 sites that shoehorn campers in. The campground stays open year-round, and the main reason it gets so much action is because it's reservable from late May through September. If you want a surefire location in summer, this is your place, but if you want serenity and space, journey on. Bring your bike and ride it around the village area – just watch out for RVs!

Dorst Campground　　　CAMPGROUND $
(Generals Hwy; campsites $20; ☻late Jun-early Sep) Of the over 200 sites at the park's second-largest campground, some are definitely better than others. The quieter back sites are for tents only, while the front loops

can get jam-packed with RVs. It's sometimes possible to find a last-minute spot here when Lodgepole Campground is full.

FOOTHILLS

These lower-elevation campgrounds are very hot and dry, especially in summer, when they often get packed with groups and are sometimes rowdy.

Potwisha Campground　　　CAMPGROUND $
(Generals Hwy; campsites $18; ☻year-round) A bigger, noisier campground with decent shade and swimming spots on the Kaweah River.

Buckeye Flat Campground　　　CAMPGROUND $
(off Generals Hwy; campsites $18; ☻Apr-Sep) A few sites tucked in a canyon near the river; down a winding road off-limits to RVs and trailers.

South Fork Campground　　　CAMPGROUND $
(South Fork Rd, off Hwy 198; campsites May–mid-Oct $12, Nov-Apr free; ☻year-round) Remote, little-used tent-only campground on the river, 13 miles from Three Rivers down a mostly dirt road.

MINERAL KING

Two first-come, first-served campgrounds sit near the end of remote Mineral King Rd (no trailers or RVs allowed). After the water taps are turned off in mid-October (so pipes don't freeze), camping is free for the remaining two weeks of the season. From late May through mid-October, pay showers are usually available at Silver City Mountain Resort.

Cold Springs Campground　　　CAMPGROUND $
(Mineral King Rd; campsites $12; ☻late May-Oct) A quick walk from the ranger station, this campground has a peaceful creekside location with ridge views and a gorgeous forest setting of conifers and aspen. If you spend the night here at 7500ft, you'll be well on your way to acclimatizing for high-altitude hikes. Cold Springs often fills up on summer weekends, including its secluded walk-in sites.

Atwell Mill Campground　　　CAMPGROUND $
(Mineral King Rd; campsites $12; ☻late May-Oct) Smaller and quieter, Atwell Mill has sites scattered under sky-obscuring forest canopy on the Kaweah River, inside a sequoia grove that was partly logged for timber. Getting a site here is rarely a problem.

GENERALS HIGHWAY

Developed USFS campgrounds off the Generals Hwy in the Sequoia National Forest are usually open from mid-May through

SEQUOIA NATIONAL PARK CAMPGROUNDS

CAMP-GROUND	LOCATION	DESCRIPTION	NO OF SITES	ELEVATION
Buckeye Flat	Foothills	Hot, exposed and sometimes rowdy; tent only	28	2800ft
Potwisha	Foothills	Hot in summer, no snow in winter; near the Kaweah River	40	2100ft
South Fork	Foothills	Remote oak and evergreen-shaded river sites; tent only	10	3600ft
Big Meadows	Generals Hwy	Spacious but primitive forest campsites	45	7600ft
Buck Rock	Generals Hwy	Remote primitive campsites near a fire lookout	11	7600ft
Horse Camp	Generals Hwy	Primitive wooded campsites; metal horse corral	5	7600ft
Stony Creek	Generals Hwy	Comfortable woodsy roadside campsites, including creekside	49	6400ft
Upper Stony Creek	Generals Hwy	Primitive, mostly quiet sites near Stony Creek Lodge	18	6400ft
Dorst	Lodgepole	Sprawling campground; quieter tent-only sites in back	204	6800ft
Lodgepole	Lodgepole	Busy family campground with closely packed sites; some features available summer only	214	6700ft
Atwell Mill	Mineral King	Well-spaced sites under forest canopy; tent only	21	6650ft
Cold Springs	Mineral King	Pretty creekside setting in high-elevation valley; tent only (some walk-in sites)	40	7500ft

All campgrounds have bear-proof boxes, picnic tables, fire pits and trash cans.

 Drinking Water   *Flush Toilets*   *RV Dump Station*   *Wheelchair Accessible*   *Dogs Allowed (On Leash)*   *Great for Families*

late September. Primitive campsites and dispersed camping off Big Meadows Rd may be available until mid-November, or whenever snow closes Forest Service roads. The only reservable **campsites** (☎518-885-3639, 877-444-6777; www.recreation.gov; ⊘reservations accepted for summer) are at Stony Creek. For dispersed camping, pick up a free campfire permit (required) from the Kings Canyon Visitor Center in Grant Grove or the USFS Hume Lake District Office (see p189).

The market at Stony Creek Lodge sells tokens for showers, usually available from mid-May to mid-October.

Stony Creek Campground CAMPGROUND $
(Generals Hwy; campsites $20; ⊘mid-May–late Sep) A mile north of Sequoia National Park, this spacious, shady forest campground is especially well-liked by families. Keep an eye out for the very persistent marauder bears!

Upper Stony Creek Campground CAMPGROUND $
(Generals Hwy; campsites $16; ⊘late May–mid-Sep) With fewer than 20 sites, this primitive campground, accessed via unpaved roads, is blissfully under-visited, but habituated bears are known to be active here, too.

Big Meadows Campground CAMPGROUND $
(Big Meadows Rd; campsites free; ⊘late May–mid-Oct) More than 40 primitive campsites are spacious, shady and relatively peaceful. Although there's no potable water, there's a creek nearby. The campground is off paved Big Meadows Rd – Forest Service (FS) road 14S11 – about 5 miles off the Generals Hwy.

Buck Rock Campground CAMPGROUND $
(FS Rd 13S04, off Big Meadows Rd; campsites free; ⊘mid-Jun–Oct) Less than a dozen primitive campsites (no water), near a high-elevation fire lookout, deep in the forest (for directions, see p166).

OPEN (APPROX)	RESERVATION REQUIRED?	DAILY FEE	FACILITIES	PAGE
Apr-Sep	no	$18		181
year-round	no	$18		181
May–mid-Oct	no	$12 (free Nov-Apr)		181
late May–mid-Oct	no	free		185
mid-Jun–Oct	no	free		182
late May–mid-Oct	no	free		183
mid-May–late Sep	yes	$20		182
late May–early Sep	yes	$16		182
late Jun–early Sep	yes	$20		181
year-round	yes (May-Oct)	$10-20		181
late May-Oct	no	$12		181
late May-Oct	no	$12		181

 Grocery Store Nearby   *Restaurant Nearby*   *Payphone*   *Ranger Station Nearby* *Summertime Campfire Program*

SEQUOIA & KINGS CANYON NATIONAL PARKS SLEEPING

Horse Camp
CAMPGROUND **$**
(Big Meadows Rd; campsites free; ☉late May–mid-Oct) Primitive forest campground (no water) with a metal horse corral for overnight stock use.

Lodging
LODGEPOLE VILLAGE & WUKSACHI
Bearpaw High Sierra Camp CABINS **$$**
(🖉reservations 801-559-4930, 866-807-3598; www.visitsequoia.com; tent cabin per person incl breakfast & dinner $175; ☉mid-Jun–mid-Sep) An 11.5-mile trek on foot from Giant Forest via the High Sierra Trail, this rustic collection of cabins in a high-elevation meadow is ideal for exploring the backcountry without lugging in your own camping gear. Rates for the six tent cabins, each equipped with two twin beds, include bedding, towels and showers in the shared bathhouse, and two meals. Boxed lunches and wine by the glass cost extra. Reservations are taken by phone starting at 7am (PST) January 2, and often sell out immediately. Call to check for last-minute vacancies.

Wuksachi Lodge HOTEL **$$$**
(🖉559-565-4070, 866-807-3598; www.visitsequoia.com; 64740 Wuksachi Way, off Generals Hwy; r $90-335; 🛜) Built in 1999 when the hotel complex at Giant Forest was closed, the Wuksachi Lodge is the most upscale lodging and dining option in the park – but don't get too excited, folks. The wood-paneled atrium lobby has an inviting stone fireplace and forest views, but the disappointingly charmless motel-style rooms with oak furniture and thin walls have an institutional feel. The lodge's location, just north of Lodgepole Village, can't be beat. Wi-fi is available only in the main lobby.

Pear Lake Ski Hut CABIN **$**
(🖉559-565-3759; www.sequoiahistory.org; dm per person $40; ☉mid-Dec–late Apr) In winter, experienced backcountry adventurers with reservations can stay in one of 10 bunk beds inside

KINGS CANYON NATIONAL PARK CAMPGROUNDS

CAMP-GROUND	LOCATION	DESCRIPTION	NO OF SITES	ELEVATION
Canyon View	Cedar Grove	Some sites with shade and canyon views; tent only	23	4600ft
Moraine	Cedar Grove	Large, well-spaced but only partly shaded; used as overflow	120	4600ft
Sentinel	Cedar Grove	Centrally located at Cedar Grove Village; fills up fast	82	4600ft
Sheep Creek	Cedar Grove	Pretty riverside loops; almost as crowded as Sentinel	111	4600ft
Azalea	Grant Grove	Shady forest sites near giant sequoias	110	6500ft
Crystal Springs	Grant Grove	Quieter campsites are wooded and well-spaced	36	6500ft
Sunset	Grant Grove	Huge evergreen-shaded forest campground near the village	157	6500ft
Hume Lake	Hume Lake	Lakeside campsites popular with families and anglers	74	5200ft
Landslide	Hume Lake	Primitive forested sites are well-spaced	9	5800ft
Princess	Hume Lake	Meadow-edged sites off scenic byway, convenient for RVs	88	5900ft
Tenmile	Hume Lake	Bigger but still primitive woodsy campground	13	5800ft
Convict Flat	Kings Canyon Scenic Byway	Secluded primitive sites with tree-sheltered canyon views	5	3000ft

All campgrounds have bear-proof boxes, picnic tables, fire pits and trash cans.

 Drinking Water   *Flush Toilets*   *RV Dump Station*   *Wheelchair Accessible*   *Dogs Allowed (On Leash)*   *Great fo Familie*

this CCC-built pine-and-granite building. You'll be oh-so-glad to see it after a strenuous 6-mile cross-country ski or snowshoe trek uphill from Wolverton Meadow. Reservations are assigned by a lottery in early November; consult the SNHA website for full details.

MINERAL KING

Silver City Mountain Resort   CABINS **$$$**
(☑summer 559-561-3223, winter 805-561-3223; www.silvercityresort.com; Mineral King Rd; cabins $120-195, chalets $250-395; ☺late May-late Oct; ☎♠) The only food and lodging option anywhere near these parts, this rustic, old-fashioned and family-friendly place rents everything from cute and cozy 1950s-era cabins to modern chalets (one is wheel-chair-accessible) that sleep up to eight. There's a ping-pong table, outdoor swings, and nearby ponds to splash around in – younger kids will love it. All guests must bring their own sheets and towels. Most cabins don't have electricity, and the property's generator usually shuts off around 10pm.

The rustic resort stands about 3.5 miles west of the Mineral King ranger station.

GENERALS HIGHWAY

Sequoia High Sierra Camp   CABINS **$$$**
(☑877-591-8982; www.sequoiahighsierracamp.com; r with shared bath incl all meals per adult/child 3-11yr $250/100; ☺mid-Jun–early Oct) Accessed via a 1-mile hike deep in the Sequoia National Forest, this off-the-grid, all-inclusive resort is nirvana for active, sociable people who don't think 'luxury camping' is an oxymoron. Canvas cabins are spiffed up by pillow-top mattresses, down pillows and cozy wool rugs, with shared restrooms and a shower house. Reservations are required. From the Generals Hwy, drive Big Meadows Rd northeast for 10 miles, then turn right onto signed Marvin Pass Rd for 2.5 unpaved miles to find the trailhead parking for guests.

Montecito Sequoia Lodge   LODGE, CABINS **$$$**
(☑559-565-3388, 800-227-9900; www.montecito sequoia.com; 63410 Generals Hwy; lodge r $89-299,

OPEN (APPROX)	RESERVATION REQUIRED?	DAILY FEE	FACILITIES	PAGE
mid-May–mid-Oct	no	$18		186
mid-May–early Sep	no	$18		186
late Apr-Sep	no	$18		186
mid-May–mid-Nov	no	$18		186
year-round	no	$10-18		186
late May–mid-Sep	no	$18		186
late May-early Sep	no	$18		186
late May-early Sep	yes	$20		186
late May-early Sep	no	free		186
mid-May–late Sep	yes	$18		186
late May–mid-Nov	no	free		187
late Apr–mid-Nov	no	free		187

 Grocery Store Nearby *Restaurant Nearby*   *Payphone* *Ranger Station Nearby*   *Summertime Campfire Program*

cabins with shared bath $99-249, all per person incl meals; ≋🛜👪) Also called Montecito Lake Resort, this rustic mountain-view forest lodge is booked as a family vacation camp almost every night from Memorial Day through Labor Day, and kiddies rule the roost year-round. Accommodations are showing their age, with cramped motel-style rooms and airy freestanding cabins (no TVs). Besides an outdoor swimming pool and hot tub, there's a small private lake with waterskiing and sailing. Horseback riding, mountain biking, tennis and even archery are also offered. In winter, cross-country skiing, snowshoeing, ice skating and sledding are open to nonguests as well.

Stony Creek Lodge LODGE **$$**
(☑559-335-5500, 866-522-6966; www.sequoia -kingscanyon.com; 65569 Generals Hwy; r $109-189; ☺mid-May–mid-Oct; 🛜👪) A low-key option that's very accommodating to families, this small wood-and-stone lodge encapsulates 11 modest motel-style rooms (no TVs). Rooms are small and furnishings well-worn, but rollaway beds are available to fit everyone in. Folksy patchwork bed coverings and emerald green carpeting perk things up a bit. When evenings are nippy, a fire gets lit in the high-beamed foyer (wi-fi available).

Big Meadows Guard Station CABIN **$$**
(☑information 559-338-2251, reservations 518-885-3639, 877-444-6677; www.fs.fed.us/r5/sequoia /recreation/rec_rentals.html, www.recreation.gov; Big Meadows Rd; cabin $125; ☺mid-Jun–mid-Oct) For a rustic overnight stay, this restored 1930s USFS patrol station built by the CCC is available as a recreational rental that sleeps six people. Just over 4 miles east of the Generals Hwy between the parks, the one-bedroom cabin sits at an elevation of 7600ft. Although you'll need to bring your own bedding and towels, the cabin is equipped with hot water, electricity, a refrigerator, stove, cookware, an outdoor fire ring and a picnic table.

Kings Canyon National Park

Camping

All park campgrounds are first-come, first-served (reservations only accepted for large-group sites). For campground amenities and elevations, consult the chart on p184.

GRANT GROVE

Pay showers are usually available from late May through late November in Grant Grove Village (buy tokens from the lodge's lobby registration desk).

Sunset Campground CAMPGROUND $
(Generals Hwy; campsites $18; ☺late May–early Sep; ⑭) Grant Grove's biggest campground, Sunset has more than 150 decent sites in open stands of evergreens. With nightly campfire programs in summer, it's just a quarter-mile walk from the village.

Azalea Campground CAMPGROUND $
(Generals Hwy; campsites $10-18; ☺year-round) With lots of amenities and scenic stands of evergreens, this busy campground offers over 100 sites and stays open year-round. From the campground, it's a short walk downhill to the General Grant Tree Grove.

Crystal Springs Campground CAMPGROUND $
(Generals Hwy; campsites $18; ☺late May–mid-Sep) With over 50 sites (14 reserved for groups), Crystal Springs is the smallest campground in the Grant Grove area, and it's usually overlooked in favor of the bigger ones. Sites are wooded, well spaced and quiet.

CEDAR GROVE

Open from late spring through early fall, these campgrounds are spread out alongside the Kings River. The Cedar Grove Village market sells tokens for showers, which are usually available from mid-May through mid-October.

Sentinel Campground CAMPGROUND $
(Hwy 180; campsites $18; ☺late Apr-Sep; ⑭) If you want to unzip your sleeping bag in the morning and be within staggering distance of hot showers and a cooked breakfast, aim for here. It's Cedar Grove's busiest and most centrally located campground, with riverside sites at the beginning of the first loop filling fastest.

Sheep Creek Campground CAMPGROUND $
(Hwy 180; campsites $18; ☺mid-May–mid-Nov) Just a quarter-mile drive, cycle or walk west of Sentinel, Cedar Grove's second-biggest campground has shady waterfront loops that are especially popular with RVers. Don't expect much quiet at night, though.

Canyon View Campground CAMPGROUND $
(Hwy 180; campsites $18; ☺late May–mid-Oct) East of the village, Canyon View has a fair amount of shade and 23 spacious tent-only sites, some with canyon ridge views. Five large-group sites can make it fairly rambunctious.

Moraine Campground CAMPGROUND $
(Hwy 180; campsites $18; ☺mid-May–early Sep) About 120 well-spaced, but often sunny and exposed, sites may open only intermittently as overflow space is needed (eg summer weekends and holidays). Because it's further east of the village, you can usually find a last-minute site here, unless you roll in very late.

HUME LAKE & KINGS CANYON SCENIC BYWAY

Developed USFS campgrounds off the Kings Canyon Scenic Byway and Hume Lake Rd in the Sequoia National Forest are usually open from mid-May through late September. The only reservable **campsites** (☎518-885-3639, 877-444-6777; www.recreation.gov; ☺reservations accepted for summer) are Hume Lake and Princess Campgrounds. For dispersed camping, pick up a free campfire permit from the Kings Canyon Visitor Center in Grant Grove or the USFS Hume Lake District Office (see p189).

Hume Lake Campground CAMPGROUND $
(Hume Lake Rd; campsites $20; ☺late May-early Sep; ⑭) Almost always full, but still with a laid-back atmosphere, this campground offers almost 75 relatively uncrowded, shady campsites, a handful with lake views. Families love the proximity to swimming holes, plus a nearby store and restaurant. Reservations recommended.

Princess Campground CAMPGROUND $
(Hwy 180; campsites $18; ☺mid-May–late Sep) Just off the Kings Canyon Scenic Byway, with evocative sequoia stumps at the camper registration area, here you'll find almost 90 reservable sites on the edge of a pretty meadow. It's especially popular with RVers. Hume Lake is 4 miles away.

Landslide Campground CAMPGROUND $
(Hume Lake Rd; campsites free; ☺late May-early Sep) Primitive but spacious and woodsy sites just a few miles uphill from Hume Lake's Sandy Cove.

Tenmile Campground CAMPGROUND $
(Hume Lake Rd; campsites free; ⊘late May–mid-Nov) Bigger, forested campground another 1.5 miles uphill from Landslide Campground, with a seasonal camp host on-site.

Convict Flat Campground CAMPGROUND $
(Hwy 180; campsites free; ⊘late Apr–mid-Nov) Five secluded, primitive sites near Yucca Point with tree-sheltered views of cliffs deep inside Kings Canyon. It's remote, so personal safety can be an issue.

Lodging
GRANT GROVE
Wi-fi is available near the lobby registration desk in Grant Grove Village.

John Muir Lodge LODGE $$
(☑559-335-5500, 866-522-6966; www.sequoia-kingscanyon.com; Grant Grove Village, off Generals Hwy; r $69-190) An atmospheric wooden building hung with historical black-and-white photographs, this year-round hotel is a place to lay your head and still feel like you're in the forest. Wide porches have wooden rocking chairs, and homespun, if thin-walled, rooms contain rough-hewn wood furniture and patchwork bedspreads (but no TVs). Cozy up to the big stone fireplace on chilly nights with a board game.

Grant Grove Cabins CABINS $$
(☑559-335-5500, 866-522-6966; www.sequoia-kingscanyon.com; Grant Grove Village, off Generals Hwy; cabins $65-140) Set amid towering sugar pines, around 50 cabins range from decrepit tent-top shacks (open from early June until early September) to rustic but comfortable heated duplexes (a few are wheelchair-accessible) with electricity, private bathrooms and double beds. For lovebirds, number 9 is the lone hard-sided, free-standing 'Honeymoon Cabin' with a queen bed, and it can book up to a year in advance.

CEDAR GROVE
Cedar Grove Lodge LODGE $$
(☑559-335-5500, 866-522-6966; www.sequoia-kingscanyon.com; Cedar Grove Village, Hwy 180; r $119-135; ⊘mid-May–mid-Oct; ❋❄☎) The only indoor sleeping option in the canyon, the riverside lodge offers 21 motel-style rooms, some with air- con. Hallways tend toward dingy, bathrooms are cramped and the bedspreads scream frumpy, but the three ground-floor rooms with shady furnished patios have spiffy river views

and kitchenettes. All rooms have phones but no TVs. The check-in desk is just inside the village market.

EATING & DRINKING

Sequoia National Park
LODGEPOLE VILLAGE & WUKSACHI
Wuksachi Lodge Dining Room AMERICAN $$
(☑559-565-4070; www.visitsequoia.com; 64740 Wuksachi Way, off Generals Hwy; breakfast $8-13, lunch $10-15, dinner $14-27; ⊘7-10am, 11:30am-2:30pm & 5-10pm; ☎❄) The lodge's dining room has a breakfast buffet and soup-and-salad lunch fare, but dinners aim somewhat successfully to be more gourmet, with mains like pan-seared trout and crab-and-shrimp cakes. Decadent desserts top it all off. Decent wine list and children's menu available.

Lodgepole Market, Snack Bar & Deli GROCERIES, TAKE-OUT $
(Generals Hwy; mains $6-10; ⊘market & snack bar 9am-6pm mid-Apr–late May & early Sep–mid-Oct, 8am-8pm late May-early Sep, deli 11am-6pm mid-Apr–mid-Oct; ❄) The park's most extensive market sells all kinds of groceries, camping supplies and snacks. Inside, a fast-food snack bar slings burgers and grilled sandwiches, and dishes up breakfast. The adjacent deli is a tad more upscale and healthy, with focaccia sandwiches, veggie wraps and picnic salads.

Wolverton Meadow BBQ BUFFET $$
(Wolverton Rd, off Generals Hwy; dinner adult/child $22/10; ⊘6-7pm nightly mid-Jun–early Sep, weather permitting; ❄) Buy tickets at Wuksachi Lodge or Lodgepole Market for this popular all-you-can-eat outdoor BBQ with all the fixin's, including ribs, cornbread and homemade desserts. Tickets include the evening living-history program designed for families.

MINERAL KING
Silver City Mountain Resort AMERICAN $
(☑559-561-3223; Mineral King Rd; mains $6-10; ⊘8am-8pm Thu-Mon & 8am-5pm Tue-Wed late May-late Oct; ☎) This little country store serves simple fare on wooden picnic tables under the trees (on Tuesday and Wednesday, only homemade pie and coffee are served). It's about 3 miles west of Mineral King ranger station.

GENERALS HIGHWAY

Stony Creek Lodge has a small **market** (☺7am-8pm (to 9pm Fri & Sat) mid-Jun–mid-Sep, 8am-7pm (to 8pm Fri & Sat) mid-May–mid-Jun & mid-Sep–mid-Oct), and a basic **restaurant** (pizzas & mains $8-20; ☺4-6:30pm (to 7:30pm Fri & Sat) mid-May–mid-Jun & mid-Sep–mid-Oct, 11am-2pm & 4-7:30pm mid-Jun–mid-Sep). Montecito Sequoia Lodge (see p184) offers a decent all-you-can-eat **dinner buffet** (adult/child $20/10).

Kings Canyon National Park

GRANT GROVE

Pizza Parlor　　　　　　　　AMERICAN **$$**
(Grant Grove Village, off Generals Hwy; pizzas $12-22; ☺2-9pm late May–early Sep, variable off-season hr; ⏺) Off the back porch of Grant Grove's restaurant, this casual spot has satisfying crisp-crust pies and a decent salad bar, and shows nonstop movies in a cozy wood-beamed room adorned with old-timey snow-sports paraphernalia.

Grant Grove Restaurant　　　AMERICAN **$$**
(Grant Grove Village, off Generals Hwy; mains $7-16; ☺7-10:30am, 11am-4pm, 5-9pm late May–early Sep, 9am-2pm & 5-7pm (to 8pm Fri & Sat) early Sep–late May; ⏺⏺) More of a diner, this is where most visitors chow down, and there can be a wait at times. There's a breakfast buffet, lunch sandwiches and filling full dinners. Vegetarians can always find at least one option, and children get their own menu.

Grant Grove Market　　　　　GROCERIES **$**
(Grant Grove Village, off Generals Hwy; ☺9am-7pm mid-Apr–late May & early Sep–mid-Oct, 8am-9pm late May–early Sep, 9am-6pm mid-Oct–mid-Apr) On the village's north end, this good-sized market has firewood, camping supplies and packaged food, with a small selection of fruits and veggies. Outside summertime the market is open an hour later on Friday and Saturday.

Espresso Cart　　　　　　　　COFFEE **$**
(Grant Grove Village, off Generals Hwy; ☺usually 8am-5pm late May–early Sep; ⏺) Caffeine junkies gulp down so-so espresso in the village's central outdoor courtyard.

CEDAR GROVE

Cedar Grove Market　　　　　GROCERIES **$**
(Cedar Grove Village, Hwy 180; ☺8am-7pm mid-May–mid-Jun & mid-Sep–mid-Oct, 7am-8pm mid-Jun–mid-Sep) This small market is the hub of the small village complex, hawking packaged food and all the camping supplies you forgot to pack.

Cedar Grove Restaurant　　　AMERICAN **$**
(Cedar Grove Village, Hwy 180; ☺usually 7-10:30am, 11am-2pm & 5-8pm mid-May–mid-Oct; ⏺⏺) More of a snack bar, the restaurant adjacent to the market has ho-hum grill food and sandwiches for order at the counter, with a riverview deck outside.

INFORMATION

For 24-hour recorded information, including winter road conditions, call ☎559-565-3341; the comprehensive park website is www.nps.gov/seki.

Books & Maps

Books and maps are sold at the Giant Forest Museum and all park visitor centers (Lodgepole has the biggest selection).

Internet Access

Find free wi-fi in the lobby of Wuksachi Lodge, near the lodging check-in desk in Grant Grove Village, and at Stony Creek Lodge in the Sequoia National Forest.

　No internet-access terminals are currently available in either park.

Laundry

Coin-op laundry is available seasonally at Lodgepole Village, Grant Grove Village and Stony Creek Lodge.

Money

Find ATMs at Lodgepole, Grant Grove, Cedar Grove and Stony Creek.

　No foreign-currency exchange is available in the parks.

Post

Grant Grove (☺9am-3:30pm Mon-Fri, 10am-noon Sat)

Lodgepole (☺8am-1pm & 2-4pm Mon-Fri)

Showers

Pay showers are available only seasonally at Lodgepole, Grant Grove Village, Cedar Grove Village, Stony Creek Lodge and Silver City Mountain Resort.

Telephone

Cell-phone coverage is nonexistent, except for limited reception at Grant Grove.

Payphones are found at all village areas and visitor centers, plus some campgrounds.

Visitor Centers & Ranger Stations

Cedar Grove Visitor Center (☑559-565-3793; ⊙9am-5pm late May-early Sep) Small visitor center in Cedar Grove Village. The wilderness permit station, which rents bear canisters, is 6 miles further east at Road's End.

Foothills Visitor Center (☑559-565-3135; ⊙8am-4:30pm, to 6pm late May-early Sep) One mile north of Ash Mountain Entrance. Rents bear canisters and issues wilderness permits.

Kings Canyon Visitor Center (☑559-565-4307; ⊙9am-5pm Mar-late May, 8am-6pm late May-early Jul & late Aug-early Sep, 8am-7pm early Jul-late Aug, 8am-5pm early Sep-late Nov, 9am-4:30pm late Nov-Feb) In Grant Grove, 3 miles east of the Big Stump Entrance. Rents bear canisters and issues NPS wilderness and USFS campfire permits.

Lodgepole Visitor Center (☑559-565-4436; ⊙9am-4:30pm mid-Apr–mid-May, 8am-4:30pm mid-May–late Jun & early Sep–mid-Oct, 7am-6pm late Jun-early Sep) Maps, information, exhibits, Crystal Cave tickets, rental bear canisters and wilderness permits in Lodgepole Village.

Mineral King Ranger Station (☑559-565-3768; ⊙8am-4pm late May-early Sep) Small outpost 24 miles east of Hwy 198 issues wilderness permits and rents bear canisters.

USFS Hume Lake District Office (☑559-338-2251; www.fs.fed.us/r5/sequoia; 35860 E Kings Canyon Rd, Dunlap; ⊙8am-4:30pm Mon-Fri) Information, maps and permits for the Sequoia National Forest.

GETTING AROUND

For information on the Sequoia Shuttle buses that run between Visalia and the Giant Forest Museum, see Getting There & Away, p231.

Free Shuttles

Shuttle buses run every 15 minutes from the Giant Forest Museum to Moro Rock and Crescent Meadow (Gray Route) or to the General Sherman Tree parking areas and Lodgepole Village (Green Route). The Purple Route links Lodgepole, Wuksachi Lodge and Dorst Campground every 30 minutes. All routes are free and currently operate from late May to late September.

Fuel

Gas is not available in either national park, but is sold on USFS land year-round at Hume Lake and from early May through late October at Stony Creek. Kings Canyon Lodge has last-chance gas on the Kings Canyon Scenic Byway, but be prepared for sky-high prices and, when we visited, exceptionally surly service.

Road Conditions

For current road conditions, call ☑559-565-3341. Expect road delays and closures along the Generals Hwy during and after snowstorms. In winter, the Kings Canyon Scenic Byway (Hwy 180) to Cedar Grove closes, usually from mid-November through mid-April, while Sequoia's Mineral King Rd typically closes from late October through late May.

AROUND SEQUOIA & KINGS CANYON NATIONAL PARKS

Entering the parks from the south, Hwy 198 passes through the city of Visalia and the tiny gateway town of Three Rivers, which borders Sequoia National Park. To the north, Hwy 180 accesses Kings Canyon, but no sizable towns are located along the way from Fresno. In the Eastern Sierra, trailheads around Lone Pine and Onion Valley allow backpackers to set off into remote wilderness areas of the parks or, most famously, to summit Mt Whitney.

Southern Route

VISALIA
☑559 / POP 122,100 / ELEV 330FT

In the middle of the hotter-than-hell Central Valley, Visalia is the main southern gateway to the parks, and the last sizable population center on your way up to Sequoia's Foothills area. Downtown is walkable, although blistering summer heat will have you scouting for shade. Hwy 198 runs just south of the middle of town; Main St is the major east–west commercial strip.

You can stock up on camping, fishing and outdoor-sports equipment at **Big 5 Sporting Goods** (☑559-625-5934; www.big5sportinggoods.com; 1430 S Mooney Blvd; ⊙10am-9pm Mon-Fri, 9am-9pm Sat, 10am-7pm Sun), less than a mile south of Hwy 198.

🛏 Sleeping

Chain motels and hotels line Hwy 198 and are scattered around downtown.

Spalding House
B&B $

(☎559-739-7877; www.thespaldinghouse.com; 631 N Encina St; r incl breakfast $85-95; ❀@) Built by a lumber baron, this atmospheric 1901 Colonial Revival home feels like a private mansion, with a formal library and 1923 Steinway piano. Three unique guest suites have private sitting rooms and gorgeous details such as mosaic-tiled sinks, a stained-glass ceiling or a sleigh bed.

Lamp Liter Motel
MOTEL $

(☎559-732-4511, 800-662-6692; http://lampliter .net; 3300 W Mineral King Ave; r $75-115; ❀❀ 🛜🏊🐾) It could be a run-of-the-mill two-story courtyard motel, but this family-owned establishment surprises with its 100 spotlessly clean rooms and four country cottages facing the outdoor pool. The Sequoia Shuttle stops here.

🍴 Eating & Drinking

Tazzaria
CAFE $$

(208 W Main St; drinks & snacks $2-6, mains $7-18; ⊘7am-3pm Mon-Wed, 7am-9pm Thu-Sat; 🛜) This sidewalk cafe in the middle of downtown brews up espresso drinks and bakes almond croissants and fruit-topped French toast for the morning crowds. Californian and Mediterranean salads, sandwiches, tapas and more substantial mains like curried halibut fill out the eclectic lunch and dinner menus.

Brewbakers
BREWPUB $$

(www.brewbakersbrewingco.com; 219 E Main St; mains $6-22; ⊘11:30am-10pm, bar till late; 🐾) Always popular, Brewbakers beckons the thirsty with awesome beer, like the Sequoia Red and heavy Possum Porter, and housemade sodas. A huge bar-and-grill menu offers homemade stuffed pretzels, burgers, pizzas, pastas and market-fresh salads. Expect long waits.

Watson's
VEGETARIAN $

(www.watsonshealthfoods.com; 615 W Main St; mains $6-8; ⊘store 9am-6pm Mon-Thu, 8am-5pm Fri, deli 10am-4pm Mon-Fri; 🍴) At this organic-minded deli inside a health-foods store, you'll be spoiled for choice with seven kinds of veggie burgers, Mediterranean nibbles, salads, healthily stuffed wraps and homemade soup bowls.

Visalia Farmers Market – Downtown
MARKET $

(www.visaliafarmersmarket.com; cnr Main & Church Sts; ⊘5-8pm Thu mid-Mar–late Oct) Fresh produce downtown.

UTOPIAN DREAMS: THE KAWEAH CO-OPERATIVE COLONY

A few years before Sequoia National Park was created, an idealistic organization of union workers, skilled craftspeople and social progressives settled in the foothills around Three Rivers. The radical group planned a utopian community based on cooperative assets and collective land ownership. In 1886 they applied for inexpensive land grants and got to work setting up a logging business in the Giant Forest.

As the socialist colony toiled to build a logging road, local citizens grew concerned about their unusually large claims. At the time, it wasn't uncommon for railroads and other corporations to fraudulently purchase huge tracts of land, quietly expanding their monopolies. George Stewart, the editor of the Visalia *Delta* newspaper led a campaign for Congress to protect the giant sequoias, and jumpstarted an inquiry into colonists' land claims. Ironically, the Kaweah Colony was suspected of the very capitalist motives it abhorred.

By the summer of 1890, the colony finished a rough road to the edge of the mature sequoia groves and logging began. But within months, Sequoia National Park was created, shielding the sequoias from destruction, which became the colony's undoing. Their settlement sat squarely inside the national park, so their claims and sweat equity were now worthless.

Besides the descendants of this economic experiment, a number of relics remain from the colony's heyday, including the Kaweah Post Office, north of Three Rivers town. In Sequoia National Park, the Squatters Cabin at Crescent Meadow is another legacy of the colony's failed attempts at land ownership and logging, while Old Colony Mill Rd, stretching between Kaweah's North Fork Rd and Sequoia's Crystal Cave Rd, is the difficult passage they forged.

Visalia Farmers Market –
Sequoia Mall   MARKET $
(www.visaliafarmersmarket.com; cnr Mooney Blvd
& Caldwell Ave; ⊘8am-11:30am Sat) Year-round
market, rain or shine.

☆ Entertainment
Visalia Fox Theater   CINEMA, MUSIC
(☑559-625-1369; www.foxvisalia.org; 300 W Main
St) A 1930s 'talkie' movie palace, the Fox
has a stunning East Indian temple–themed
interior and occasionally hosts film screen-
ings, live music concerts, stand-up comedy
and special events.

ⓘ Information
Tulare County Library (www.tularecounty
library.org; 200 W Oak Ave; ⊘9am-8pm Tue-
Thu, noon-6pm Fri, 9am-5pm Sat; @) Free
public internet access.

Visalia Convention & Visitors Bureau (☑559-
334-0141; www.visitvisalia.org; 303 E Acequia
Ave) Inside the convention center.

ⓘ Getting There & Away
Amtrak (☑800-872-7245; www.amtrak.com)
San Joaquin trains to/from the San Francisco
Bay Area and Sacramento via Merced (with bus
connections to/from Yosemite Valley) stop in
Hanford, with onward Amtrak Thruway buses to
Visalia (35 minutes).

Sequoia Shuttle (☑877-287-4453; www.sequoia
shuttle.com; one way/round-trip $7.50/15; ⊘late
May-late Sep) Five daily buses equipped with
two-bicycle racks between Visalia and Sequoia
National Park (70 minutes to Foothills, 2½ hours
to Giant Forest); advance reservations required.

THREE RIVERS
☑559 / POP 2550 / ELEV 830FT
Just southwest of Sequoia National Park
and named for the nearby convergence of
three Kaweah River forks, Three Rivers is
a friendlysmall town populated mostly by
retirees and artsy newcomers. The town's
main drag, Sierra Dr (Hwy 198), is sparsely
lined with motels, eateries and shops.

◎ Sights & Activities
Kaweah Post Office   LANDMARK
(43795 North Fork Dr; ⊘1-2pm Mon-Fri) Founded by the utopian Kaweah Co-operative
Colony, this is the smallest and oldest
still-operating post office in the USA. Look
for the rustic wooden building around
2.7 miles north of Hwy 198.

FREE Three Rivers Historical
Museum   MUSEUM
(www.3rmuseum.org; 42268 Sierra Dr; ⊘9am-5pm
Apr-Sep, 9am-3pm Oct-Mar) Holds a modest
collection of local ranching, mining and
domestic artifacts, as well as an archive
of historical photographs and newspaper
clippings.

Kaweah Whitewater
Adventures   WHITE-WATER RAFTING
(☑559-740-8251, 800-229-8658; www.kaweah
-whitewater.com; ⊘Apr-Jul) Local outfitter runs
thrilling white-water rafting trips down the
Kaweah River (for more details, see p39).

Lake Kaweah   SWIMMING, FISHING
(☑559-597-2005; 34443 Sierra Dr, Lemon Cove)
Want to slough off the heat in summertime?
Just west of Three Rivers, Slick Rock Recreation Area has pools amid big boulders
that make for cool swimming spots. You
can rent boats from Lemon Hill's marina,
which also sells fishing tackle.

🛏 Sleeping
Lodgings in Three Rivers are modest and
may not have phones or TVs.

Sequoia Village Inn   CABINS, COTTAGES $$
(☑559-561-3652; www.sequoiavillageinn.com; 45971
Sierra Dr; d $120-235; ❄�📶🐾♿🐕) Across the
street from the Buckeye Tree Lodge, these 10
pretty, modern cottages, cabins and chalets
(many with kitchens), border the park and
are great for families or groups. Most have
outdoor woodsy decks and BBQs, and the
largest can sleep 12. Pet fee $10.

Buckeye Tree Lodge   MOTEL $$
(☑559-561-5900; www.buckeyetreelodge.com;
46000 Sierra Dr; d incl breakfast $125-150;
❄🔽🐾🐕) Sit out on your grassy back patio
or perch on the balcony and watch the
river ease through a maze of boulders.
Modernwhite-brick motel rooms, some
with kitchenettes, manage to feel airy and
bright. Pet fee $10.

Rio Sierra Riverhouse   INN $$
(☑559-561-4720; www.rio-sierra.com; 41997 Sierra
Dr; d $125-275; ❄🔽♿) Right on the river beach
in the middle of town, this cottage-style inn
rents four suites, each with a TV and DVD
player, telephone, minifridge and micro-
wave. For more privacy, rent the tree-shaded
RV out back that has its own BBQ grill.

In-town RV parks may let you pitch a
tent, sometimes right on the river.

Horse Creek Campground   CAMPGROUND $
(☑info 559-597-2301, reservations 518-885-3639,
877-444-6777; www.reserveamerica.com; Hwy 198;
campsites $20-25) At Lake Kaweah, about

SEQUOIA & KINGS CANYON NATIONAL PARKS AROUND SEQUOIA & KINGS CANYON NPS

3 miles east of the dam, this developed family campground has all the amenities, including hot showers, flush toilets and an RV dump station. Between mid-April and mid-July flooding may close all campsites.

✖ Eating & Drinking

We Three Bakery & Restaurant CAFE $
(43368 Sierra Dr; mains $6-11; ⏱7am-4pm; 🛜) Cinnamon French toast, biscuits with gravy, and diner-style coffee lure in the breakfast crowd, while hot and cold sandwiches make it a delish lunch spot. Chow down on the outdoor patio under a shady oak.

River View Restaurant
& Lounge BAR & GRILL $$
(42323 Sierra Dr; lunch $6-12, dinner $12-26; ⏱6:30am-9pm, to 10pm Fri & Sat, bar open late) With a breezy back patio on the river and live bands on weekends, this casual honky-tonk stays busy; the bar ceiling is plastered with $1 bills. Burgers, hot sandwiches and full chicken or sirloin steak dinners are filling enough.

Sierra Subs & Salads DELI, TAKE-OUT $
(www.sierrasubsandsalads.com; 41717 Sierra Dr; mains $5-9; ⏱10:30am-6pm Tue-Sat, 10:30am-5pm Sun) Roadside sandwich shop offering a choice of fresh breads along with healthy wraps, salads, fruit smoothies and cheesy quesadillas.

Three Rivers Village
Market GROCERIES, TAKE-OUT $
(40869 Sierra Dr; ⏱10:30am-6pm Tue-Sat, 10:30am-5pm Sun) Supermarket with take-out deli goods for picnic salads, sandwiches and BBQ chicken, ribs and tri-tip.

❶ Information

Kaweah Commonwealth (www.kaweah commonwealth.com) For local information and area history, the weekly newspaper prides itself as 'a journal for those who labor and think.'

Sierra Foothills Chamber of Commerce (☎559-561-3300, 877-530-3300; www .threerivers.com; 42268 Sierra Dr; ⏱9am-5pm, off-season hr vary) Shares space with the town museum, and has tourist maps and information.

Tulare County Library (www.tularecounty library.org; 42052 Eggers Dr, off Hwy 198; ⏱noon-5pm & 6-8pm Tue & Thu, 10am-1pm & 2-6pm Wed & Fri; @) Free public internet access.

❶ Getting There & Away

Sequoia Shuttle (☎877-287-4453; www .sequoiashuttle.com; one way/round-trip $7.50/15; ⏱late May-late Sep) Five daily round-trip buses equipped with two-bicycle racks between Visalia (one hour) and Sequoia National Park (35 minutes to Foothills, two hours to Giant Forest); advance reservations required.

MT WHITNEY PERMITS & SHUTTLES

Perhaps the biggest obstacle to reaching the top of Mt Whitney is obtaining a wilderness permit ($15), which is required for all overnight trips and for day hikes past Lone Pine Lake (about 3 miles from Whitney Portal trailhead). A quota system limits daily access to 60 overnight and 100 day-hikers from May 1 through November 1. Because of huge demand for this hike, enter the online permit lottery, currently between February 1 and March 15. Check with the **Inyo National Forest Wilderness Permit Office** (☎760-873-2483; www.fs.usda.gov/inyo) for details.

If you don't want the hassle of getting a permit for the Mt Whitney Trail, you can always summit via the back door route from Sequoia or Kings Canyon National Parks. It takes about six days from Sequoia's Crescent Meadow via the High Sierra Trail to the John Muir Trail, with no Whitney Zone advance permit required (although you'll still need an NPS wilderness permit, for which seasonal trailhead quotas do apply; see p176). Within the Whitney area, you must carry out your poop (free 'pack-out kits' available at Crabtree Meadow) and use an approved bear canister (see p242).

One-way hikers can book one of the many trailhead shuttle services, including:

» **High Sierra Transportation** (☎760-258-6060; www.highsierratransportation.com; Bishop)

» **Mt Whitney Shuttle Service** (☎760-876-1915; www.mtwhitneyshuttle.com; Lone Pine)

» **Sequoia Sightseeing Tours** (☎559-561-4189; www.sequoiatours.com; Three Rivers)

Eastern Route

LONE PINE

☑760 / POP 2035 / ELEV 3730FT

The last outpost on the way up to Mt Whitney, Lone Pine is also a convenient stopover for drivers on Hwy 395 in the Eastern Sierra. The town was once a popular set location for movie Westerns. A few basic motels, restaurants and shops flank Hwy 395 (Main St). Whitney Portal Rd heads west at the lone stoplight.

◎ Sights & Activities

Alabama Hills　　　　　NATURAL FEATURE

Located on Whitney Portal Rd, the warm colors and rounded contours of these hills stand in stark contrast to the jagged snowy Sierras just behind. The setting for countless ride-'em-out movies and the *Lone Ranger* TV series, it's a beautiful place to catch dawn or dusk. Drive, walk or mountain-bike along dirt roads rambling by boulders and along Tuttle and Lone Pine creeks. To get here, head west on Whitney Portal Rd and turn right onto Movie Rd after 3 miles.

Museum of Lone Pine Film History　　　　　MUSEUM

(☑760-876-9909; www.lonepinefilmhistorymuseum .org; 701 S Main St; adult/child under 12 $5/free; ◎10am-6pm Mon-Wed, to 7pm Thu-Sat, to 4pm Sun) To get a sense of local lore, this museum exhibits Western movie paraphernalia and screens movies in its small Wild West Theater (call for schedules).

FREE **Southern Inyo Museum**　　　　　MUSEUM

(127 W Bush St; ◎9am-5pm Thu-Sat) Located downtown, this tiny spot has a mildly interesting collection of regional artifacts.

Elevation　　　　　OUTDOOR GEAR

(☑760-876-4560; www.elevation.com; 150 S Main St, cnr Whitney Portal Rd; ◎call for hr) Rents bear canisters and crampons, and sells hiking, backpacking and climbing gear.

Lone Pine Sporting Goods　　　　　OUTDOOR GEAR

(☑760-876-5365; 220 S Main St; ◎call for hr) Sells camping gear, fishing licenses (cash only) and maps.

⌂ Sleeping

Dow Hotel & Dow Villa Motel　　HOTEL, MOTEL $$

(☑760-876-5521, 800-824-9317; www.dowvilla motel.com; 310 S Main St; r with/without bath from $102/54; ❋❄☎⌨) John Wayne and Gene Autry are among the stars who have stayed at this venerable hotel. Built in 1922, the place has been restored but retains much of its rustic charm. Bigger motel-annex rooms are comfy and bright, if generic. Wi-fi available in hotel lobby.

Whitney Portal Hostel　　　　　HOSTEL $

(☑760-876-0030; www.whitneyportalstore.com; 238 S Main St; dm/q $20/$60; ❋@☎⌨) A popular launching pad for Whitney trips and for post-hike wash-ups (public showers available), the carpeted bunk bed rooms have towels and TVs to reacclimatize the weary, plus there's free coffee in the communal kitchenette (but no stove). Reserve ahead for July and August.

Tuttle Creek　　　　　CAMPGROUND $

(www.blm.gov/ca/st/en/fo/bishop/camping/tuttle .html; Horseshoe Meadows Rd; campsites $5) Off Whitney Portal Rd, this first-come, first-served USFS campground has primitive sites with panoramic 'pinch-me!' views of the Sierras, White Mountains and the rosy Alabama Hills. There's not much shade, though.

Lone Pine Campground　　　　　CAMPGROUND $

(☑reservations 518-885-3639, 877-444-6777; www .recreation.gov; Whitney Portal Rd; campsites $15-17) About midway between Lone Pine and Whitney Portal, this popular creekside USFS campground (elevation 6000ft) offers flush toilets and potable water.

✖ Eating

Seasons　　　　　NEW AMERICAN $$$

(☑760-876-8927; 206 N Main St; mains $18-30; ◎5-10pm Apr-Oct, 5-9pm Mon-Sat Nov-Mar) Seasons has everything you fantasized about the last time you choked down freeze-dried backpacking rations: sautéed trout, roasted duck, elk medallions, filet mignon and plates of carb-replenishing pasta, along with Californian wines and beer.

Alabama Hills Café & Bakery　　　　　DINER $

(111 W Post St; mains $6-10; ◎6am-2pm Mon-Fri, 7am-2pm Sat & Sun) Swing by early in the morning to line up for lumberjack-sized breakfasts (think eggs with corned beef hash, or wholegrain pancakes), then grab a deli sandwich stacked on home-baked bread for a trailside lunch.

Joseph's Bi-Rite　　　　　SUPERMARKET $

(119 S Main St; ◎8am-9pm May-Oct, to 8pm Nov-Apr) Stock up on groceries.

❶ Information

Eastern Sierra Interagency Visitor Center
(☎760-876-6200; cnr Hwy 395 & SR 136; www
.fs.usda.gov/inyo; ⊗8am-6pm May-Oct, 8am-
5pm Nov-Apr) Both a visitor center and a ranger
station, this is the one-stop shop for wilderness
permits and regional recreation information,
including books and maps.

Espresso Parlor (123 N Main St; ⊗6am-6pm;
🛜) Free wi-fi.

Inyo County Library (www.inyocounty.us
/library; cnr Bush & Washington Sts; 12:30-7pm
Mon & Wed, 10am-noon & 1-5pm Tue & Thu-Fri,
10am-1pm Sat; @) Free public internet access.

Lone Pine Chamber of Commerce (☎760-
876-4444; www.lonepinechamber.org; 120
S Main St; ⊗8:30am-4:30pm Mon-Fri) Free
movie-location maps and brochures.

❶ Getting There & Away

Eastern Sierra Transit (☎760-872-1901, 800-
922-1930; www.easternsierratransitauthority
.com) Weekday CREST bus service to/from
Bishop ($6, 70 minutes, three daily); limited
onward connections to Mammoth Lakes, Lee
Vining and Reno, Nevada.

AROUND LONE PINE
Mt Whitney

Mt Whitney (14,505ft), the tallest point in
the continental US and the southern terminus of the John Muir Trail, sits smack
on the eastern border of Sequoia National
Park. The mystique of Mt Whitney captures the imagination, and bagging its
superlative summit becomes an obsession
for many.

The main summit trail leaves from
Whitney Portal, 13 miles west of Lone
Pine via Whitney Portal Rd (closed during
winter), and it climbs some 6000ft over 11
miles. It's a super-strenuous, *really* long
hike that'll wear out even experienced
mountaineers, but, between mid-July
and mid-September, reaching the summit
doesn't usually require technical skills.
Earlier or later in the season, you'll likely
need an ice axe and crampons.

Many people in good physical condition
make it to the top, although only superbly
conditioned, previously acclimatized hikers should attempt this as a day hike.
Breathing becomes difficult at these
elevations and altitude sickness (see p235)
is a common problem. Consider spending
at least a night at **USFS campgrounds**
(☎reservations 518-885-3639, 877-444-6777;
www.recreation.gov; campsites $10-19; ⊗mid-
May–late Oct) at the trailhead or Whitney

Portal to acclimatize, then another night at
a backcountry camp along the route: Outpost Camp (3.5 miles from the trailhead) or
Trail Camp (6 miles).

For environmental reasons, toilets are
no longer available along the trail. Hikers
must now pack out their human waste: free
'pack-out kits' are available when you pick
up your permit. Pack a few extra plastic
bags too, just in case.

When considering an ascent, do your
homework. One recommended book is
*Mt Whitney: The Complete Trailhead-to-
Summit Hiking Guide* by Paul Richins
Jr. Before setting out, call or stop by Lone
Pine's **Eastern Sierra Interagency Visitor
Center** (left) to get the latest scoop about
weather and trail conditions. An excellent
website with up-to-date info and tips for
first-timers is the **Whitney Portal Store**
(www.whitneyportalstore.com).

Manzanar National Historic Site

A stark wooden guard tower alerts drivers to one of the darkest chapters in US
history, which unfolded on a barren and
windy sweep of land some 10 miles north
of Lone Pine. Little remains of the infamous WWII internment camp, a dusty
square mile where more than 10,000
people of Japanese ancestry from the
West Coast were unjustly corralled during
WWII following the attack on Pearl Harbor.
This supposedly precautionary step against
espionage included US citizens and young
children.

The camp's former high-school audi-
torium now houses a superb **interpretive center** (☎760-878-2194; www.nps.gov
/manz; admission free; ⊗9am-5:30pm Apr-Oct,
to 4:30pm Nov-Mar). Watch the 22-minute
documentary, then explore the thought-
provoking exhibits that chronicle the stories of the families who nevertheless built a
vibrant community while imprisoned here.
Afterwards, take a self-guided 3.2-mile
driving tour around the grounds, which
takes you past a reconstructedmess hall
and housing barracks, ruined gardens and
the haunting camp cemetery.

On the last Saturday of April, a pilgrim-
age by family members of former internees
takes place at Manzanar, keeping alive the
memory of this national tragedy.

Independence

About 16 miles north of Lone Pine, this
sleepy highway town is home to the

Eastern California Museum (www.inyo
county.us/ecmuseum; 155 N Grant St; donation
requested; ⊙10am-5pm). It contains one of
the most complete collections of Paiute
and Shoshone baskets in the country,
as well as artifacts from the Manzanar
relocation camp, and historic photographs of primitively equipped local rock
climbers scaling Sierra peaks, including
Mt Whitney.

About 15 miles west of town via Onion
Valley Rd (Market St in town), pretty **Onion
Valley** (elevation 9600ft) harbors the trailhead for **Kearsarge Pass** (9.5 miles round-
trip), an old Paiute trade route. This is the
quickest eastside access to the John Muir
and Pacific Crest National Scenic Trails, and
Kings Canyon National Park.

Hwy 395 through town offers a handful
of humble roadside motels. Onion Valley Rd
has three **USFS campgrounds** (✆reserva-
tions 518-885-3639; 877-444-6777; www.recreation
.gov; campsites $14-16; ⊙Mar-Oct) alongside
Independence Creek.

Next to the courthouse, **Jenny's Café** (246
N Edwards St; lunch $7-9, dinner $12-22; ⊙6am-
9pm Thu-Tue) serves rib-sticking burgers,
sandwiches and steaks in a country kitchen
with rooster-print curtains. Upscale and
unexpected in such a flyspeck town, bright,
artistic **Still Life Café** (✆760-878-2555; 135
S Edward St; lunch $10-16, dinner $20-25; ⊙11am-
3pm & 6-9:30pm Wed-Mon) prepares escargot,
steak au poivre and other French bistro
faves.

Understand
Yosemite, Sequoia
& Kings Canyon

The Parks Today

California Dreaming

The economic recession has created an upswing in domestic tourism, with Americans taking shorter vacations and staying closer to home. After ebbing to a low of 3.4 million in 2005, Yosemite's visitation numbers have risen steadily, getting closer to reaching the all-time 4.2 million peak of 1996. Visitation at Sequoia & Kings Canyon has been inching up too.

And those folks aren't just circling the sights and calling it a day. In both parks, the number of backcountry hiking permits has also increased, spiking in 2008. In a time of federal and California state budget cuts, parks and other public lands soldier on, trying to do more with less, and many of the surrounding national forests and state parks have had to reduce their services.

» Highest point of Yosemite: Mt Lyell (13,114ft)

» Highest point of Sequoia: Mt Whitney (14,505ft)

The Balancing Act

The parks continue to dance the tricky footwork of facilitating preservation while accommodating tourism. Yosemite, especially Yosemite Valley, still teeters on the edge of being loved to pieces, with little movement towards the conservation goals outlined in its 1980 General Management Plan or the 2000 Yosemite Valley Plan. Many Yosemite Valley visitors decide to forgo their cars and whiz around by shuttle or bicycle, but Yosemite's planners occasionally hatch some head-scratching schemes to enhance the visitor experience, like cutting down Valley trees to open up scenic views.

Still, Yosemite has taken a few more recent steps to cut back the impact of visitors. One new project is restoration of the area surrounding Tenaya Lake, rerouting people around sensitive habitats. The number of incidents between humans and bears has decreased significantly over the last decade, due to increased education and ranger outreach. But the boldest

Top Books

» **An Uncertain Path: A Search for the Future of National Parks** (Bill Tweed, 2010) A retired Sequoia park planner hikes and ponders park management in an era of climate change.

» **Yosemite in Time: Ice Ages, Tree Clocks, Ghost Rivers** (2005)

A coffee-table photo essay on Yosemite's iconic views, past and present.

» **Off the Wall: Death in Yosemite** (Michael Ghiglieri & Butch Farabee, 2007) A cautionary compendium of fatalities and daring search and rescue operations.

On Film

» **The National Parks: America's Best Idea** (2009) Documentary series on US park history.

» **Star Trek V: The Final Frontier** (1989) Captain Kirk does El Capitan.

» **The Eiger Sanction** (1975) Clint Eastwood *really* climbs.

Seasonal visitation – Yosemite

(% of annual visitors)

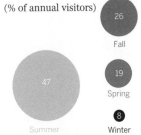

26 Fall
19 Spring
47 Summer
8 Winter

if 100 people visited Yosemite, where would they enter

35 South Entrance
29 Arch Rock
26 Big Oak Flat
9 Tioga Pass
1 Hetch Hetchy

measure – and to some the most draconian – has been to limit the number of daily hikers summiting Half Dome. Recent deaths on the Half Dome cables and from the Mist Trail waterfalls fuel the perpetual conversation about the parks' duty to warn visitors about dangers in the natural world and the responsibility that people must take for their actions.

In 2009, the 40,000-acre John Krebs Wilderness was designated in the Mineral King region of Sequoia & Kings Canyon, and the twin parks have initiated an extensive plan to assess wilderness stewardship.

Looking Ahead

The year 2016 marks the centennial of the National Parks Service, a time of reflection, assessment and celebration for the nation's almost 400 national parks and monuments.

Traveling through the region, you'll encounter some of the issues that the national parks and forests face as they struggle with everything from global warming, to forest fires, to the impact of millions of visitors every year.

Climate change is a biggie. Glaciers such as the Lyell Glacier are rapidly receding as temperatures rise. Small, upper-elevation mammals such as the beloved little pika (a tiny relative of the rabbit) have moved to higher, previously uninhabitable elevations and abandoned their lower stomping grounds. Hand in hand with climate change, fire suppression has transformed the natural world throughout the Sierras, and the park service continues to educate visitors about controlled burning and preventing fires. As cliché as it sounds, the future of the parks lies in public hands – the more time you spend up here, the more obvious that becomes.

Yosemite is a mispronunciation of the Miwok word *Oo-hoo'-ma-te* or *uzumate*, meaning 'grizzly bear'

Best Maps

» **National Geographic** (www.nationalgeographic.com) One Sequoia/Kings Canyon and five hiking maps for Yosemite in its Trails Illustrated series.

» **Tom Harrison** (www.tomharrisonmaps.com) Waterproof topo maps of the Sierra Nevada; the John Muir Trail map pack is the gold standard.

» **DeLorme California Atlas and Gazetteer** (www.delorme.com) Excellent driving atlas.

» **Eastern Sierra: Bridgeport to Lone Pine** Produced and sold locally by Sierra Maps; detailed recreation information.

Souvenirs

» 'Restore Hetch Hetchy' bumper sticker.

» 'Go Climb a Rock' T-shirt, sold at the Curry Village Mountain Shop.

» A small, special-edition print from the Ansel Adams Gallery.

History

History unfolds here at varying rates of speed: the timelessness of the physical landscape; the presence of its first people, Native American tribes who still call it home; the decomposing ghost towns left behind by California's early settlers and miners; and the record-setting feats of modern rock climbers and mountaineers have all left their mark. The names you'll encounter as you explore – Tenaya, Whitney, Ahwahnee, Muir – tell the story of the parks' peopled past.

During the gold-rush era, conflict between miners and Native American tribespeople escalated until the Mariposa Battalion marched into Yosemite in 1851, finally forcing the capitulation of Chief Tenaya and his Ahwahneechee people. In 1855 San Francisco entrepreneur James Hutchings guided the first tourists to Yosemite Valley, and before long tourist inns and roads began springing up.

Alarmed by tourist development, conservationists petitioned Congress to protect the area – with success. In 1864 President Abraham Lincoln signed the Yosemite Grant, which ceded Yosemite Valley and the Mariposa Grove of Giant Sequoias to California as a state park. This landmark decision eventually paved the way for the US national park system, of which Yosemite, Sequoia and General Grant (now Kings Canyon) became a part in 1890, thanks in part to efforts by conservationist John Muir.

The parks' popularity with tourists soared during the 20th century. By the mid-1970s, traffic had draped them in a smoggy haze. Today, park managers strive to balance visitors' needs with the preservation of the natural beauty that draws them here in the first place.

Native Americans

Archeologists believe that indigenous peoples had been living in the Sierra Nevada – and the Yosemite Valley, with its abundance of natural resources – for several thousand years before Spanish explorers and, later, American pioneers first arrived.

Best Historical Sights

» Yosemite Museum & Indian Village of Ahwahnee, Yosemite Valley

» Pioneer Yosemite History Center, Wawona, Yosemite National Park

» Hospital Rock & Mineral King, Sequoia National Park

» Bodie State Historic Park

TIMELINE

AD 1400	1833	1848
The Ahwahneechee ('people of the gaping mouth'), a subtribe of the Sierra Miwok, settle in Yosemite Valley and become its first known permanent residents.	American fur trapper, trader and scout Joseph Reddeford Walker and his party become the first Europeans to cross the Sierra Nevada from east to west.	Mexico cedes California to the US under the Treaty of Guadalupe Hidalgo; gold is discovered at Sutter's Mill, starting the great California gold rush.

THE AHWAHNEECHEE

Before Europeans arrived, the Sierra Miwok referred to the Yosemite Valley as Ahwahnee (or Awahni), meaning 'place of the gaping mouth,' describing its shape. Native American tribespeople who lived in the valley were known as the Ahwahneechee. Before the arrival of Europeans, a fatal illness decimated their numbers, and the survivors dispersed to join other tribes. By the mid-19th century, Chief Tenaya, an Ahwahneechee chief born and raised with the Mono Lake Paiute in the Eastern Sierra, had gathered together other Ahwahneechee descendants and reestablished his people's ancestral home in Yosemite Valley.

Most Sierra Nevada tribes migrated with the seasons and, although they established warm-weather hunting sites in the High Sierra, they generally kept to lower elevations. Heavy snow cover on the western slopes of the Sierra discouraged year-round habitation above 5000ft, but the oak forests of the lower western foothills and piñon-juniper forests on the eastern escarpments were hospitable year-round.

As American explorers made their way across the Sierra Nevada, both sides of the mountain range were already occupied by distinct linguistic groups. The western slopes of today's Yosemite region were home to the Sierra Miwok. To the south, the Western Mono (or Monache) and the Tuba-tulabal inhabited the western slopes of what is today Sequoia and Kings Canyon National Parks, with the Yokut residing in the lowest-elevation foothills and across the Central Valley. The Eastern Sierra was home to the Mono Lake Paiute to the north and the Owens Valley Paiute to the south.

While most tribal groups traveled only when migrating or when hunting and gathering, both trading and warring parties regularly crossed the Sierra on foot to exchange goods and fight battles. Obsidian and pine nuts from the Eastern Sierra were in great demand by western slope and coastal peoples, who traded them for acorns and seashells. Early Euro-American explorers making their way over the Sierra often found themselves on these ancient trade routes – as do hikers and backpackers today.

Early Explorers

As early as the 18th century, Spanish explorers described a great *sierra nevada* – a snow-covered mountain range – glimpsed from the San Joaquin Valley. On January 6, 1805, a Spanish military expedition stumbled across a great canyon in the southern Sierra and named the river *El Río de los Santos Reyes,* having discovered it on the Christian Feast of Epiphany.

Before California became a US state in 1850, American trappers and explorers were making incursions into the region from the east. Jedediah

First published in 1965, Francis P Farquhar's excellent *History of the Sierra Nevada* is still one of the region's definitive books on the subject and continues to be an extremely enjoyable read for armchair travelers.

1851	1853	1858	1864
Members of the Mariposa Battalion, led by James Savage in paramilitary pursuit of Native Americans, become the first white men to enter Yosemite Valley.	Chief Tenaya, the last chief of the Ahwahneechee, is killed under still-mysterious circumstances, and the last of his people disperse from Yosemite Valley.	Homesteader Hale Tharp becomes the first white man to enter the grove of giant sequoias that would later be named the Giant Forest in Sequoia National Park.	President Lincoln signs the Yosemite Grant, establishing the Yosemite Valley and Mariposa Grove as a state park, the first such park in the world.

MOUNTAINEERING

Part history and
part adventure
writing, Clarence
King's *Moun-
taineering in the
Sierra Nevada*
(1872) is a
dramatic account
of his exploits in
the Sierras and
a gripping read
to boot.

Smith made his trailblazing way to San Gabriel Mission (in present-day Los Angeles County) in 1826–27, then wandered north to become the first European to cross the Sierra Nevada. In 1833, frontiersman Joseph Walker led the first party of American emigrants across the range, likely becoming the first nonindigenous person to look down into Yosemite Valley, although he was too exhausted to appreciate the extraordinary sight.

Over the next decade, rumors of rich farmlands in Alta California (a province still held by Mexico) reached emigrants on the Oregon Trail. Several immigrant groups made the difficult trans-Sierra trek, which inevitably ended at the region's only pioneer settlement: Sutter's Fort, a nascent utopian community on the Sacramento River created by Swiss immigrant John Sutter.

The Gold Rush Is On

In February 1848, during construction of John Sutter's sawmill in the Sierra Nevada foothills, foreman James Marshall found flecks of gold in the water. News of Marshall's discovery immediately spread around the world, setting off a stunning reconfiguration of the Sierra Nevada's physical and demographic landscapes. As many as 200,000 people poured into the Sierra Nevada over the next decade alone. Men (and a few women) eventually made their way to the Sierra mines from Europe and the eastern US, but in the early gold-rush years, many of the miners were Chinese, South American and Mexican.

The news was not good for Native Americans in the Sierra Nevada, however. Genocide that began with diseases (introduced in the earlier Spanish mission period) progressed to enslavement and outright slaughter under the Americans. As Native Californians took up arms, raids upon settlers increased and the state sanctioned the creation of militias to settle any conflicts the new arrivals had with indigenous inhabitants.

Mariposa Battalion

During the gold-rush era, prospector James Savage began mining on the Merced River. After clashes with local tribes culminated in the burning of his trading post, Savage sought revenge by creating a militia called the Mariposa Battalion. When Savage learned that the raiding tribespeople might belong to a holdout group of Sierra Miwok from a valley further upriver, the militia hastily marched to root them out.

On March 27, 1851, after a brief encounter with Ahwahneechee Chief Tenaya, the Mariposa Battalion entered Yosemite Valley. Determined to drive out the valley's indigenous inhabitants, the battalion burned Native American camps and provisions, but failed to find many tribespeople on their first expedition. (Among the battalion was a young recruit named Lafayette Bunnell. Apparently the only one among the men who was

1868

Hired to watch over a flock of sheep and its wayward herder, naturalist John Muir makes his first visit to the Sierra Nevada mountains and Yosemite Valley.

1879

Despite consistently unproductive silver-mining claims in Mineral King Valley, the Mineral King Rd is built, creating the first wagon access to what is now Sequoia National Park.

» Frontier building in Bodie State Historic Park (p146)

moved by the scenery, Bunnell proceeded to name the features he saw. Bunnell gave the valley the name Yosemite, a corruption of the Miwok word *Oo-soo'-ma-te,* meaning 'grizzly bear.')

In continuation of their gruesome pursuit, the Mariposa Battalion made several forays into the Yosemite region that spring and forced Tenaya and most of his people from their Yosemite Valley home to a reservation near Fresno. The following winter, the chief and some of his people were allowed to return to Yosemite. But hostilities continued in the following years, and in circumstances that are still a matter of debate, Chief Tenaya was killed in Yosemite Valley, allegedly by Mono Lake Paiute tribespeople angered over the theft of some horses.

The Secret Is Out

Tales of cascading waterfalls and towering stone columns followed the Mariposa Battalion out of Yosemite and soon raised public awareness. In 1855 an entrepreneurial Englishman named James Hutchings led the first tourist party into Yosemite Valley. The party's enthusiastic reports spurred other groups to visit later that same summer, during which Yosemite received a grand total of 42 visitors.

Among the visitors in the summer of 1855 was Galen Clark, who returned the following year to establish a homestead near the Mariposa Grove of giant sequoias, where he lived for several decades. From the start, Clark's camp served as a lodge and artists camp. Clark himself took on the role of Yosemite guardian, a title that became official when the park became public land in 1864.

As word got around, entrepreneurs and homesteaders began arriving to divvy up the real estate of Yosemite Valley, creating ramshackle residences and roads, cutting down forests and planting the meadows with gardens and orchards. They brought in livestock, and started running sheep into the high mountain meadows where the trampling hooves destroyed wildflowers and delicate grasses.

Despite a flurry of silver-mining claims that were filed in the optimistically named Mineral King area of present-day Sequoia National Park, the area failed to turn up much of value.

It was ranching that brought the region's first homesteader, Hale Tharp, to the southern Sierra. In 1858, led by a Native American guide, Tharp became the first white man to enter the Giant Forest, where he famously fashioned a cabin inside a fallen giant sequoia tree.

Road to Protection

In 1860 Thomas Starr King, a Unitarian minister, orator and respected nature writer, helped rescue Yosemite from runaway commercialism. King wrote a series of widely read letters to the *Boston Evening Transcript*

Thousands of pages of digital books fill the Yosemite Online Library (www .yosemite.ca.us /library), including the complete texts of numerous authors and century-old newspaper articles.

1890	1892	1899	1900
In late September, President Harrison authorizes the creation of Sequoia National Park; one week later, Congress passes the Yosemite Act, establishing Yosemite National Park.	The Sierra Club is founded with 182 charter members, and John Muir is elected its first president; its first task is to defeat proposed reductions in Yosemite's boundaries.	David and Jennie Curry establish Camp Curry, offering home-cooked meals and board in military-style canvas tents for $2 – half of Yosemite Valley's going hotel rate.	The first automobile sputters into Yosemite Valley, but a ban on cars inside the park is immediately established by park rangers, citing vehicular disturbance to livestock and tourists.

describing his trip. Shortly after the publication of King's letters, an exhibition opened in New York featuring photographs of Yosemite by Carleton E Watkins. The exhibition was a critical success, and Watkins' work caught the attention of California Senator John Conness.

Meanwhile, Frederick Law Olmsted, the landscape architect who designed New York's Central Park, brought his ideals to bear on Yosemite. He believed that government should play a role in preserving natural spaces that nourished the human spirit. Olmsted met with San Francisco businessman Israel Ward Raymond, who had become concerned about the fate of Yosemite's giant sequoias.

In February 1864 Raymond wrote a letter to Senator Conness, proposing a bill that would grant Yosemite Valley and the Mariposa Grove to the State of California. Conness presented the bill to Congress, and on June 30, 1864, in the midst of the Civil War, President Abraham Lincoln signed the Yosemite Grant into law. This marked the first time that the US federal government had ever mandated the preservation and protection of a natural area for public use, making Yosemite the first state park.

Whitney vs Muir

Even as the gold rush waned, interest in California's natural resources grew. In 1860 the newly appointed California State geologist, Josiah Whitney, assembled a crew of scientists, surveyors and cartographers to map out those resources.

Officially the California Geological Survey, Whitney's team explored Yosemite in 1863, and the Kings Canyon and Mt Whitney regions the following year. During their expeditions, they surveyed and named lakes, passes and peaks – Mt Dana, Mt Hoffman and Mt Lyell in Yosemite, and Mt Whitney, Mt Tyndall and Mt Brewer in Sequoia & Kings Canyon are just a few examples.

As Whitney's survey cobbled together its theories on Yosemite's formation, a naturalist named John Muir, who first visited Yosemite Valley in 1869, began to put forth his own ideas. Muir attributed the Valley's formation to glaciers, a theory Whitney himself vehemently shot down, but that would later prove correct.

Meanwhile, the Scottish-born Muir, a prolific writer and indefatigable advocate for conservation, would become Yosemite's most adamant and successful defender (see also the boxed text, p220).

New National Parks

In 1889 John Muir took Robert Underwood Johnson, publisher of the national magazine *Century,* on a camping trip to Tuolumne Meadows. Under the stars, the two men hammered out a plan to save the area from 'hoofed locusts' (what Muir infamously called sheep) and commercial interests.

To immerse yourself in the yesteryear world of the Sierra Nevada, you can do no better than to dive into John Muir's many books and collections of essays, including *Our National Parks* (1901), *My First Summer in the Sierra* (1911) and *The Yosemite* (1912).

Written while exploring with the California Geological Survey between 1860 and 1864, chemistry professor William Brewer's entertaining journal *Up and Down California* makes scaling a mountain sound like a Sunday picnic.

1903	1916	1923	1927
Led by Colonel Charles Young, a regiment of 'Buffalo Soldiers,' the African American cavalry and infantry regiments of the US Army, arrive for duty in Sequoia National Park.	Congress authorizes establishment of the National Park Service, and Stephen T Mather becomes its first director; Tioga Rd and the John Muir Trail under construction.	Construction of O'Shaughnessy Dam finished, costing $100 million and 68 lives, damming the Tuolumne River and flooding Hetch Hetchy Valley, which John Muir had likened to a holy temple.	Yosemite's luxurious Ahwahnee Hotel, which was dreamed up to promote tourism by National Park Service director Stephen Mather, opens on the site of a former indigenous tribal village.

The two men's plan drew upon the precedent set by Yellowstone, established as the country's first national park in 1872. Muir agreed to write some articles promoting the concept, which were published in *Century* the following summer, while Johnson exercised his considerable political influence in Washington DC.

Around the same time, the giant sequoia groves south of Yosemite were falling at an alarming rate beneath the saws of lumber companies acquiring enormous tracts of old-growth forest through government loopholes. Visionary Visalia newspaper editor George Stewart began pushing for federal protection of a sequoia grove that Muir had baptized the Giant Forest. Muir, Johnson and others quickly joined Stewart's fight.

On September 25, 1890, President Benjamin Harrison signed a bill into law that protected the Giant Forest, thus creating Sequoia National Park, California's first national park. A week later, Congress passed the Yosemite Act, creating Yosemite National Park (although Yosemite Valley and Mariposa Grove remained under state control) *and* General Grant National Park, which encompassed Grant Grove and would later be incorporated into Kings Canyon National Park.

Johnson realized that the creation of national parks might not be enough to protect the Sierra Nevada from a large and vocal contingent that saw the whole idea of public land as an affront to the Western ethic of free enterprise. He encouraged Muir to organize an advocacy association, which became the Sierra Club, chartered in 1892 with Muir as its first president.

JOHN MUIR

The Sierra Club's online John Muir Exhibit (www .sierraclub.org /john_muir _exhibit) is a storehouse of everything Muir, featuring the author's complete books, as well as photos, essays and historical pieces.

Enter the Army

With the Sierra parks designated federal land in 1890, the Department of the Interior assumed responsibility for protecting the wilderness from its new owners – the American public.

During the US Army's tenure in charge of Yosemite, highly skilled trackers blazed most of the current trails through the backcountry (while chasing pioneer cattlemen and sheepherders) and created maps with far more detail than those made by the Whitney Survey. The army planted trout in the streams and lakes, educated visitors about trash disposal and forest fires, and stood up against poachers and elite hunting parties.

In 1906, after lobbying by John Muir and the Sierra Club, the State of California finally ceded Yosemite Valley and the Mariposa Grove to Yosemite National Park, and the army promptly moved its headquarters from Wawona to Yosemite Valley. There it faced the challenge of bringing nearly 10,000 annual visitors in line with park conservation policies. But even after all of its hard work, the army was not destined to stay: in 1916, Congress established an all-civilian National Park Service (NPS).

1935	1940	1970	1978
After years of work, the Generals Hwy is extended from the Giant Forest to General Grant National Park; it's immediately declared one of the nation's most scenic roads.	Congress creates Kings Canyon National Park, encompassing General Grant National Park and including a large part of the namesake canyon John Muir once called 'a rival to the Yosemite.'	On July 4, a riot rocks Yosemite Valley as mounted rangers are beaten while trying to remove people illegally camped in Stoneman Meadow; the National Guard is called in.	Mineral King Valley, a glacially formed canyon of vast natural beauty, is added to Sequoia National Park, preventing the Walt Disney Company from building a ski resort there.

Growing the Parks

Hotels came and went in Yosemite Valley's early years. Hastily erected of wood and canvas to house the ever-increasing hordes of tourists, many of the early hotels burned down when sparks escaped from stoves, or when lanterns got too close to curtains. Tourism started off more slowly in Sequoia National Park. In 1898, two Tulare County ranchers set up a horse-and-mule packing service to bring visitors to see the big trees of the Giant Forest, housing them in a simple tent hotel.

In 1899, when a night in Yosemite's popular Sentinel Hotel cost $4, David and Jennie Curry established a tourist camp at the base of Glacier Point in Yosemite Valley. At Camp Curry, campers were provided with a bed in a large canvas tent, shared bath facilities and home-cooked meals for a mere $2 a day. What's more, Camp Curry offered an evening program of music, stunts, nature talks and views of the nightly 'firefall' (see the boxed text, p69).

The first automobile sputtered into Yosemite Valley in the summer of 1900, but cars were quickly prohibited from the park on the grounds that they spooked livestock and ruined tourists' experience (those were the days!). The ban was lifted in 1913, and a couple of years later a serviceable dirt road opened through Tioga Pass. Annual visitation spiked to more than 30,000, and by 1922 it had surpassed 100,000.

In Sequoia National Park, the first automobile didn't arrive until 1904, and in 1926 the Generals Hwy opened between the park's foothills and the Giant Forest. It took almost another decade to push the highway through to General Grant National Park, connecting the Giant Forest with what would later become Kings Canyon National Park. Although the Generals Hwy was one of the country's most scenic (and expensive) roads, the park only received a quarter of the visitors that Yosemite did.

Although the automobile certainly increased visitation to all three parks, it was the enthusiastic – and sometimes extreme – policies of the NPS's first director, Stephen T Mather, that really sent the numbers

Pick up the historical novel *Gloryland* by Yosemite ranger Shelton Johnson, a well-known historian of the African American 'Buffalo Soldiers' who served as the Sierra Nevada's first national park rangers.

BUFFALO SOLDIERS

Beginning in 1899, US Army infantry and calvary troops drawn from well-respected, though segregated, African American regiments of 'Buffalo Soldiers' were sent to patrol the Sierra Nevada's new national parks. In Sequoia and what was then General Grant National Park, the troops were impressively productive, building roads, creating a trail system and setting a high precedent as stewards of the land. The troops were commanded by Captain (later Colonel) Charles Young, who at the time was the only African-American captain in the army. In 1903 he became the first African American acting superintendent of a US national park.

1984	1996	1997	2006
Unesco declares Yosemite National Park a World Heritage site; Congress passes the sweeping California Wilderness Act, designating almost 90% of Yosemite as specially protected wilderness.	Annual visitation to Yosemite National Park peaks at over 4 million people, then abruptly declines over the next decade, not bouncing back until 2010.	Massive New Year's Day flooding on the Merced River washes out sections of Hwy 140 and damages campgrounds, trails, bridges and more; Yosemite National Park closes for several months.	In August, four cave researchers discover the Ursa Minor cave in Sequoia National Park, said to be one of the most significant cave discoveries in recent history.

climbing. During his tenure between 1917 and 1929, Mather oversaw the development of Yosemite's Wawona Golf Course, the Yosemite Museum, the Ahwahnee Hotel and the ice rink at Camp Curry, and he initiated nature walks and interpretive programs at all three parks.

War & the Plan

In 1940, just before the US entered WWII, Congress passed a law creating Kings Canyon National Park, which absorbed General Grant National Park into its much larger boundaries. As the national war effort gobbled up federal funds, Sequoia and Kings Canyon National Parks were merged into a single administrative body in 1943.

In Yosemite, the Ahwahnee Hotel became a wartime naval hospital and the US Army set up camps at Wawona and Badger Pass. The California National Guard was stationed at Hetch Hetchy to protect the public water supply, while 90,000 troops occupied Yosemite Valley. At the height of the war in 1943, public visitation plummeted to just 116,000 people.

But after WWII, families taking vacations in their shiny new automobiles started rolling into Yosemite in record numbers, and even the backcountry began to get crowded. By the 1970s, Yosemite in summer had become an unsavory place for average tourists, as 'hippies and freaks' swarmed into the Valley, and theft, drug abuse and noise pollution rose.

Tensions came to a head on July 4, 1970, during the Stoneman Meadow Riot, when Yosemite park rangers on horseback forcefully removed partying youth who were illegally camped in Stoneman Meadow. Rangers were pulled from their horses and beaten, dozens of revelers suffered injuries, and by morning, 135 people had been arrested and the National Guard called in.

In Yosemite, annual spikes in visitation and the Stoneman Meadow Riot prompted the park service to introduce one-way roads and a free shuttle service, as well as a quota system for backcountry use. Still, with visitor numbers hitting almost 2.5 million in 1980 and more than one million vehicles driving into the Valley each year, the NPS decided it was time for a plan.

In 1980 Yosemite drew up its first General Management Plan, calling for restrictions on private cars, increases in public transportation, changes to Merced River campgrounds and relocation of many commercial services outside the park. Mired in political and public opposition, however, the plan foundered and underwent many changes over the years. Finally, in 1997, a major flood in Yosemite Valley forced the plan into its final revision, adopted just in time for the 21st century. It proposes $441 million in work to Yosemite Valley with the objective of minimizing human impact.

'The pack that walks like a man,' early 20th-century mountaineer Norman Clyde pioneered many first ascents in the Sierra Nevada while carrying a famously heavy backpack, outfitted with a skillet, fishing gear, books, axe, hammer, firearm, boots and multiple cameras.

HISTORY WAR & THE PLAN

Just exactly how much is planned in that Yosemite Valley Plan anyway? Find out on the NPS website (www.nps.gov/archive/yose/planning/), which details all the current plans for the park.

JOHN ELK III/LONELY PLANET IMAGES ©

2007	2010
The Yosemite Valley Visitor Center opens the doors to its new $1.3 million exhibit hall, which hadn't been upgraded in 40 years.	Yosemite institutes a permit reservation system to control backcountry access for hikers planning to scale Half Dome; profiteers try illegally re-selling the permits on Craigslist.

» Tour 'bus' passing Yosemite Falls (p64)

Geology

Poetically nicknamed the 'Range of Light' by conservationist John Muir, the Sierra Nevada is a 400 mile–long range of 14,000ft peaks that gives California much of its astonishing geological diversity. When the range reached its current height around 12 million years ago, it created a towering wall that captures clouds and douses the western slopes in water, while shutting off the supply of rain to the eastern slopes and the Great Basin desert beyond. Stretching ever skyward, the Sierra Nevada provides living, earth-shaking evidence of the irresistible geological forces still at work shaping the landscape today.

Top Roadside Geology Viewpoints

» Glacier Point, Yosemite National Park

» Tunnel View, Yosemite Valley

» Olmsted Point, Tioga Road, Yosemite National Park

» Moro Rock, Sequoia National Park

» Junction View, Kings Canyon Scenic Byway

The Lay of the Land

Geologists call the Sierra Nevada a tilted fault-block range – and it's a particularly impressive example at that, spreading over 40 to 60 miles wide, with hundreds of peaks over 10,000ft. Picture a tilted fault block as an iceberg listing to one side while floating in the earth's crust. In the Sierra Nevada, that imaginary 'iceberg' is actually an immense body of granite known as a batholith that formed deep within the earth's crust, then 'floated' up and became exposed on the surface over millions of years. Today park visitors can see the tip of this batholith, though it's obscured in places where older rocks (mostly metamorphic) still cling, like pieces of a torn cloak, or where newer rocks (mostly volcanic) have been added on top, like icing.

Drifting on Ancient Seas

Around 225 million years ago, the area that is now the Sierra Nevada was actually a shallow sea lying off the coast of a young North American continent. Material from island volcanoes exploding offshore, plus tons of debris that were eroding from the continental landmass, gradually began filling in this sea with weighty layers of sediment.

At the same time, the continental North American Plate started drifting westward and riding over the leading edge of the oceanic Pacific Plate. With almost unimaginable force, this movement drove the edge of the Pacific Plate down to depths where it melted into magma, later cooling to form the Sierra Nevada batholith (a term derived from the Greek words for 'deep rock').

Today's Sierra Nevada and Cascade mountain chains mark the edge of this submerged, melting plate. The force of the continental and oceanic plates colliding and crushing together also generated such enormous heat and pressure that old sedimentary and volcanic rocks turned into the metamorphic rocks now found throughout the Sierra Nevada range.

Building Mountains: Batholiths & Plutons

As it made its huge, continual push over the Pacific Plate, the North American Plate buckled so strongly that it formed a proto-Sierra Nevada mountain range of folded rock that may have reached as high as 15,000ft.

This initial phase of building the Sierra Nevada ceased about 130 million years ago, when the older mountains began a long erosional phase that reduced them to gently rolling uplands by 50 million years ago, leaving the batholith exposed on the earth's surface.

Between 80 and 210 million years ago, the Sierra Nevada batholith began as magma deep in the earth's crust, cooling to form giant blocks of rock over 100 different times. Each magma event formed a discrete body of granitic rock known as a pluton (from Pluto, the Roman god of the underworld), each with a characteristic composition and appearance. Hikers today can trace the layout of these well-mapped plutons by examining the mix of minerals and the size of the crystals within rocks alongside park trails.

Pushing Up, Sliding Down

About 10 million years ago, the Sierra Nevada's granite batholith began to lift and bulge upward between parallel sets of faults (that is, cracks in the earth's crust). Regions of much older rocks were uplifted on the newly forming crest of the Sierra Nevada. Remnants of old rocks perched on top of granite ridges are today called roof pendants, of which Yosemite's Mt Dana is an outstanding example.

The Sierra Nevada batholith has continued to lift, reaching its current height an estimated two million years ago. Since then, the counterbalancing forces of uplift and erosion have created an equilibrium that keeps the Sierra Nevada at more or less the same size, although the range continues to slowly grow at a miniscule, yet measurable, rate.

From two million years ago until about 10,000 years ago, Ice Age glaciers covered portions of the Sierra Nevada with snow and ice. The largest ice field was a giant cap of ice that covered an area 275 miles long and 40 miles wide between Lake Tahoe and Yosemite. From high-elevation ice fields, rivers of ice (glaciers) flowed down and scoured out rugged river canyons, simply enlarging some or beautifully sculpting others, like Yosemite Valley and the upper portions of Kings Canyon.

After the Ice Age came a warm period when there were no glaciers in the Sierra, but during the last thousand years or so, about 99 glaciers and 398 glacierets (small glaciers or pockets of ice) reformed during the Little Ice Age. The largest remaining glaciers are on Mt Lyell and Mt Maclure in the Yosemite region, and on the Palisades in the John Muir Wilderness

California claims both the highest point in contiguous US (Mt Whitney, 14,505ft) and the lowest elevation in North America (Badwater, Death Valley, 282ft below sea level) – and they're only 90 miles apart, as the condor flies.

GEOLOGY THE LAY OF THE LAND

SIERRA NEVADA ROCKS: A PRIMER

The Sierra Nevada is one of the world's premier granite landscapes, yet these mountains include much more than just granite!

» **Metamorphic rocks** are older volcanic and sedimentary rocks whose structure has been dramatically altered by intense heat and pressure deep within the earth's crust. These rocks pre-date the Sierra Nevada batholith, and their reddish, purplish or greenish hues are a distinctive change from the speckled grays of granite.

» **Granite** describes a broad category of rocks formed when molten magma cools within the earth's crust (called lava when it erupts or flows onto the earth's surface). Sierra Nevada granite is actually composed of five separate minerals occurring in complex combinations that produce a characteristic salt-and-pepper appearance.

» **Volcanic rocks** in the Sierra Nevada have mostly weathered away except for high, uplifted pockets. Chemically identical to rocks that form deep within the earth's crust, volcanic rocks change as they erupt on the surface as lava. Gases injected into the liquid rock give it a pockmarked or bubbled appearance. Rocks that cool deep underground do so very slowly, forming large, visible crystals; liquid rock exposed to air cools so quickly that crystals can't form.

in the Eastern Sierra further south. However, due to global warming, these glaciers are all melting rapidly and are in danger of disappearing entirely within decades.

The Forces at Work

The dramatic tale of how the Sierra Nevada range first formed is only the beginning of the geologic story – as soon as its rocks were exposed on the earth's surface, a host of new forces shaped them into what you see today. Hugely powerful glaciers have played a dramatic role, but erosion and weathering have also done their part, as have lava and ash eruptions.

Glaciers

Most of the Sierra Nevada's landscape has been substantially shaped by glaciers. In fact, of all the forces that have contributed to the landscape, none have had greater impact than the relentless grinding caused by millions of tons of ice over a period of two million years. Evidence of this dramatic grinding process is often right at your feet in areas of the Sierra Nevada where glaciers have worn granite surfaces down to a smooth, shiny finish. Along the road at Tenaya Lake, for example, flat granite shelves are so polished they glisten in the early morning light. In contrast, hikers to high-alpine nunataks (peaks and plateaus that were too high to be glaciated) such as Mt Conness will find rough-textured, sharp-edged and jagged granite formations.

Glaciers arise where snowfields fail to melt completely by summer's end. Over time, delicate snow crystals dissolve into tiny spheres that connect and fuse into solid ice. True glacial ice forms after hundreds of years, with the original snowflakes becoming nine times heavier and 500 times stronger in the process. These ice fields develop in high mountain valleys where snowdrifts readily accumulate, and from there they flow downhill at the rate of inches or yards per day. The longest known glacier in the Sierra Nevada was a 60-mile tongue that flowed down the Tuolumne River canyon about 20,000 years ago.

In some Sierra Nevada valleys, the ice field once measured 500ft to 4000ft thick. Hundreds of thousands of cubic feet of ice thus created an unbelievable amount of pressure and shearing strength that completely altered the landscape. Massive boulders were plucked up and dragged along like giant rasping teeth on a file's edge. Smaller rocks and sand carried along the glacier's bottom acted like sandpaper that polished underlying bedrock. Every rock that was loose or could be pried loose was caught up and transported for miles.

The vast wilderness of the High Sierra (lying mostly above 9000ft) presents an astounding landscape of glaciers, sculpted granite peaks and remote canyons, beautiful to look at but difficult to access on foot or horseback – presenting one of the greatest challenges for 19th-century settlers attempting to reach California.

SHAKY GROUND

Uplift of the Sierra's batholith continues to occur along its eastern face, where a zone of geologic activity keeps life exciting for folks living between Mammoth Lakes and Lone Pine.

In 1872 the Eastern Sierra jerked upward 13ft in a single earthquake, while over the past two decades Mammoth has endured a nerve-wracking series of minor earthquakes and tremors. The Sierra crest is estimated to lift as much as 1.5in per century and as a result of this skewed tilting the eastern face of the Sierra is now an abrupt wall rising up to 11,000ft high while the western face is a long gentle incline.

Due to uplift along the eastern face, rivers flowing down the west slope have picked up speed and cut progressively deeper canyons into the formerly flat, rolling landscape. Today, over a dozen major river canyons mark the west slope, and the rock that formerly filled those canyons now buries the Central Valley under 9.5 miles of sediment. Talk about rolling stones!

Glaciers have the funny effect of rounding out landscape features that lie below the ice while sharpening features that rise above the ice. The same grinding force that smoothes out valleys also quarries rocks from the base of peaks, resulting in undercutting that forms towering spikes. In Tuolumne Meadows this effect is particularly dramatic – compare the smooth domes on the valley floor, like Lembert and Pothole, with the sheer spires of Cathedral and Unicorn Peaks visible nearby.

Rocks: Cracking, Fracturing & Weathering

The distinctive granite of the Sierra Nevada owes its appearance not only to the tremendous sculpting power of glaciers but also to something far more subtle – the internal properties of the rock itself, and how it behaves in its natural environment.

The first rule of thumb is that granite tends to crack and separate along regular planes, often parallel to the surface of the rocks. Everywhere you travel in the High Sierra, you'll easily be able to see evidence of this ongoing cracking.

At Olmsted Point along the Tioga Pass Rd, visitors can see a surrealistic view of vast granite walls peeling off like onion layers below Clouds Rest. This exfoliation is the result of massive rock formations expanding and cracking in shell-like layers as the pressure of overlying materials erodes away. Over time, sharp angles and corners give way to increasingly rounded curves that leave us with distinctive landmarks like Yosemite Valley's Half Dome and Moro Rock in Sequoia National Park.

Weathering breaks granite down through a process different from glacial erosion or internal cracking, yet its effects are equally profound. Joints in the granite allow water to seep into deep cracks where the liquid expands during winter's freezing temperatures. This pushes open cracks with pressures up to 1000 pounds per sq inch and eventually forces square-angled blocks to break off from the parent formation.

Granite rock edges and corners are further weathered over time to create rounded boulders. Rain and exposure to the elements wear down granite's weaker minerals, leaving an unstable matrix of hard, pale minerals (quartz and feldspar) that crumble into fine-grained rubble called grus. Hikers walking on granite slabs might experience the unnerving sensation of slipping on tiny pebbles of grus that roll underfoot like ball bearings. In the presence of water, grus eventually break down into crumbly soil.

On the western slopes of the Sierra Nevada, granites are mostly fine-grained, with joints spaced fairly widely. As a result, rock formations tend to be massive structures shaped by exfoliation, like Yosemite's Half Dome. Further east, granites are more likely to be coarse-grained and to have closely spaced joints. There the process of water seeping into cracks and pushing rocks apart results in characteristically jagged, sawtooth ridges such as those in the Cathedral Range of Yosemite's high country.

Volcanoes

Between five and 20 million years ago, a series of lava and mud flows covered about 12,000 sq miles of the Sierra Nevada north of Yosemite, with some volcanic activity extending south to the area now enclosed by the national park. While much of this violent geological history has since eroded away, caps of old volcanic material still exist at Sonora Pass, an otherworldly landscape of eroding debris.

About three million years ago, the zone of volcanic activity shifted from the region north of Yosemite to the slopes east of the Sierra Nevada crest. Massive eruptions between Mammoth Lakes and Mono Lake created a series of calderas and volcanic mountains, including Mammoth

---

Can't see yourself backpacking for days into the Sierra Nevada to glimpse a glacier, or hanging around for weeks in Yosemite Valley just hoping to witness a rock-fall? Download the free video podcast series 'Yosemite Nature Notes,' available on iTunes and from www.nps.gov /yose/photos multimedia /ynn.htm.

The highest single-tier waterfall in North America is not Yosemite Falls – it's Ribbon Fall, which plummets 1612ft from a precipice west of El Capitan. With three distinct falls, Yosemite Falls gets disqualified, despite measuring an astonishing 2425ft from top to bottom.

GEOLOGY THE FORCES AT WORK

Mountain itself. Mono Lake gained two islands and a small chain of hills on its southern side during this period of activity, which is still ongoing. Over time, the volcanic landscape at Mono Lake has undergone dramatic changes, with the last eruption taking place as recently as 640 years ago.

The most familiar and popular landmark formed in the current (geologically speaking) era of volcanic activity is Devils Postpile, a national monument located west of Mammoth Lakes. About 80,000 to 100,000 years ago, a violent volcanic vent filled a river canyon and a natural lake with lava 400ft deep. The lava cooled so quickly that it formed one of the world's most spectacular examples of columnar basalt, today reaching up to 60ft high. These multisided columns are virtually perfect in their symmetry, and the iconic formation can be viewed by taking just a short hike.

The rawness and relative newness of all of these volcanic formations reminds us how active and ongoing the Sierra Nevada's evolution is. For example, just consider how the Ice Age glaciers retreated a mere 10,000 years ago, not even enough time for soil to develop in most places! This is a remarkably young range, still jagged and sharp, still rising – and yes, still shaking.

Take a virtual field trip into the Sierra Nevada, courtesy of the myriad links put together by the California Geological Survey at www.conservation.ca.gov/cgs/geotour.

Wildlife

Wildlife in the Sierra Nevada ranges from lumbering bears and soaring birds to skittering lizards and fleeting butterflies, all scattered across a vast and wild region. Only in a few places do animals congregate in conspicuous numbers. But if you remain patient and alert, you might be rewarded with lifelong memories.

Mammals

Black Bears

Arguably the animal that park visitors would most like to see is the black bear. Weighing in at around 350lb, these bears can be formidable fighters, but they generally shy away from human contact. For safety tips for bear encounters, see p236.

Whether climbing trees, poking under logs and rocks or crossing rivers, bears are basically big noses in search of food – they'll eat almost anything. Bears may spend a considerable amount of time grazing like cows on meadow plants. Later in the summer, they switch over to berries and acorns, with insects (including ants, beetles, termites and wasps) making up about 10% of their diet.

Mule Deer

The most common large mammals in the Sierra Nevada, mule deer dwell in all forest habitats below the timberline. In parks, they have become remarkably unconcerned about human observers and tend to frequent meadows from late afternoon until sunset. White-spotted fawns first appear in mid- to late July, while tannish adults with big floppy ears become numerous in early winter, when deep snows push them out of the high country and they forage below 5500ft. At all times, deer favor leaves and young twigs as a source of food; in late fall, they feed heavily on acorns.

Big Cats

You'll rarely glimpse a mountain lion bounding into the woods. Reaching up to 8ft from nose to tail tip and weighing as much as 150lb, this solitary and highly elusive creature makes a formidable predator. In the Sierra Nevada, mountain lions roam all forested habitats below the timberline in search of mule deer and, occasionally, endangered bighorn sheep. Humans are rarely more than a curiosity or nuisance to be avoided, although a few attacks have occurred. Hikers are more likely to see the handsome bobcat, looking like a scaled-up version of the domestic tabby, with a brown-spotted, yellowish-tan coat and a cropped tail.

Wild Dogs

The ubiquitous coyote and its much smaller cousin, the gray fox, share the same grayish-brown coat. Both have adapted to human habitats, becoming altogether too comfortable around roads, campgrounds and

---

Top Wildlife Watching Spots

» Yosemite Valley, Yosemite National Park

» Glacier Point, Yosemite National Park

» Tioga Road, Yosemite National Park

» Giant Forest, Sequoia National Park

» Kings River, Kings Canyon National Park

California's mountain forests are home to an estimated 25,000 to 35,000 black bears, whose fur actually ranges in color from black to dark brown, cinnamon or even blond.

any food left unguarded. You stand a good chance of seeing a coyote during the daytime, especially around meadows, where they hunt rodents. Foxes mainly come out at night, when you might spy one crossing a road or trail.

Rodents

That odd little 'bleating' call coming from jumbles of rocks and boulders is likely a pika. A careful search will reveal the hamsterlike vocalist peering from under a rock with small beady eyes. Pikas typically live on talus slopes above 8000ft, especially in the alpine realm of mountain hemlock, whitebark pine and heather plants.

The golden-mantled ground squirrel is often mistaken for a chubby chipmunk. However, ground squirrels have no stripes on their heads and shoulders, while chipmunks are striped all the way to the tip of their noses. Ground squirrels spend the winter hibernating, so in late summer they start gaining an extreme amount of weight.

A large cousin of the chipmunk, the western gray squirrel, with its long, fluffy tail trailing behind, tends to live at low to mid-elevations on the western slope of the Sierra. The smaller Douglas squirrel, recognized by its slender tail and rusty tone, lives in conifer forests up to the timberline.

Birds

Whether you enjoy the aerial acrobatics of swifts and falcons over Yosemite Valley's waterfalls, the flash of brilliant warblers in oak woodlands, or the bright, inviting lives of more than 250 other bird species found in the Sierra Nevada, it goes without question that birding is a highlight here.

No other bird commands attention quite like the ubiquitous Steller's jay, found in virtually every forested habitat and around campgrounds. Flashing a shimmering cloak of blue feathers and an equally jaunty attitude, these noisy birds wander fearlessly among picnic tables and parked cars in pursuit of overlooked crumbs.

Another conspicuous bird, the small mountain chickadee, with its distinctive black cap, is a perennial favorite with children because its merry song sounds like 'cheese-bur-ger.' You'll hear this song often in forested areas above 4000ft.

In the highest mountain forests, hikers can expect greetings from the raucous and inquisitive Clark's nutcracker, a hardy resident of subalpine forests recognized by its black wings and white tail. A flock of

You'll be amazed by the 2800 hand-drawn watercolor illustrations and easy-to-understand descriptions of more than 1700 species found in *The Laws Field Guide to the Sierra Nevada*, by John Muir Laws.

MOUNTAIN KINGS

Among the most curious mammals in the Sierra high country, the yellow-bellied marmot inhabits rock outcrops and boulder fields above 7500ft. Sprawled lazily on sun-warmed rocks, marmots scarcely bear notice until closely approached, when they jolt upright and send out shrieks of alarm to the entire marmot neighborhood. Marmots have a great appetite – they spend four to five months putting on weight (incredibly, up to 50% of their body weight can be fat) before starting a long, deep hibernation until the following spring.

Another high-elevation dweller, but one that's less likely to be seen, is the endangered Sierra Nevada bighorn sheep. Although bighorns once numbered in the thousands, their wild population has declined to just 125 animals as the result of 19th-century hunting and exposure to diseases from domesticated livestock. Your best chance of spotting bighorns is during summer as they scale granite slopes and peaks above 10,000ft in the Eastern Sierra to graze on alpine plants and escape from predators.

YOSEMITE'S BIRDS OF PREY

While 11 species of owls live in the Yosemite region, no other evokes the mystery of the nocturnal realm quite like that rare phantom, the great gray owl. Easily the most famous and sought-after bird in Yosemite, this distinctive owl stands 2ft tall. A small population (about 150 individuals) of these birds survive in the park. These majestic owls have been spotted at Crane Flat, where they hunt around large meadows in the late afternoon.

You'll also be fortunate if you see the peregrine falcon, a species that has climbed back from the brink of extinction and now is present in healthy numbers. This stream-lined, fierce hunter with long, pointed wings and a black 'moustache' mark on its cheek now nests in cliffs in the Yosemite Valley, where seasonal rock-climbing route closures protect chicks until they've fledged, usually by late summer.

nutcrackers will survive the winter by gathering and storing up to four million pine nuts each fall, burying the nuts in thousands of small caches.

John Muir favored the American dipper (formerly known as a water ouzel) for its ceaseless energy and good cheer even in the depths of winter. This 'singularly joyous and lovable little fellow' rarely leaves the cascading torrents of cold, clear mountain streams, where it dives to capture underwater insects and larvae.

Amphibians

Among the region's several unique amphibians is the Yosemite toad. This endemic, high-elevation toad used to abound, but in recent years it has mysteriously disappeared from many of its former haunts. At lower elevations, the western toad is still quite common and often observed moving along trails or through campgrounds at night. To identify a toad, look for a slow, plodding walk and dry, warty skin, which easily distinguishes them from smooth-skinned, quickly hopping frogs.

Another unusual amphibian of the High Sierra is the scarce mountain yellow-legged frog, whose numbers have declined sharply in alpine lakes stocked with trout. This strong jumping and diving frog resides on lake margins. The abundant Pacific treefrog, by contrast, is extremely wide-spread and diverse in habitat preferences. Treefrogs have the familiar 'ri-bet' call that nearly everyone associates with singing frogs (thanks to Hollywood movies that feature this frog in their soundtracks).

Oddest among amphibians is the rare Mt Lyell salamander, first discovered in Yosemite in 1915 when accidentally captured in a trap. This granite-colored salamander resides on domed rocks and talus slopes from 4000ft to 12,000ft, where it uses its webbed toes and strong tail to climb sheer cliffs and boulders in search of food.

Reptiles

The most abundant and widespread reptile is the western fence lizard, a 6in-long creature you're likely to see perched on rocks and logs or scam-pering across the forest floor. During breeding season, you'll notice gray males bob energetically (doing 'push ups') as they conspicuously display their iridescent-blue throats and bellies.

Found in forest-floor debris, southern alligator lizards wiggle off noisily like clumsy snakes when disturbed. These 10in-long yellow-tan lizards with crossbars on their backs reside from the lower foothills up into the mixed conifer zone.

The region has over a dozen snake species, including garter snakes, which live in the widest diversity of habitats and are the snakes you're most likely to see. Two kinds of garter snake sport mainly black skin,

The Yosemite Conservancy (www.yosemite conservancy.org) is a nonprofit group that publishes books and teaches a wide variety of natural history classes about the Sierra Nevada, including family-friendly outings and art workshops in Yosemite Valley.

Want to learn more about the local ecosystem? For an explanation of just about everything, check out *Sierra Nevada Natural History* (University of California Press), by Tracey Storer, Robert Usinger and David Lukas.

with yellow or orange stripes running the length of their bodies. A third species, restricted to low to mid-elevation rivers, features a black checkerboard pattern on an olive-gray body.

No other snake elicits as much fear as the western rattlesnake. Even if they're not rattling, you can quickly recognize rattlers by their bluntly triangular heads perched on remarkably slender necks. Rocky or brushy areas below 8000ft are the preferred haunts of this venomous though generally docile snake. See p237 for information on rattlesnakes and what to do if bitten.

Often confused with deadly coral snakes (which don't live in California), the mountain king snake – with bright orange, black and white-colored bands around its body – is harmless to humans, and lives throughout the Sierra Nevada.

Best Wild-flower Blooms

» Tuolumne Meadows, Yosemite National Park

» McGurk Meadow, Yosemite National Park

» Wawona Meadow, Yosemite National Park

» Crescent Meadow, Sequoia National Park

» Zumwalt Meadow, Kings Canyon National Park

Fish

The most widely distributed fish in the Western Sierra is the rainbow trout. Formerly limited to the lower reaches of streams below insurmountable barriers (eg waterfalls), rainbow trout have been introduced into countless alpine and eastern creeks and lakes for sportfishing. Now threatened with extinction, the California golden trout – the state's official fish – inhabits the Kern River drainage of Sequoia & Kings Canyon National Parks.

Further complicating the natural order of things, non-native species such as brook trout, lake trout, brown trout and kokanee salmon have been successfully introduced throughout the Sierra Nevada. Introduced fish have had a devastating impact on aquatic ecosystems, especially in formerly fishless alpine areas, where fragile nutrient cycles and invertebrate populations have changed dramatically as a result.

Insects

Most visitors won't notice the amazing variety of insects in the Sierra Nevada, except for a handful of conspicuous butterflies and other charismatic insects. Foremost among the large, showy butterflies are the five swallowtail species. The Western tiger swallowtail, yellow in color with bold black bars and beautiful blue and orange spots near its 'tail,' follows stream banks from the lower foothills to subalpine forest. Restricted to the foothill zone, the stunning, iridescent-blue pipevine swallowtail flits in large numbers along foothill canyons and slopes almost year-round.

Plants

The Sierra Nevada boasts one of the richest selections of plants found anywhere in North America. Yosemite National Park alone is home to over 20% of California's 7000 plant species, even though it encompasses less than 1% of the state's total land.

Wildflowers

You can see flowering plants from early March until late August, and taking time out to find them will enrich your park experience.

At low elevations in early spring, when wildflowers carpet low-elevation hillsides, you can't miss the brilliant orange, native California poppy, each with four floppy, silken petals. At night and on cloudy days, poppy petals fold up and become inconspicuous.

At least a dozen species of Indian paintbrush of varying colors and shapes can be found in the region. Most are red or orange in color and seem somewhat hairy. Surprisingly, the flowers themselves are hidden and accessible only to hummingbirds (the plants' pollinators), while a set of specialized colored leaves take on the appearance of petals. Paintbrushes are semiparasitic, often tapping into the roots of their neighbors to draw nourishment. So are snow plants, which feed on fungi in the soil and shoot up fleshy stems with brilliant red flowers that bloom early and often at the edges of melting snow banks.

Mountaineers climb into a rarified realm rich in unique flowers, and if you need a single target flower to hunt for, one that's rare and mysterious like a distant peak, you couldn't make a better choice than the Sierra primrose. Confined to a handful of high subalpine slopes and peaks, this brilliant magenta beauty is a real find for the lucky hiker. Arising from clumps of toothed, succulent leaves, primroses sometimes grow in large patches sprawling across rocky slopes.

Highest and showiest of all is the aptly named sky pilot. Usually found only above 11,000ft, this plant erupts into flagrant displays of violet-blue flowers arranged in dense, ball-like clusters. After a long and grueling ascent, hikers to the highest peaks will better understand its name, a slang term for a military chaplain or priest said to lead others to heaven.

Trees

While flowers rise and fade with ephemeral beauty, trees hold their majesty for centuries. Given a few simple tips, you can learn to identify many of the region's prominent species and appreciate the full sweep of trees cloaking the parks' landscape.

Pines are conifers whose needles appear in tight clusters, with two, three or five needles per cluster. Named for its straight, slender trunk, the abundant lodgepole pine has two-needled clusters and globular cones that are less than 2in long. Lodgepoles are the most common tree around mountain meadows because this species has adapted to survive in waterlogged soils or in basins where cold air sits at night (so-called frost pockets).

THE SMALL KINGDOM OF GIANT SEQUOIAS

The Sierra Nevada's most famous tree, the giant sequoia, is also the source of much legend and ballyhoo. Even information as basic as the trees' maximum height and width remains uncertain because loggers and claim-seekers who cut down many of the original giants found it beneficial to exaggerate records. Today, the General Sherman tree of Sequoia National Park, which measures 275ft tall and over 100ft in circumference, is recognized as the largest known living specimen (and it's still growing!).

Giant sequoias cluster in fairly discrete groves on the western slopes of the Sierra Nevada. You can recognize them by their spongy, cinnamon-red bark and juniperlike needles. Despite claims that these are the world's oldest trees, it's now thought that the longest they can live is just over 3000 years, far short of the age reached by ancient bristlecone pines.

Between five and 25 million years ago, the giant sequoias' arboreal ancestors covered a vast area between the Sierra Nevada and the Rocky Mountains. Migrating westward, possibly through low mountain passes, these trees got a foothold on the west slope of the Sierra Nevada just as the range began to reach its current height. The formation of the Sierra Nevada isolated those sequoias on the west slope while at the same time creating a rain shadow that killed off the main population of sequoias to the east.

Giant sequoias survive today in 67 scattered groves. In Yosemite National Park the Tuolumne Grove and Merced Grove along Hwy 120 and the Mariposa Grove along Hwy 41 are relatively small groves, while the 20-plus groves in Sequoia and Kings Canyon National Parks are generally more extensive because the soils are deeper and better developed in areas that weren't covered by glaciers.

The ponderosa pine, with some examples of the Jeffrey pine mixed in, covers vast tracts of low to mid-elevation Sierra Nevada slopes. Three-needled clusters characterize both trees. Virtually identical in appearance, the two species do have distinct cones; on ponderosa cones the barbs protrude outward, and on Jeffrey pines they curve inward. If you're unsure of the identification, simply hold a cone in your hand and remember the adage: 'Gentle Jeffrey, prickly ponderosa.'

The wide variety of deciduous trees in the region includes the quaking aspen, with its smooth, white bark and oval leaves. Every brief gust sets these leaves quivering on their flattened stems. Aspens consist of genetically identical trunks arising from a single root system that may grow to be more than 100 acres in size. By sprouting repeatedly from this root system, aspens have what has been called 'theoretical immortality,' and some aspens are thought to be over 80,000 years old.

Magnificent black oaks grow up to 80ft high at mountain elevations between 2000ft and 7000ft, where their immense crops of acorns are a food source for many animals, including bears, deer and woodpeckers.

Located in the stunning terrain of the southern Sierra, the Sequoia Natural History Association (www.sequoiahistory.org) has one of the best outdoor classrooms in the region, offering guided hikes and underground cave tours and other family fun.

Shrubs

No other shrub may be as worthy of note as poison oak, which can trigger an inflammatory skin reaction in people who come into contact with it. The shrub is distinguished by shiny, oak-like leaves that occur in groups of three; clusters of white berries appear by late summer. If you'll be exploring the western slopes of the Sierra Nevada, learn how to identify this common trailside plant (see the boxed text, p40).

At higher elevations, huckleberry oak and greenleaf manzanita form a dense, nearly impenetrable habitat, known as montane chaparral, that carpets the high country around granite boulders and outcrops. Here bears, deer, rabbits and many other animals find food and shelter not provided in nearby forests.

At lower elevations, you'll find foothill chaparral characterized by whiteleaf manzanita. The two manzanitas feature the same smooth, reddish bark and small, red, apple-like berries (manzanita is Spanish for 'little apple'), but they differ in the color of their leaves. During late summer, the scat of animals like black bears, coyotes and foxes is chock-full of partly digested manzanita berries.

Conserving the Parks

Ever since the discovery of gold in 1848, the natural world of the Sierra Nevada has been forever altered by a rush of new settlers. The 19th-century human stampede to find gold and profit at any cost had a devastating impact on both Native Americans and the landscape. Today, California is the most populous US state with the highest projected growth rate in the nation, which strains the region's precious natural resources. Tourism also impacts, with over five million people visiting these national parks each year.

Water

Without doubt, the greatest benefit that the Sierra Nevada provides to the state of California is an abundant supply of fresh, clean water. Ironically, the greatest harm to the Sierra Nevada has come from using, managing and collecting this essential resource.

During the mid-19th century, rivers were diverted, rocks moved and entire hillsides washed away to reveal gold deposits north of Yosemite. More than 1.5 billion tons of debris and uncalculated amounts of poisonous mercury flowed downstream, with harsh consequences for aquatic ecosystems and watershed health, which are still felt today in both the Sierra Nevada and Central Valley.

Early 20th-century construction of Yosemite's Hetch Hetchy Dam to supply San Francisco with water allegedly broke conservationist John Muir's heart. In the Eastern Sierra, the diversion of water for the city of Los Angeles contributed to the destruction of Owens Lake and its fertile wetlands, and the degradation of Mono Lake.

Throughout the 20th century, dams drawn across the Sierra Nevada severely altered aquatic habitats and eliminated spawning habitat for fish such as salmon. Native fish populations and aquatic ecosystems have been further decimated by the introduction of dozens of non-native fish species, mostly through sportfishing.

But there's good news, too. In 2004, the removal of the Cascades Diversion Dam west of Yosemite Valley has helped to restore the wild and scenic Merced River. In the Eastern Sierra, the ongoing restoration of Mono Lake is another water-conservation success story. Lake levels have already risen over 10ft since reaching their lowest point in 1982.

Air

Perhaps the most pernicious environmental issue today is air pollution. In 2004 Yosemite joined a growing list of national parks that violate federal smog standards, and the situation in Sequoia & Kings Canyon is much worse. Monitoring stations in Yosemite detect high ozone levels 30 to 40 times per year, and it's not uncommon for park views to be

Visitors can do their part to 'green' the parks by recycling, reusing and reducing as much waste as possible during their visit. For more Leave No Trace tips to help minimize your impact on the parks, see p38.

Known as the little organization that triumphed over Los Angeles, the Mono Lake Committee (www.monolake.org) has matured into a successful environmental powerhouse in the Eastern Sierra, offering field seminars and naturalist-guided walks, talks and kayak tours.

JOHN MUIR: A MAN OF THE MOUNTAINS

Arriving in San Francisco in the spring of 1868, John Muir started out to walk across California's Central Valley to the then scarcely known landmark of Yosemite Valley, where his wanderings and writings later earned him lasting worldwide fame.

This Scotsman's many treks led him into the highest realms of Yosemite's backcountry, where he took little more than a wool overcoat, dry crusts of bread and a bit of tea on his wanderings. Though not a scientist by training, Muir looked at the natural world with a keen curiosity, investigating glaciers, trees, earthquakes, bees and even the most plain-coated of Sierra birds, recording them in great detail.

Not only did Muir's prolific and poetic writings span the gap between literature and science, but his articles and lobbying efforts became the foundation of the campaign that established Yosemite as a national park in 1890. Despite that success and his other accomplishments with the Sierra Club, Muir was unable to save Hetch Hetchy Valley, which he said rivaled Yosemite Valley in beauty and grandeur. Muir lost that final battle in 1913, when Hetch Hetchy Valley was sacrificed to the water and power needs of a growing San Francisco.

obscured by haze all summer long. Tighter regulations are slowly making California's air cleaner, but plenty of pollution still drifts up from the Central Valley.

Tourism also has a detrimental effect on air quality, as every visitor arriving by car or bus contributes to the overall impact of vehicle emissions – and traffic jams. Visitors can help the parks' air quality by leaving their cars behind and riding shuttle buses or – even better – renting or bringing their own bikes. Drivers can turn the engine off rather than letting it idle at roadside viewpoints.

Co-founded by John Muir in 1892, the Sierra Club (www.sierra club.org) was the USA's first conservation group and it remains the nation's most active, offering educational programs, group hikes, organized trips and volunteer vacations.

Livestock & Logging

Following the mid-19th-century gold rush, ranchers began driving millions of sheep into the Sierra Nevada's mountain meadows, where they wreaked havoc. The result? Sheep turned meadows into choking dustbowls by devouring fragile plants before they could flower and produce seeds.

Even now, over a hundred years later, the pattern of vegetation in the high mountains largely reflects this grazing history, with many hillsides still dry, barren or choked with species that 'hoofed locusts' didn't like.

Fortunately, the Sierra Nevada's mountain environments can be so extreme that few weed species ever took hold. The opposite is true of its foothill slopes, though, where weed species introduced by humans and their livestock now utterly dominate and choke out native plants. Global climate change has further imperiled native plants all across the Sierra Nevada.

John Muir's concern over destructive logging practices, especially those that felled giant sequoia trees, played an important part in the establishment of Yosemite National Park, but Muir didn't live long enough to see the worst of what could happen. Industrial-scale logging took off after WWII, when gasoline-powered chainsaws, logging trucks and heavy equipment were brought in to the national forests surrounding the parks, causing lasting damage to the soil and watersheds, and causing devastating forest fires.

Since the 1960s, national forest management directives have begun to reverse course, aiming to better balance conservation and public recreation with big-business tree 'harvesting.' Toward the end of the 20th century, both national forests and parks also changed their minds about wildfire management. Wildfires that were once suppressed have been shown to be part of the healthy life cycle of the parks' forests. Today, they may be allowed to burn naturally when they don't endanger park visitors or infrastructure.

Survival Guide

Directory A–Z

Accommodations

Accommodations options in both Yosemite and Sequoia & Kings Canyon National Parks run the gamut from basic to bourgeois. You can shack up in rustic tent cabins in both parks, sleep in comfort at one of the lodges within or around the parks or go totally overboard staying somewhere like Yosemite's famous Ahwahnee Hotel. And, of course, you can camp.

Accommodations in this book are listed in order of preference.

Seasons

» Most campgrounds, many lodges and some B&Bs close during the winter season (generally October through March, April or May), but you'll find something open in and around both national parks year-round.

» If an accommodations option or campground is open only part of the year, we've included its opening hours following the '☺' sign.

Pricing

Throughout this book, you can easily identify how much a place charges by the number of dollar signs it receives. Prices listed are for peak-season travel before taxes.

» Budget options ($) are less than $100 and range from campgrounds to tent cabins and cheap motels found along the gateway routes into the park.

» Midrange double accommodations ($$) run $100 to $200 and are generally (though not always) comfortable motels, some lodges and B&Bs. At the upper end of the midrange spectrum, you can expect good beds, hot water and private bathrooms as a bare minimum.

Prices for tent cabins and many ho-hum motels fall into the midrange spectrum during the summer high season.

» A top-end joint ($$$) costs over $200. You can generally expect solid service, comfy beds, private bathroom, hot water, spacious accommodations and, depending on the place, amenities like telephone, room service and (mostly outside the parks) cable TV.

Reservations

» If you want to stay within either park, make a reservation no matter what time of the year you plan to visit. Anyone hoping to sleep in Yosemite during the peak months of May through September should reserve *far* in advance.

» If you don't have a reservation, don't write off your trip – you might get lucky, especially if you're camping in May, early June or September and you turn up before noon.

B&Bs

There are no bed and breakfasts per se in the national parks. But they are easily found in towns along the gateway routes into the parks. B&Bs generally average around $150 and offer intimate accommodations, usually in an old house or small historical building. Service is always personal (often by the owners themselves), and breakfasts are generally wholesome and filling.

Campgrounds
TYPES OF CAMPGROUNDS

» Most of the parks' sites are designated for car camping, meaning you pull up, unload your car and pitch your tent.

» Some sites are walk-in campgrounds, meaning you have to park your vehicle in a designated lot and carry your camping equipment and supplies to the campsite.

BOOK YOUR STAY ONLINE

For more accommodations reviews by Lonely Planet authors, check out hotels.lonelyplanet.com. You'll find independent reviews, as well as recommendations on the best places to stay. Best of all, you can book online.

PRACTICALITIES

» Major US newspapers are available from coin-operated newspaper boxes in Yosemite and Sequoia & Kings Canyon.

» The National Weather Service broadcasts regular updates (frequency 162.450MHz) from its Yosemite tower.

» Local FM and AM radio stations can be picked up within Yosemite Valley.

» US domestic electrical current is 110V, 60Hz (same as Canada).

» The USA uses the imperial system of weights and measures; road signs are in miles.

» To convert between metric and imperial, see the inside back cover.

» Smoking is prohibited in restaurants and bars throughout California, and many accommodations are completely nonsmoking.

The advantage of walk-in sites is the lack of cars and RVs, which makes for a more 'natural' experience.

» Yosemite has three backpacker campgrounds to accommodate people heading into or out of the backcountry. You must have a wilderness permit to stay in these. There are no backpacker campgrounds in Sequoia and Kings Canyon National Parks.

INSIDE THE PARKS

Camping inside the parks offers the distinct advantage of putting you closest to what you came to see. You likely won't have to drive to the trailhead nor (and this pertains primarily to Yosemite) face the day-parking nightmare that day-trippers face. On the other hand, park campgrounds generally fill up the fastest.

OUTSIDE THE PARKS

The advantage of staying outside the park is that you'll likely pay a little less (though the amount is generally negligible) and reservations are often easier to make closer to the date you wish to camp.

» Campgrounds outside the national parks are either privately owned or operated by the **US Forest Service** (USFS; www.fs.fed.us).

» Campgrounds at lower elevations are open year-round, while upper-elevation campgrounds usually open only seasonally.

» Although not covered in this book, there are many free car-accessible campgrounds within the national forests surrounding the parks, though they generally lie at the end of long dirt roads and don't offer access to the parks.

RESERVATIONS

All reservable park and USFS campgrounds are bookable through **Recreation.gov** (☑toll free 877-444-6777, international 518-885-3639; www.recreation.gov).

FIRST-COME, FIRST-SERVED

Some campgrounds, both within and around the parks, operate on a first-come, first-served basis. For folks without reservations (especially those heading to Yosemite), these generally offer the only hope. The key to scoring a first-come, first-served campsite is arriving between 8am and noon. Arrive too early and the previous night's guests haven't yet left; too late and sites are full with new campers.

In Yosemite, seven campgrounds operate on a first-come, first-served basis. In Sequoia and Kings Canyon 12 of the 14 campgrounds are first-come, first served.

Even in the heat of summer, getting a first-come, first-served campsite isn't that difficult if you arrive early enough. The park recommends 9am, but on weekdays you'll probably be fine before noon. The method is simple: drive or walk around the campground loops until you see an unoccupied site – that means no tents, equipment or hired bodyguards there to hold it, and no receipt hanging from the site's little signpost. If it's free, take it, because if you're too picky it might be gone the next time you drive by. Remember that check-out time is not until noon at most campgrounds, so late risers may not clear out until close to lunchtime. Take a look at the check-out date printed on the campsite receipt for some guidance. And be patient.

Once you have claimed a site, head back to the campground entrance and follow instructions listed there for paying and properly displaying your receipt. Pay for as many days as you expect to stay; and if you extend your stay, just pay again in the morning before check-out time.

WILDERNESS CAMPING

Also called 'backcountry camping' or 'dispersed camping,' wilderness camping is just what it sounds like: camping in the wilderness. Provided you meet certain requirements, you can camp wherever you want. Along popular trails there are often established wilderness campsites; in heavily visited areas (such as Little Yosemite Valley) pit toilets minimize camper impact. Although sleeping in an established campsite might not seem your idea of wilderness camping, doing so helps minimize impact on other areas.

Hostels

There are very few hostels in the area. In fact, we know of two: the hostel-cum-lodge of Yosemite Bug Rustic Mountain Resort (p137), on Hwy 140 just outside of Yosemite National Park, and the Whitney Portal Hostel in Lone Pine.

Hotels

Most hotels are found outside the parks. Two exceptions are the Wawona Hotel and the famous Ahwahnee Hotel, both in Yosemite, and the Wuksachi Lodge in Sequoia.

Lodges

The word 'lodge' usually connotes a stately structure with stone fireplaces, beamed ceilings and rustic but well-kept rooms. Lodges in and around the parks often fit the stereotype, and most offer choices of rooms in the main lodge (which sometimes have shared bathrooms) or cabins (with private bathrooms). Rates can start as low as $80 off-season and climb as high as $500 for a cabin in July and August. The latter may seem high, but when you consider that cabins can hold up to several families, the price is more manageable.

Tent Cabins

Tent cabins are a sort of in-between option: not quite camping, not quite a hotel. Generally, these consist of cement walls with canvas roofs, and amenities mean a light bulb, an electrical outlet and cots. Bedding usually costs extra, so you're better off (and more comfortable) bringing your own. All parks have tent cabins. Sleeping up to four (sometimes more) and costing anywhere from $80 off-season to $100 in summer, they're an affordable alternative to lodges. If you're staying in a tent cabin

in spring or winter, remember that they lack heating and get very cold.

Business Hours

Businesses and services maintain opening hours based on a wide range of factors: some close for the winter, and 'winter' can begin and end on different dates each year. Others stay open year-round, but maintain shorter hours in winter and their longest hours in summer.

Specific opening hours are provided for establishments and services throughout this book only when they differ significantly from the following standard hours or when they open only seasonally. Note that even when opening hours are listed, they're still subject to change based on weather, demand and budgetary constraints.

» Cafés and restaurants generally serve breakfast from 7am to 10:30am, lunch from 11am to 2:30pm and dinner from about 5pm to 9pm.

» Bars in the parks are usually open from approximately 5pm to 10pm. Outside the parks they may close as late as 2am.

» Shops and services are open from about 9:30am to 5:30pm.

Courses

Both parks and surrounding areas offer a wide range of learning opportunities, from fun family-style nature walks to photography excursions and college-credit courses. For information on climbing, wilderness and other activity-related courses, see the Activities chapter, p31. For kid-specific courses, such as Yosemite's Junior Ranger program, see p44.

Yosemite

Art Yosemite Art & Education Center runs inexpensive, informal art classes.

Astronomy and stargazing See p68 for programs at Glacier Point and throughout the park.

Outdoor education and hikes Yosemite Conservancy (☑209-379-2317; www.yosemiteconservancy.org), the park's main support organization, presents a huge range of classes and guided hikes. **NatureBridge** (formerly the Yosemite Institute; ☑209-379-9511; www.nature bridge.org) runs outdoor environmental education programs for youths.

Park ranger and naturalist-led walks Check the Yosemite Guide or stop by a visitor center for a schedule.

Photography Free photography walks are offered through the park service and the Ansel Adams Gallery.

Around Yosemite

Mono Lake Committee (☑760-647-6386; www .monolake.org) Affordable and highly respected programs and seminars with the goal of educating people about the unique lake and its surroundings.

Sequoia & Kings Canyon

Sequoia Natural History Association ((☑559-565-3759; www.sequoiahistory.org) 'Ed Venture' backpacking trips, natural history hikes and backpacking skills courses.

Discount Cards

» All National Park Service (NPS) passes cover the cardholder and up to three adult occupants of their vehicle and can be purchased at park entrances. An annual pass for Yosemite costs $40; for Sequoia & Kings Canyon it's $30.

» Annual Pass: costs $80 and grants the holder (and everyone in his or her vehicle) entrance to any national park or federal recreation area for one year.

» Two 'America the Beautiful' passes are valid for life and available to US citizens and permanent residents: the $10 Senior Pass (62 years or over) and the free Access Pass for people with permanent disabilities. These passes cover free entry to all US national parks and federal recreation areas, plus deep discounts on some campgrounds and services.

» The parks offer no student or youth discount cards. Children under 16 enter the parks free of charge with a paying adult.

Food

Restaurants

BOOK SYMBOL	PRICE PER MAIN COURSE
$	<$10
$$	$10-20
$$$	>$20

Self-Catering

» Small grocery stores inside both parks stock items such as cooking oil, canned foods, ice, beer and other staples as well as junk food, but you'll be charged top dollar. It's best to buy food en route to the parks.

» Most campsites have fire pits (you can grill your food if you bring a grill), and most have picnic tables.

Bear-Proof Lockers

» All campsites, most trailheads and many parking lots have bear-proof metal storage boxes. You are required by law to store *all* your food (including canned goods, beverages and coolers) and all scented products (toothpaste, shampoo, sunscreen etc) in these boxes at all times.

» Never leave food unattended in your car, especially in Yosemite, whether you're taking a multiday backpacking trip or just spending a few

hours meandering through the museum. It may seem like a hassle to put your picnic lunch in a locker, but having a bear break your window, ransack your car and tear up your upholstery is even more hassle. What's more, you can be fined for leaving anything in your car (or in your bike's panniers).

» Proper storage helps keep bears from becoming 'problems,' which can mean a bad end for the bear.

» Backcountry hikers must use bear-proof canisters, which can be rented when you pick up your wilderness permit or bought at stores in and nearby the parks.

Insurance

If you're traveling very far to get here (and especially if you're flying), it's a good idea to get some travel insurance. Although most travel-insurance policies won't cover your $1500 digital Canon camera ($500 is usually the max on a single piece of electronic equipment), they will cover baggage theft, trip cancellation and, most importantly, medical emergency. When choosing a policy, read the fine print; some policies will not cover 'extreme' activities, which could include anything from river rafting to rock climbing. Domestic rental and home-owners insurance policies often cover theft while you're on the road. Look into it.

Worldwide travel insurance is available at www.lonelyplanet.com/bookings, and you can buy, extend and make a claim online anytime – even if you're already on the road. For auto insurance, see p232; for health insurance, see p234.

Internet Access

» Most lodgings in and outside the parks offer free wireless for their guests. Free internet access can be

found in most public libraries (including two in Yosemite).

» For details on access in Yosemite, see p131; for Sequoia & Kings Canyon, see p188.

Public Holidays

The parks (and the areas surrounding the parks) are at their absolute busiest during the summertime school-holiday period, which runs roughly from mid-June through August. During this period, *everything* is packed, and reservations are a must. The greatest numbers of visitors also hit the parks during the following public holidays.

New Year's Day January 1
Martin Luther King Jr Day Third Monday in January
Presidents' Day Third Monday in February
Easter A Friday through Sunday in March or April
Memorial Day Last Monday in May
Independence Day July 4
Labor Day First Monday in September
Columbus Day Second Monday in October
Veterans' Day November 11
Thanksgiving Day Fourth Thursday in November
Christmas December 25

Solo Travelers

» Aside from the fact that you usually end up paying more for camping and lodging (with no one to split it with), there is generally no problem traveling alone in the region.

» Group hikes and other park programs are good options for meeting other travelers.

Telephone

» In the parks, you'll find pay phones at almost every developed location. Cell-phone reception is patchy

INTERNATIONAL VISITORS

Entering the Country

» For up-to-date information on travel to the US, as well as current procedures, visit the websites of the **US Department of State** (www.travel.state.gov) and the **US Customs and Border Protection** (www.cbp.gov). It is highly recommended that you check and confirm all entry requirements with a US consulate in your home country before leaving.

» Citizens of the 36 Visa Waiver Program (VWP) countries – including Australia, France, Germany, New Zealand, Spain and the UK – can enter the US as tourists for up to 90 days without obtaining a visa. They need to register with the US government online (https://esta.cbp.dhs.gov) at least three days before their visit. The registration is valid for two years.

» Your passport should be valid for at least another six months after you leave the US.

Embassies & Consulates

» **Australia** (Los Angeles; ☎310-229-2300; www.usa.embassy.gov.au)

» **Canada** (Los Angeles; ☎213-346-2700; www.canadainternational.gc.ca)

» **France** (Los Angeles; ☎310-235-3200; www.ambafrance-us.org)

» **Germany** (Los Angeles; ☎323-930-2703; www.germany.info)

» **Ireland** (San Francisco; ☎415-392-4214; www.consulateofirelandsanfrancisco.org)

» **Japan** (Los Angeles; ☎213-617-6700; www.us.emb-japan.go.jp)

» **Netherlands** (San Francisco; ☎877-388-2443; http://sanfrancisco.the-netherlands.org)

» **New Zealand** (Los Angeles; ☎310-566-6555; www.nzembassy.com/usa)

» **UK** (Los Angeles; ☎310-481-0031; www.ukinusa.fco.gov.uk)

Money

» If you're arriving from abroad and need to change money, do so at the airport or at an exchange bureau or bank in a major city. It is nearly impossible to exchange money in most small towns throughout the Sierras.

» Major credit cards (Visa, MasterCard, Amex) are widely accepted throughout the region and are often required as deposits when renting a car or reserving a hotel room.

» Traveler's checks (in US dollars) are a good way to carry a large amount of money that is replaceable in the event of loss or theft.

Post

» Nearly every town around the national parks has a post office. Yosemite National Park has four and Sequoia & Kings Canyon National Parks has two.

» Sending a postcard domestically costs $0.29 to $0.44, depending on its size. The international rate averages $0.98

» A letter costs $0.44 domestically and about $1.82 internationally.

Telephone

» For up-to-date information on international cell-phone technology (including world phones, GSM, quad-band phones etc), check out www.kropla.com.

» For important numbers, see p19.

Time

» From November to mid-March, California is on Pacific Standard Time, which is eight hours behind Coordinated Universal Time (UTC or Greenwich Mean Time).

» At 2am on the second Sunday in March, clocks are set forward one hour to Pacific Daylight Time (aka daylight saving time). On the first Sunday in November clocks revert to Pacific Standard Time.

through the Sierra region, depending on your carrier, though there's excellent reception in some parts of Yosemite. Once you ascend out of the valley, reception often gets even better. In Tuolumne, there's usually reception in the Wilderness Center parking lot. Cellphone reception is spotty to nonexistent in Wawona. In Sequoia & Kings Canyon, forget it.

» When breaking out that cell phone, consider the reality of noise pollution. Hearing someone's cell phone ring in a neighboring campsite or at a scenic lookout is annoying at best, while being subjected to a loud and lengthy phone conversation is grounds for a pine-coning.

Tourist Information

Tourist information offices (known as visitor centers) are found throughout Yosemite and Sequoia & Kings Canyon, and in nearly every town in the Sierras.

California Travel & Tourism Commission (www.visit california.com) The official state tourism website.

Yosemite National Park (209-372-0200; www.nps.gov /yose) Information on every-thing from road conditions and wilderness permits to employment opportunities and lodging.

Useful sources for areas around the national parks include the following:

Inyo National Forest (www .fs.usda.gov/inyo)

Sierra National Forest (www.fs.usda.gov/sierra)

Stanislaus National Forest (www.fs.usda.gov/stanislaus)

Yosemite Sierra Visitors Bureau (559-683-4636; www.yosemitethisyear.com)

Tours

The park-affiliated Yosemite Conservancy and the Sequoia Natural History Association nonprofits offer multiday courses and seminars that are great alternatives to tours. See p31.

Discover Yosemite Tours (559-642-4400; www .yosemitetours.com) Operates bus tours year-round from Oakhurst, Fish Camp and Bass Lake.

DNC Parks & Resorts (209-372-4386, 209-372-1240; www.yosemitepark.com) Yosemite's main conces-sionaire runs the Valley's traditional tram tours, which include a wheelchair-accessible two-hour Valley Floor Tour, an all-day Grand Tour, a Big Trees Tram Tour to Mariposa Grove and a Moonlight Tour. It also offers tours to Tuolumne Meadows and Glacier Point. Reserva-tions can be made online, by telephone, at the Curry Village registration desk, at the Yosemite Lodge tour

desk (inside the lobby) or by dialing extension 1240 from any park courtesy phone. Prices start at $25/23/13 for adults/seniors/children for the Valley Floor Tour and top out around $82/69/46 for the Grand Tour.

Green Tortoise (415-956-7500, 800-867-8647; www .greentortoise.com) Runs backpacker-friendly two-day (about $186) and three-day (about $295) trips to Yosemite from San Francisco where travelers sleep in the converted bus or in campgrounds, cook collectively and choose among activities like hiking, swimming or just hanging out (and there's always some great hanging out). Prices (which change annually) include most meals and the park entry fee.

Incredible Adventures (415-642-7378, 800-777-8464; www.incadventures.com) This outfit uses biodiesel vans for its San Francisco–based tours to Yosemite, from one-day sightseeing tours ($140) to three-day camping tours ($325). Park entry fees and most meals are included, and it provides all cooking and camping gear except sleeping bags.

Yosemite Bug Bus (866-826-7108; www.yosemitebug bus.com) The Yosemite Bug Rustic Mountain Resort (see p137) offers multiday backpacking tours through-out Yosemite. It picks up passengers in San Francisco, stops at its hostel (just outside the park) and continues into Yosemite.

Travelers with Disabilities

» Both national parks publish an **accessibility brochure** (Yosemite www .nps.gov/yose/planyourvisit /accessibility.htm; Sequoia & Kings Canyon www.nps .gov/seki/planyourvisit

---

LOST & FOUND

There are two numbers to call if you lose or find an item in Yosemite. For anything left or recovered in restaurants, hotels, gift shops or on buses, call **DNC Lost & Found** (209-372-4357). For items astray elsewhere, call the **NPS** (209-379-1001). If you're still in the Valley, you can also just go to the information desk at the Yosemite Val-ley Visitor Center, where rangers keep a stash of things found. The park service will ship most items to their owners free of charge.

In Sequoia & Kings Canyon, each visitor center main-tains its own lost and found.

/accessibility.htm) and have an accessibility coordinator. Both are excellent sources of information on everything from hotels and campgrounds to visitor sites and ranger-led activities. If you need to make arrangements in advance, call any park visitor center or contact the coordinator prior to your arrival.

» Many sights and campgrounds within the park are wheelchair accessible; for a complete and detailed list, download the accessibility brochure.

» All lodging options within Yosemite have wheelchair-accessible rooms.

» Shuttle buses in Yosemite all have wheelchair lifts and tie-downs, and the drivers can assist disabled passengers on and off. The Yosemite Lodge Bike Stand and the Curry Village Rental Stand both have wheelchairs for rent; call ☑209-372-8319 for reservations.

» For hearing-impaired visitors, a ranger may be available during summer months for American Sign Language (ASL) interpretation during park-led walks and talks. For information, contact one of the visitor centers or call ☑209-372-4726 (TTY). For paid tours, ASL interpretation can be arranged through the **Yosemite Lodge tour desk** (☑209-372-1240).

» Based in Mammoth Lakes, the nonprofit organization **Disabled Sports Eastern Sierra** (☑760-934-0791; www .disabledsportseasternsierra .org) offers a variety of educational opportunities for disabled travelers, including skiing and climbing courses.

» See p225 for information on discount passes for people with disabilities.

Volunteering

Besides helping the national parks, volunteering is a great way to see a side of Yosemite and Sequoia & Kings Canyon that most tourists never do. It's also a great way to meet locals and fellow volunteers – contacts that can last a lifetime. As a volunteer you can do everything from weeding and sweeping to working on restoration projects, monitoring bears and leading educational walks. Most volunteer positions require advanced application and background checks.

» There are several resources to explore when researching volunteer opportunities. A great place to start is calling the **Yosemite Park Volunteer Coordinator** (☑209-379-1850; www.nps.gov/yose) or the **Sequoia & Kings Canyon Park Volunteer Coordinator** (☑559-565-3132; www.nps.gov/seki). Both park websites maintain updated information on volunteering in their respective 'Support Your Park' sections.

» The **Volunteer.gov/gov** (www.volunteer.gov/gov) website maintains a comprehensive database on positions available at all national parks and federal recreation areas, allowing you to browse openings by category, eg backcountry, fish and wildlife, historical preservation.

» The **Yosemite Conservancy** (☑209-379-2317; www.yosemiteconservancy .org) runs an established volunteer program for its members that includes restoration and revegetation projects as well as staffing information stations. Long-term volunteers receive free camping, a small stipend and bookstore discounts.

» The **Habitat Protectors of Yosemite** (HaPY; www.nps .gov/yose/planyourvisit/happy .htm) weekly drop-in program does hands-on-the-dirt activities like removing invasive plants in some of the most scenic areas of the park.

» Earth Day (April 22) celebrations in Yosemite feature chances to help out the park and includes cleanup projects and tree planting as well as kids' educational events, a vendors' fair, and live music and poetry.

» The **Sierra Club's LeConte Memorial Lodge** (☑volunteer info winter 209-372-4542, summer 209-403-6676; www.sierraclub.org /education/leconte) in Yosemite puts Sierra Club members to work as volunteers assisting in the operation of the lodge for one-week stints between May 1 and mid-September.

TIPS FOR TEACHERS

Educational and scientific groups who want to study in Yosemite can get their entrance fees waived if they apply in advance and provide the proper documentation. The trip must be for educational purposes, not simply recreation. For details, contact the **Yosemite Fees Office** (☑209-372-0207) or check the Yosemite website at www .nps.gov/yose/planyourvisit/waivers.htm.

Both Yosemite and Sequoia & Kings Canyon National Parks run field-trip programs specifically for teachers who wish to bring their students to study in the parks. Teachers can contact **Yosemite's education office** (☑209-375-9503) or the **Sequoia & Kings Canyon Education Coordinator** (☑559-565-4303). Also check under 'For Teachers' in the Yosemite and Sequoia & Kings Canyon sections of the NPS website.

Work

» Most workers inside the parks are employed either by the NPS or by park concessionaires. Most employment opportunities within the parks are seasonal – roughly Memorial Day (the last Monday in May) through Labor Day (the first Monday in September). Applications are almost always due at least six months in advance.

» **DNC Parks & Resorts** (DNC; ☑209-372-1236; www.yosemitepark.com), Yosemite's chief concessionaire, runs nearly all of the park's businesses and transportation and is your best bet – it employs about 1800 people per summer. For a list of jobs it has available, see 'Employment Opportunities' (under 'About Us') on its website. If you're already in the Valley and are struck by the need to stay and work, drop by the Human Resources department in the DNC administration offices in Yosemite Village. DNC occasionally hires people on the spot if they're short staffed. Eligible international applicants are interviewed via Skype.

» In Kings Canyon & Sequoia, the main concessionaires are **Sequoia-Kings Canyon Park Service Company** (☑559-335-5500; www.sequoia-kingscanyon.com) in Kings Canyon, and the office of **DNC** (☑559-565-4070, ext 605 www.visitsequoia.com) in Sequoia.

» Seasonal and year-round positions with the NPS are posted at www.usajobs.gov. Only US citizens are eligible for NPS employment.

Transportation

GETTING THERE & AWAY

Air

» **Transport Security Administration** (www.tsa .gov) Comprehensive, up-to-date information on all US federal security requirements.

Airports

Major international airports three to five hours' driving time from Yosemite and Sequoia & Kings Canyon:

Los Angeles International (LAX; ☑310-646-5252; www .lawa.org)

McCarran International (LAS; ☑702-261-5211; www .mccarran.com) In Las Vegas.

Mineta San José International (SJC; ☑408-277-4759; www.sjc.org)

Oakland International (OAK; ☑510-563-3300; www .flyoakland.com)

Sacramento International (SMF; ☑916-929-5411; www .sacairports.org)

San Francisco International (SFO; ☑650-821-8211; www.flysfo.com)

Reno-Tahoe International (RNO; ☑775-328-6870; www .renoairport.com)

Two smaller, closer, airports:

Fresno Yosemite International Airport (FAT; ☑559-621-4500; www .flyfresno.org) Approximately 90 miles southwest of Yosemite and 60 miles west of Sequoia & Kings Canyon.

Mammoth Yosemite Airport (MMH; www.visit mammoth.com/airport) Closest airport to the east side of Yosemite (it's 2.5 hours' drive from Yosemite Valley); see p151.

Bicycle

Cycling is a great way to get to the national parks, but roads are narrow, grades are steep and summer temperatures can climb well over 90°F (32°C).

» Long-distance cyclists can overnight in Yosemite's backpacker campgrounds.

» **Better World Club** (☑866-238-1137; www.better worldclub.com) offers emergency roadside assistance for cyclists for an annual membership fee of about $40.

Bus

Greyhound (☑800-231-2222; www.greyhound.com) runs to the parks' hub cities – Merced for Yosemite and Visalia for Sequoia & Kings Canyon.

To/From Yosemite

Yosemite Area Regional Transportation System (YARTS; ☑209-388-9589, 877-989-2787; www.yarts.com) buses run along Hwy 140 from Merced into Yosemite Valley (3¼ hours, $25 round trip including park entry fee). Children 12 and under and seniors (62 or over) pay $18 for the round-trip ticket. With each adult ticket, one child rides free. Bicycles can be

---

CLIMATE CHANGE & TRAVEL

Every form of transport that relies on carbon-based fuel generates CO_2, the main cause of human-induced climate change. Modern travel is dependent on aeroplanes, which might use less fuel per kilometer per person than most cars but travel much greater distances. The altitude at which aircraft emit gases (including CO_2) and particles also contributes to their climate change impact. Many websites offer 'carbon calculators' that allow people to estimate the carbon emissions generated by their journey and, for those who wish to do so, offset the impact of the greenhouse gases emitted with contributions to portfolios of climate-friendly initiatives throughout the world. Lonely Planet offsets the carbon footprint of all staff and author travel.

ROUTES INTO THE PARKS

Yosemite National Park

Yosemite operates three entrance stations on the west side of the Sierra Nevada: the South Entrance on Hwy 41 (Wawona Rd) north of Fresno – convenient from southern California; the Arch Rock Entrance on Hwy 140 (El Portal Rd) east of Merced – convenient from northern California; and the Big Oak Flat Entrance on Hwy 120 W (Big Oak Flat Rd) east of Manteca – the quickest route from the Bay Area. Roads are generally kept open all year, though in winter (usually November to April), drivers may be required to carry tire chains.

The Tioga Pass Entrance, along Hwy 120 E (Tioga Rd) on the east side of the park, is open from about June to October, depending on when the snow is cleared. From Tioga Pass, drivers connect with Hwy 395 and points such as Reno and Death Valley National Park.

Sequoia & Kings Canyon National Parks

The two routes into Sequoia & Kings Canyon approach from the west, departing Hwy 99 from Fresno or Visalia. From Visalia, Hwy 198 leads 46 miles east into Sequoia National Park. From Fresno, Hwy 180 east leads 57 miles east to Kings Canyon. The two roads are connected by the Generals Hwy, inside Sequoia. There is no access to either park from the east, and no internal roads between the parks.

transported along with all your gear. Buses originate from the Merced Transpo Center & Greyhound Terminal and stop at Merced's Amtrak station before heading to Yosemite.

Reservations for YARTS buses are not required, but it's best to obtain tickets before boarding. You can purchase tickets from area motels, the visitor center in Mariposa and the Yosemite Bug Lodge & Hostel in Midpines. Bus drivers also sell tickets. Inbound buses from Merced stop at all Valley hubs.

YARTS also offers a round-trip bus service between Yosemite Valley and Mammoth Lakes once daily in July and August; see p136.

To/From Sequoia & Kings Canyon

From the San Joaquin Valley town of Visalia, the **Sequoia Shuttle** (☑877-287-4453; www.sequoiashuttle.com) runs to Giant Forest Museum (2½ hours) in Sequoia National Park during summer, via Three Rivers and other towns en route. The $15 round-trip fare includes park entry. Advance reservations required.

Car & Motorcycle

Driving is by far the most popular way to get to and around both national parks. In Yosemite, this means traffic, smog and sometimes frustrating battles for parking spaces during peak summer months.

Automobile Associations

American Automobile Association (AAA; www.aaa.com; 24hr roadside assistance 800-222-4357) Has free maps and discounts on accommodations, theme parks and other services.

Better World Club (☑866-238-1137; www.betterworldclub.com) Similar services to AAA and donates 1% of its revenue to environmental clean-up and advocacy.

Driver's License

Non-US residents can legally drive in the US for up to a year with only their home driver's license and passport, but proffering an international driver's license if you get pulled over can make things easier on everyone. Most car-rental companies don't require an international driver's license, but claim that having one makes the rental process easier.

Rental

Most rental companies require that you be at least 25 years old, have a valid driver's license and a major credit card. Rentals are available at all airports and major cities. Most agencies rent car seats with advance notice.

The following car-rental companies maintain branches at major airports and throughout California:

Alamo (☑877-222-9075; www.alamo.com)

Avis (☑800-331-1212; www.avis.com)

Budget (☑800-527-0700; www.budget.com)

Dollar (☑800-800-3665; www.dollar.com)

Enterprise (☑800-261-7331; www.enterprise.com)

Fox (☑800-225-4369; www.foxrentacar.com)

Hertz (☑800-654-3131; www.hertz.com)

National (☑800-227-7368; www.nationalcar.com)

Thrifty (☑800-847-4389; www.thrifty.com)

DRIVING DISTANCES & TIMES

FROM	DISTANCE, TIME TO YOSEMITE VALLEY	DISTANCE, TIME TO SEQUOIA
San Francisco	210 miles, 4hr	280 miles, 5.5hr
Los Angeles	276 miles, 6hr	225 miles, 4hr
Las Vegas	400-475 miles, 8-8.5hr	400 miles, 6.5hr

For motor home rentals, try **El Monte** (www.elmonterv.com), **Cruise America** (www.cruiseamerica.com) or **Happy Travel Campers** (www.camperusa.com).

Insurance

» California requires drivers to have a minimum of $45,000 in injury liability insurance and $5000 for property damage; proof must be carried in the car at all times.

» Credit cards or your own auto-insurance policy (be sure to check both) often cover insurance for rentals; if not, you can purchase optional liability insurance that adds between $15 and $30 per day to the rental rate.

» If you're driving a friend's car, you'll be insured under their policy (assuming they have one).

Road Rules

» Cars drive on the right-hand side of the road.

» Unless signed otherwise, it's legal to make a right turn on a red light after coming to a complete stop.

» Distances and speed limits are shown in miles.

» On a two-lane highway, you can pass cars on the left-hand side if the center line is broken (not solid yellow).

» Talking on a hand-held cell phone or texting while driving is illegal.

» For a complete list of California road rules, see the *California Driver Handbook* at the website of **California Department of Motor Vehicles** (DMV; www.dmv.ca.gov).

Train

No trains serve the parks directly, but **Amtrak** (☎800-872-7245; www.amtrak.com) offers daily service to the transport hubs of Merced and Lancaster for Yosemite, and Visalia (via Hanford) for Sequoia & Kings Canyon, where bus service is available into the parks.

At Merced station transfer directly to the YARTS bus – you can pay for this part of your journey when you purchase your Amtrak ticket (but curiously not online). The park entry is included in the fare, and you're guaranteed a seat on the YARTS bus. From Lancaster there is a bus service to Mammoth, where onward bus connections run to Yosemite when Hwy 120 is open; see p136.

For Sequoia & Kings Canyon, you get off the train in Hanford (20 miles west of Visalia), where an Amtrak bus picks you up and takes you to Visalia. From there, you transfer to the Sequoia Shuttle (summer only).

From most major airports, the first leg of Amtrak service is often by bus to the nearest train station. The earlier you book your Amtrak ticket, the cheaper the fare.

GETTING AROUND

Bicycle

» The easiest way to get around Yosemite Valley is by bike. Cycling other areas of the park, like Tioga Rd or Glacier Point Rd, is for experienced cyclists.

» All trails within the national parks are off-limits to mountain bikes – head to Mammoth Lakes instead.

Bus

» Yosemite has an excellent free shuttle system, making it easy to get around Yosemite Valley and other areas. For information on YARTS buses over Tioga Rd as far as Mammoth Lakes, see p230.

» Sequoia National Park has three free shuttle routes within the park; Kings Canyon has no shuttles.

» There is no public transportation *between* any of the parks.

Car & Motorcycle

The vast majority of visitors get around the parks by car. It's the most convenient way to see Sequoia & Kings Canyon, as well as the greater Yosemite area. During peak summer season, however, the traffic can be extremely frustrating in Yosemite Valley. A good option is to park in a day parking lot and take the excellent free shuttles that operate in Yosemite and Sequoia.

Fuel & Spare Parts

» Fuel and spare parts become more expensive as you near the parks.

» The nearest place to Yosemite Valley for fuel is El Portal, about 14 miles west of Yosemite Village on Hwy 140.

» There are no gas stations in Sequoia & Kings Canyon; the nearest are at Kings Canyon Lodge, Stony Creek Lodge (both open mid-April to mid-October only) and Hume Lake.

Road Conditions

Both parks are accessible year-round, and almost all

RVS & TRAILERS

For the most part, all three parks are RV- and trailer-friendly. Consider the following if you're visiting Yosemite National Park:

» There are no electrical hookups.
» Generators can be used sparingly in campgrounds during daylight hours.
» In Yosemite Valley, maximum length for RVs is 40ft, for trailers it's 35ft.
» No vehicles over 25ft on Mariposa Grove Rd; trailers aren't permitted.
» No vehicles over 25ft on Hetch Hetchy Rd; maximum width 8ft mirror-to-mirror.
» No trailers or vehicles over 30ft on Glacier Point Rd past the Sentinel Dome/Taft Point trailheads.
» RVs over 24ft are not recommended for Yosemite Creek and Tamarack Flat campgrounds or for Porcupine Flat or White Wolf.
» Yosemite's only year-round dump station is in Yosemite Valley near the Upper Pines Campground. Wawona and Tuolumne Meadows stations open in summer.
» More information at www.nps.gov/yose/planyourvisit/rvcamping.htm.

The following applies to Sequoia & Kings Canyon National Parks:

» Generator hours vary, but they exist.
» No RVs or trailers permitted on Mineral King Rd.
» Vehicles over 22ft are not recommended on Crystal Cave Rd, at Panoramic Point or on the Moro Rock–Crescent Meadow road between Potwisha and the Giant Forest Museum.

---

roads are paved. In Yosemite, there are a few unpaved roads unsuitable for long trailers or large RVs. Outside the parks lies an endless network of fire and forest-service roads, many leading to remote campgrounds and lakes. While many of these roads are drivable with a standard-clearance vehicle, potential explorers would be better off with above-average clearance and 4WD.

Snow closes Yosemite's Tioga Rd (Hwy 120 east of Crane Flat) all winter long. In Sequoia & Kings Canyon, the Kings Canyon Scenic Byway and the Generals Hwy both close periodically in winter. Mineral King Rd, in Sequoia, closes November 1 to late May.

Caltrans (☎800-427-7623; www.dot.ca.gov) Current road conditions for highways throughout California.

Yosemite road information (☎209-372-0200)

Sequoia & Kings Canyon road information (☎559-565-3341)

Road Hazards

Speeding motorists represent one of the parks' principal road hazards. Not only does speeding put humans in danger, it also endangers park wildlife. Many animals, including bears, deer and coyotes, are hit by motorists every year.

Snow and ice present hazards and road closures. During snowy months motorists will encounter 'chain controls' on many mountain roads; continuing past these without snow tires or four- or all-wheel drive is illegal. Unless you're properly equipped, your only option is to buy or rent chains or turn back. If you plan to drive to the parks when there's any chance of snow, the easiest solution is to bring your own chains, as renting or purchasing at or near chain controls is expensive. Permitted workers along the roadside will fit the chains for a modest fee, and save your knuckles in the process. If you plan to put your chains on yourself, bring gloves.

A smart precaution in winter is to pack emergency food and water and a sleeping bag for each person in the car. If you're on a country road and get stuck or lose control and slide off the road, assistance could be hours or days away. Provisions and warmth in the car can literally save your life.

Hitchhiking

Hitchhiking is never entirely safe anywhere in the world, and we don't recommend it. That said, hitching is quite common in Yosemite and the Eastern Sierra and is sometimes necessary to get to or from a trailhead. While hitchers are generally viewed with suspicion in the US, Sierra backpackers will often get a break. If you're trying to get home from Yosemite, check the bulletin board at Camp 4 for rides offered and needed. To get a ride to the parks, check out the rideshare forums on **Craigslist** (www.craigslist.org).

Health & Safety

IN THE PARKS

The parks are not immune from crime – and it's no wonder, considering they see millions of visitors each year. However, the majority of crimes are small-time theft, vandalism and public drunkenness. Car break-ins are more often the work of opportunistic bears than burglars. Carry money and valuables with you; if you leave anything in the car, store it out of sight in the trunk. When possible, avoid leaving your vehicle at an isolated trailhead and instead park in a more heavily used area within reasonable walking distance of the trail, or ride park shuttle buses.

Keeping safe while visiting the parks depends on your predeparture preparations, daily routines and how you handle any dangerous situations that develop. While the potential problems can seem quite frightening, in reality few park visitors experience anything worse that a skinned knee.

BEFORE YOU GO

If you're planning on doing any hiking, start getting regular physical exercise a few weeks prior to your trip. When possible, visitors from lower elevations should allow at least a day or two to acclimatize before undertaking any strenuous activity.

Insurance

Review the terms of your health insurance policy before your trip; some policies won't cover injuries or emergency evacuation sustained as a result of 'dangerous' activities like backpacking, rock climbing or mountaineering. Some policies require you to get pre-authorization for medical treatment from a call center before seeking help. Be sure to keep all receipts and documentation.

For travel insurance, see p225.

Websites

Yosemite National Park – Your Safety (www.nps.gov /yose/planyourvisit/yoursafety .htm)

Sequoia & Kings Canyon National Park– Your Safety (www.nps.gov /seki/planyourvisit/yoursafety .htm)

Wilderness Medicine Institute (www.nols.edu /wmi/) Certification classes and helpful case studies, articles and course book updates.

Further Reading

Backcountry First Aid and Extended Care (Buck Tilton, Falcon, 2007) Inexpensive pocket-sized wilderness survival manual.

NOLS Wilderness Medicine (Tod Schimelpfenig, National Outdoor Leadership School, 2006) Comprehensive wilderness first-aid curriculum.

Availability of Health Care

For emergencies, call ☏911. Inside the parks, cell phones often won't work. A satellite phone or personal locator beacon (PLB) is your best option for backcountry trips. Park rangers with medical training can provide basic first aid, free of charge. For more serious ailments, drive yourself to the nearest hospital emergency room (ER) or urgent-care clinic. Search-and-rescue (SAR) and helicopter evacuations are only for truly life-threatening emergencies. SAR operations are very costly for the parks and put employees' lives at risk.

Yosemite Area

In Yosemite Valley, **Yosemite Medical Clinic** (☏209-372-4637; ⊘9am-5pm) and **Yosemite Dental Clinic** (☏209-372-4200) are on Ahwahnee Rd, near Yosemite Village.

Hospitals near Yosemite include:

Doctors Medical Center (☏209-578-1211; www.dmc -modesto.com; 1441 Florida Ave, Modesto; ⊘24hr) The region's largest medical facility.

MEDICAL CHECKLIST

In addition to any prescription or over-the-counter medications you typically take, consider adding these to your first-aid kit:

» acetaminophen/paracetamol (eg Tylenol) or aspirin
» adhesive or paper tape
» antibacterial ointment for cuts and abrasions
» antidiarrhea and antinausea drugs
» antifungal cream or powder
» antihistamines (for hay fever and allergic reactions)
» anti-inflammatory drugs (eg ibuprofen)
» bandages, gauze, gauze rolls
» calamine lotion, sting-relief spray or aloe vera
» cortisone (steroid) cream for allergic rashes
» elasticized support bandage for knees, ankles etc
» eye drops
» insect repellent
» moleskin (for blisters)
» nonadhesive dressings
» oral rehydration mix
» pocketknife
» scissors, safety pins, tweezers
» sunscreen and lip balm
» thermometer

John C Fremont Hospital
(☎209-966-3631; www.jcf
-hospital.com; 5189 Hospital
Rd, Mariposa; ◷24hr)

Mammoth Hospital (☎760-934-3311; www.mammoth
hospital.com; 85 Sierra Park
Rd, Mammoth Lakes; ◷24hr)

Sequoia & Kings Canyon Area

First-aid is available at ranger stations. Hospitals near the parks include:

Community Regional Medical Center (☎559-459-6000; www.communitymedical
.org; 2823 Fresno St, Fresno;
◷24hr) The region's major trauma center.

Kaweah Delta Medical Center (☎559-624-2000;
www.kaweahdelta.org; 400
W Mineral King Ave, Visalia;
◷24hr) Busy emergency room.

Sierra Kings District Hospital (☎559-638-8155;
www.skdh.org; 372 W Cypress

Ave, Reedley; ◷24hr) Limited emergency services.

Infectious Diseases

Amoebic Dysentery

Serious diarrhea caused by contaminated water is an increasing problem in heavily used backcountry areas. If diarrhea occurs, fluid replacement is key: drink weak black tea with a little sugar or a soft drink allowed to go flat and 50% diluted by water.

With severe diarrhea, a rehydrating solution is necessary to replace minerals and salts. Commercially available oral rehydration salts are useful. Gut-paralyzing drugs such as diphenoxylate or loperamide can be used to bring relief from the symptoms but do not actually cure the problem.

Giardiasis

If you drink snowmelt, stream, lake or groundwater, you risk being infected by waterborne parasites. Giardiasis is an intestinal disease marked by chronic diarrhea, abdominal cramps, bloating, fatigue and weight loss; symptoms can last for weeks. Though not usually dangerous, giardiasis requires treatment with antibiotics. To protect yourself, always boil, filter or chemically treat water before drinking. Refrain from brushing your teeth or doing dishes with untreated water.

Environmental Hazards

Altitude

Most people adjust to altitude within a few hours or days. Acute Mountain Sickness (AMS) occasionally occurs, usually at elevations greater than 8000ft. Being physically fit offers no protection; the risk increases with faster ascents, higher altitudes and greater exertion. When traveling to high altitudes, avoid overexertion, eat light meals and abstain from alcohol.

Initial symptoms of AMS may include headaches, nausea, vomiting, dizziness, weakness, shortness of breath, insomnia and loss of appetite. The best treatment is descent. If symptoms are severe or don't resolve promptly, seek medical help. AMS can be life-threatening.

Bears

Only black bears live in California. They're active day and night throughout the Sierra Nevada. While wild black bears often flee at the sight, sound or smell of people, many park bears have lost their natural fear of people.

So what's the big deal if a bear nabs a little human food? Well, it could mean death for the bear. Bears that associate people with

BEAR ENCOUNTERS: DOS & DON'TS

To many visitors, bears represent a mix of the fascinating and the frightening. It's not often we get to see such powerful, majestic animals in the wild – at the same time, some visitors would just as soon not see one while in the park. Bears entering developed areas in search of human food should be treated differently to wild bears observed in their natural environment.

Be Loud in the Campground

If you spot a bear, do not drop your food and run. Gather others together and wave your arms to look big and intimidating. Make noise by banging pots and pans, clapping your hands and yelling.

Do not attempt to retrieve food from a bear, and don't corner the bear – give it plenty of room to escape.

Never throw rocks, which can seriously injure or kill a bear.

Be Deferential on the Trail

Do not drop your pack or run, which may trigger the bear's instinct to chase – you can't outrun a bear!

Stay together and keep small children next to you, picking up little ones. Give the bear lots of room (300ft or more). If a bear chuffs (ie huffs and puffs), stamps its feet and paws the ground, you're *way* too close.

Never get between a sow and her cubs. If you spot a lone cub, its mother and siblings are likely nearby.

Stand still and watch the bear (nonflash photos are OK) but don't linger too long. If a bear starts moving toward you, step far off-trail and let it pass by, making sure not to block its escape routes.

A bear may 'bluff charge' to test your dominance. Stand your ground by making yourself look as big as possible (eg wave your arms above your head) and shouting menacingly.

It's extremely rare for a black bear to attack humans, but if one does, fight back using any means available.

---

food become increasingly bold about approaching people, to the point where they become dangerously aggressive. Once a bear becomes a serial campground bandit, or begins charging visitors, rangers may be obligated to 'haze' or eventually kill it.

Habituated bears regularly break into vehicles and raid campgrounds and back-country campsites in search of food. You must remove *all* scented items from your car, including any food, trash (scour the car for empty potato-chip bags, soda cans, recyclables etc) and products such as gum, toothpaste, soap and sunscreen. Cover up anything in your car that even resembles food or a cooler. Place all food and scented items in bear canisters – large metal storage lockers found in most parking lots, every park campsite and a few popular backcountry campgrounds.

At campsites, think of the bear box as your refrigerator: keep it shut and latched when you are not actively using it. Keep all food within arm's reach at all times. Bears can sneak up and steal food from picnic tables or campsites when your back is turned, even just for a second. In national parks, failure to use bear boxes may result in a fine (law-enforcement rangers do regular campground and parking-lot monitoring).

Backpackers without a park-approved bear-resistant food container must usually rent one from a wilderness permit office, visitor center or park store. Hanging your food in a tree (the counter-balancing method) no longer works, as too many black bears have figured out that trick.

For more information, check out http://sierra wild.gov/bears and www .tahoewildbears.org.

Bites & Stings

Do not attempt to pet, handle or feed any wild animal, including squirrels and deer, that may bite humans. Any animal bite or scratch should be promptly and thoroughly cleansed with soap and water, followed by application of an antiseptic (eg iodine, alcohol) to prevent infection. Ask local health authorities about the advisability of rabies treatments.

SNAKES

Snakes frequent areas below 5000ft, so keep your eyes on the trail, wear hiking boots and don't stick your hands into any places that you can't see (eg under rocks).

Rattlesnakes usually give warning of their presence. Backing away (slowly!) from rattlers usually prevents confrontation. Most rattle-snake bites are caused by people intentionally picking up the snake or poking it with a stick. Rattlesnake bites are seldom fatal and adult rattlers don't always inject venom when they bite (younger ones are more prone to inject venom, as they haven't yet learned self-discipline!).

If bitten, place a light, constricting bandage above the bite, keep the wounded part below the level of the heart and move it as little as possible. Stay calm and get to a medical facility as soon as possible. Bring the dead snake for identification if you can, but don't risk being bitten again.

The use of tourniquets and sucking out the poison are now comprehensively discredited.

INSECTS & SPIDERS

Much of the Sierra Nevada teems with annoying mosquitoes, especially in mid-summer. You're more likely to get bitten near standing water or snowmelt. Apply insect repellent and wear long-sleeved shirts and long pants. Backpackers should bring a lightweight tent or mosquito net to sleep under.

Present in brush, forest and grassland, ticks may carry Lyme disease (borrelia). Early symptoms are similar to the flu (eg chills, high fever, headache, digestive problems, general aches). Also look for a blotchy red rash. Check your clothes, hair and skin after hiking, and your sleeping bag if it has been outside. If you find unattached ticks, simply brush them off. Otherwise,

carefully grab the tick's head with tweezers, then gently pull upwards – do not twist or force it.

Some spider bites (eg from black widows or brown recluses) contain toxic venom, which children are more vulnerable to; apply ice or cool water to the affected area, then seek medical help.

Cold

HYPOTHERMIA

Temperatures in the mountains can quickly drop from balmy to below freezing. A sudden downpour and high winds can also rapidly lower your body temperature.

Seek shelter when bad weather is unavoidable. Woolen clothing and synthetics, which retain warmth even when wet, are superior to cottons. Always carry waterproof layers and high-energy, easily digestible snacks like chocolate or dried fruit.

Symptoms of hypothermia include exhaustion, numbness (especially in fingers and toes), shivering, stumbling, slurred speech, disorientation or confusion, dizzy spells, muscle cramps and irrational or even violent behavior.

To treat early stages of hypothermia, get victims out of the wind or rain, remove any wet clothing and replace it with dry, warm clothing. Give victims hot liquids (no alcohol or caffeine) and high-calorie, easily digestible food.

In advanced stages, gently place victims in warm sleeping bags cocooned inside a waterproof outer wrapping. Do not rub a victim's skin.

FROSTBITE

Frostbite refers to the freezing of extremities, including fingers, toes and nose. Signs and symptoms include a whitish or waxy cast to the skin, as well as itching, numbness and pain.

Warm the affected areas by immersion in warm (not hot) water, only until the skin becomes flushed. Frostbitten

body parts should not be rubbed, and blisters should not be broken. Pain and swelling are inevitable. Seek medical attention immediately.

Heat

DEHYDRATION

To prevent dehydration drink plenty of fluids (minimum one gallon per day). Eat enough salty foods – when you sweat, you lose electrolytes, too. Avoid diuretics like caffeine and alcohol.

Because your body can only absorb about a quart (liter) of water per hour, prehydrate hours before starting a long hike.

HEAT EXHAUSTION

It's easy to forget how much fluid you are losing via perspiration while you are hiking, particularly at cooler, higher elevations or if a strong breeze is drying your skin quickly.

Symptoms of heat exhaustion include feeling weak; headache; irritability; nausea or vomiting; dizziness; muscle cramps; heavy sweating and/or cool, clammy skin; and a fast, weak pulse.

Treatment involves getting out of the heat and/or sun to rest, removing clothing that retains heat (cotton is okay), cooling skin with a wet cloth and fanning continuously, and rehydrating with water. Recovery is usually rapid, though you may feel weak for days afterward.

HEATSTROKE

Heatstroke is a serious, life-threatening condition that occurs when body temperature rises to dangerous levels. Symptoms come on suddenly and include weakness; nausea; hot, flushed and dry skin (sweating stops); elevated body temperature; dizziness; confusion; headaches; hyperventilation; loss of coordination; and, eventually, seizures, collapse and loss of consciousness.

Seek medical help immediately. Meanwhile, rapidly cool the person by getting them into the shade; removing clothes; covering them with a wet cloth or towel; fanning vigorously; and applying ice or cold packs to the neck, armpits and groin. Give fluids if they're conscious.

SUNBURN

You face a greater risk from sun exposure at high elevations. Sunburn is possible on hazy or cloudy days, and even when it snows. Use sunscreen and lip moisturizer with UV-A and UV-B protection and an SPF of 30 or greater, and reapply throughout the day. Wear a wide-brimmed hat and sunglasses; consider tying a bandanna around your neck for extra protection.

Safe Hiking

Avoid poison oak by paying attention to the shrubbery on low-elevation hikes (see the boxed text, p40).

Waterfalls, Cliffs & Rockfall

Smooth granite beside rivers, streams and waterfalls is often slippery, even when dry. Approach any waterfall with caution and, above all, don't get into the water. If you slip, the current will drag you over the top of the fall, likely killing you. Despite warning signs in several languages and protective

railings in many places (eg on Yosemite's Mist Trail), people have died after wading above waterfalls.

Use caution when hiking around cliff edges and precarious viewpoints. Some park overlooks have railings, but plenty of others don't.

Always be alert to the danger of rockfall, especially after heavy rains. If you accidentally let loose a rock on a trail, loudly warn other hikers below.

Crossing Streams & Rivers

On some backcountry trails, you may have to ford a river or stream swollen with snow-melt that is fast-flowing and cold enough to be a potential risk. Before stepping out from the bank, ease one arm out of the shoulder strap of your pack and unclip the belt buckle – should you lose your balance and be swept downstream, it will be easier to slip out of your backpack.

If you're linking hands with others, grasp at the wrist or cross arms at the waist, both tighter grips than a simple handhold. If you're fording alone, plant a stick or your hiking poles upstream to give you greater stability and help you to lean against the current.

Walk side-on to the direction of flow so that your body presents less of an obstacle to rushing water.

Lightning & Storms

Before starting your hike – especially if you're heading

to the top of an exposed peak or dome – check the weather forecast at a visitor center or ranger station. Regardless of the forecast, if you're planning a long hike carry rain gear and be prepared for the worst. Changeable weather in the mountains is a given in the mountains.

When a storm is brewing, avoid exposed ridges, summits and granite domes (eg Yosemite's Half Dome, Sequoia's Moro Rock). Lightning has a penchant for crests, lone trees, small depressions, gullies and cave entrances, as well as wet ground.

If you are caught out in the open, crouch or squat on dry ground with your feet together; keep a layer of metallic-free insulation (eg sleeping pad) between you and the ground; and place all metal objects (eg metal-frame backpacks and hiking poles) far away from you.

Rescue & Evacuation

If someone in your group is injured or falls ill and can't move, leave somebody with them while one or more others go for help. If there are only two of you, leave the injured person with as much warm clothing, food and water as it's sensible to spare, plus a whistle and flashlight. Mark the position with something conspicuous (eg orange bivvy bag, a large stone cross on the ground).

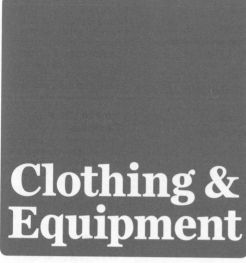

Clothing & Equipment

Much of what you should bring to the parks depends on when you're visiting and what activities you plan to do. If you're going backpacking, you'll be shouldering everything for a few days, so a comfortable pack weight is crucial. Pare down to the essentials, and make sure that what you bring isn't unnecessarily bulky; having a clean shirt every morning is nowhere near as important as how your back feels at day's end. Use a checklist to ensure all the important stuff gets remembered.

Clothing

Layering

A secret of comfortable walking is to wear several layers of light clothing, which you can easily take off or put on as you warm up or cool down. Most hikers use three main layers: a base layer next to the skin, an insulating layer and an outer, shell layer for protection from wind, rain and snow.

» For the upper body, the base layer is typically a shirt of synthetic material such as polypropylene for wicking moisture away from the body.

» The insulating layer retains heat next to your body, and is often a windproof synthetic fleece or down jacket.

» The outer shell should be a waterproof jacket that protects against cold winds.

» For the lower body, the layers generally consist of either shorts or loose-fitting pants; polypropylene 'long-john' underwear; and waterproof rain pants (long leg zippers let you easily pull them on and off over hiking boots).

Waterproof Shells

The ideal specifications are:
» breathable, waterproof fabric (Gore-Tex is a popular choice)
» a hood that is roomy enough to cover headwear but still allows peripheral vision
» a capacious map pocket
» a heavy-gauge zipper protected by a storm flap

If heavy rain is unlikely, a poncho is a good lightweight option.

Footwear, Socks & Gaiters

Trail running shoes are fine over easy terrain, but for more difficult trails and across rocks and scree, the ankle support offered by boots is invaluable.

» Hiking boots should have a flexible midsole and an insole that supports the arch and heel. Nonslip soles (such as Vibram) provide the best grip.

» Buy boots in warm conditions or go for a walk before trying them on, so that your feet can expand slightly as they would on a walk.

» Most hikers carry a pair of river sandals to wear at night, at rest stops and/or when fording waterways.

» For longer hikes, synthetics wick away moisture better than cotton and wool. Also consider wearing lightweight liner socks for comfort and to avoid blisters.

» If you'll be hiking through snow, deep mud or scratchy vegetation, gaiters will protect your legs and help keep your socks dry. Choose gaiters made of strong fabric, with a robust zip protected by a flap, that secure snugly around your hiking boots.

Navigation

Maps & Compass

Carry a good map of the area you are hiking, and know how to read it.

» Before setting off, ensure that you understand the contours and map symbols, plus the main ridge and river systems in the area.

» Familiarize yourself with the true north–south directions and the general direction in which you are heading.

» On the trail, try to identify major landforms (eg mountain peaks) and locate them on your map. This will give you a better grasp of the region's geography.

» Buy a compass and learn how to use it. The attraction of magnetic north varies in different parts of the

EQUIPMENT CHECKLIST

Your list will depend on the kind of hiking you do, whether you're car camping or backpacking, and the weather.

Clothing

» broad-brimmed sun hat
» hiking boots, socks, gaiters and spare laces
» hat (warm), scarf and gloves
» jacket (waterproof) and rain pants
» shorts and lightweight trousers or skirt
» sweater or fleece jacket
» thermal underwear
» T-shirt and collared long-sleeved shirt

Equipment

» backpack with waterproof liner or cover
» first-aid kit*
» insect repellent
» map, compass and guidebook
» pocketknife
» sunglasses, sunscreen and lip balm
» survival blanket or bivvy bag
» toilet paper and trowel
» flashlight or headlamp, spare batteries and bulb
» watch
» water containers
» whistle

Overnight Hikes

» bear canister
» cooking, eating and drinking utensils
» sleeping bag and liner
» sleeping mat (and if inflatable, patch kit)
» spare cord and sewing/repair kit
» stove, fuel and lighter/matches
» tent, pegs, poles and guylines
» towel
» water-purification filter or tablets

Optional Items

» camera, film/charger and batteries
» cell phone**
» emergency distress beacon
» GPS receiver and spare batteries
» groundsheet
» mosquito net
» swimsuit
» walking/hiking/trekking poles

*see Medical Checklist (p235)
**see Telephone (p225)

world, so compasses need to be balanced accordingly. Compass manufacturers have divided the world into five zones. Make sure your compass is balanced for your destination zone. There are also 'universal' compasses on the market that can be used anywhere in the world.

How to Use a Compass

This is a very basic introduction to using a compass and will only be of assistance if you are proficient in map reading. For simplicity, it doesn't take magnetic variation into account. Before using a compass we recommend you obtain further instruction.

READING A COMPASS
Hold the compass flat in the palm of your hand. Rotate the bezel so the red end of the needle points to the N on the bezel. The bearing is read from the dash under the bezel.

ORIENTING THE MAP
To orient the map so that it aligns with the ground, place the compass flat on the map. Rotate the map until the needle is parallel with the map's north–south grid lines and the red end is pointing to north on the map. You can now identify features around you by aligning them with labeled features on the map.

TAKING A BEARING FROM THE MAP
Draw a line on the map between your start and end points. Place the edge of the compass on this line with the direction of travel arrow pointing towards your destination. Rotate the bezel until the meridian lines are parallel with the north–south grid lines on the map and the N points to north on the map. Read the bearing from the dash.

FOLLOWING A BEARING
Rotate the bezel so that the intended bearing is in line

with the dash. Place the compass flat in the palm of your hand and rotate the base plate until the red end points to N on the bezel. The direction-of-travel arrow will now point in the direction you need to walk.

DETERMINING YOUR BEARING

Rotate the bezel so the red end points to the N. Place the compass flat in the palm of your hand and rotate the base plate until the direction-of-travel arrow points in the direction in which you have been walking. Read your bearing from the dash.

GPS

Originally developed by the US Department of Defense, the Global Positioning System (GPS) is a network of 30 earth-orbiting satellites that continually beam encoded signals back to earth. Small, computer-driven devices (GPS receivers) can decode these signals to give users an extremely accurate reading of their location – to within 15m, anywhere on the planet, any time, in almost any weather.

» The cheapest hand-held GPS receivers now cost less than $100 (although these may not have a built-in averaging system that minimizes signal errors). Other important factors to consider when buying a GPS receiver are its weight and battery life.

» Remember that a GPS receiver is of little use to hikers unless used with an accurate topographical map. The receiver simply gives your position, which you must then locate on the local map.

» GPS receivers will only work properly in the open. The signals from a crucial satellite may be blocked (or bounce off rock or water) directly below high cliffs, near large bodies of water or in dense tree cover and give inaccurate readings.

» GPS receivers are more vulnerable to breakdowns

(including dead batteries) than the humble magnetic compass – a low-technology device that has served navigators faithfully for centuries – so don't rely on them entirely for your navigational needs.

Altimeter

Altimeters determine altitude by measuring air pressure. Because pressure is affected by temperature, altimeters are calibrated to take lower temperatures at higher altitudes into account. However, discrepancies can still occur, especially in unsettled weather, so it's wise to take a few precautions when using your altimeter.

» Reset your altimeter regularly at known elevations such as spot heights and passes. Do not take spot heights from villages where there may be a large difference in elevation from one end of the settlement to another.

» Use your altimeter in conjunction with other navigation techniques to fix your position. For instance, taking a back bearing to a known peak or river

confluence, determining the general direction of the track and obtaining your elevation will usually give you a pretty good fix on your position.

» Altimeters are also barometers and are useful for indicating changing weather conditions. If the altimeter shows increasing elevation while you are not climbing, it means the air pressure is dropping and a low-pressure weather system may be approaching.

Equipment

Backpacks & Daypacks

» For day hikes, a daypack (1800 to 2450 cu inches, or 30L to 40L) usually suffices. Those with built-in hydration systems are convenient.

» For multiday hikes you will need a backpack of between 2750 and 5500 cu inches (45L and 90L) capacity.

» A good backpack should be made of strong fabric, have a lightweight internal or external frame and an adjustable, well-padded harness that evenly distributes weight

---

ROUTE FINDING

While accurate, our maps are not perfect. Inaccuracies in altitudes are commonly caused by air-temperature anomalies. Natural features such as river confluences and mountain peaks are in their true position, but sometimes the location of trails is not always so. This may be because the size of the map does not allow for detail of the trail's twists and turns. However, by using several basic route-finding techniques, you should have few problems following our hike maps and descriptions:

» Be aware of whether the trail should be climbing or descending.

» Check the north-point arrow on the map and determine the general direction of the trail.

» Time your progress over a known distance and calculate the speed at which you travel in the given terrain. From then on, you can determine with reasonable accuracy how far you have traveled.

» Watch the path – look for boot prints, broken branches, cut logs, cairns and other signs of previous passage.

(internal frames distribute weight better than external).

» Look for backpacks with robust, easily adjustable waist-belts that can support the entire load; shoulder straps should serve only to steady the pack.

» Even if the manufacturer claims your pack is water-proof, use heavy-duty liners or a pack cover.

Tents

» A three-season tent will usually suffice, except during winter, when you'll need a sturdy four-season tent to combat windy, wet and freezing conditions, especially in the backcountry.

» Regardless of the season, the tent's floor and outer shell, or fly, should have taped or sealed seams and covered zips to stop leaks.

» Most backpackers find tents of around 4.4lb (2kg) a comfortable carrying weight.

» Dome- and tunnel-shaped tents handle windy conditions better than flat-sided tents.

» Ultralight backpackers can ditch the tent and opt for using the fly and ground tarp during warm, dry weather.

Sleeping Bag & Mat

» Mummy bags are the best shape for weight and warmth.

» Down fillings are warmer than synthetic for the same weight and bulk, but unlike synthetic fillings do not retain warmth when wet.

» The given figure (eg 10°F/ -12°C) is the coldest temperature at which a person should feel comfort-able in the bag (but ratings are notoriously unreliable).

» An inner liner helps keep your sleeping bag clean, as well as adding an insulating layer. Silk liners are lightest, but they also come in polypropylene.

» Self-inflating sleeping mats work like a thin air cushion between you and the ground, and also insulate you from the cold. Foam mats are a low-cost, but less comfortable, alternative.

Stoves & Fuel

Fuel stoves fall roughly into four categories: propane, multifuel, methylated spirits (eg denatured alcohol) and butane gas.

» Bulky car-camping stoves run on propane canisters. This fuel is inexpensive and available everywhere, including many gas stations.

» Multifuel stoves are small, efficient and ideal for places where a reliable fuel supply is difficult to find. However, they tend to be sooty and require frequent maintenance.

» Stoves running on methylated spirits are slower and less efficient, but are safe, clean and easy to use.

» Butane gas stoves are clean and reliable, but can be slow, and the gas canisters can be awkward to carry and a potential hazardous-waste problem.

» Propane and butane stove performance decreases in below-freezing temps.

Bear Canisters

Most backcountry hikes require a bear-resistant container for storing food and toiletries.

» If you have your own canister, confirm that your model is approved for the Sierra Nevada, where black bears have learned how to open some models.

» All-black Garcia canisters, made locally in Visalia, can be rented cheaply in the parks and at US Forest Service (USFS) ranger stations.

» Buying canisters costs anywhere from $70 for a heavier Garcia to $275 for an ultralight Wild Ideas 'bearikade' model.

Buying & Renting Locally

Renting equipment is a good way to go if you've never tried an activity. Why sink money into equipment that might live in a closet forever after? That said, rentals aren't cheap if you plan to use something for more than a weekend.

Yosemite

Curry Village Mountain Shop (Yosemite Valley) Sells climbing and hiking gear, clothing, maps and books; see p61.

Yosemite Village Sport Shop (Yosemite Valley) Sells clothing, shoes, day packs and car-camping gear; see p58.

Tuolumne Meadows Sport Shop (Tuolumne Meadows) Sells climbing and hiking gear and maps; see p75.

Around Yosemite

Bell's Sporting Goods (Lee Vining) Sells car-camping gear and backpacking supplies; see p145.

Mammoth Mountaineering Supply (Mammoth Lakes) Hiking, backpacking and snow-sports gear rentals and sales, plus topo maps and shoes; see p151. Also in Bishop (p154), selling used clothing and gear too.

REI (☑559-261-4168; www.rei .com; 7810 N Blackstone Ave, Fresno; ☉10am-9pm Mon-Fri, 10am-9pm Sat, 11am-6pm Sun) Rents bear canisters and camping and backpacking equipment; sells clothing, maps, books and four-seasons outdoor gear.

Wilson's Eastside Sports (Bishop) Camping, climbing, backpacking and winter-trekking gear rentals and sells shoes, clothing and backpacks; see p154.

Sequoia & Kings Canyon

Big 5 Sporting Goods (Visalia) Camping, fishing and outdoor-sports equipment sales; see p189.

Elevation (Lone Pine) Rents bear canisters and crampons and sells hiking, backpacking and climbing gear; see p193.

Lone Pine Sporting Goods (Lone Pine) Sells camping gear, fishing licenses and maps; see p193.

behind the scenes

SEND US YOUR FEEDBACK

We love to hear from travelers – your comments keep us on our toes and help make our books better. Our well-traveled team reads every word on what you loved or loathed about this book. Although we cannot reply individually to postal submissions, we always guarantee that your feedback goes straight to the appropriate authors, in time for the next edition. Each person who sends us information is thanked in the next edition – and the most useful submissions are rewarded with a free book.

Visit **lonelyplanet.com/contact** to submit your updates and suggestions or to ask for help. Our award-winning website also features inspirational travel stories, news and discussions.

Note: We may edit, reproduce and incorporate your comments in Lonely Planet products such as guidebooks, websites and digital products, so let us know if you don't want your comments reproduced or your name acknowledged. For a copy of our privacy policy visit lonelyplanet.com/privacy.

OUR READERS

Many thanks to the travelers who used the last edition and wrote to us with helpful hints, useful advice and interesting anecdotes:

Brian Jennings, April Langley, Geoff Shepherd, Brian Stepanek

AUTHOR THANKS
Beth Kohn

Thanks to Kathleen Munnelly and Alison Lyall and the great team who made this happen! Sam Benson gets a prolonged standing ovation, plus a lifetime supply of the bear spray of her choice. Thanks also go to my fellow explorers this time around – Claude Moller, Julia and June Brashares, Woody Hastings and Pati Fuentes – plus all the helpful and patient rangers at Yosemite National Park and the Inyo National Forest.

Sara Benson

Thanks to Kathleen Munnelly, Alison Lyall and everyone else at Lonely Planet for making this book happen. Beth Kohn, you were a superstar CA! I'm grateful to everyone I met on the road who shared their local expertise and tips, especially national park and forest rangers, staff and volunteers, and also my friends and family who love playing and living in the Sierra Nevada as much as I do. Most of all, big thanks to Ranger Mike for all of those epic backcountry trips.

ACKNOWLEDGMENTS

Climate map data adapted from Peel MC, Finlayson BL & McMahon TA (2007) 'Updated World Map of the Köppen-Geiger Climate Classification', *Hydrology and Earth System Sciences*, 11, 163344.

Cover photograph: Upper and Lower Yosemite Falls. Yosemite National Park/ David Tomlinson/Lonely Planet Images. Many of the images in this guide are available for licensing from Lonely Planet Images: www.lonelyplanetimages.com.

THIS BOOK

This 3rd edition of Lonely Planet's *Yosemite, Sequoia & Kings Canyon National Parks* guidebook was researched and written by Beth Kohn and Sara Benson. The previous edition was written by Danny Palmerlee and Beth Kohn, along with David Lukas. The first edition was written by Kurt Wolff, Amy Marr, David Lukas and Cheryl Koehler. This guidebook was commissioned in Lonely Planet's Oakland office, laid out by Cambridge Publishing Management, UK, and produced by the following:

Commissioning Editor
Kathleen Munnelly
Coordinating Editors
Tom Lee, Fionnuala Twomey
Coordinating Cartographer Jolyon Philcox
Coordinating Layout Designer Paul Queripel
Managing Editors Helen Christinis, Kirsten Rawlings
Senior Editor Angela Tinson
Managing Cartographers Alison Lyall, Amanda Sierp
Managing Layout Designer Chris Girdler
Assisting Editors Kathryn Glendenning, Michala Green, Nick Newton, Katie O'Connell, Ceinwen Sinclair

Assisting Cartographers
Hunor Csutoros, Andy Rojas, Brendan Streager
Assisting Layout Designer Julie Crane
Cover Research Aude Vauconsant
Internal Image Research Sabrina Dalbesio
Color Designer Tim Newton
Indexer Marie Lorimer

Thanks to Sasha Baskett, Lucy Birchley, Ryan Evans, Suki Gear, Lee Gibson, Liz Heynes, Heather Howard, Yvonne Kirk, Trent Paton, John Taufa, Gerard Walker, Juan Winata

index

how to use this book

These symbols will help you find the listings you want:

- ⊙ Sights
- 🏄 Beaches
- 🏃 Activities
- 🎓 Courses
- ☞ Tours
- 🎊 Festivals & Events
- 🛏 Sleeping
- ✕ Eating
- 🍸 Drinking
- ☆ Entertainment
- 🛍 Shopping
- ℹ Information/Transport

Look out for these icons:

- TOP CHOICE Our author's recommendation
- FREE No payment required
- 🌿 A green or sustainable option

Our authors have nominated these places as demonstrating a strong commitment to sustainability – for example by supporting local communities and producers, operating in an environmentally friendly way, or supporting conservation projects.

These symbols give you the vital information for each listing:

- ☏ Telephone Numbers
- ⊙ Opening Hours
- ℗ Parking
- ⊖ Nonsmoking
- ❄ Air-Conditioning
- @ Internet Access
- 🛜 Wi-Fi Access
- 🏊 Swimming Pool
- 🥗 Vegetarian Selection
- 📖 English-Language Menu
- 👪 Family-Friendly
- 🐾 Pet-Friendly
- 🚌 Bus
- ⛴ Ferry
- Ⓜ Metro
- Ⓢ Subway
- ⊖ London Tube
- 🚊 Tram
- 🚆 Train

Reviews are organised by author preference.

Map Legend

Sights
- Beach
- Buddhist
- Castle
- Christian
- Hindu
- Islamic
- Jewish
- Monument
- Museum/Gallery
- Ruin
- Winery/Vineyard
- Zoo
- Other Sight

Activities, Courses & Tours
- Diving/Snorkelling
- Canoeing/Kayaking
- Skiing
- Surfing
- Swimming/Pool
- Walking
- Windsurfing
- Other Activity/Course/Tour

Sleeping
- Sleeping
- Camping

Eating
- Eating

Drinking
- Drinking
- Cafe

Entertainment
- Entertainment

Shopping
- Shopping

Information
- Post Office
- Tourist Information

Transport
- Airport
- Border Crossing
- Bus
- Cable Car/Funicular
- Cycling
- Ferry
- Metro
- Monorail
- Parking
- S-Bahn
- Taxi
- Train/Railway
- Tram
- Tube Station
- U-Bahn
- Other Transport

Routes
- Tollway
- Freeway
- Primary
- Secondary
- Tertiary
- Lane
- Unsealed Road
- Plaza/Mall
- Steps
- Tunnel
- Pedestrian Overpass
- Walking Tour
- Walking Tour Detour
- Path

Boundaries
- International
- State/Province
- Disputed
- Regional/Suburb
- Marine Park
- Cliff
- Wall

Population
- Capital (National)
- Capital (State/Province)
- City/Large Town
- Town/Village

Geographic
- Hut/Shelter
- Lighthouse
- Lookout
- Mountain/Volcano
- Oasis
- Park
- Pass
- Picnic Area
- Waterfall

Hydrography
- River/Creek
- Intermittent River
- Swamp/Mangrove
- Reef
- Canal
- Water
- Dry/Salt/Intermittent Lake
- Glacier

Areas
- Beach/Desert
- Cemetery (Christian)
- Cemetery (Other)
- Park/Forest
- Sportsground
- Sight (Building)
- Top Sight (Building)

OUR STORY

A beat-up old car, a few dollars in the pocket and a sense of adventure. In 1972 that's all Tony and Maureen Wheeler needed for the trip of a lifetime – across Europe and Asia overland to Australia. It took several months, and at the end – broke but inspired – they sat at their kitchen table writing and stapling together their first travel guide, *Across Asia on the Cheap*. Within a week they'd sold 1500 copies. Lonely Planet was born.

Today, Lonely Planet has offices in Melbourne, London and Oakland, with more than 600 staff and writers. We share Tony's belief that 'a great guidebook should do three things: inform, educate and amuse'.

OUR WRITERS

Beth Kohn

Coordinating Author: Welcome to Yosemite, Sequoia & Kings Canyon, 20 Top Experiences, Need to Know, What's New, If You Like..., Month by Month, Itineraries, Regions at a Glance, Yosemite National Park, Around Yosemite, The Parks Today, Directory A–Z, Transportation A lucky long-time resident of San Francisco, Beth lives to be playing outside or splashing in big puddles of water. For this guide, she dodged spring floods in Yosemite Valley, potholed in the high country, lugged a bear canister along the John Muir Trail and selflessly soaked in hot springs – for research purposes, of course. An author of Lonely Planet's *California* and *Mexico* guides, you can see more of her work at www.bethkohn.com.

Read more about Beth at:
lonelyplanet.com/members/bethkohn

Sara Benson

20 Top Experiences, Itineraries, Activities, Travel with Children, Travel with Pets, Sequoia & Kings Canyon National Parks, History, Geology, Wildlife, Conserving the Parks, Health & Safety, Clothing & Equipment After graduating from college in Chicago, Sara jumped on a plane to California with just one suitcase and $100 in her pocket. She has bounced around the Golden State ever since, in between stints living in Hawaii and Asia and working as a seasonal national park ranger in the Sierra Nevada. The author of 50 travel and nonfiction books, Sara trekked on snowshoes and cross-country skis and chased black bears away from her campsites while writing this guide. Follow her adventures online at www.indietraveler.blogspot.com and www.twitter.com/indie _traveler.

Read more about Sara at:
lonelyplanet.com/members/sarabenson

Published by Lonely Planet Publications Pty Ltd
ABN 36 005 607 983
3rd edition – February 2012
ISBN 978 1 74179 406 9
© Lonely Planet 2012   Photographs © as indicated 2012
10 9 8 7 6 5 4 3 2 1
Printed in Singapore